MASASHI KISHIMOTO

At age 44, I just learned that a giraffe's call sounds exactly like a fart. The world is full of things I don't know. There is still much to learn.

AKIRA OKUBO

I'm often playing some video or other while I draw the art. These days I find myself gravitating toward videos of rain or campfires.

SAMURAI 8
THE TALE OF HACHIMARU

03

SHONEN JUMP Manga Edition

Story **MASASHI KISHIMOTO**
Art **AKIRA OKUBO**

Translation/STEPHEN PAUL
Touch-Up Art & Lettering/SNIR AHARON
Design/JULIAN [JR] ROBINSON
Editor/ALEXIS KIRSCH

SAMURAI8 HACHIMARUDEN © 2019 by Masashi Kishimoto, Akira Okubo
All rights reserved.
First published in Japan in 2019 by SHUEISHA Inc., Tokyo.
English translation rights arranged by SHUEISHA Inc.

Printed in the U.S.A.

Published by VIZ Media, LLC
P.O. Box 77010
San Francisco, CA 94107

10 9 8 7 6 5 4 3 2 1
First printing, August 2020

viz.com

shonenjump.com

PARENTAL ADVISORY
SAMURAI 8 is rated T for Teen and is
recommended for ages 13 and up. This
volume contains fantasy violence.

SAMURAI 8

THE TALE OF HACHIMARU

03

KOTSUGA & RYU

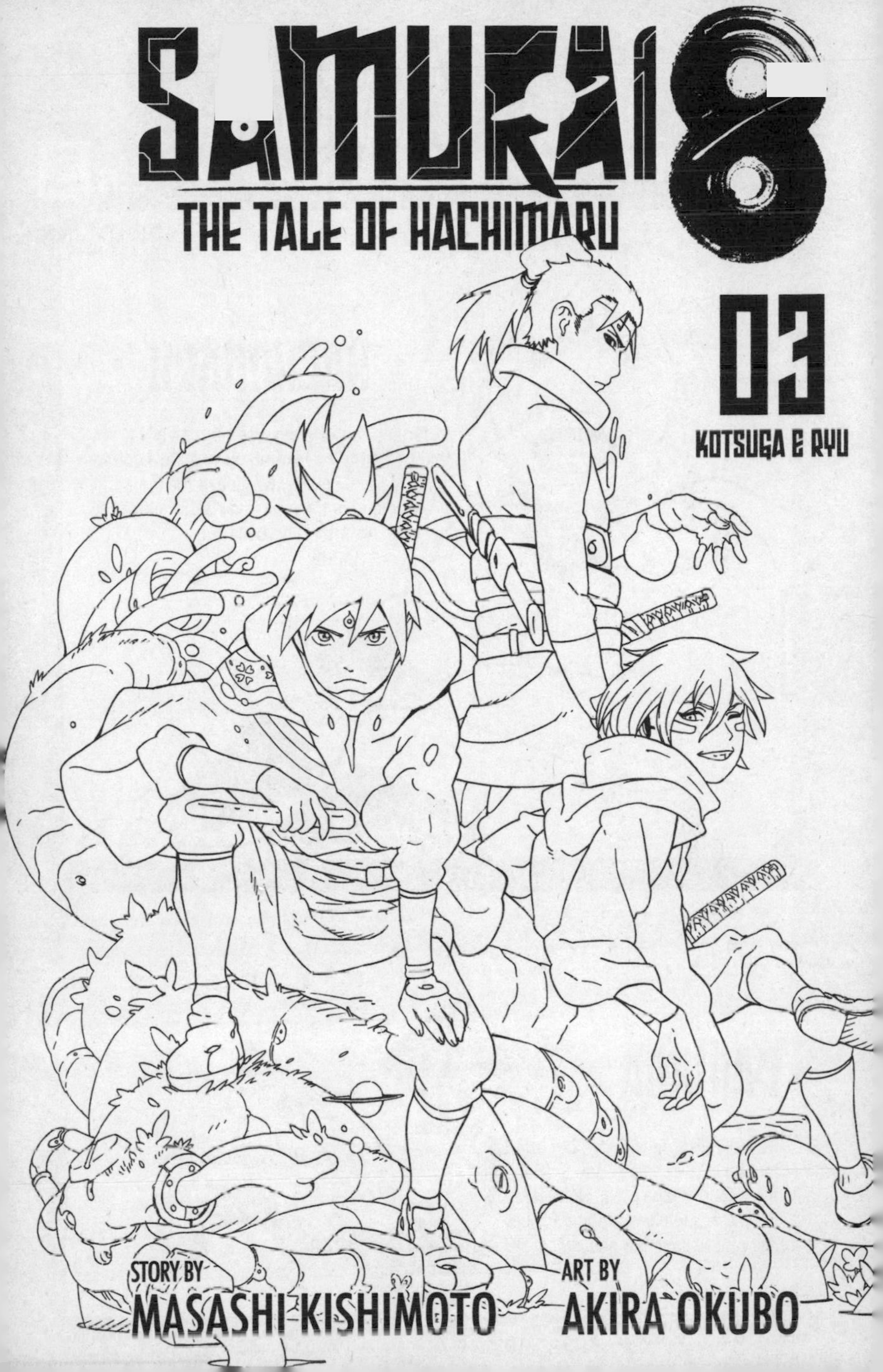

STORY BY
MASASHI KISHIMOTO

ART BY
AKIRA OKUBO

THE TALE OF HACHIMARU

CHARACTERS

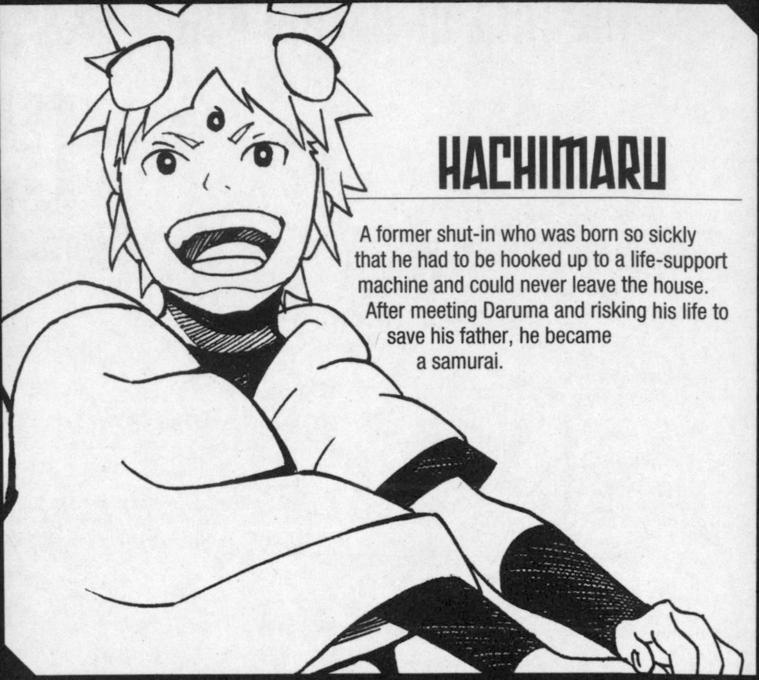

HACHIMARU

A former shut-in who was born so sickly that he had to be hooked up to a life-support machine and could never leave the house. After meeting Daruma and risking his life to save his father, he became a samurai.

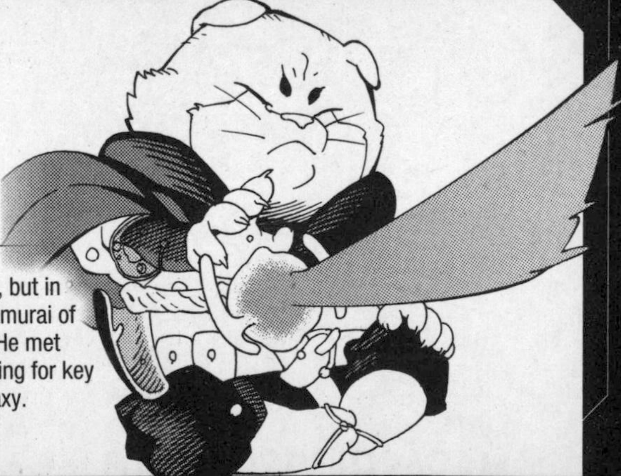

DARUMA

He looks like a lucky cat, but in fact he is a legendary samurai of the Kongo-Yasha Style. He met Hachimaru while searching for key samurai to save the galaxy.

SAMURAI 8

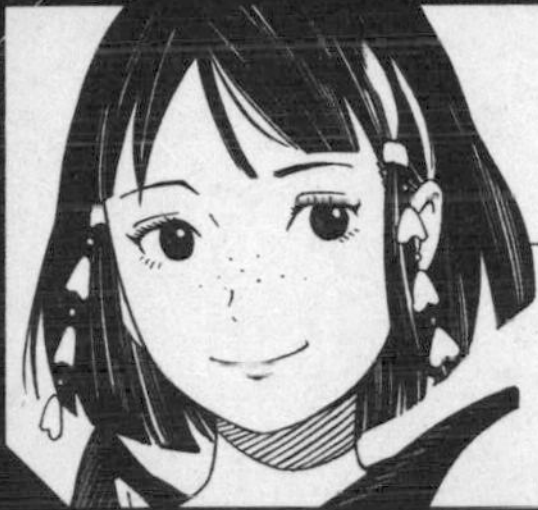

ANN

A young princess in training. She lost her Locker Ball, which is necessary to complete the samurai ritual.

HAYATARO

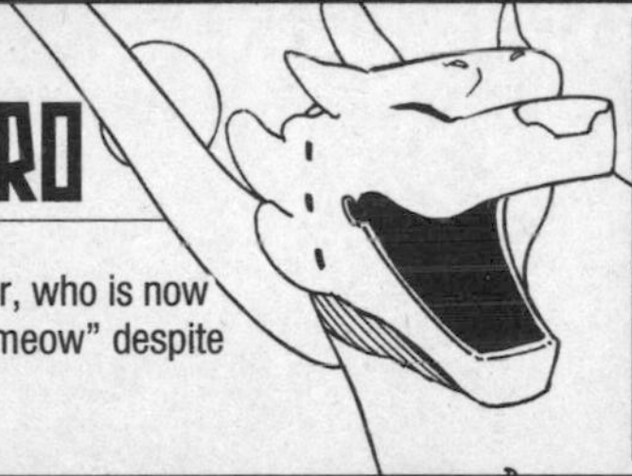

Hachimaru's Pet Holder, who is now his Key Holder. Says "meow" despite being a dog type.

WHAT IS A HOLDER?
A lifeform(?) that inhabits this galaxy. Their name changes based on their role: Pet Holder, Guard Holder, etc. Ones who serve a samurai master are called special Key Holders.

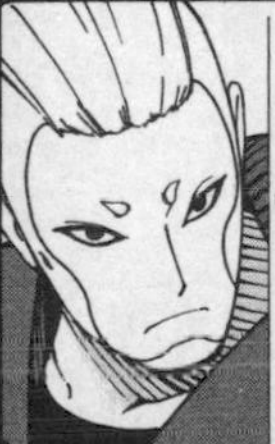

HAGAMICHI

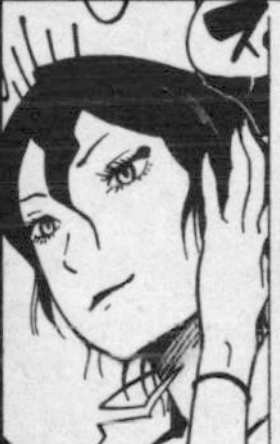

PRINCESS UN

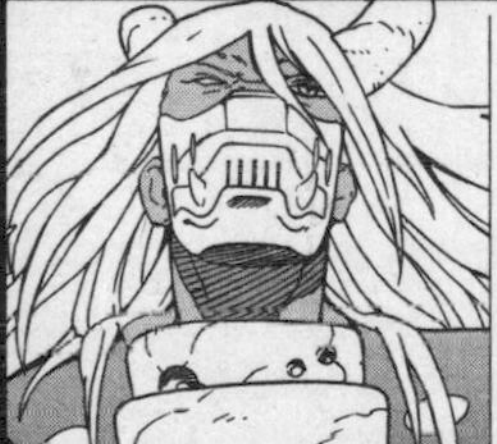

ATA

STORY

Hachimaru is a boy with a weak body. He can't survive without being hooked up to a life-support device, and believes his dream of becoming a samurai will never come true. But one day, he meets Daruma, a samurai in the body of a large, round cat. With the approval of the warrior god, Hachimaru gains the life of a samurai! He starts training under Daruma and meets his princess of fate, Ann. Things take a turn for the worse when the samurai Ata attacks Hachimaru. Hachimaru's father sacrifices his own life to drive Ata off—but it is only a clone body that he destroys. Hachimaru sees Ata with seven people who claim to be his brothers. Hachimaru then decides to make it his samurai calling to fulfill his promise to his father and protect the planet.

SAMURAI 8
THE TALE OF HACHIMARU

03

KOTSUGA E RYU

CONTENTS

CHAPTER 16: STAR-BREAKER

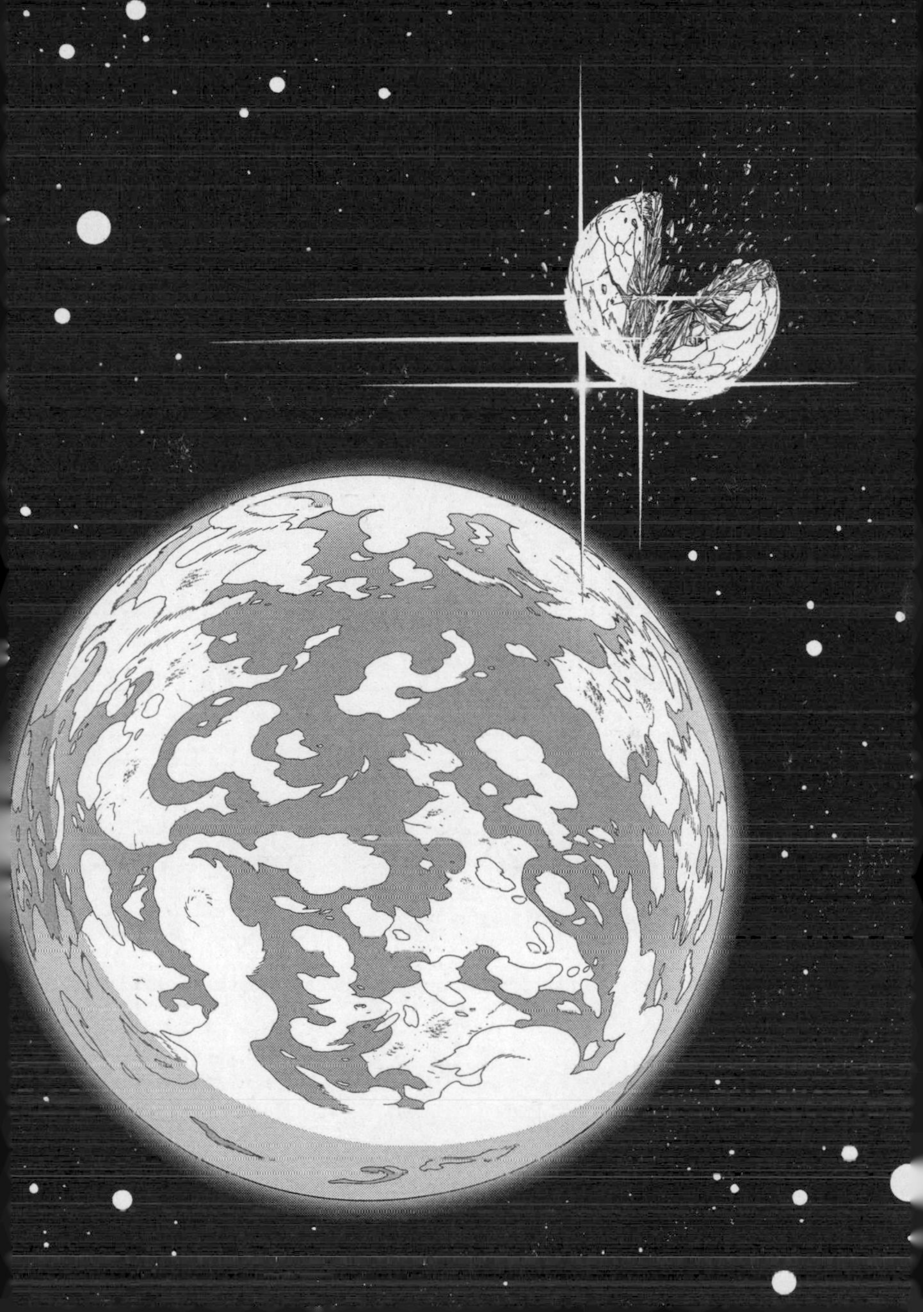

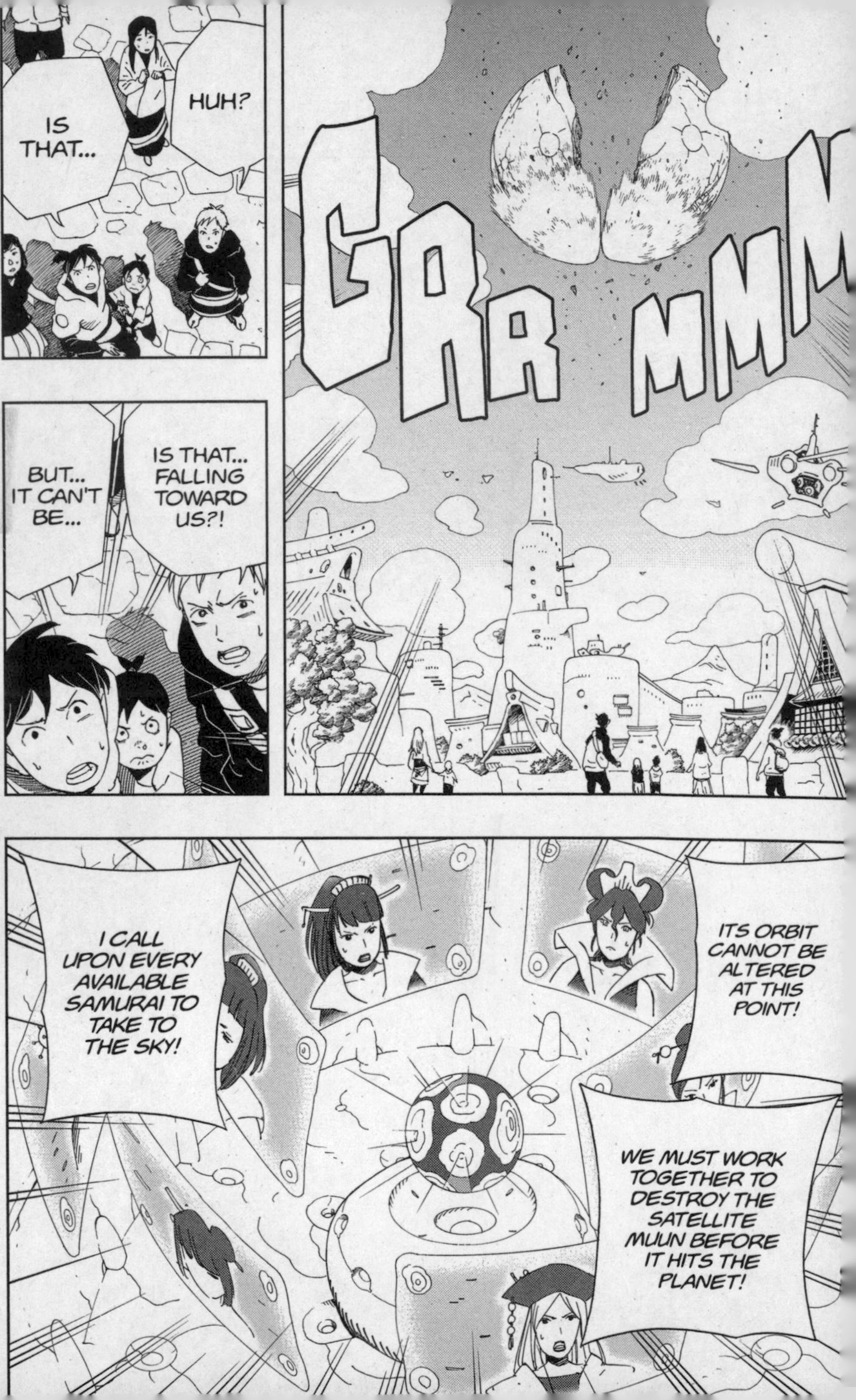
GRR MMM
HUH?
IS THAT...
IS THAT... FALLING TOWARD US?!
BUT... IT CAN'T BE...
ITS ORBIT CANNOT BE ALTERED AT THIS POINT!
I CALL UPON EVERY AVAILABLE SAMURAI TO TAKE TO THE SKY!
WE MUST WORK TOGETHER TO DESTROY THE SATELLITE MUUN BEFORE IT HITS THE PLANET!

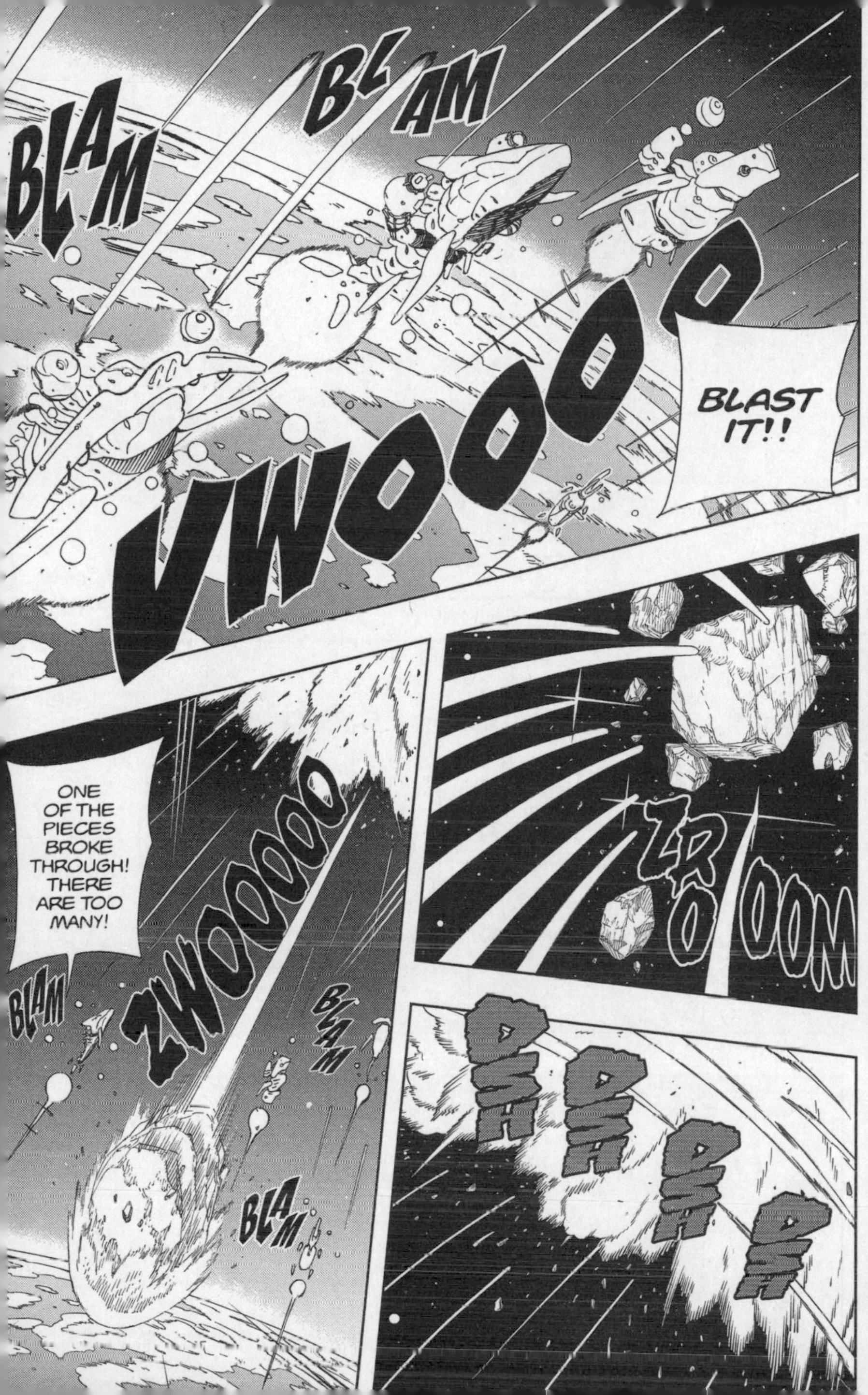
BLAST IT!!
VWOOOO
BLAM
BLAM
ZROOOM
DSH
DSH
DSH
DSH
ONE OF THE PIECES BROKE THROUGH! THERE ARE TOO MANY!
BLAM
ZWOOOOO
BLAM
BLAM

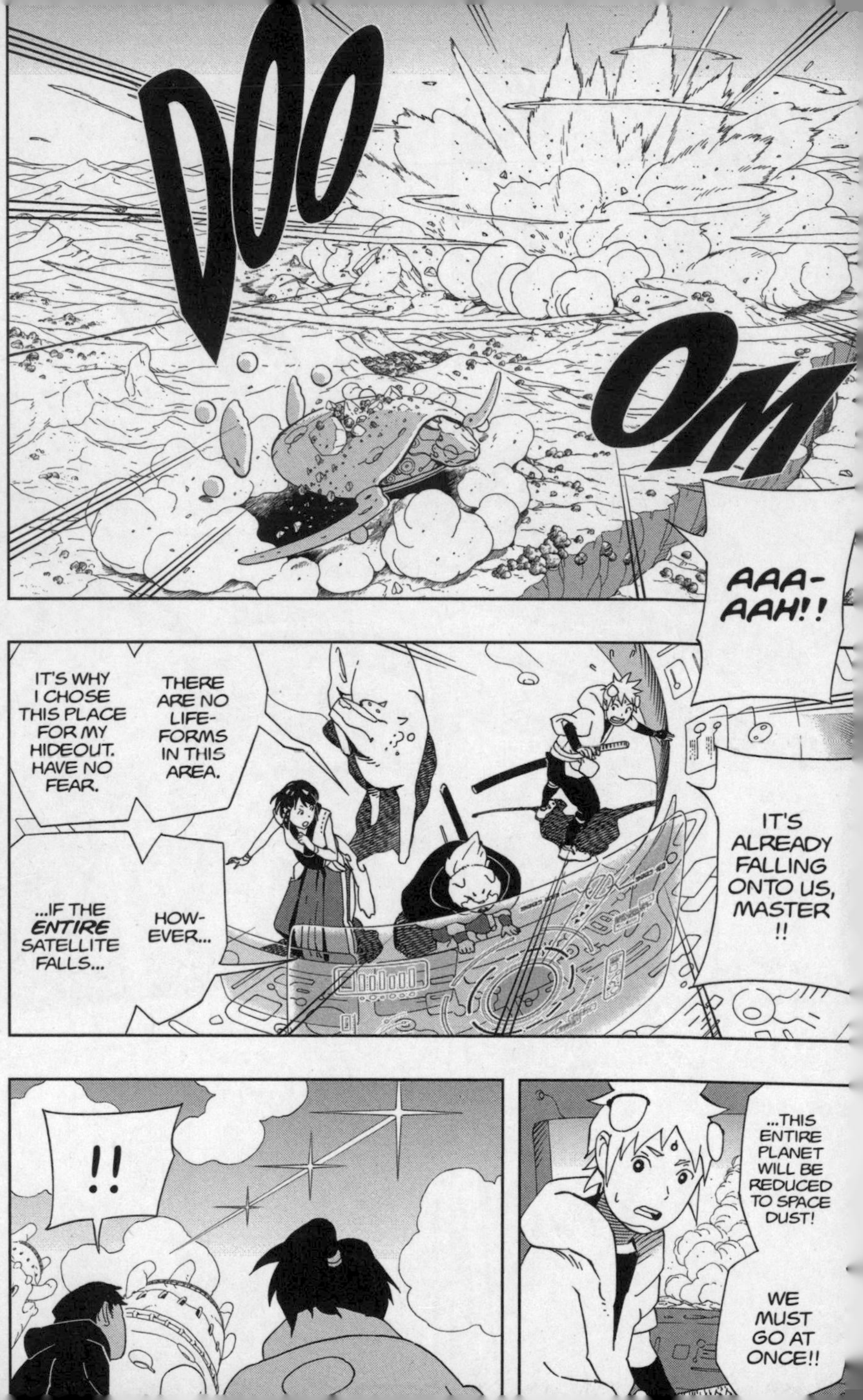
DOOOM
AAA-AAH!!
IT'S ALREADY FALLING ONTO US, MASTER!!
THERE ARE NO LIFE-FORMS IN THIS AREA.
IT'S WHY I CHOSE THIS PLACE FOR MY HIDEOUT. HAVE NO FEAR.
HOW-EVER...
...IF THE ENTIRE SATELLITE FALLS...
...THIS ENTIRE PLANET WILL BE REDUCED TO SPACE DUST!
WE MUST GO AT ONCE!!
!!

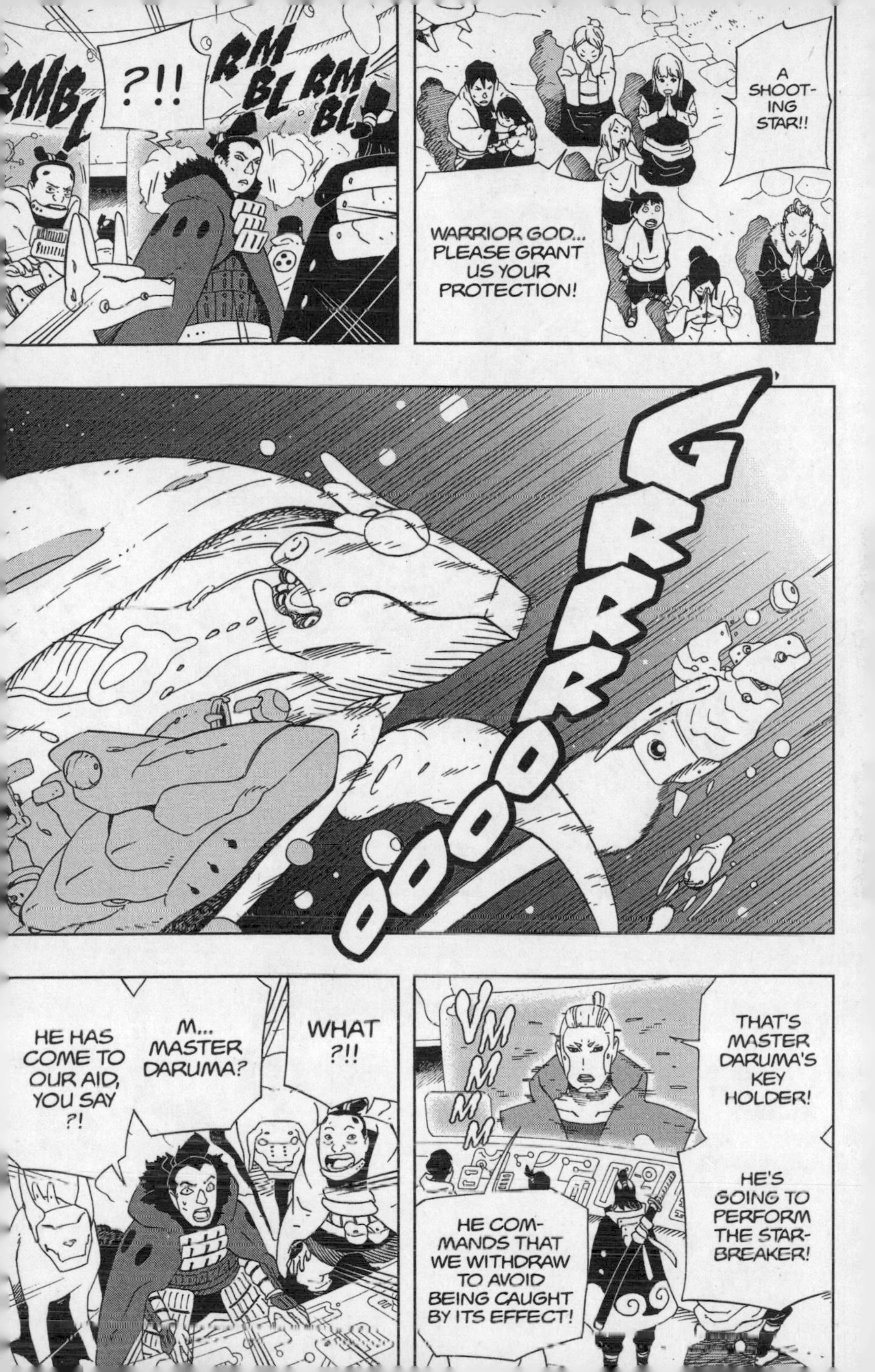
A SHOOTING STAR!!
WARRIOR GOD... PLEASE GRANT US YOUR PROTECTION!
RMBL
?!!
RM BL RM BL
GRRROOOO
THAT'S MASTER DARUMA'S KEY HOLDER!
HE'S GOING TO PERFORM THE STAR-BREAKER!
HE COMMANDS THAT WE WITHDRAW TO AVOID BEING CAUGHT BY ITS EFFECT!
VMMMM
WHAT ?!!
M... MASTER DARUMA?
HE HAS COME TO OUR AID, YOU SAY ?!

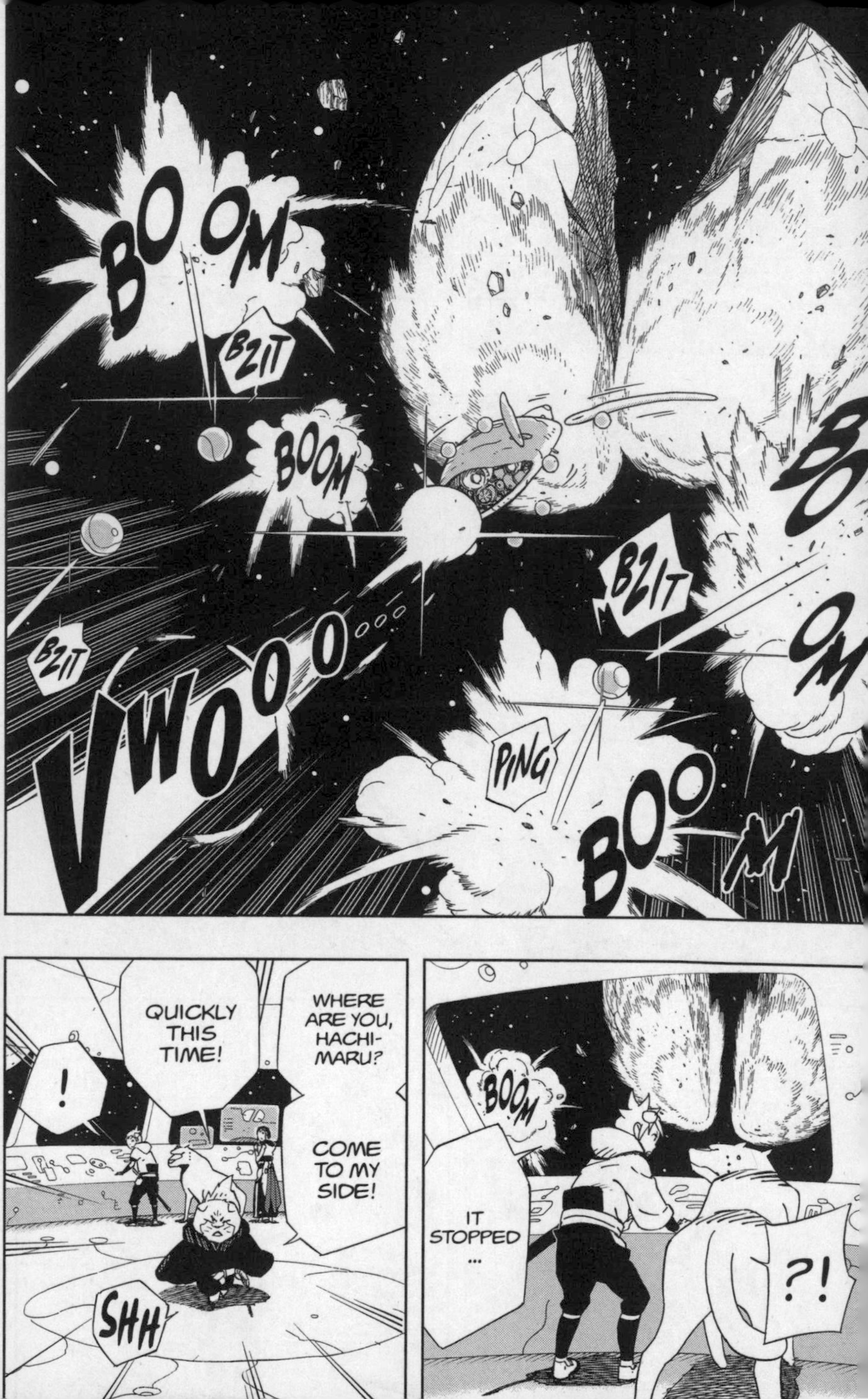
BOOM
BZIT
PING
BOOM
BOOM
BZIT
BOOM
BZIT
VWOOOooo
BOOM
IT STOPPED ...
?!
WHERE ARE YOU, HACHI-MARU?
COME TO MY SIDE!
QUICKLY THIS TIME!
!
SHH

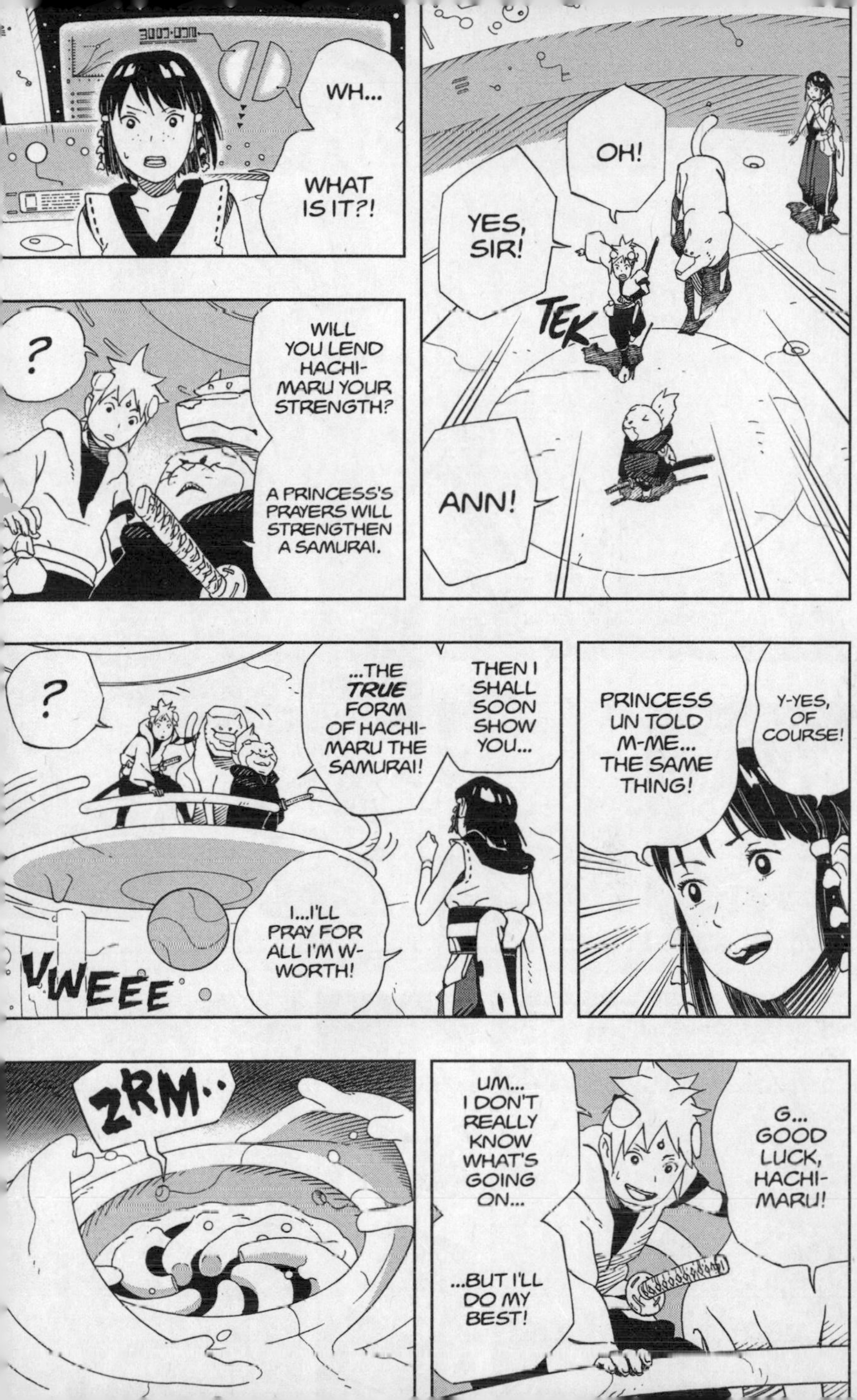
OH!
YES, SIR!
TEK
ANN!
WH...
WHAT IS IT?!
WILL YOU LEND HACHI-MARU YOUR STRENGTH?
A PRINCESS'S PRAYERS WILL STRENGTHEN A SAMURAI.
?
Y-YES, OF COURSE!
PRINCESS UN TOLD M-ME... THE SAME THING!
THEN I SHALL SOON SHOW YOU...
...THE TRUE FORM OF HACHI-MARU THE SAMURAI!
?
I...I'LL PRAY FOR ALL I'M W-WORTH!
VWEEE
G... GOOD LUCK, HACHI-MARU!
UM... I DON'T REALLY KNOW WHAT'S GOING ON...
...BUT I'LL DO MY BEST!
ZRM..

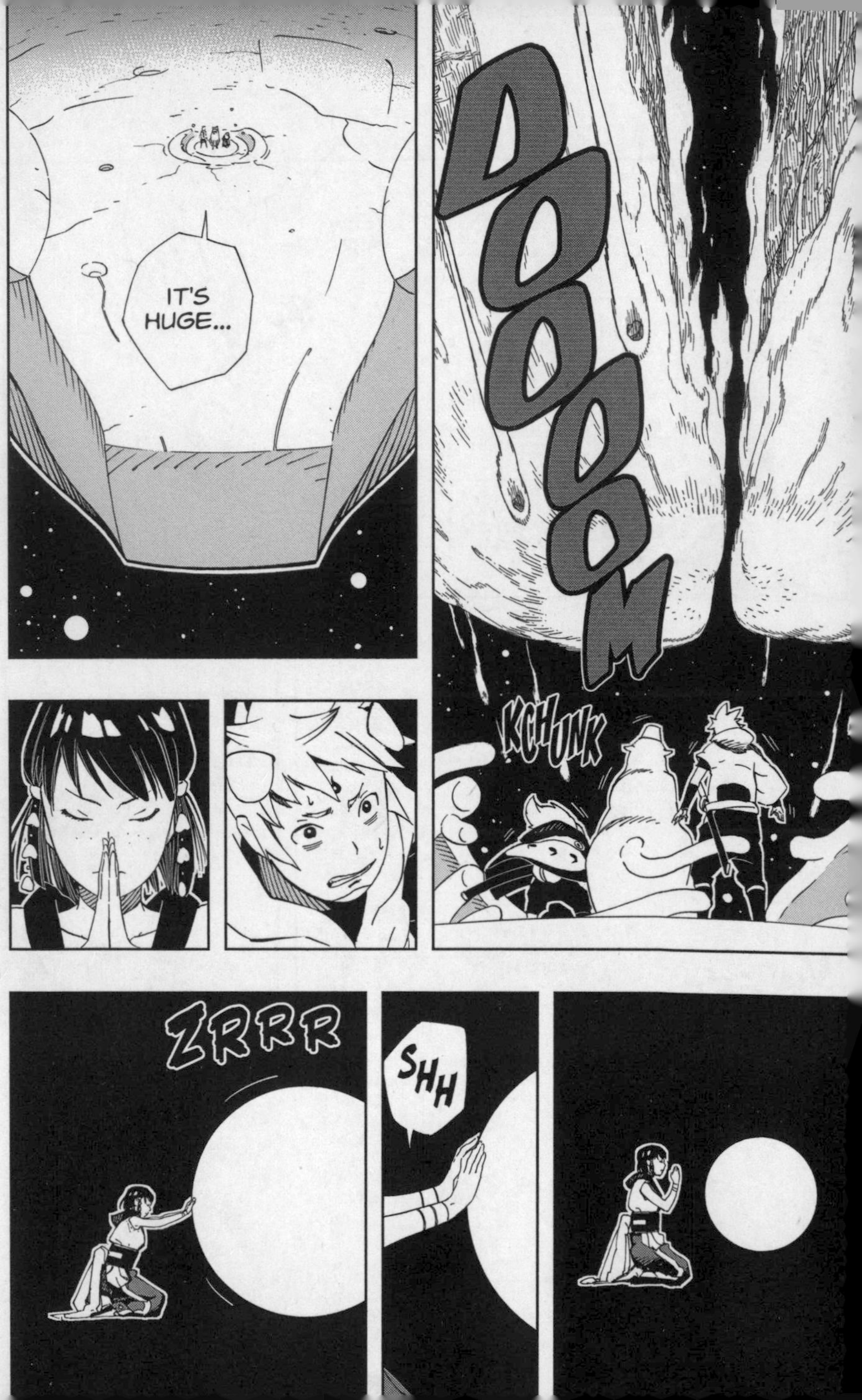
DOOOOOM
KCHUNK
IT'S HUGE...
SHH
ZRRR

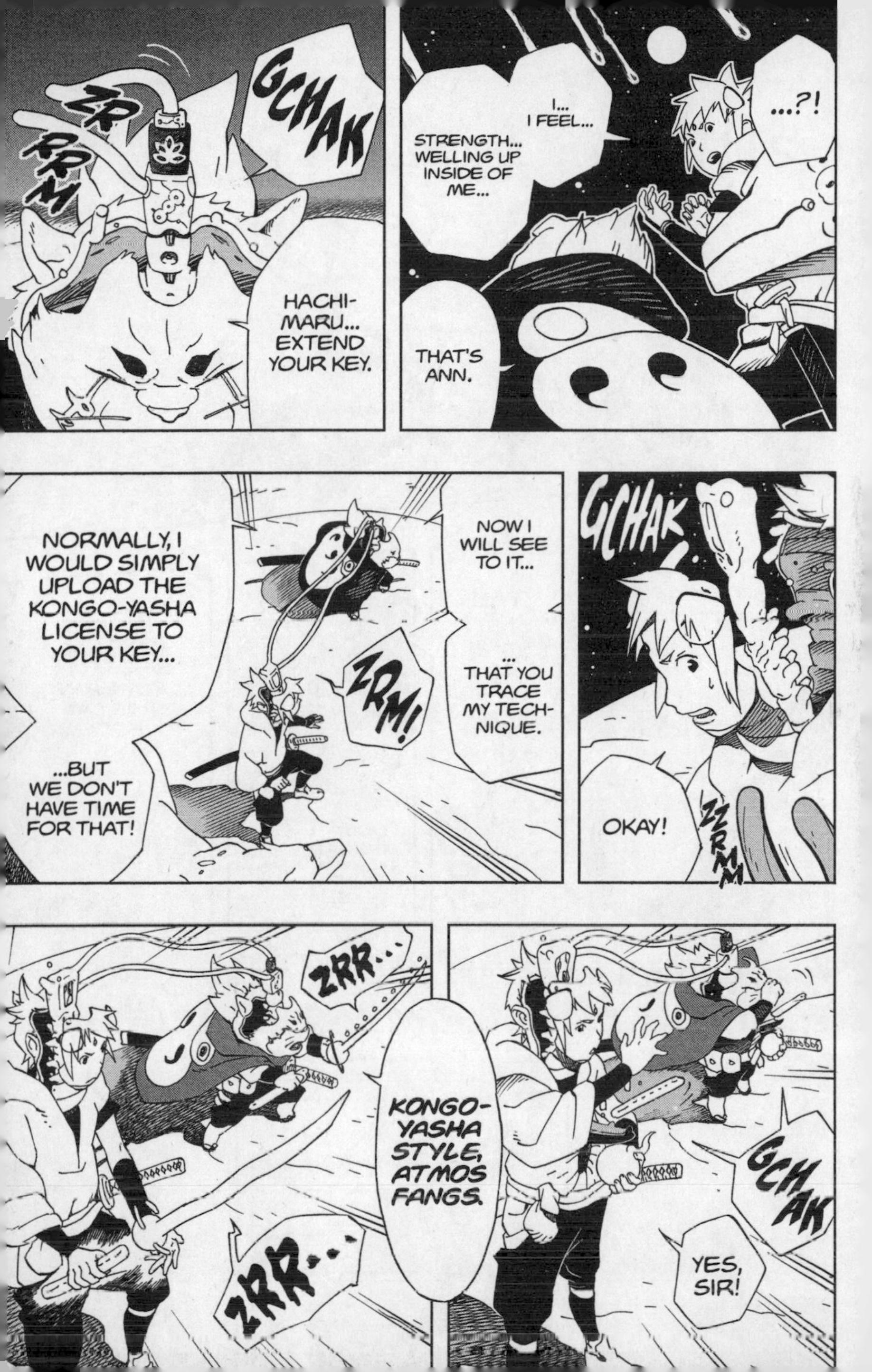
...?!
I... I FEEL...
STRENGTH... WELLING UP INSIDE OF ME...
THAT'S ANN.
GCHAK
ZR RRM
HACHI-MARU... EXTEND YOUR KEY.
GCHAK
OKAY!
ZZRMM
NOW I WILL SEE TO IT...
... THAT YOU TRACE MY TECH-NIQUE.
ZRM!
NORMALLY, I WOULD SIMPLY UPLOAD THE KONGO-YASHA LICENSE TO YOUR KEY...
...BUT WE DON'T HAVE TIME FOR THAT!
GCHAK
YES, SIR!
KONGO-YASHA STYLE, ATMOS FANGS.
ZRR...
ZRR...

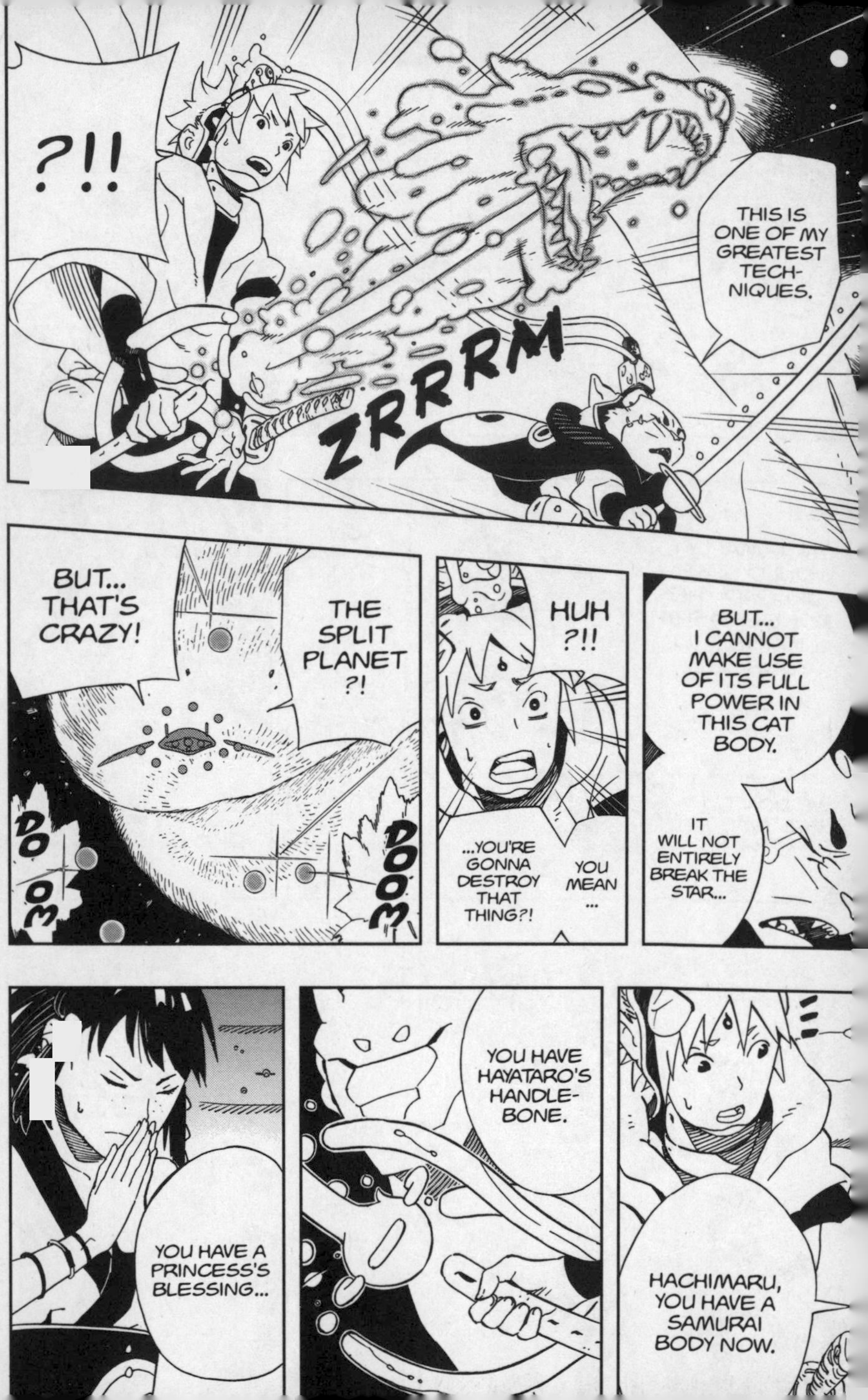
THIS IS ONE OF MY GREATEST TECH-NIQUES.
?!!
ZRRRM
BUT... I CANNOT MAKE USE OF ITS FULL POWER IN THIS CAT BODY.
IT WILL NOT ENTIRELY BREAK THE STAR...
HUH ?!!
YOU MEAN ...
...YOU'RE GONNA DESTROY THAT THING?!
THE SPLIT PLANET ?!
BUT... THAT'S CRAZY!
DOOOM
DOOM
HACHIMARU, YOU HAVE A SAMURAI BODY NOW.
YOU HAVE HAYATARO'S HANDLE-BONE.
YOU HAVE A PRINCESS'S BLESSING...

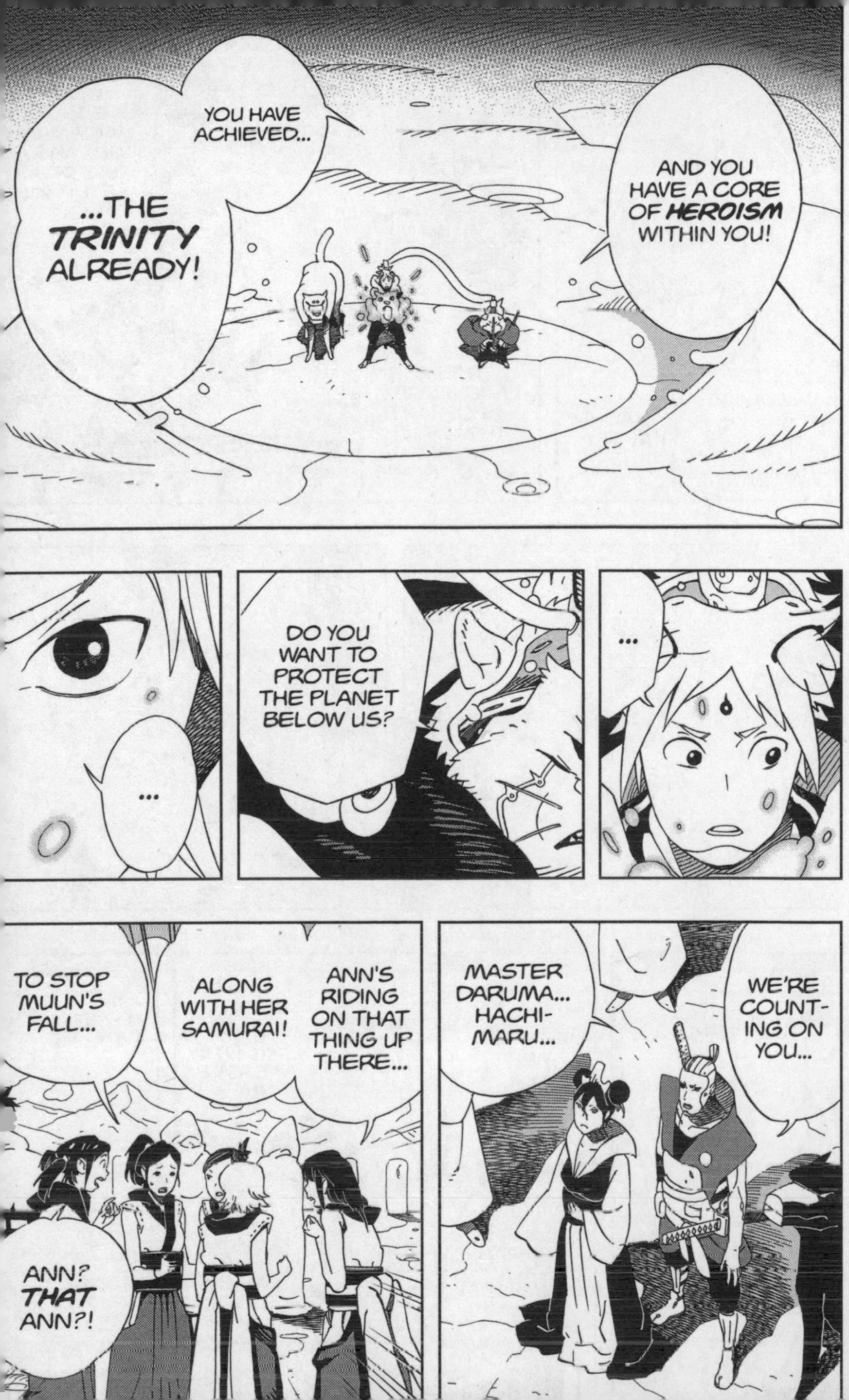
YOU HAVE ACHIEVED...
...THE *TRINITY* ALREADY!
AND YOU HAVE A CORE OF ***HEROISM*** WITHIN YOU!
...
DO YOU WANT TO PROTECT THE PLANET BELOW US?
...
MASTER DARUMA... HACHI-MARU...
WE'RE COUNTING ON YOU...
ANN'S RIDING ON THAT THING UP THERE...
ALONG WITH HER SAMURAI!
TO STOP MUUN'S FALL...
ANN? *THAT* ANN?!

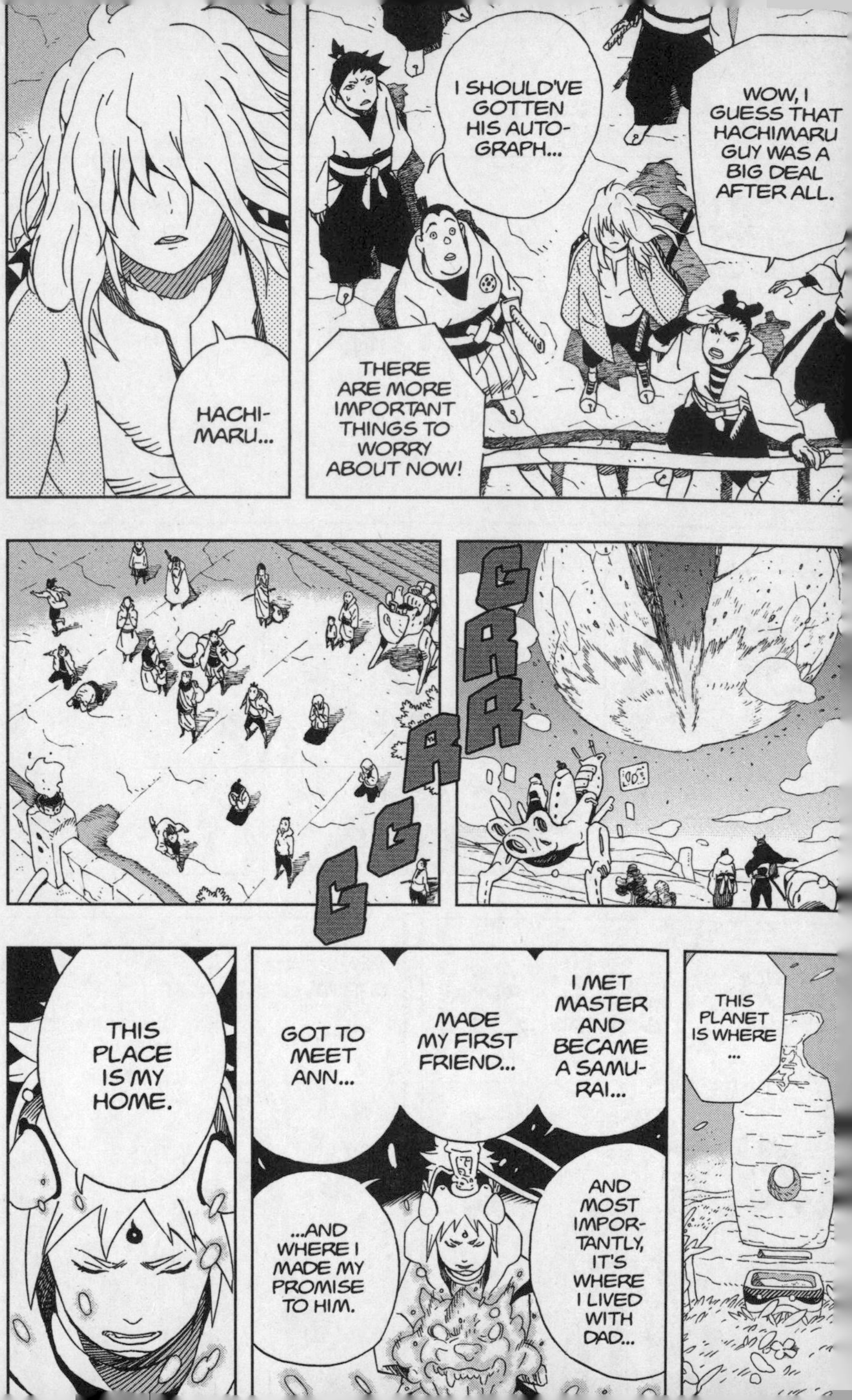
WOW, I GUESS THAT HACHIMARU GUY WAS A BIG DEAL AFTER ALL.
I SHOULD'VE GOTTEN HIS AUTOGRAPH...
THERE ARE MORE IMPORTANT THINGS TO WORRY ABOUT NOW!
HACHIMARU...
GRRRGG
THIS PLANET IS WHERE ...
I MET MASTER AND BECAME A SAMURAI...
MADE MY FIRST FRIEND...
GOT TO MEET ANN...
AND MOST IMPORTANTLY, IT'S WHERE I LIVED WITH DAD...
...AND WHERE I MADE MY PROMISE TO HIM.
THIS PLACE IS MY HOME.

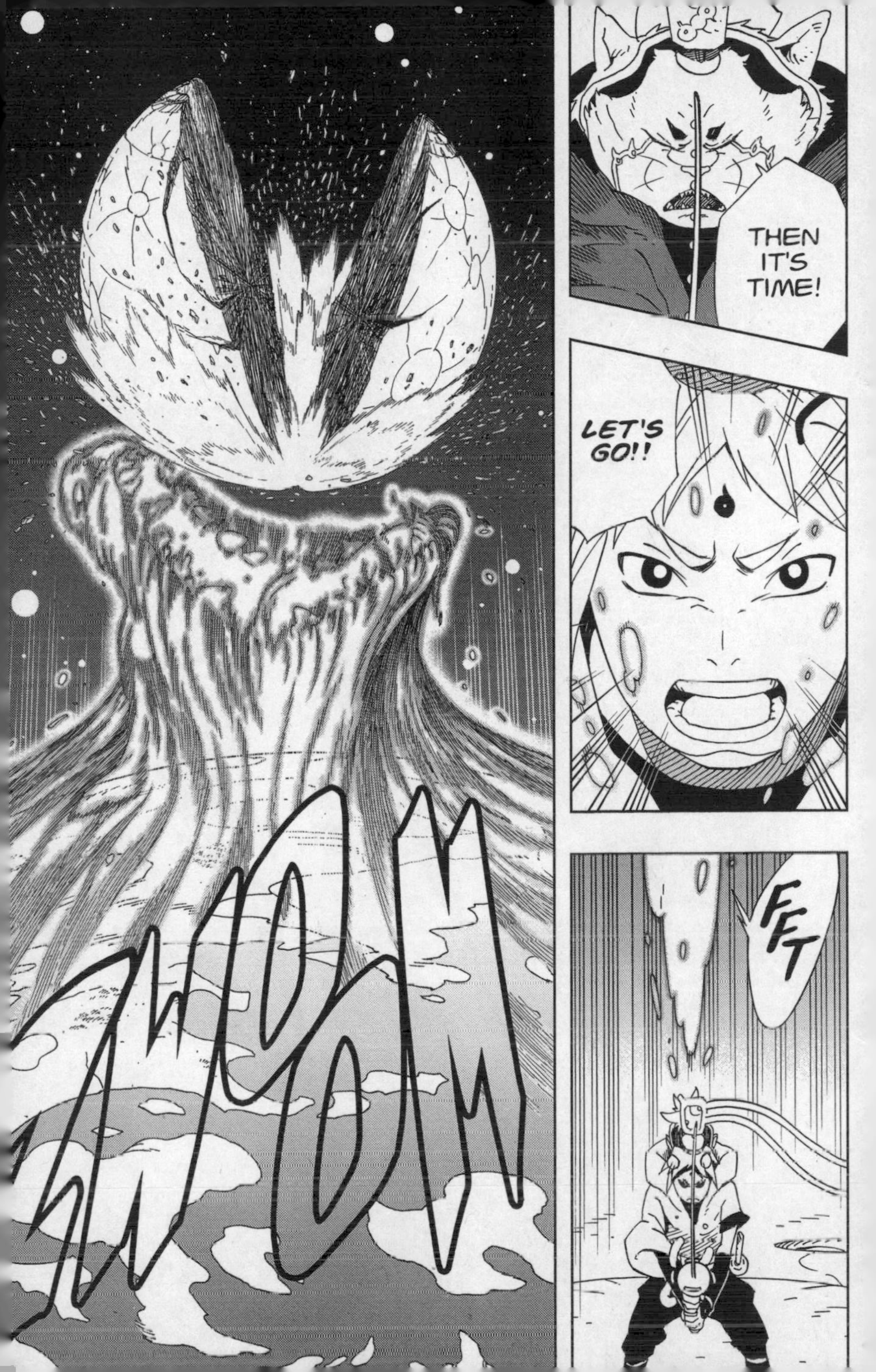
THEN IT'S TIME!
LET'S GO!!
FFT
ZWOOM

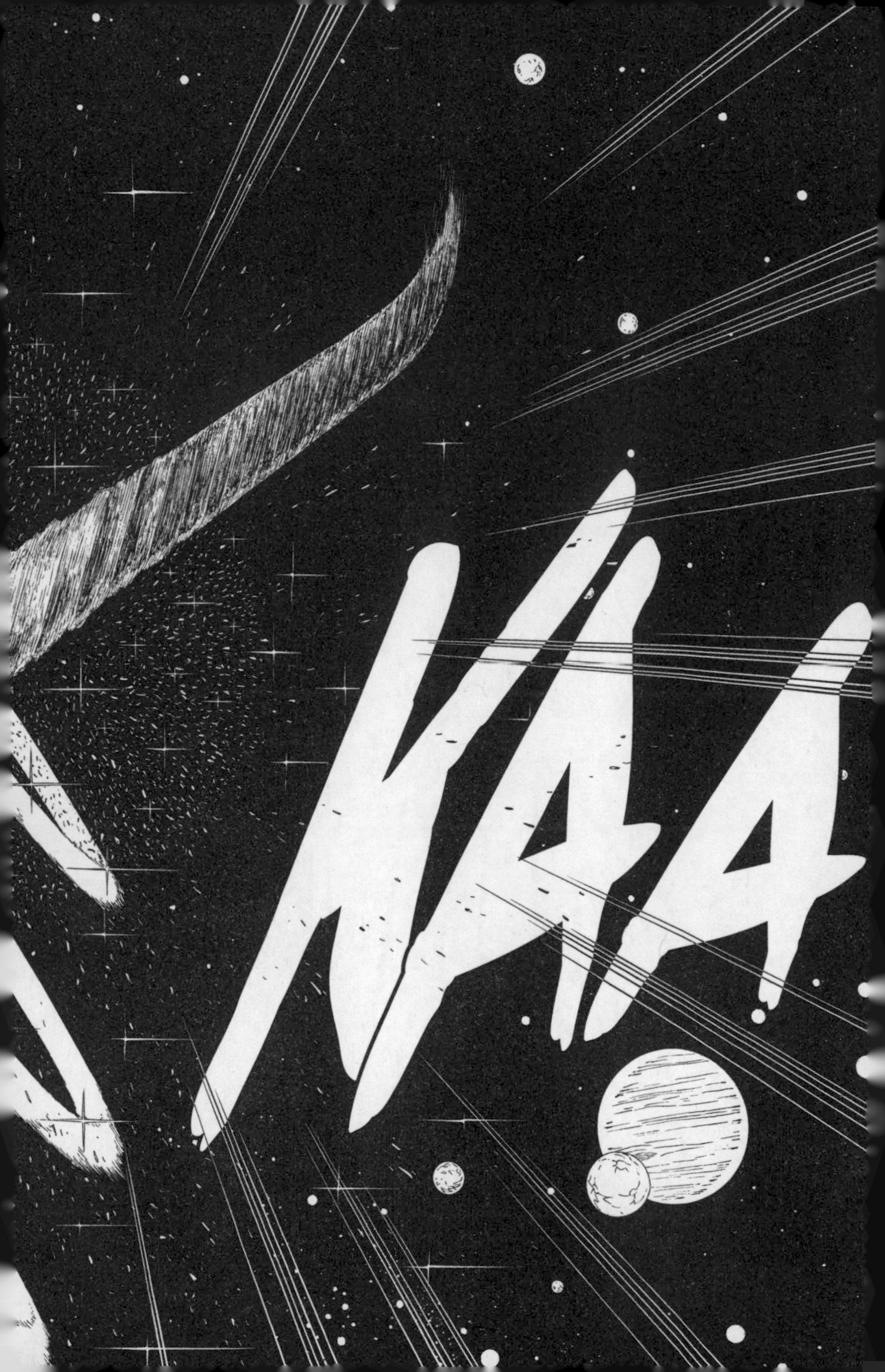

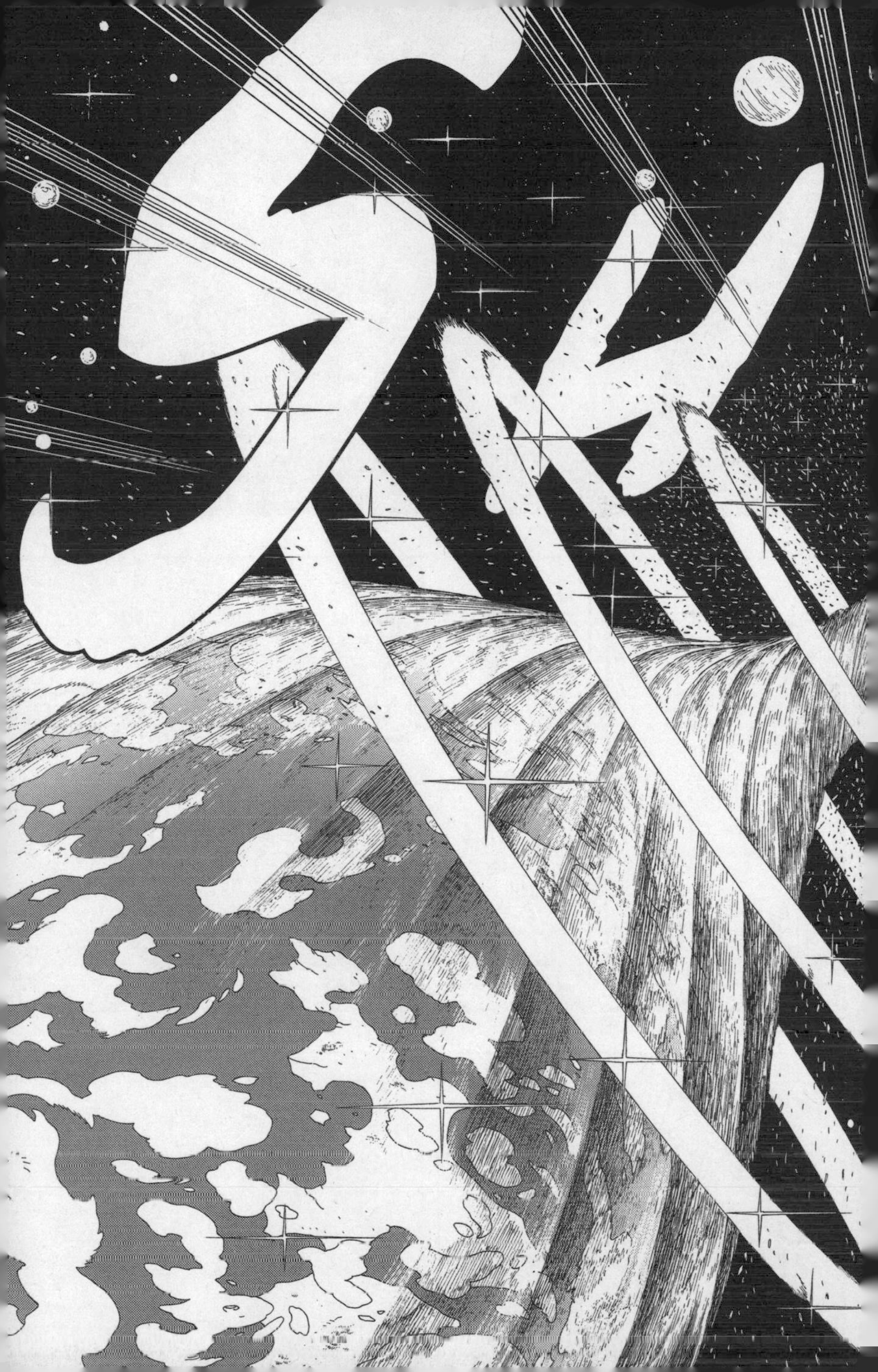

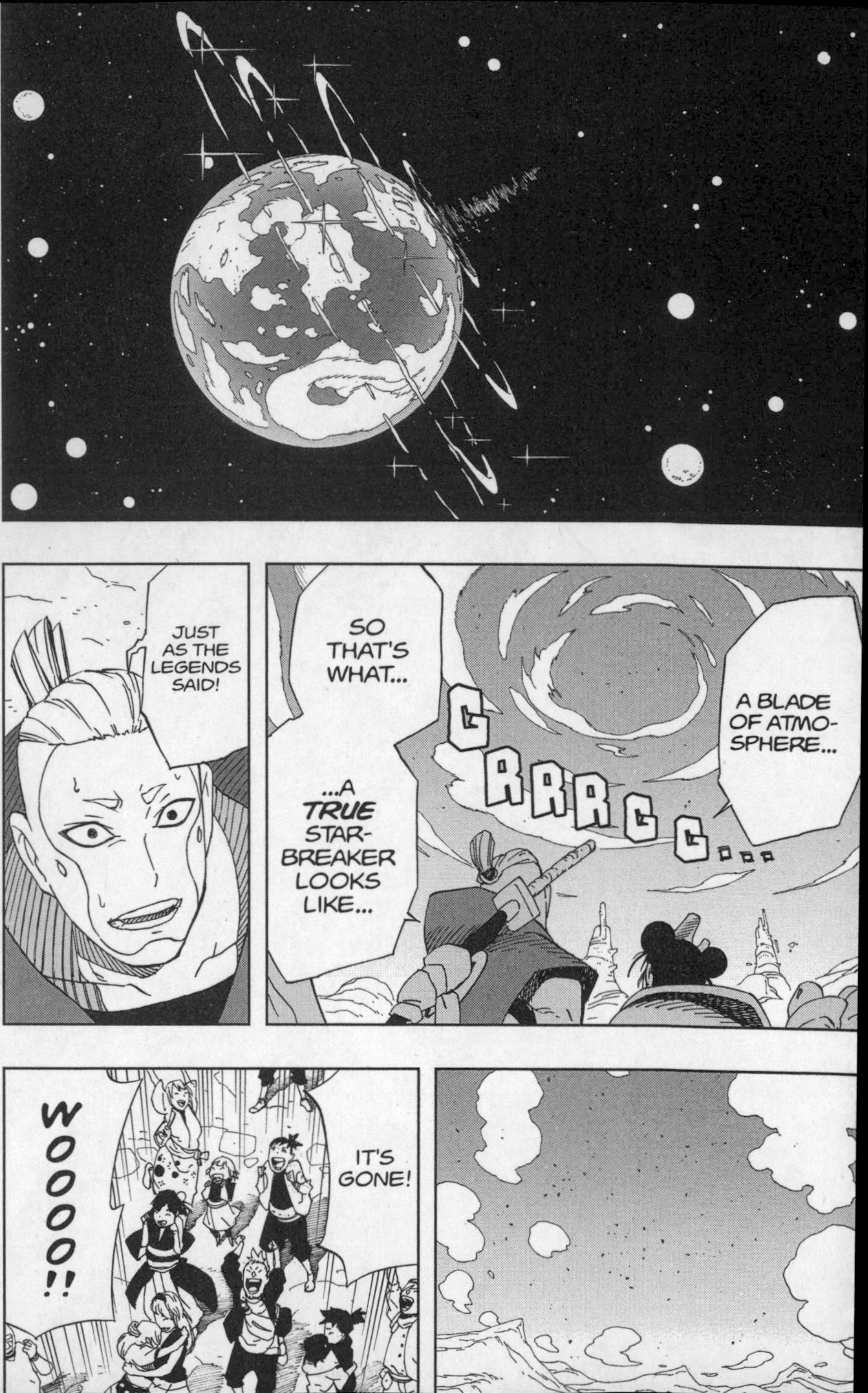
A BLADE OF ATMOSPHERE...
GRRRGG...
SO THAT'S WHAT...
...A **TRUE** STAR-BREAKER LOOKS LIKE...
JUST AS THE LEGENDS SAID!
IT'S GONE!
WOOOOO!!

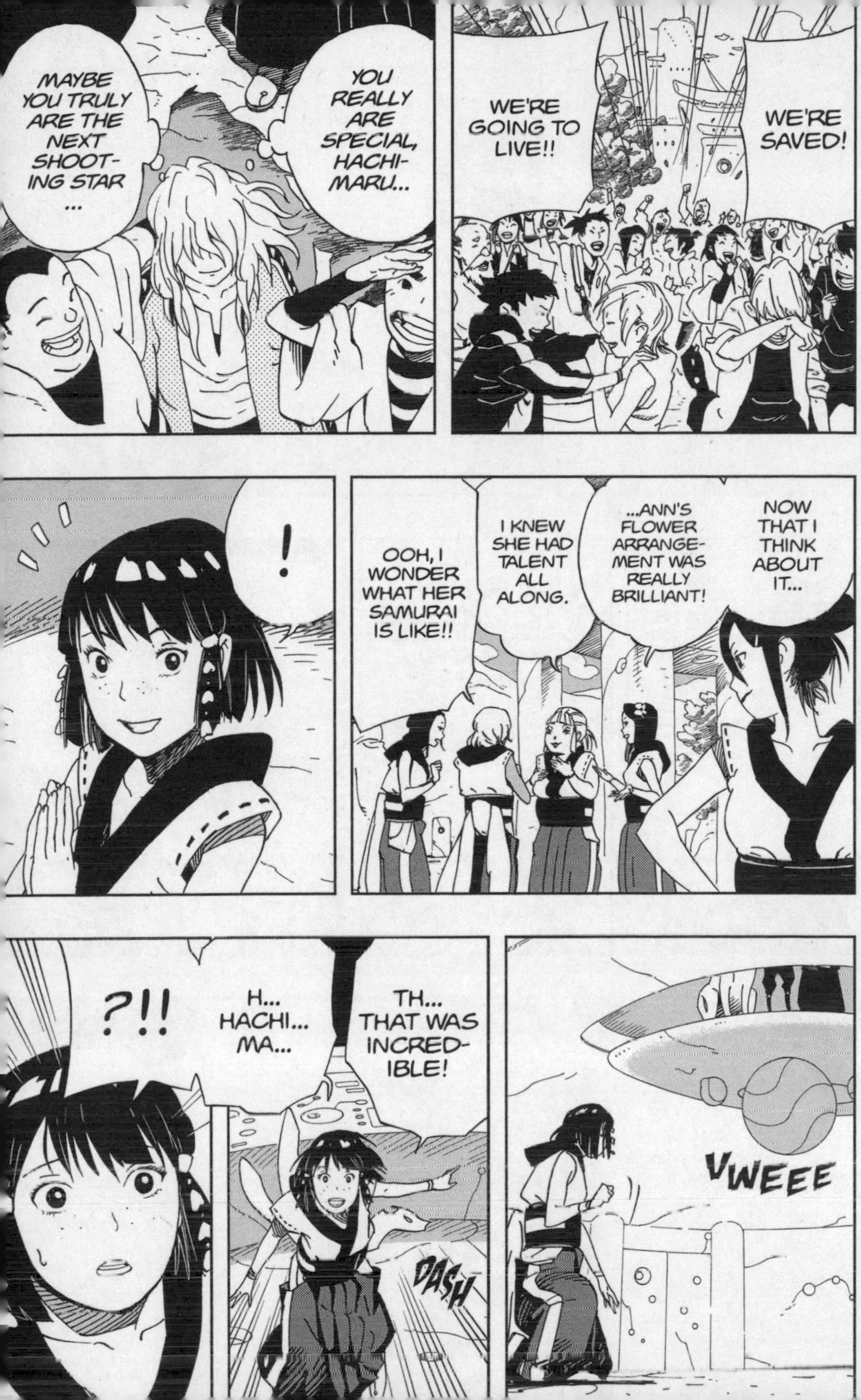
WE'RE SAVED!
WE'RE GOING TO LIVE!!
YOU REALLY ARE SPECIAL, HACHI-MARU...
MAYBE YOU TRULY ARE THE NEXT SHOOT-ING STAR ...
NOW THAT I THINK ABOUT IT...
...ANN'S FLOWER ARRANGE-MENT WAS REALLY BRILLIANT!
I KNEW SHE HAD TALENT ALL ALONG.
OOH, I WONDER WHAT HER SAMURAI IS LIKE!!
!
VWEEE
TH... THAT WAS INCRED-IBLE!
H... HACHI... MA...
DASH
?!!

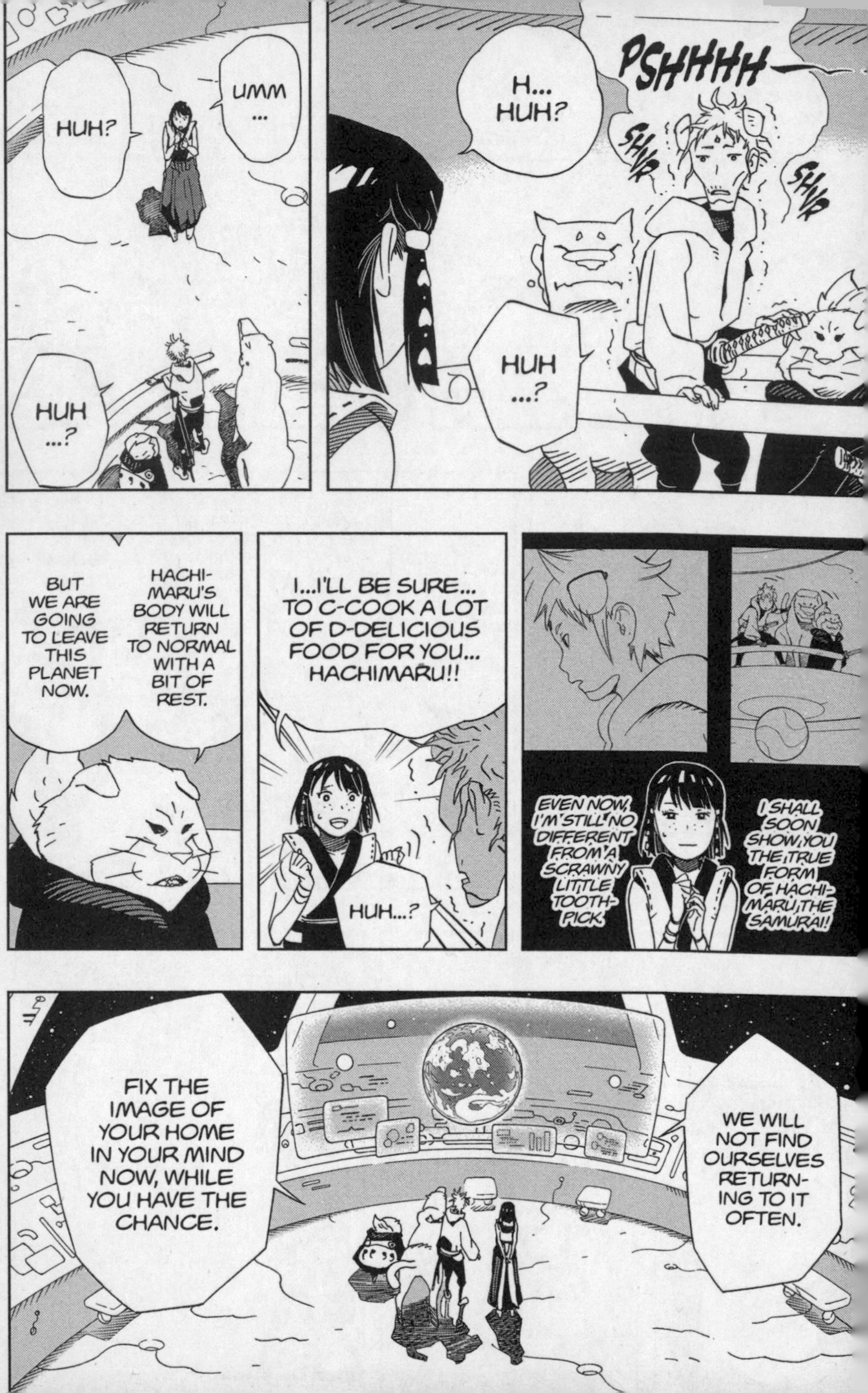
PSHHHH—
H... HUH?
SHWR
SHWR
HUH ...?
UMM ...
HUH?
HUH ...?
I SHALL SOON SHOW YOU THE TRUE FORM OF HACHI-MARU, THE SAMURAI!
EVEN NOW, I'M STILL NO DIFFERENT FROM A SCRAWNY LITTLE TOOTH-PICK.
I...I'LL BE SURE... TO C-COOK A LOT OF D-DELICIOUS FOOD FOR YOU... HACHIMARU!!
HUH...?
HACHI-MARU'S BODY WILL RETURN TO NORMAL WITH A BIT OF REST.
BUT WE ARE GOING TO LEAVE THIS PLANET NOW.
WE WILL NOT FIND OURSELVES RETURN-ING TO IT OFTEN.
FIX THE IMAGE OF YOUR HOME IN YOUR MIND NOW, WHILE YOU HAVE THE CHANCE.

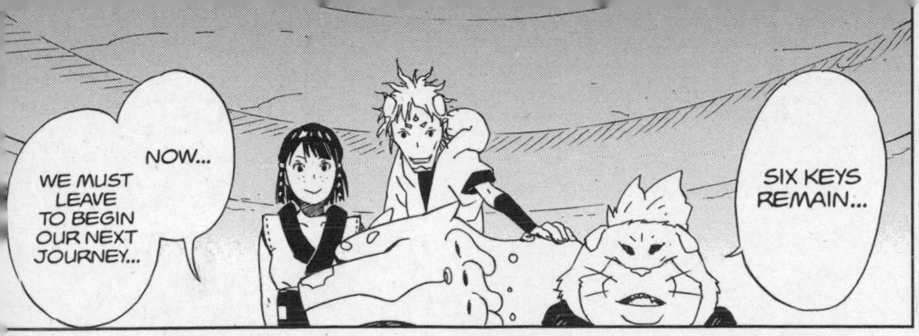
SIX KEYS REMAIN...
NOW... WE MUST LEAVE TO BEGIN OUR NEXT JOURNEY...

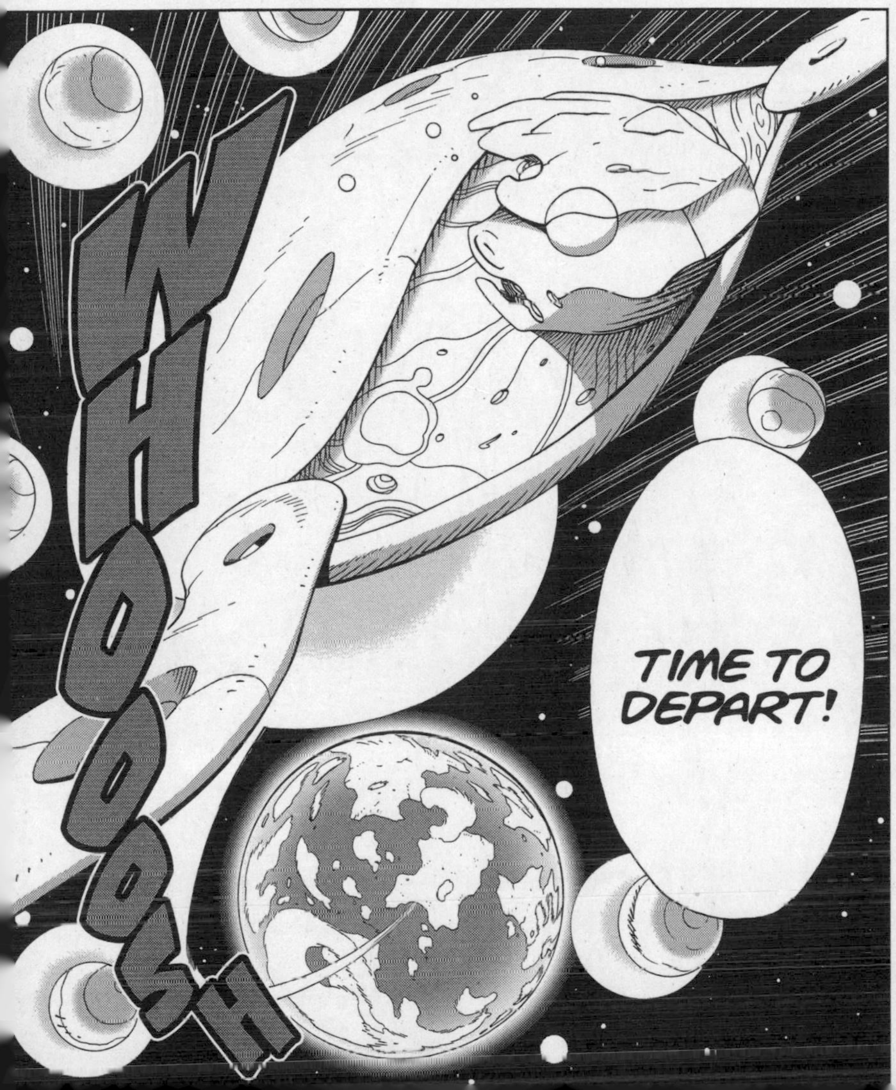
TIME TO DEPART!
WHOOOSH

Character Design Sketches: Nanashi

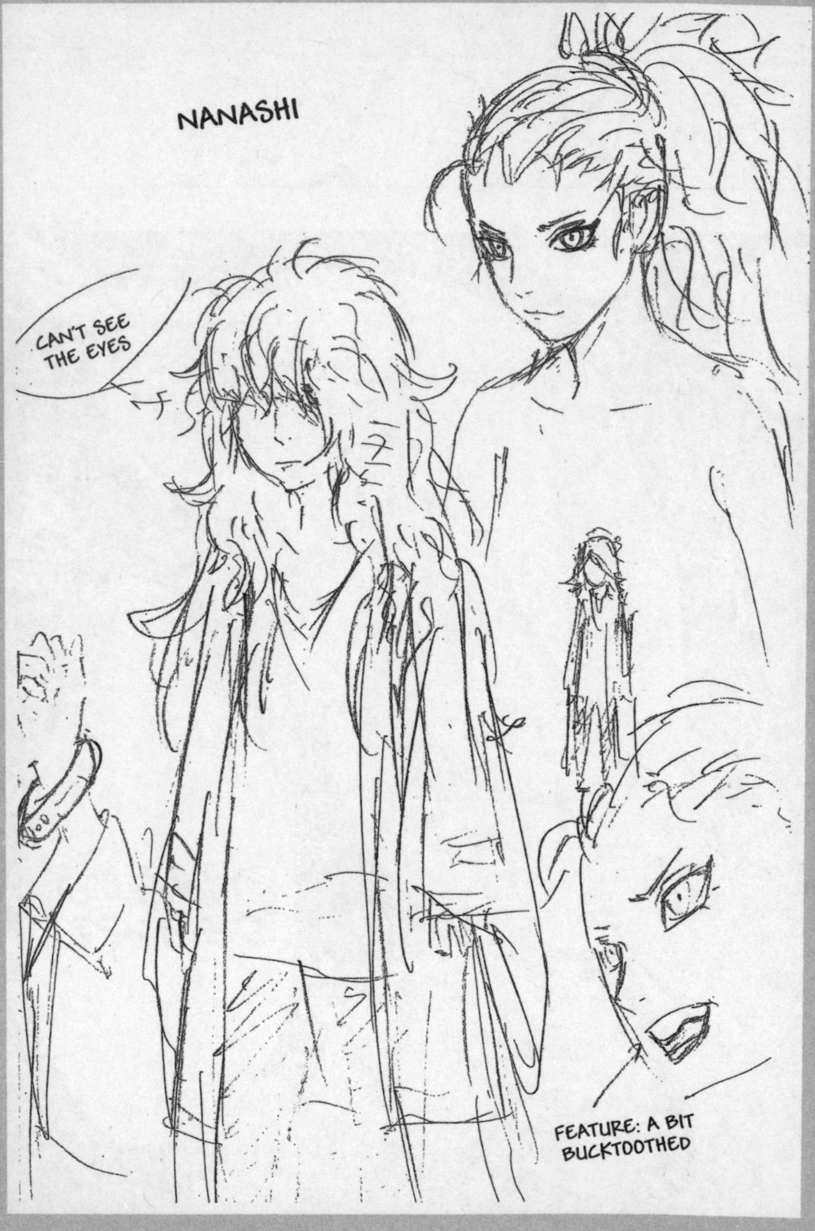
NANASHI
CAN'T SEE THE EYES
FEATURE: A BIT BUCKTOOTHED

CHAPTER 17: KOTSUGA & RYU

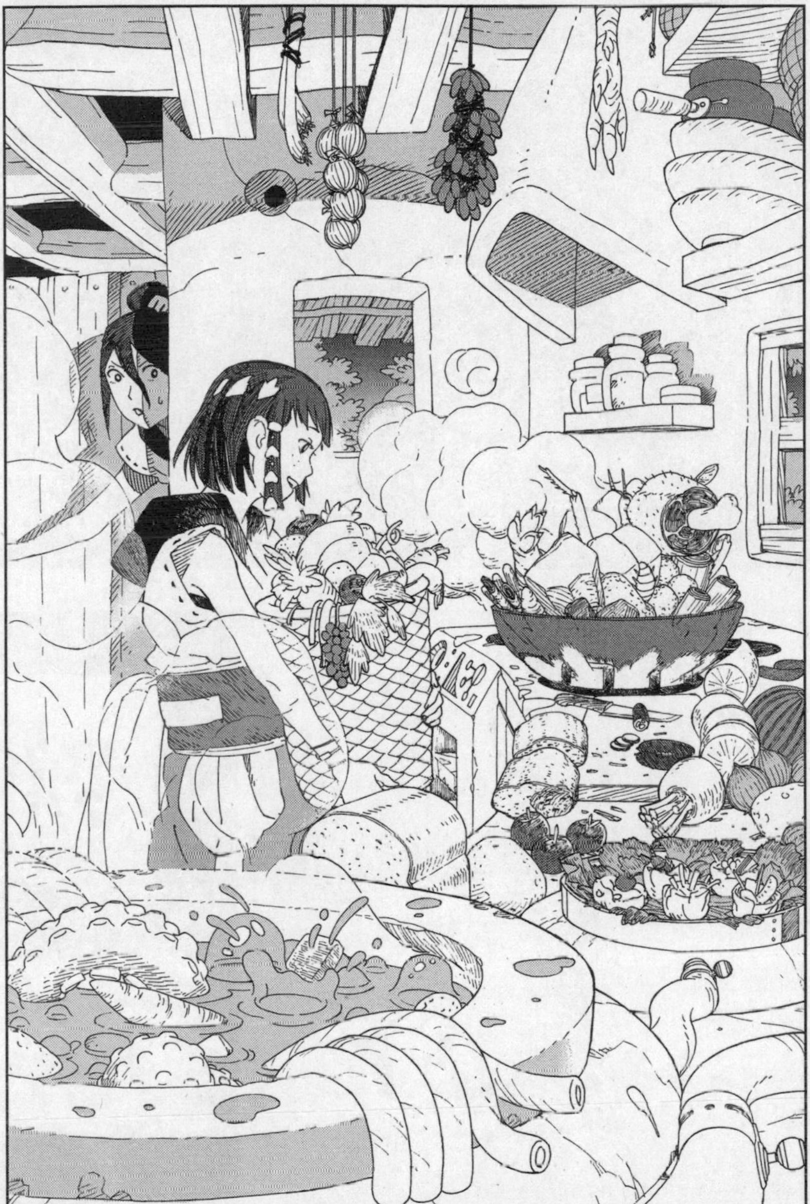

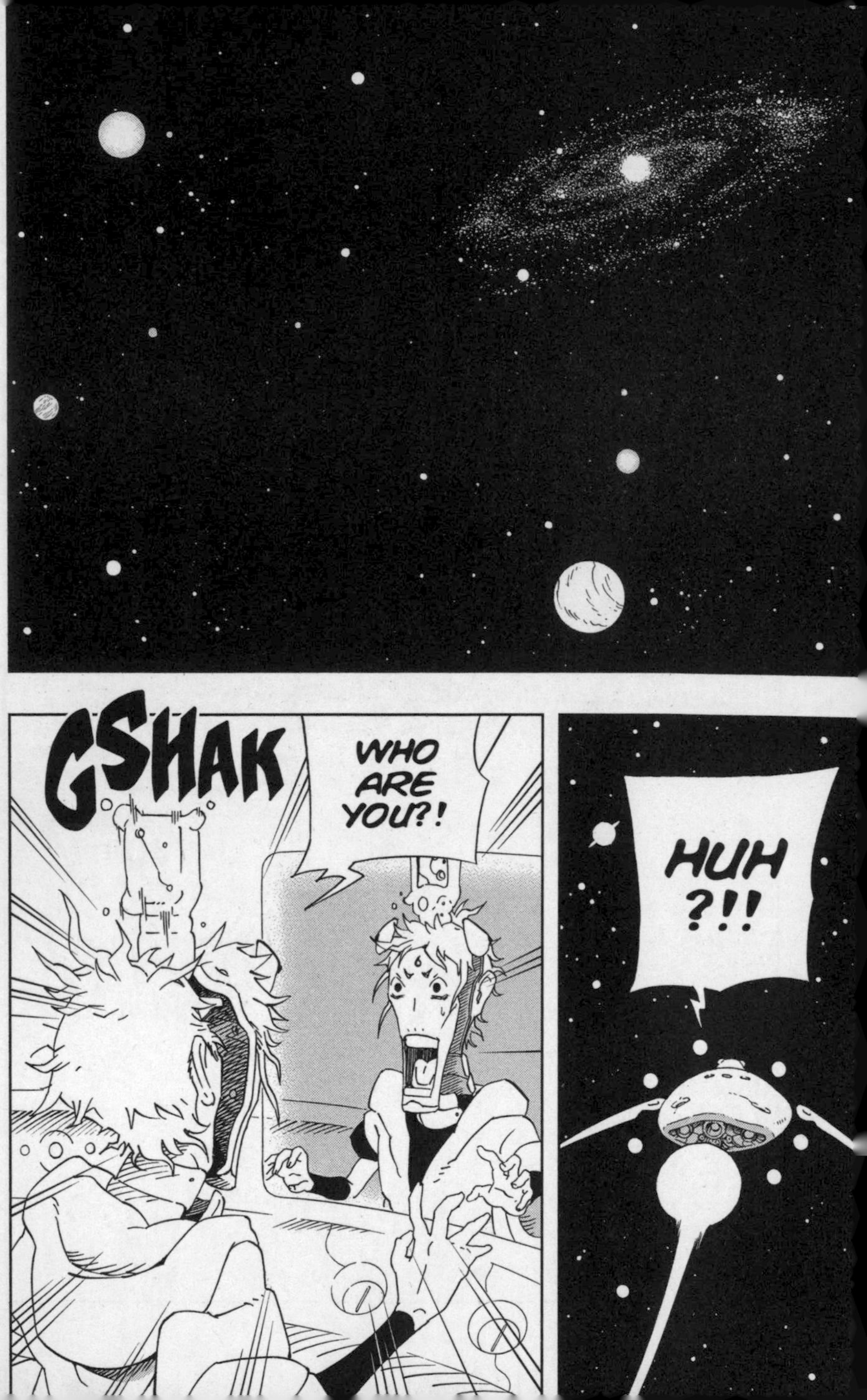
HUH ?!!
GSHAK
WHO ARE YOU?!

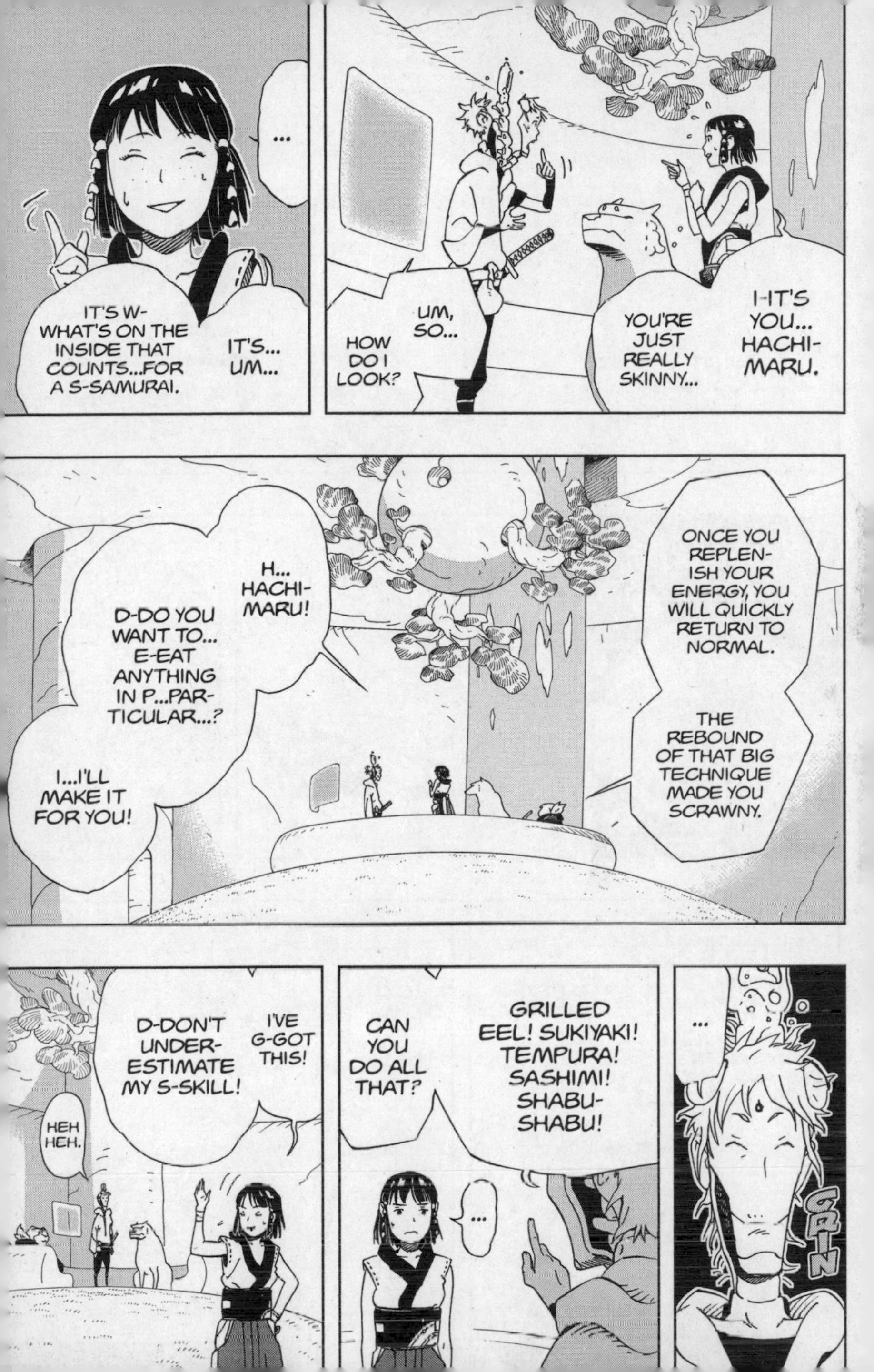
I-IT'S YOU... HACHIMARU.
YOU'RE JUST REALLY SKINNY...
UM, SO...
HOW DO I LOOK?
...
IT'S... UM...
IT'S W-WHAT'S ON THE INSIDE THAT COUNTS...FOR A S-SAMURAI.
ONCE YOU REPLENISH YOUR ENERGY, YOU WILL QUICKLY RETURN TO NORMAL.
THE REBOUND OF THAT BIG TECHNIQUE MADE YOU SCRAWNY.
H... HACHIMARU!
D-DO YOU WANT TO... E-EAT ANYTHING IN P...PARTICULAR...?
I...I'LL MAKE IT FOR YOU!
...
GRIN
GRILLED EEL! SUKIYAKI! TEMPURA! SASHIMI! SHABU-SHABU!
CAN YOU DO ALL THAT?
...
I'VE G-GOT THIS!
D-DON'T UNDERESTIMATE MY S-SKILL!
HEH HEH.

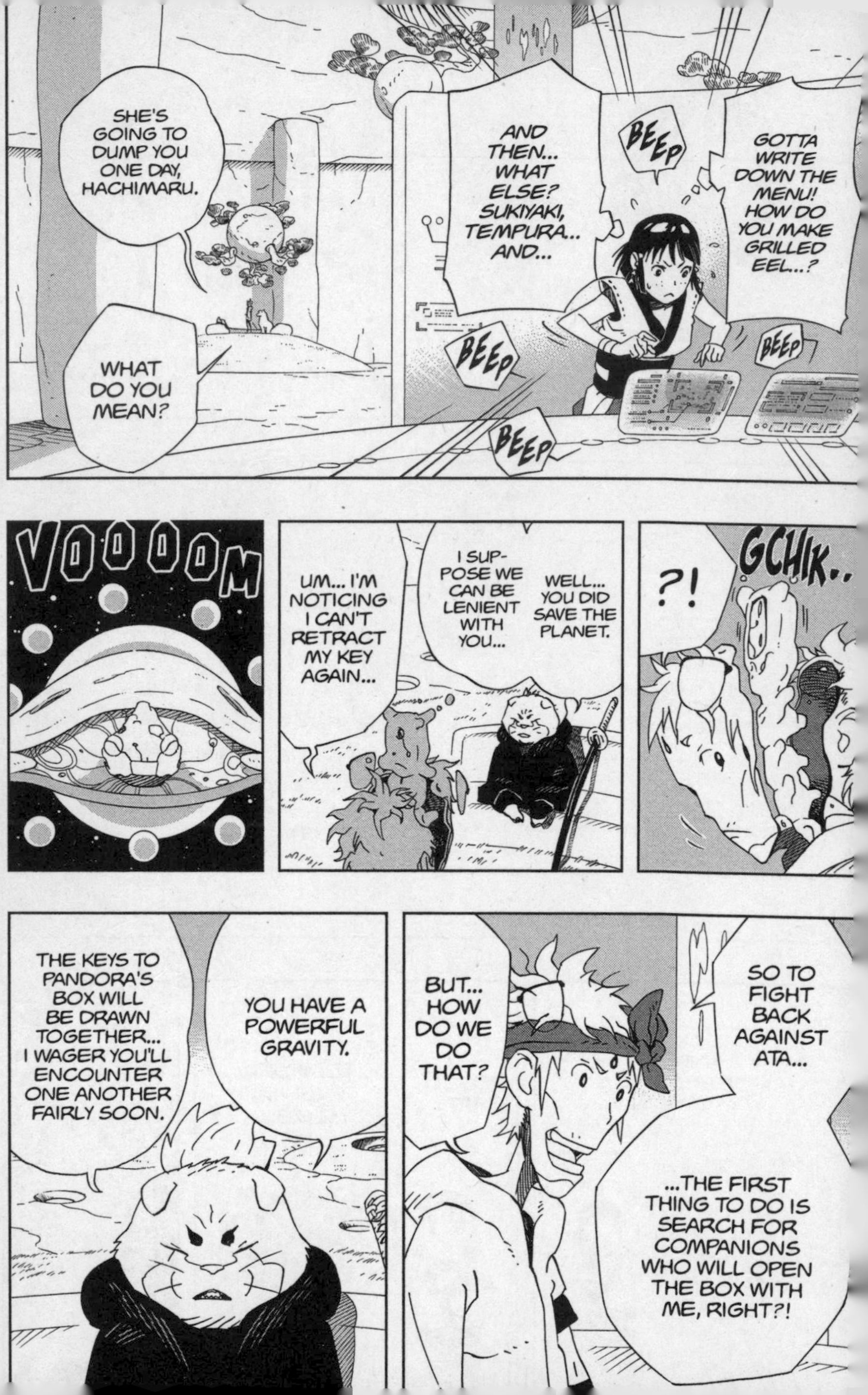
GOTTA WRITE DOWN THE MENU! HOW DO YOU MAKE GRILLED EEL...?
BEEP
AND THEN... WHAT ELSE? SUKIYAKI, TEMPURA... AND...
BEEP
BEEP
BEEP
SHE'S GOING TO DUMP YOU ONE DAY, HACHIMARU.
WHAT DO YOU MEAN?
GCHIK..
?!
WELL... YOU DID SAVE THE PLANET.
I SUP-POSE WE CAN BE LENIENT WITH YOU...
UM... I'M NOTICING I CAN'T RETRACT MY KEY AGAIN...
VOOOOM
SO TO FIGHT BACK AGAINST ATA...
...THE FIRST THING TO DO IS SEARCH FOR COMPANIONS WHO WILL OPEN THE BOX WITH ME, RIGHT?!
BUT... HOW DO WE DO THAT?
YOU HAVE A POWERFUL GRAVITY.
THE KEYS TO PANDORA'S BOX WILL BE DRAWN TOGETHER... I WAGER YOU'LL ENCOUNTER ONE ANOTHER FAIRLY SOON.

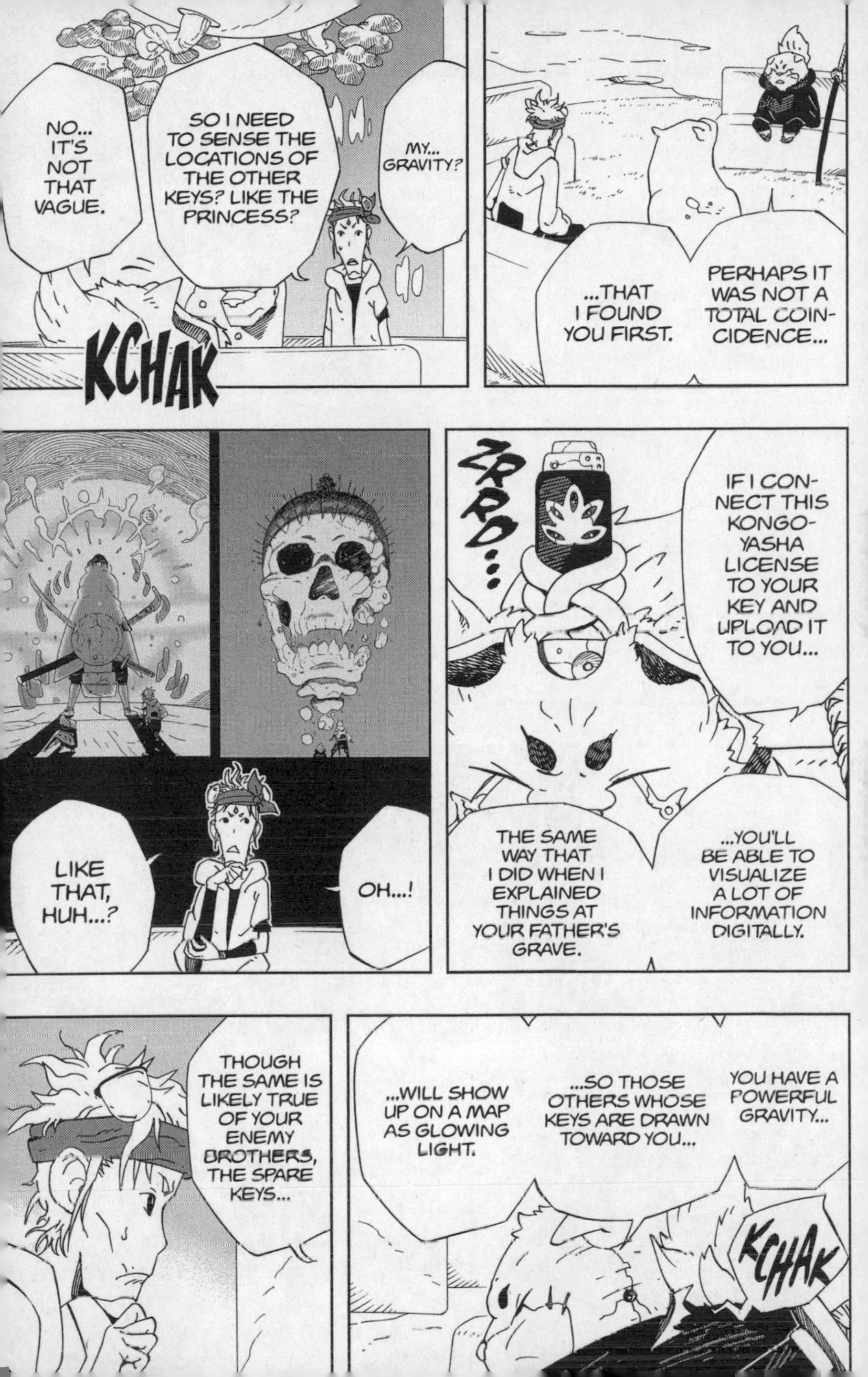
PERHAPS IT WAS NOT A TOTAL COINCIDENCE...
...THAT I FOUND YOU FIRST.
MY... GRAVITY?
SO I NEED TO SENSE THE LOCATIONS OF THE OTHER KEYS? LIKE THE PRINCESS?
NO... IT'S NOT THAT VAGUE.
KCHAK
ZRRD...
IF I CONNECT THIS KONGO-YASHA LICENSE TO YOUR KEY AND UPLOAD IT TO YOU...
...YOU'LL BE ABLE TO VISUALIZE A LOT OF INFORMATION DIGITALLY.
THE SAME WAY THAT I DID WHEN I EXPLAINED THINGS AT YOUR FATHER'S GRAVE.
OH...!
LIKE THAT, HUH...?
YOU HAVE A POWERFUL GRAVITY...
...SO THOSE OTHERS WHOSE KEYS ARE DRAWN TOWARD YOU...
...WILL SHOW UP ON A MAP AS GLOWING LIGHT.
KCHAK
THOUGH THE SAME IS LIKELY TRUE OF YOUR ENEMY BROTHERS, THE SPARE KEYS...

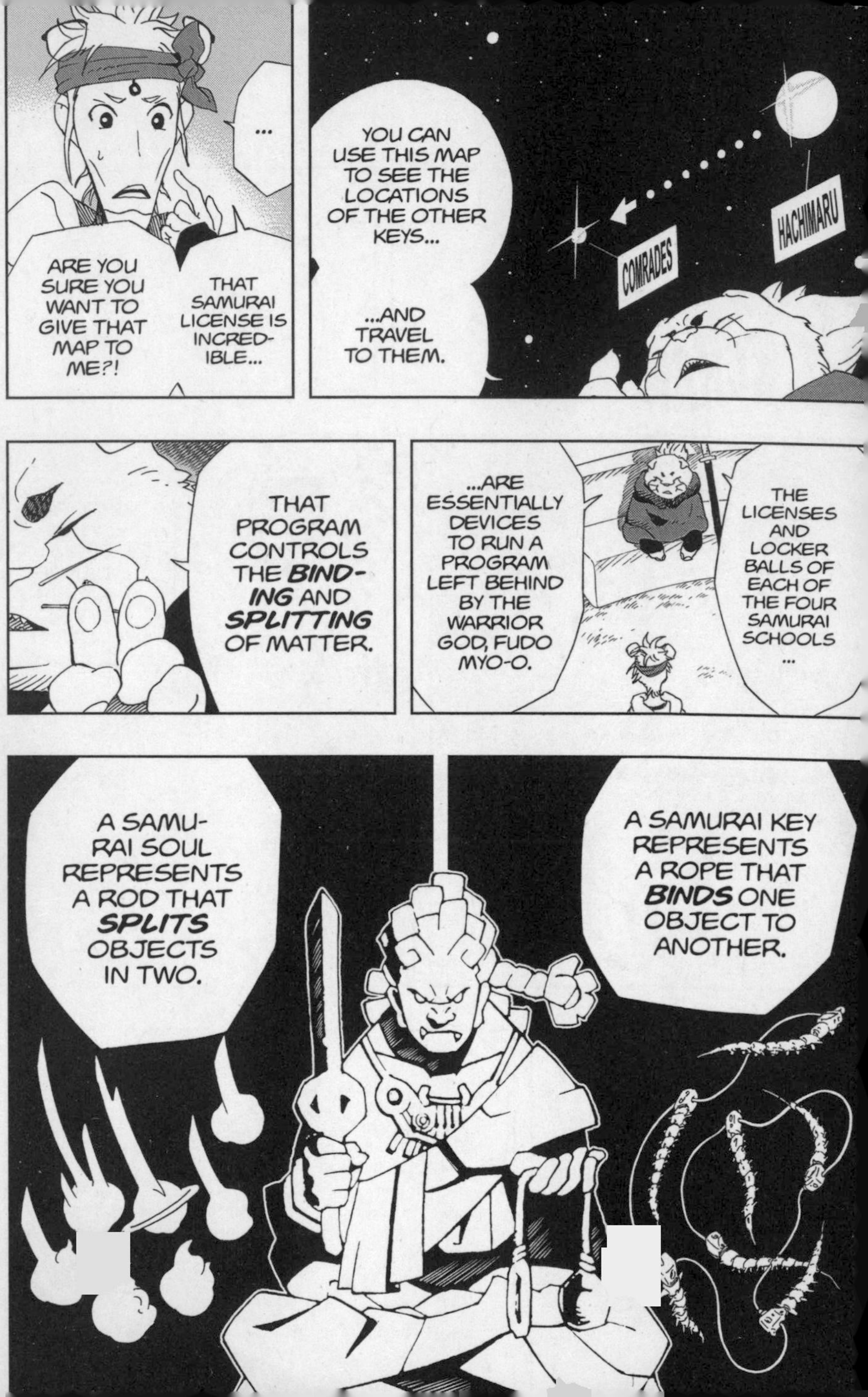
YOU CAN USE THIS MAP TO SEE THE LOCATIONS OF THE OTHER KEYS...
HACHIMARU
COMRADES
...AND TRAVEL TO THEM.
...
THAT SAMURAI LICENSE IS INCREDIBLE...
ARE YOU SURE YOU WANT TO GIVE THAT MAP TO ME?!
THE LICENSES AND LOCKER BALLS OF EACH OF THE FOUR SAMURAI SCHOOLS ...
...ARE ESSENTIALLY DEVICES TO RUN A PROGRAM LEFT BEHIND BY THE WARRIOR GOD, FUDO MYO-O.
THAT PROGRAM CONTROLS THE BINDING AND SPLITTING OF MATTER.
A SAMURAI KEY REPRESENTS A ROPE THAT BINDS ONE OBJECT TO ANOTHER.
A SAMURAI SOUL REPRESENTS A ROD THAT SPLITS OBJECTS IN TWO.

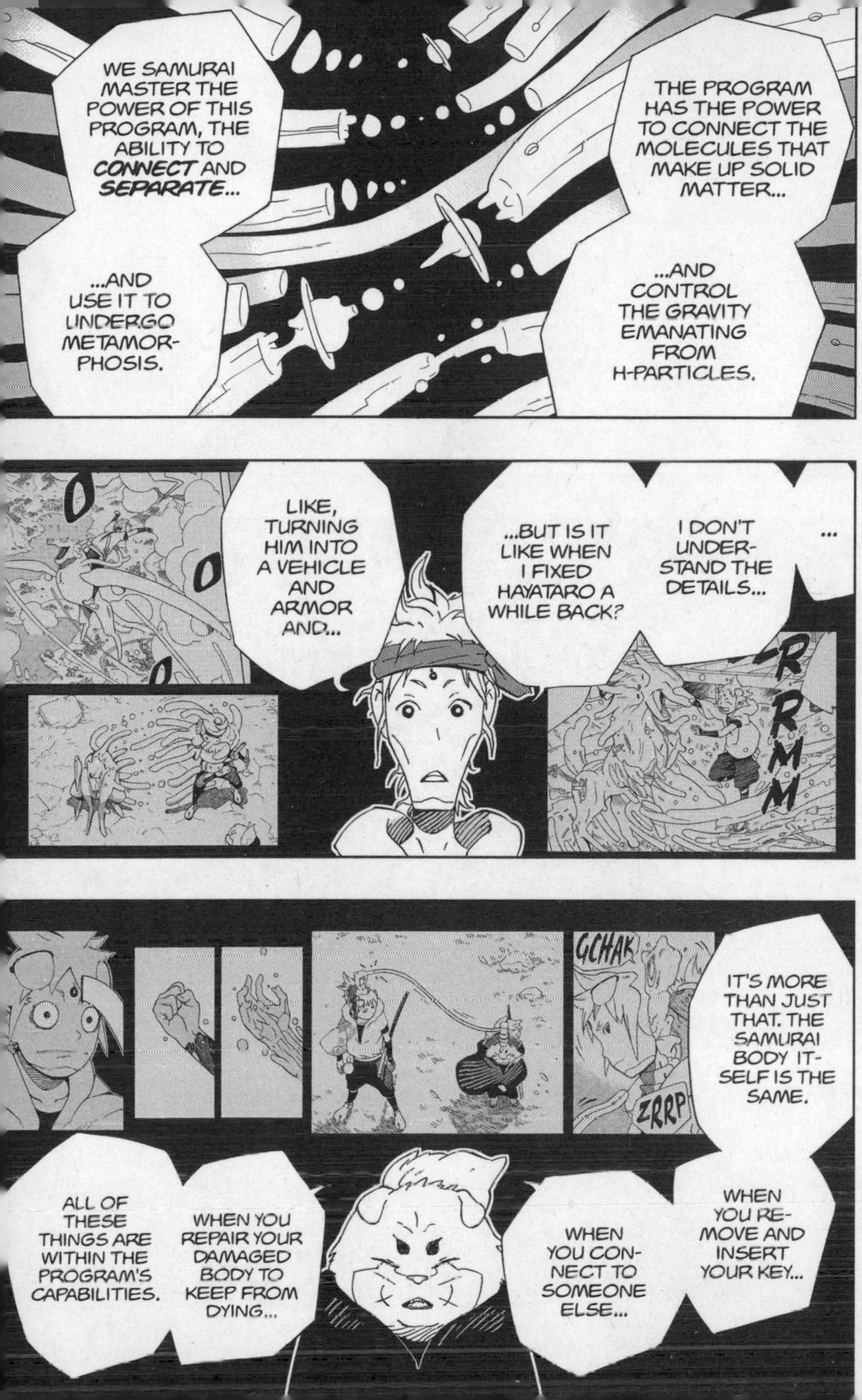
THE PROGRAM HAS THE POWER TO CONNECT THE MOLECULES THAT MAKE UP SOLID MATTER...
...AND CONTROL THE GRAVITY EMANATING FROM H-PARTICLES.
WE SAMURAI MASTER THE POWER OF THIS PROGRAM, THE ABILITY TO *CONNECT* AND *SEPARATE*...
...AND USE IT TO UNDERGO METAMORPHOSIS.
...
I DON'T UNDERSTAND THE DETAILS...
...BUT IS IT LIKE WHEN I FIXED HAYATARO A WHILE BACK?
LIKE, TURNING HIM INTO A VEHICLE AND ARMOR AND...
RRRMM
IT'S MORE THAN JUST THAT. THE SAMURAI BODY ITSELF IS THE SAME.
GCHAK
ZRRP
WHEN YOU REMOVE AND INSERT YOUR KEY...
WHEN YOU CONNECT TO SOMEONE ELSE...
WHEN YOU REPAIR YOUR DAMAGED BODY TO KEEP FROM DYING...
ALL OF THESE THINGS ARE WITHIN THE PROGRAM'S CAPABILITIES.

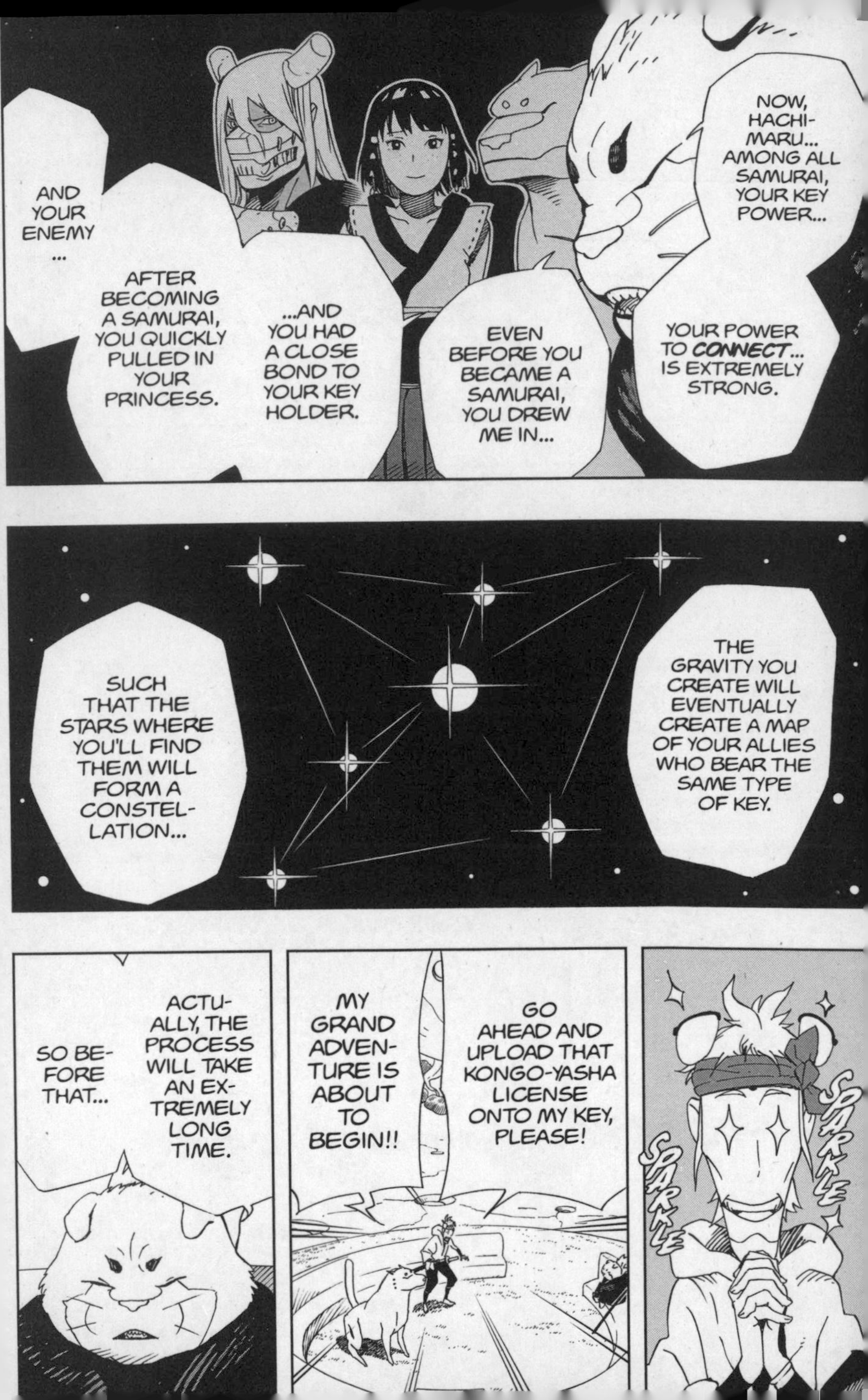

NOW, HACHIMARU... AMONG ALL SAMURAI, YOUR KEY POWER...
YOUR POWER TO ***CONNECT***... IS EXTREMELY STRONG.
EVEN BEFORE YOU BECAME A SAMURAI, YOU DREW ME IN...
...AND YOU HAD A CLOSE BOND TO YOUR KEY HOLDER.
AFTER BECOMING A SAMURAI, YOU QUICKLY PULLED IN YOUR PRINCESS.
AND YOUR ENEMY ...
THE GRAVITY YOU CREATE WILL EVENTUALLY CREATE A MAP OF YOUR ALLIES WHO BEAR THE SAME TYPE OF KEY.
SUCH THAT THE STARS WHERE YOU'LL FIND THEM WILL FORM A CONSTELLATION...
SPARKLE
SPARKLE
GO AHEAD AND UPLOAD THAT KONGO-YASHA LICENSE ONTO MY KEY, PLEASE!
MY GRAND ADVENTURE IS ABOUT TO BEGIN!!
ACTUALLY, THE PROCESS WILL TAKE AN EXTREMELY LONG TIME.
SO BEFORE THAT...

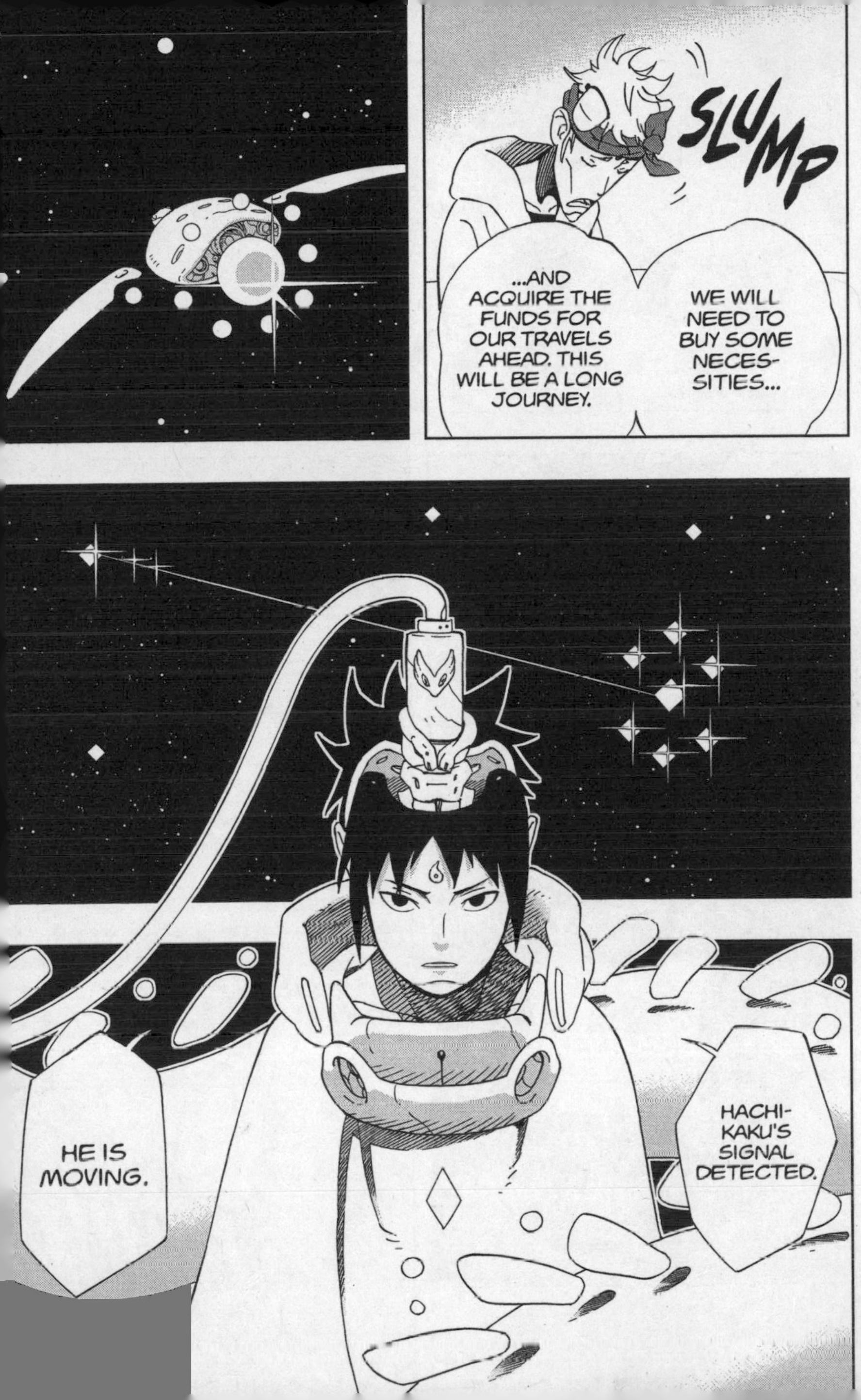
SLUMP
WE WILL NEED TO BUY SOME NECES-SITIES...
...AND ACQUIRE THE FUNDS FOR OUR TRAVELS AHEAD. THIS WILL BE A LONG JOURNEY.
HACHI-KAKU'S SIGNAL DETECTED.
HE IS MOVING.

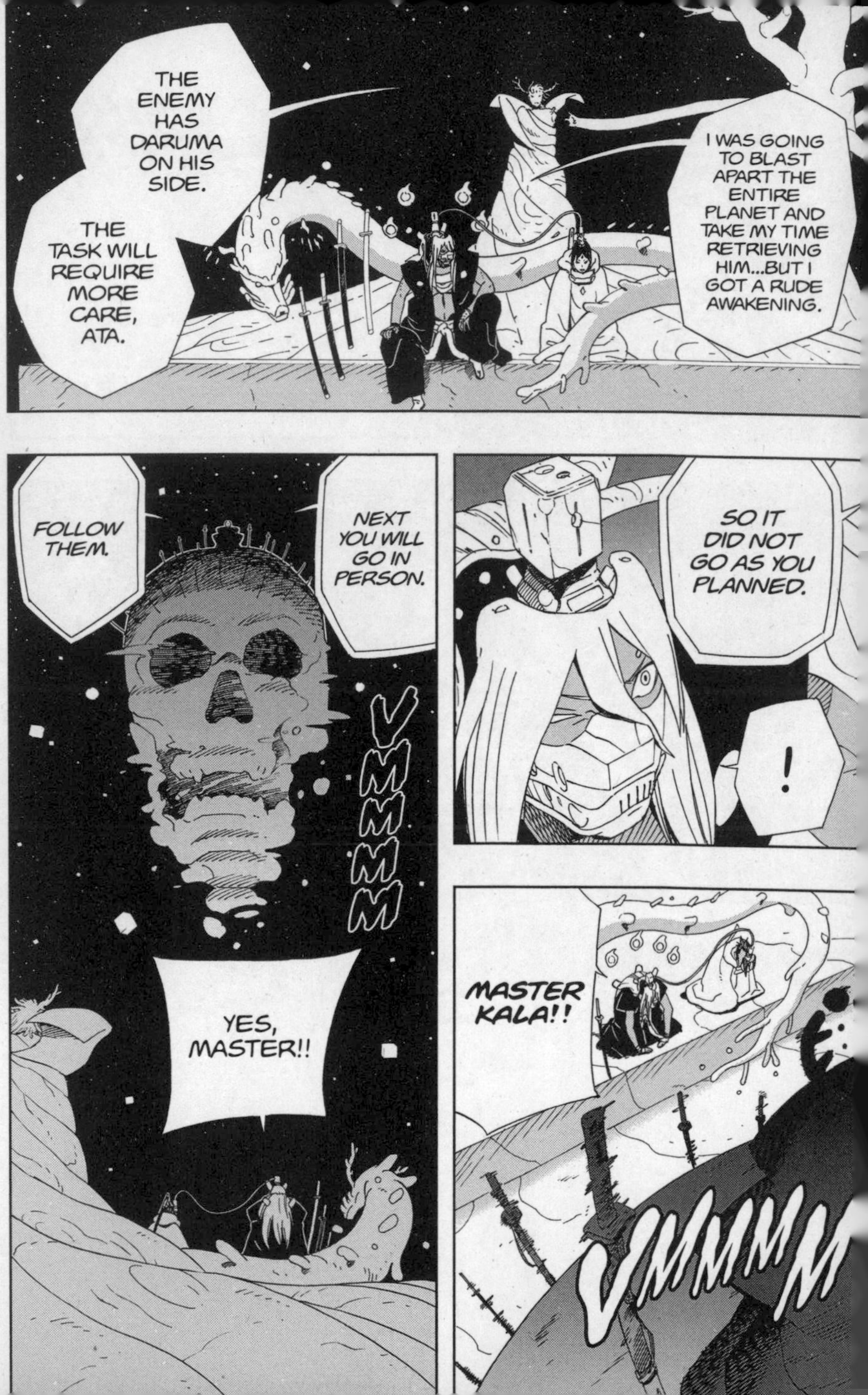
I WAS GOING TO BLAST APART THE ENTIRE PLANET AND TAKE MY TIME RETRIEVING HIM...BUT I GOT A RUDE AWAKENING.
THE ENEMY HAS DARUMA ON HIS SIDE.
THE TASK WILL REQUIRE MORE CARE, ATA.
SO IT DID NOT GO AS YOU PLANNED.
!
MASTER KALA!!
VMMMM
NEXT YOU WILL GO IN PERSON.
FOLLOW THEM.
VMMMMM
YES, MASTER!!

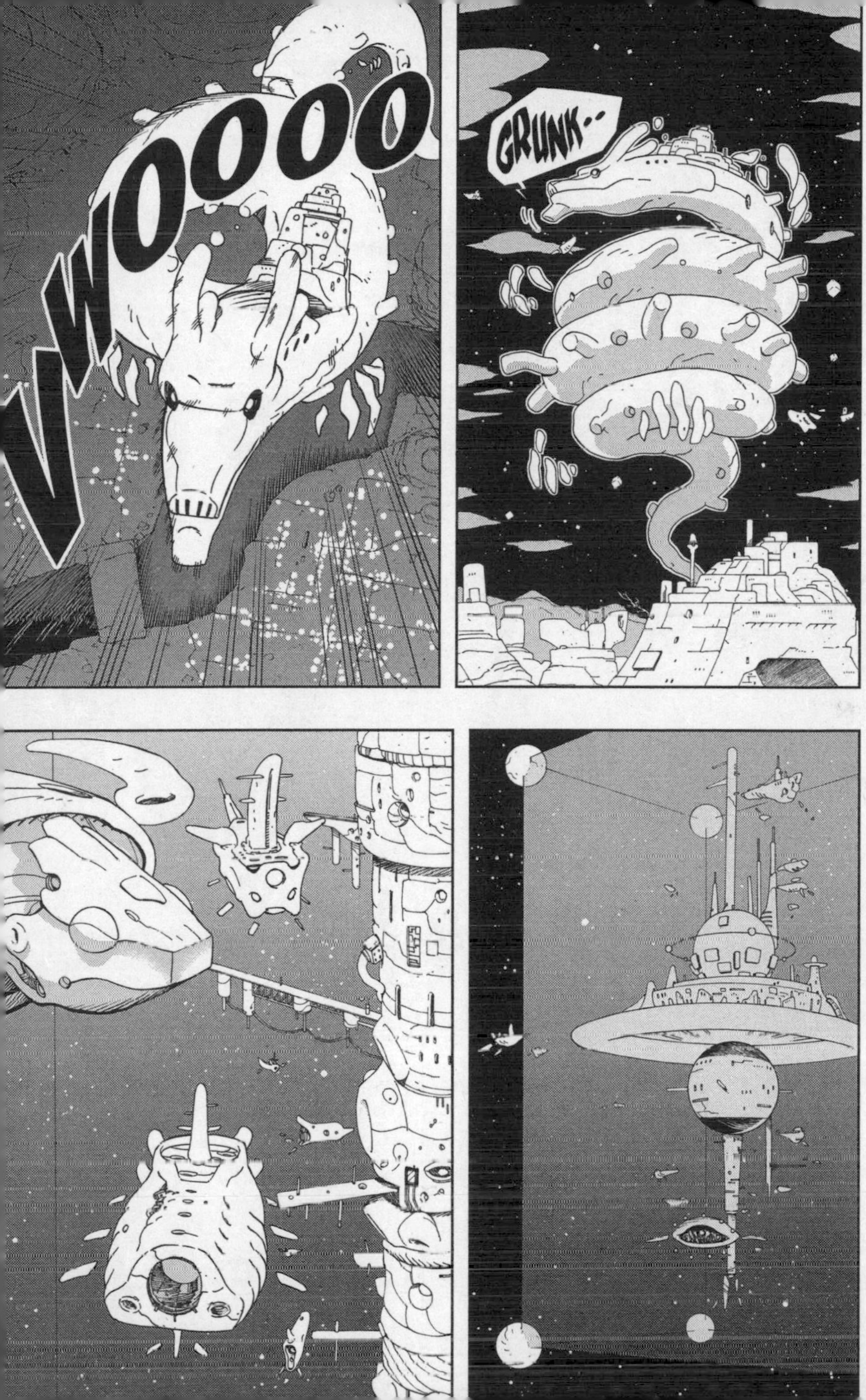
GRUNK..
VWOOOOO

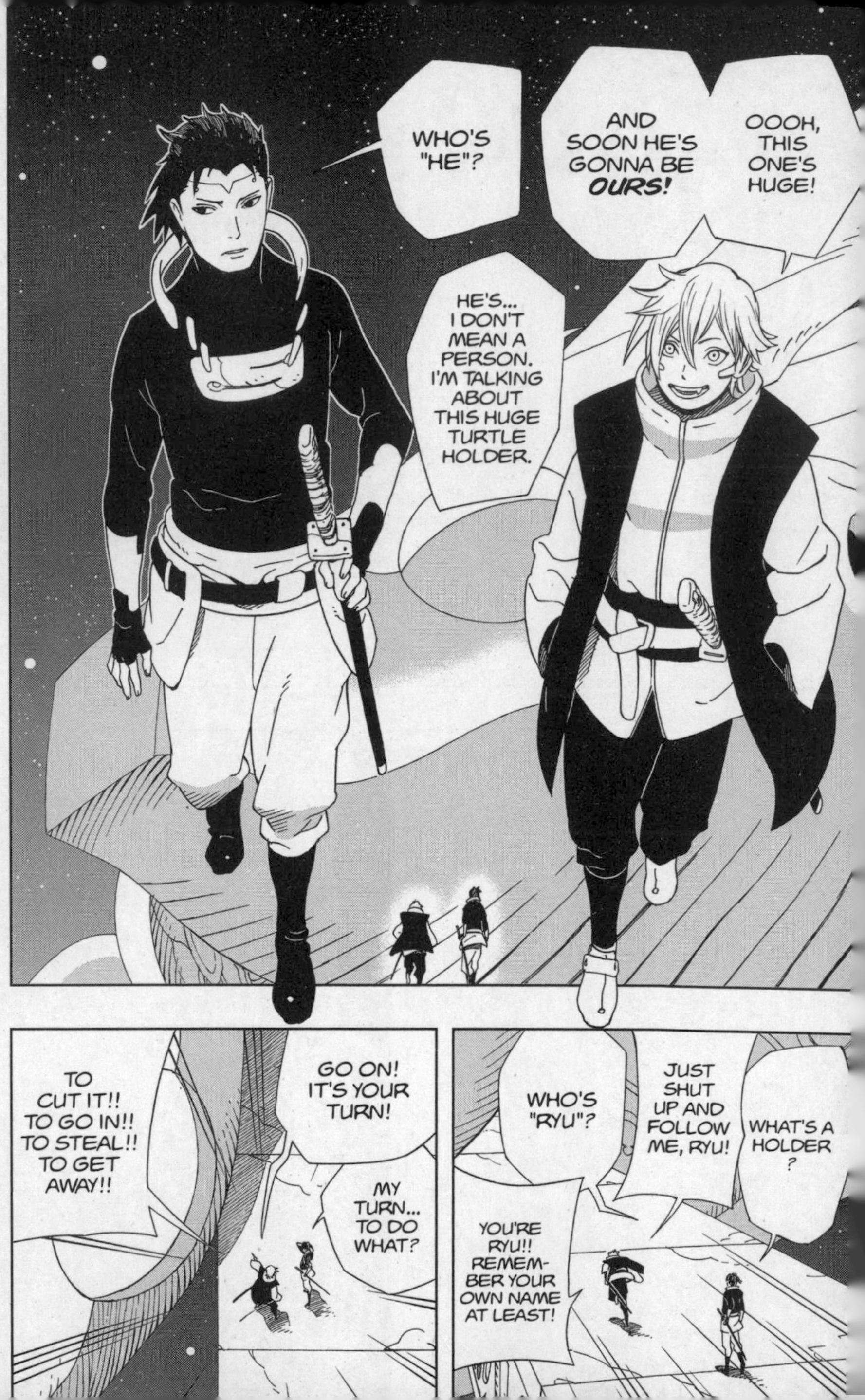
OOOH, THIS ONE'S HUGE!
AND SOON HE'S GONNA BE **OURS!**
WHO'S "HE"?
HE'S... I DON'T MEAN A PERSON. I'M TALKING ABOUT THIS HUGE TURTLE HOLDER.
WHAT'S A HOLDER ?
JUST SHUT UP AND FOLLOW ME, RYU!
WHO'S "RYU"?
YOU'RE RYU!! REMEMBER YOUR OWN NAME AT LEAST!
GO ON! IT'S YOUR TURN!
MY TURN... TO DO WHAT?
TO CUT IT!! TO GO IN!! TO STEAL!! TO GET AWAY!!

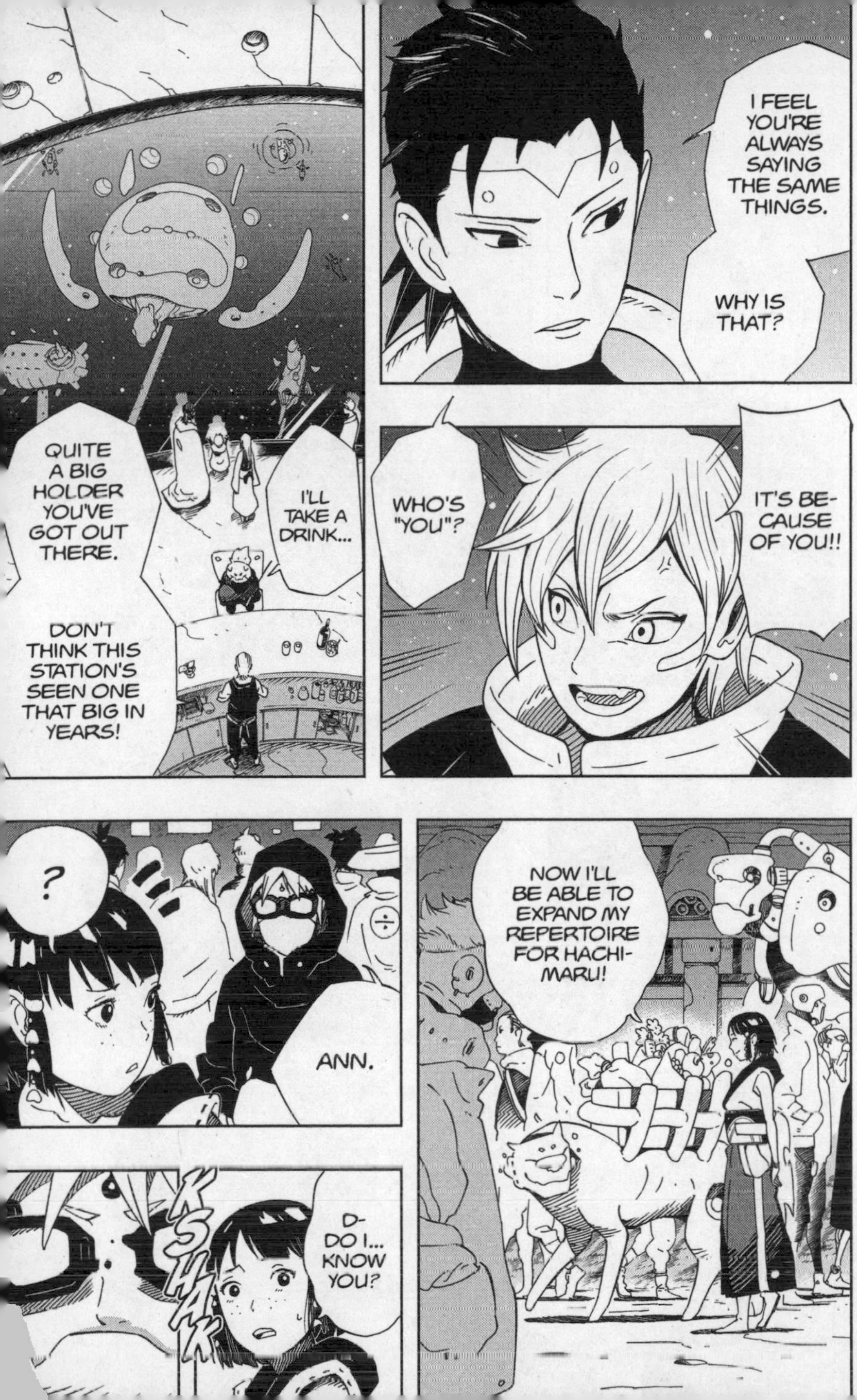
I FEEL YOU'RE ALWAYS SAYING THE SAME THINGS.
WHY IS THAT?
IT'S BE-CAUSE OF YOU!!
WHO'S "YOU"?
I'LL TAKE A DRINK...
QUITE A BIG HOLDER YOU'VE GOT OUT THERE.
DON'T THINK THIS STATION'S SEEN ONE THAT BIG IN YEARS!
NOW I'LL BE ABLE TO EXPAND MY REPERTOIRE FOR HACHI-MARU!
?
ANN.
KSHAK
D-DO I... KNOW YOU?

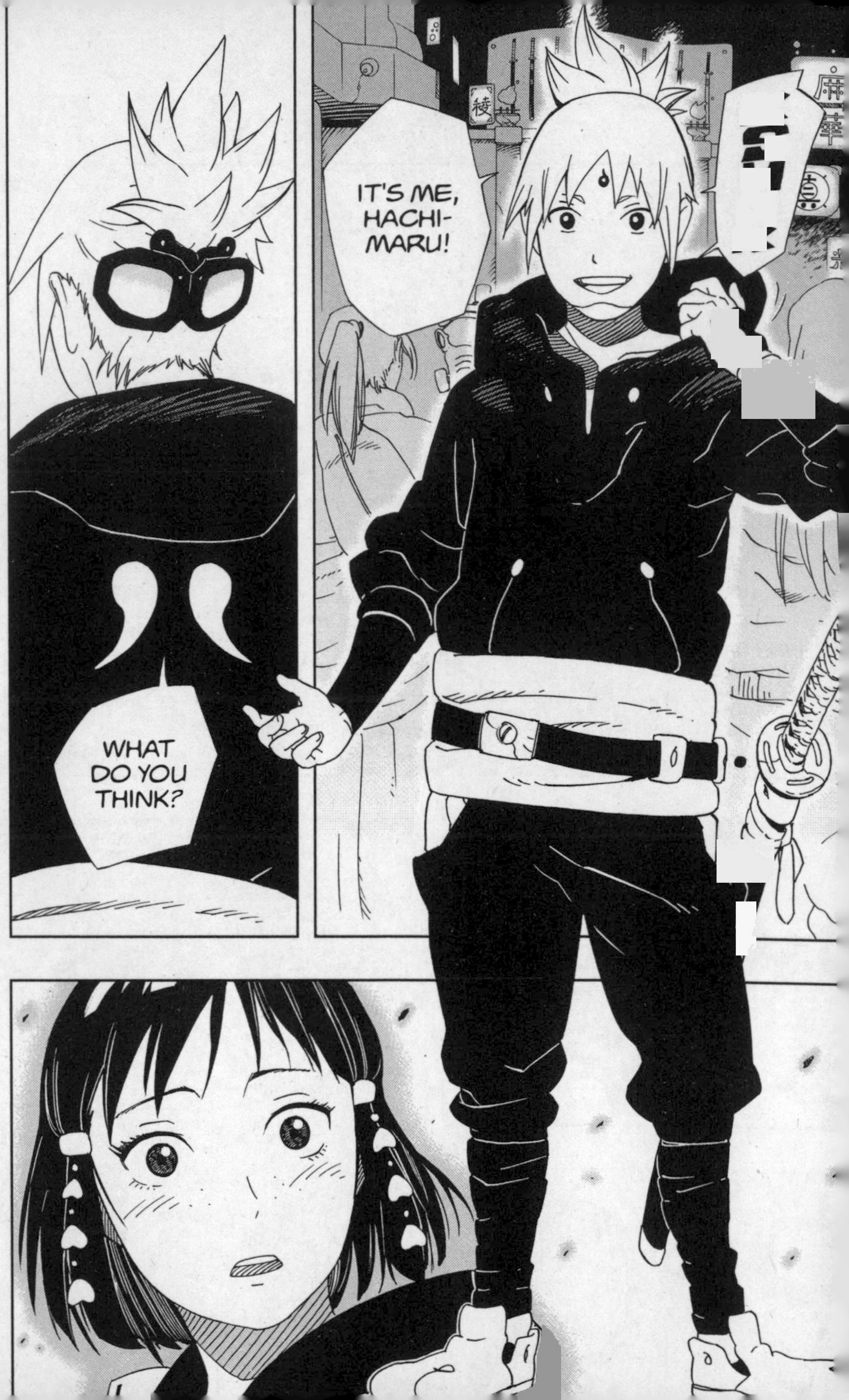
IT'S ME, HACHI-MARU!
WHAT DO YOU THINK?

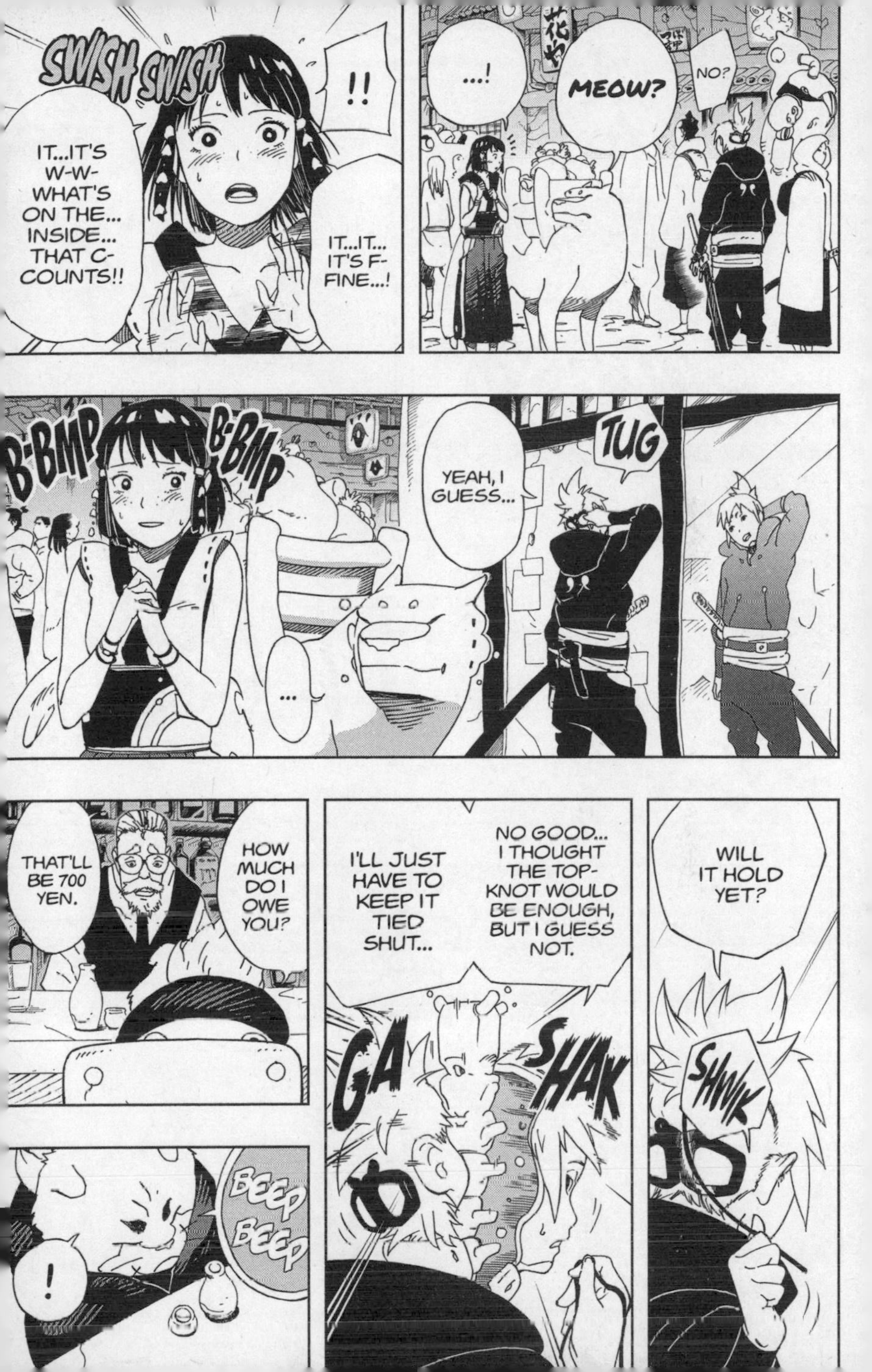
NO?
MEOW?
...!
!!
IT...IT... IT'S F-FINE...!
SWISH SWISH
IT...IT'S W-W-WHAT'S ON THE... INSIDE... THAT C-COUNTS!!
TUG
YEAH, I GUESS...
B-BMP B-BMP
...
WILL IT HOLD YET?
SHNIK
NO GOOD... I THOUGHT THE TOP-KNOT WOULD BE ENOUGH, BUT I GUESS NOT.
I'LL JUST HAVE TO KEEP IT TIED SHUT...
GA SHAK
HOW MUCH DO I OWE YOU?
THAT'LL BE 700 YEN.
BEEP BEEP
!

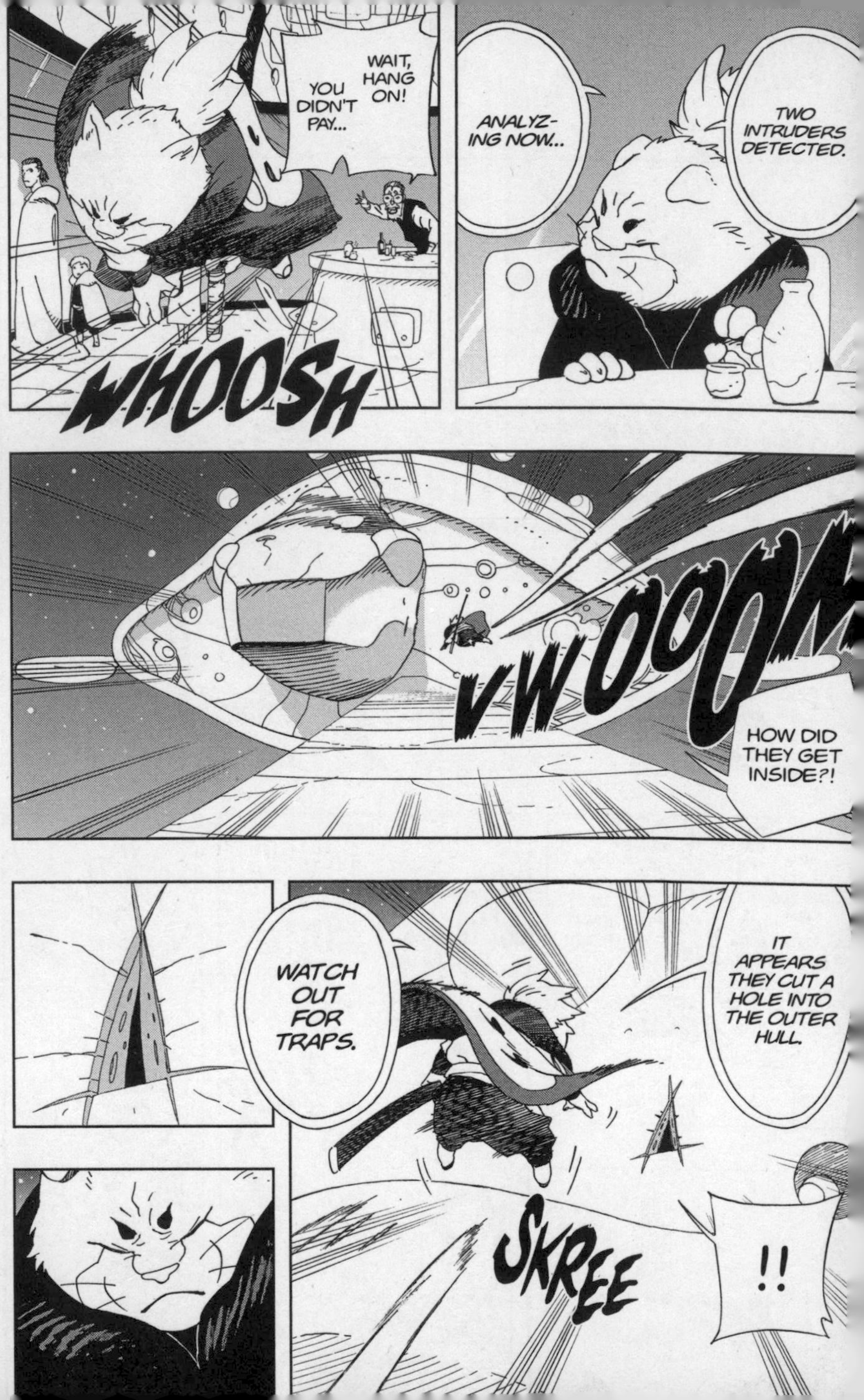
TWO INTRUDERS DETECTED.
ANALYZ-ING NOW...
WAIT, HANG ON!
YOU DIDN'T PAY...
WHOOSH
VWOOOOM
HOW DID THEY GET INSIDE?!
IT APPEARS THEY CUT A HOLE INTO THE OUTER HULL.
WATCH OUT FOR TRAPS.
SKREE
!!

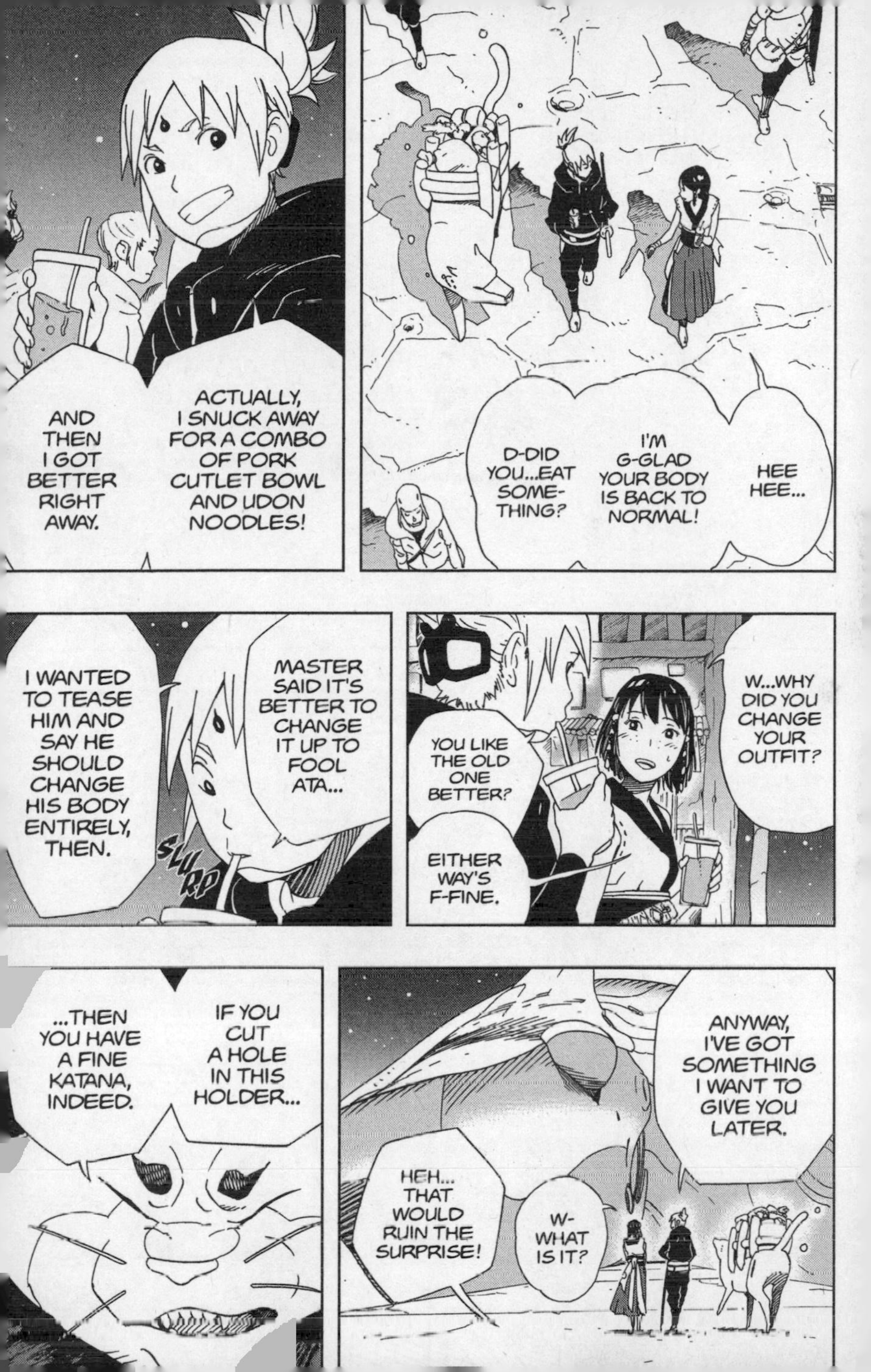
HEE HEE...
I'M G-GLAD YOUR BODY IS BACK TO NORMAL!
D-DID YOU...EAT SOMETHING?
ACTUALLY, I SNUCK AWAY FOR A COMBO OF PORK CUTLET BOWL AND UDON NOODLES!
AND THEN I GOT BETTER RIGHT AWAY.
W...WHY DID YOU CHANGE YOUR OUTFIT?
YOU LIKE THE OLD ONE BETTER?
EITHER WAY'S F-FINE.
MASTER SAID IT'S BETTER TO CHANGE IT UP TO FOOL ATA...
SLURP
I WANTED TO TEASE HIM AND SAY HE SHOULD CHANGE HIS BODY ENTIRELY, THEN.
ANYWAY, I'VE GOT SOMETHING I WANT TO GIVE YOU LATER.
W-WHAT IS IT?
HEH... THAT WOULD RUIN THE SURPRISE!
IF YOU CUT A HOLE IN THIS HOLDER...
...THEN YOU HAVE A FINE KATANA, INDEED.

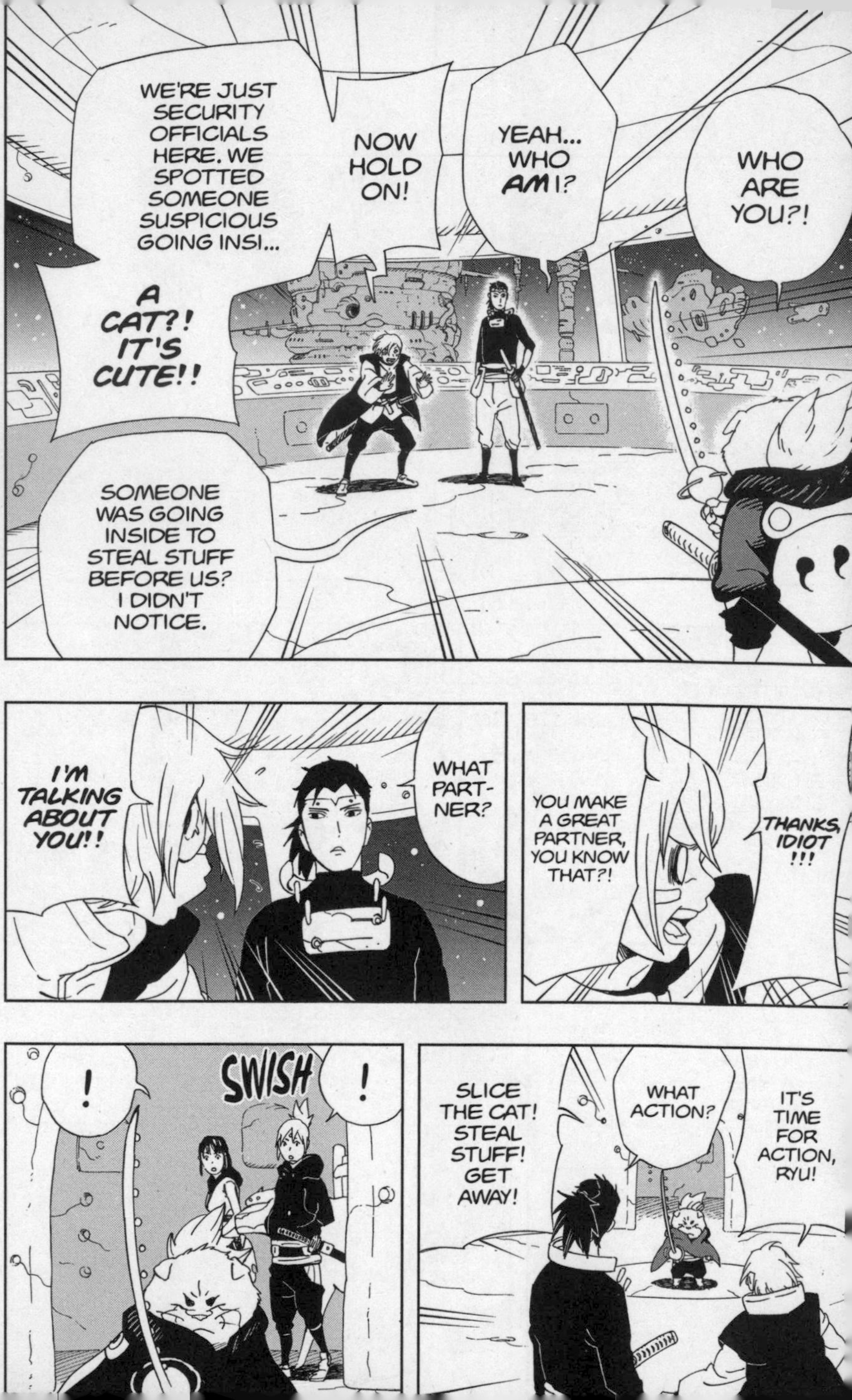
WHO ARE YOU?!
YEAH... WHO AM I?
NOW HOLD ON!
WE'RE JUST SECURITY OFFICIALS HERE. WE SPOTTED SOMEONE SUSPICIOUS GOING INSI...
A CAT?! IT'S CUTE!!
SOMEONE WAS GOING INSIDE TO STEAL STUFF BEFORE US? I DIDN'T NOTICE.
THANKS, IDIOT!!!
YOU MAKE A GREAT PARTNER, YOU KNOW THAT?!
WHAT PART-NER?
I'M TALKING ABOUT YOU!!
IT'S TIME FOR ACTION, RYU!
WHAT ACTION?
SLICE THE CAT! STEAL STUFF! GET AWAY!
!
SWISH
!

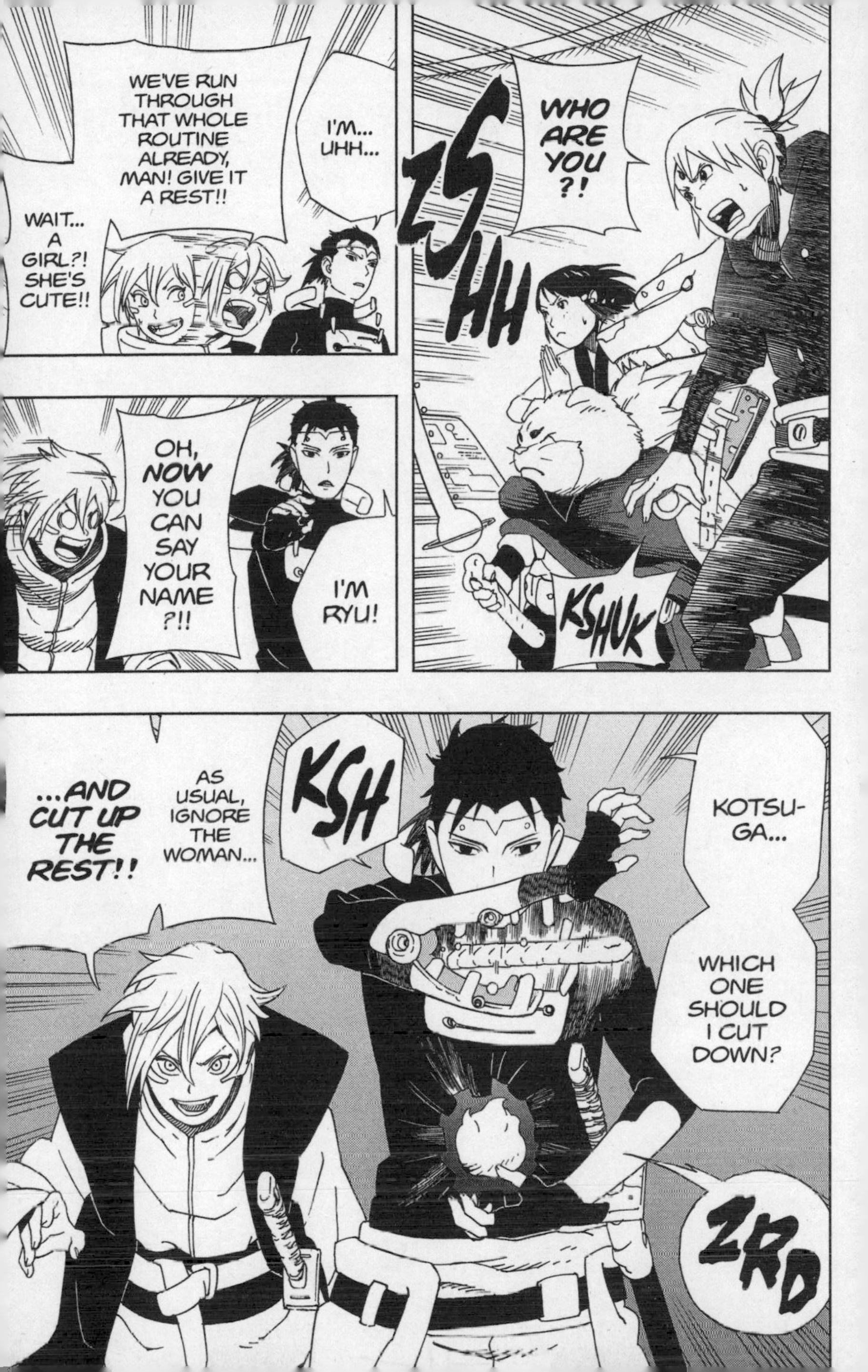
WHO ARE YOU?!
ZSHH
KSHUK
I'M... UHH...
WE'VE RUN THROUGH THAT WHOLE ROUTINE ALREADY, MAN! GIVE IT A REST!!
WAIT... A GIRL?! SHE'S CUTE!!
I'M RYU!
OH, NOW YOU CAN SAY YOUR NAME?!!
KOTSU-GA...
WHICH ONE SHOULD I CUT DOWN?
ZRD
KSH
AS USUAL, IGNORE THE WOMAN...
...AND CUT UP THE REST!!

Character Design Sketches: Hagamichi

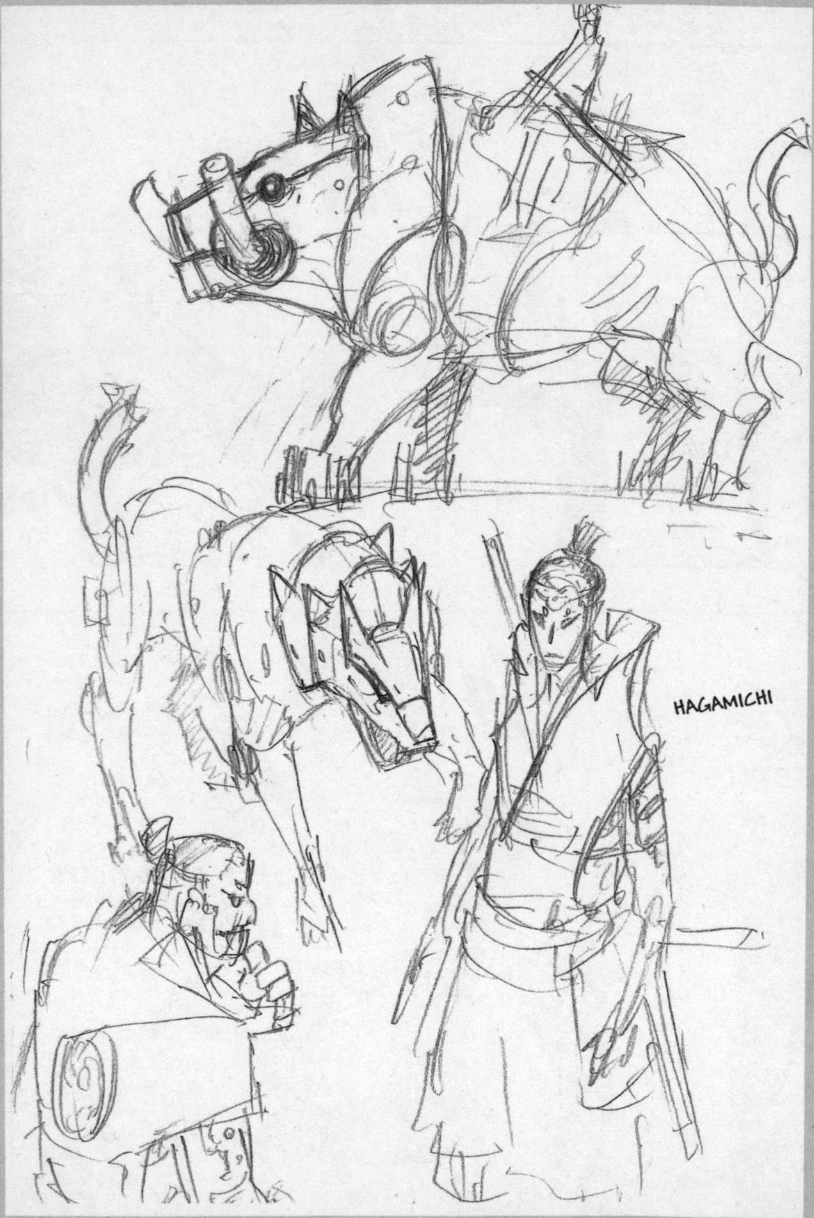
HAGAMICHI

CHAPTER 18: ALWAYS SHOP RESPONSIBLY

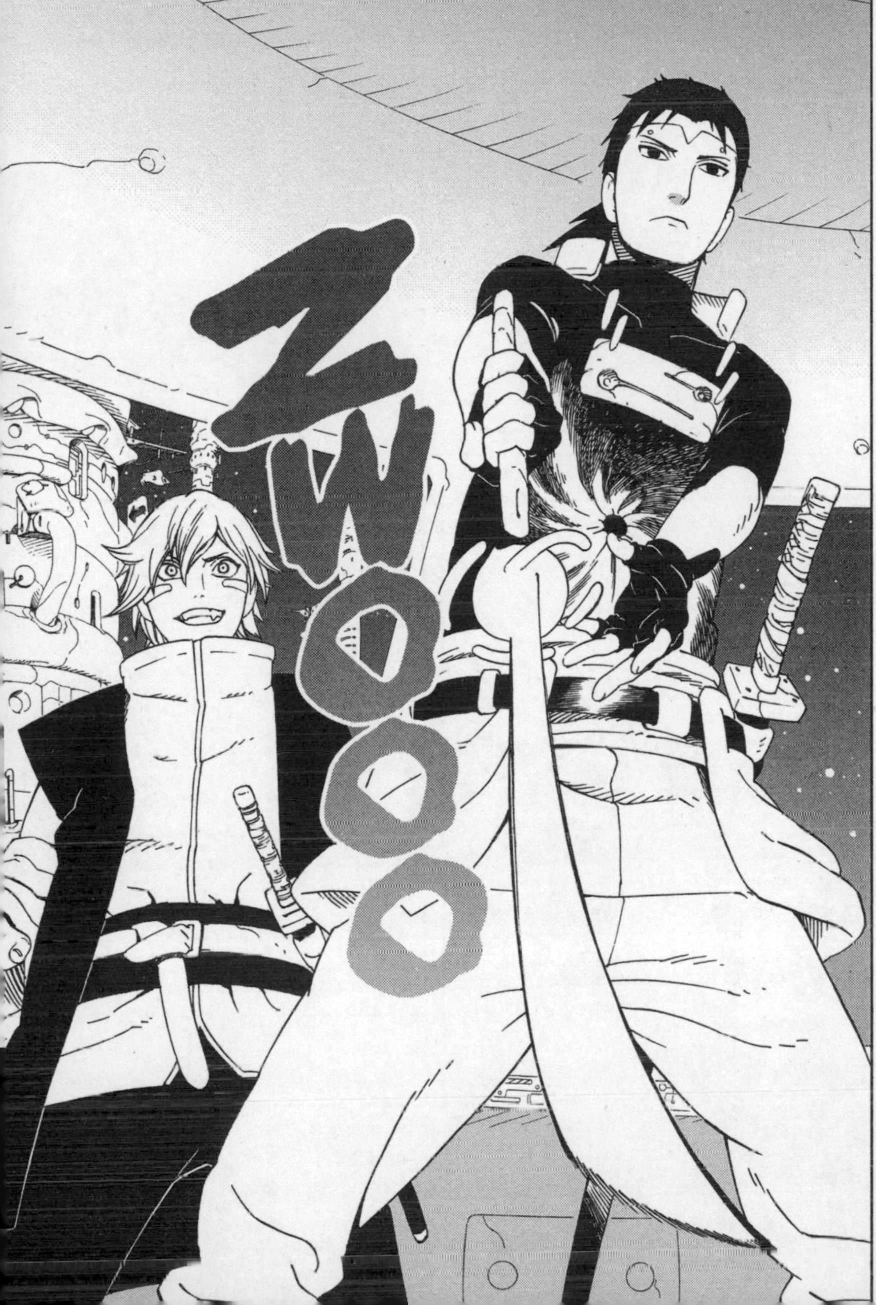
ZWOOO

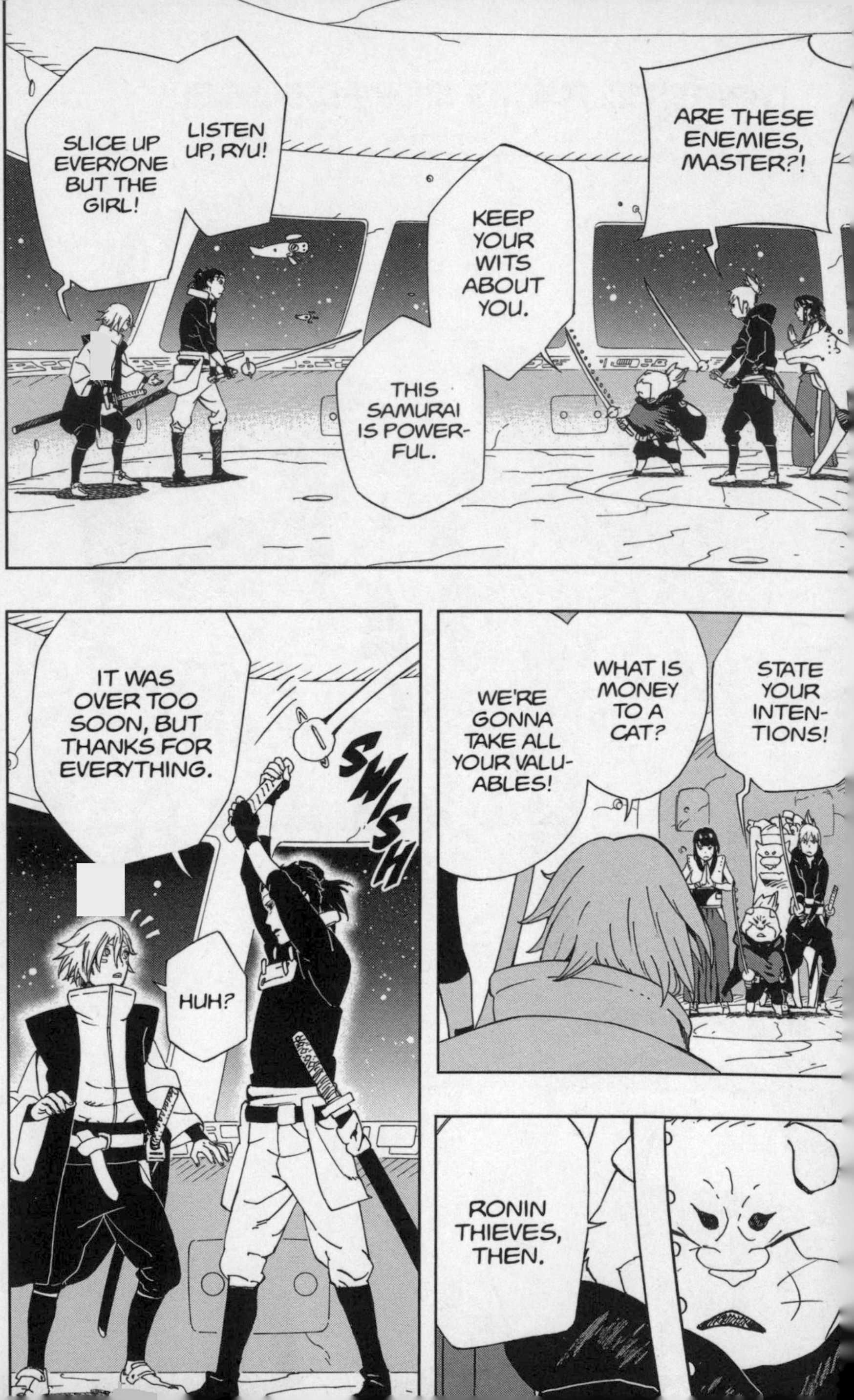
ARE THESE ENEMIES, MASTER?!
KEEP YOUR WITS ABOUT YOU.
THIS SAMURAI IS POWER-FUL.
LISTEN UP, RYU!
SLICE UP EVERYONE BUT THE GIRL!
STATE YOUR INTEN-TIONS!
WHAT IS MONEY TO A CAT?
WE'RE GONNA TAKE ALL YOUR VALU-ABLES!
RONIN THIEVES, THEN.
IT WAS OVER TOO SOON, BUT THANKS FOR EVERYTHING.
SWISH
HUH?

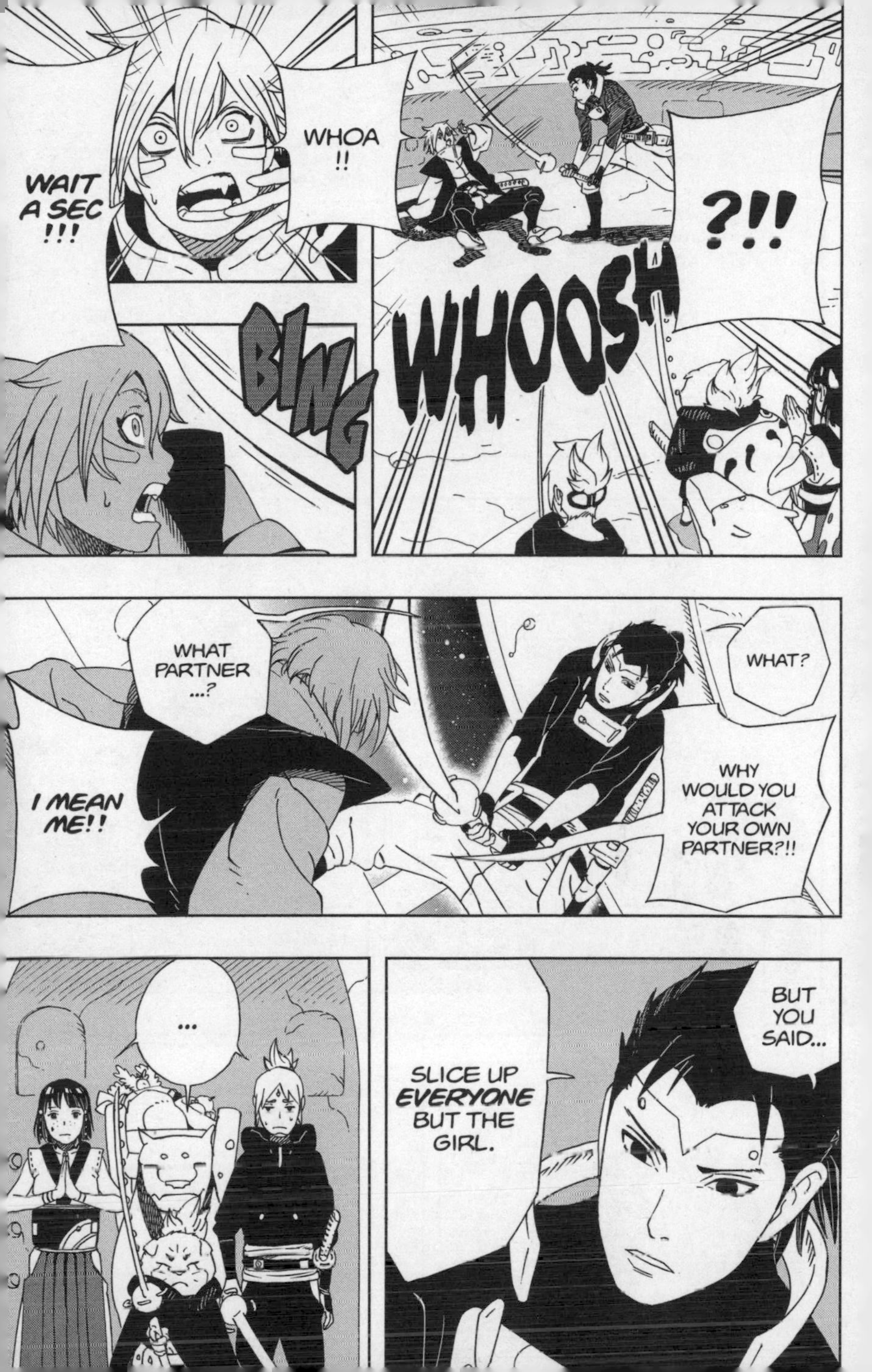
?!!
WHOA !!
WHOOSH
WAIT A SEC !!!
BING
WHAT?
WHY WOULD YOU ATTACK YOUR OWN PARTNER?!!
WHAT PARTNER ...?
I MEAN ME!!
BUT YOU SAID...
SLICE UP EVERYONE BUT THE GIRL.
...

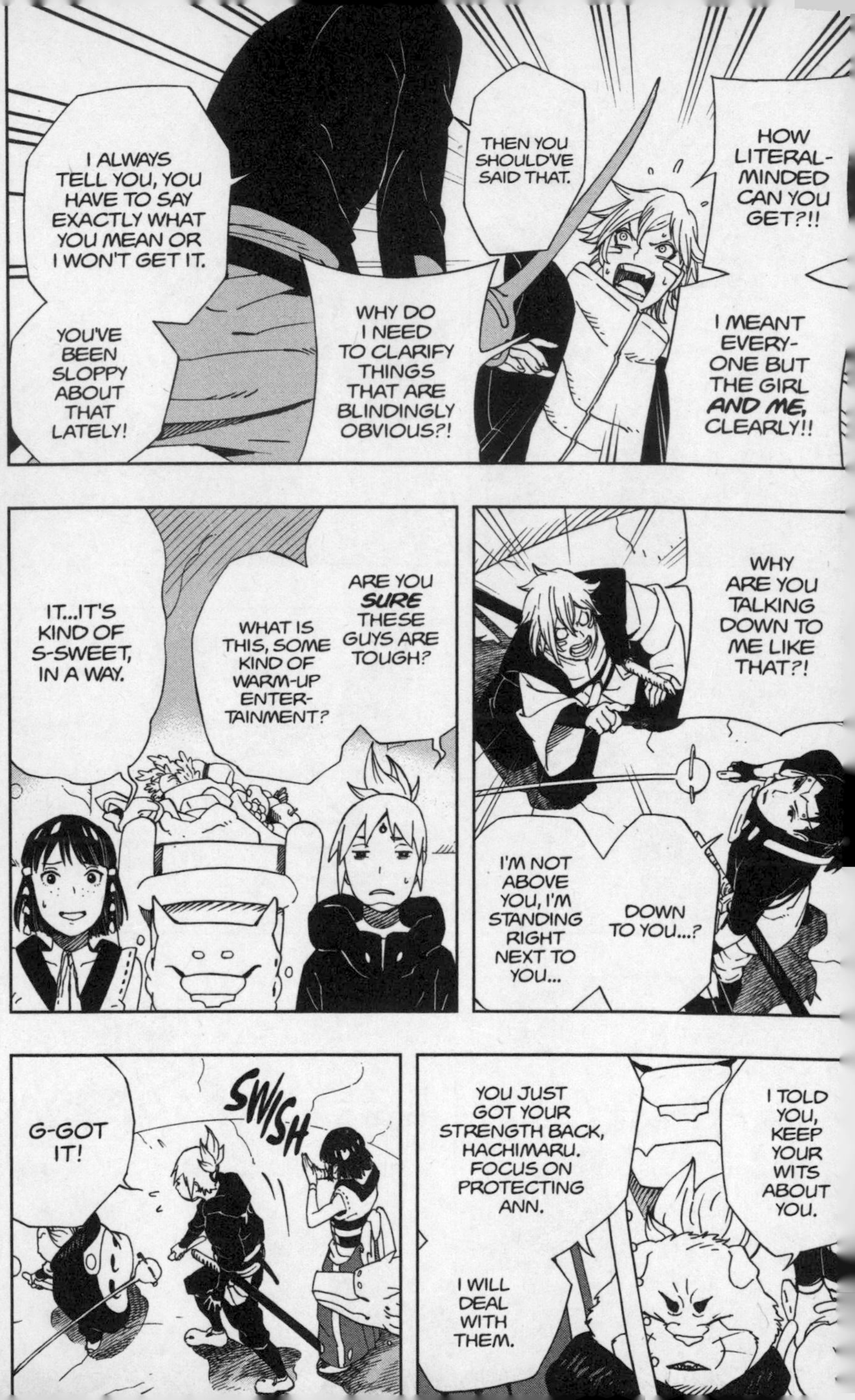
HOW LITERAL-MINDED CAN YOU GET?!!
I MEANT EVERYONE BUT THE GIRL **AND ME,** CLEARLY!!
THEN YOU SHOULD'VE SAID THAT.
WHY DO I NEED TO CLARIFY THINGS THAT ARE BLINDINGLY OBVIOUS?!
I ALWAYS TELL YOU, YOU HAVE TO SAY EXACTLY WHAT YOU MEAN OR I WON'T GET IT.
YOU'VE BEEN SLOPPY ABOUT THAT LATELY!
WHY ARE YOU TALKING DOWN TO ME LIKE THAT?!
DOWN TO YOU...?
I'M NOT ABOVE YOU, I'M STANDING RIGHT NEXT TO YOU...
ARE YOU **SURE** THESE GUYS ARE TOUGH?
WHAT IS THIS, SOME KIND OF WARM-UP ENTERTAINMENT?
IT...IT'S KIND OF S-SWEET, IN A WAY.
I TOLD YOU, KEEP YOUR WITS ABOUT YOU.
YOU JUST GOT YOUR STRENGTH BACK, HACHIMARU. FOCUS ON PROTECTING ANN.
I WILL DEAL WITH THEM.
SWISH
G-GOT IT!

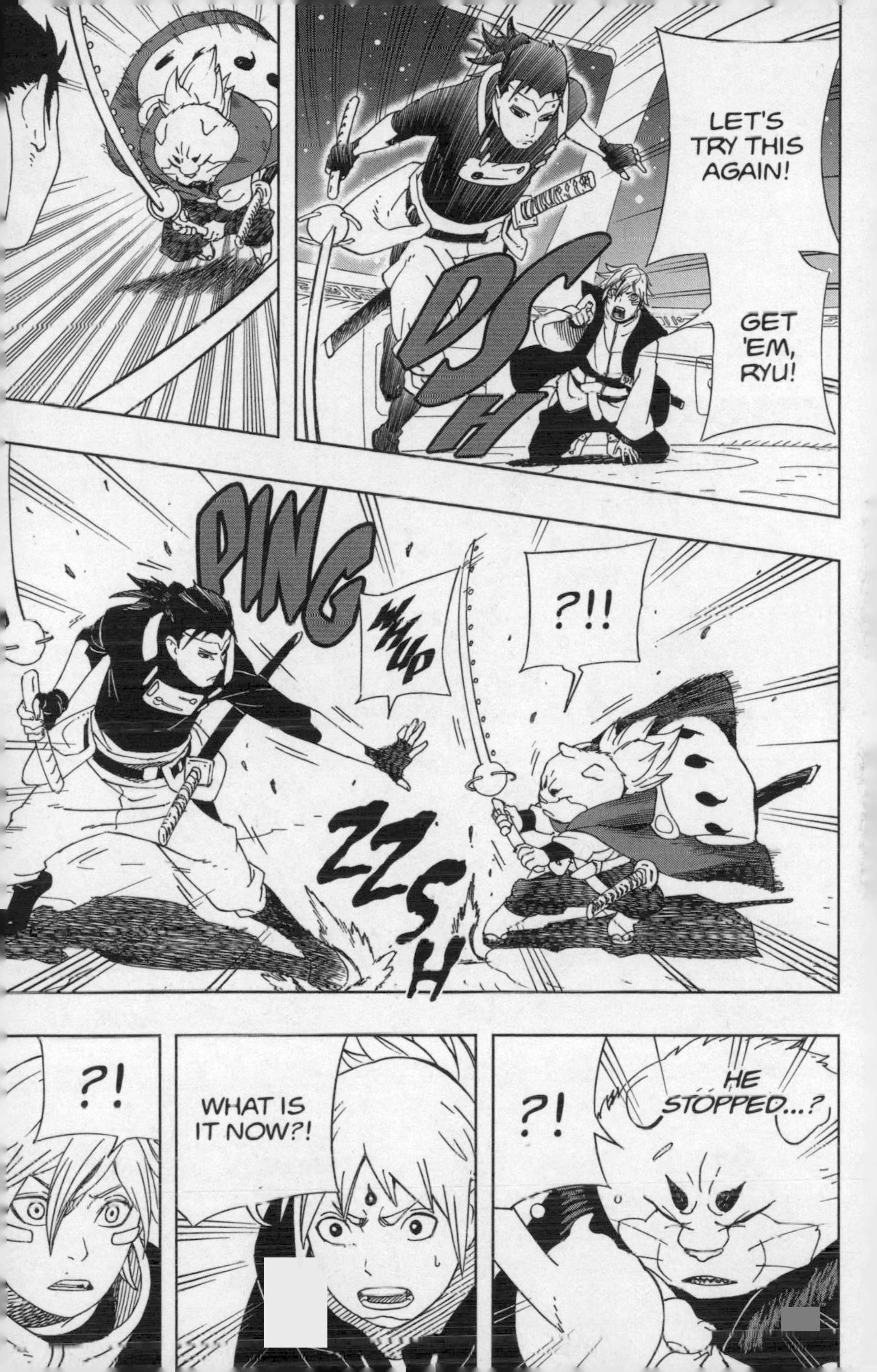
LET'S TRY THIS AGAIN!
GET 'EM, RYU!
DSH
?!!
WHUP
PING
ZZSH
HE STOPPED...?
?!
WHAT IS IT NOW?!
?!

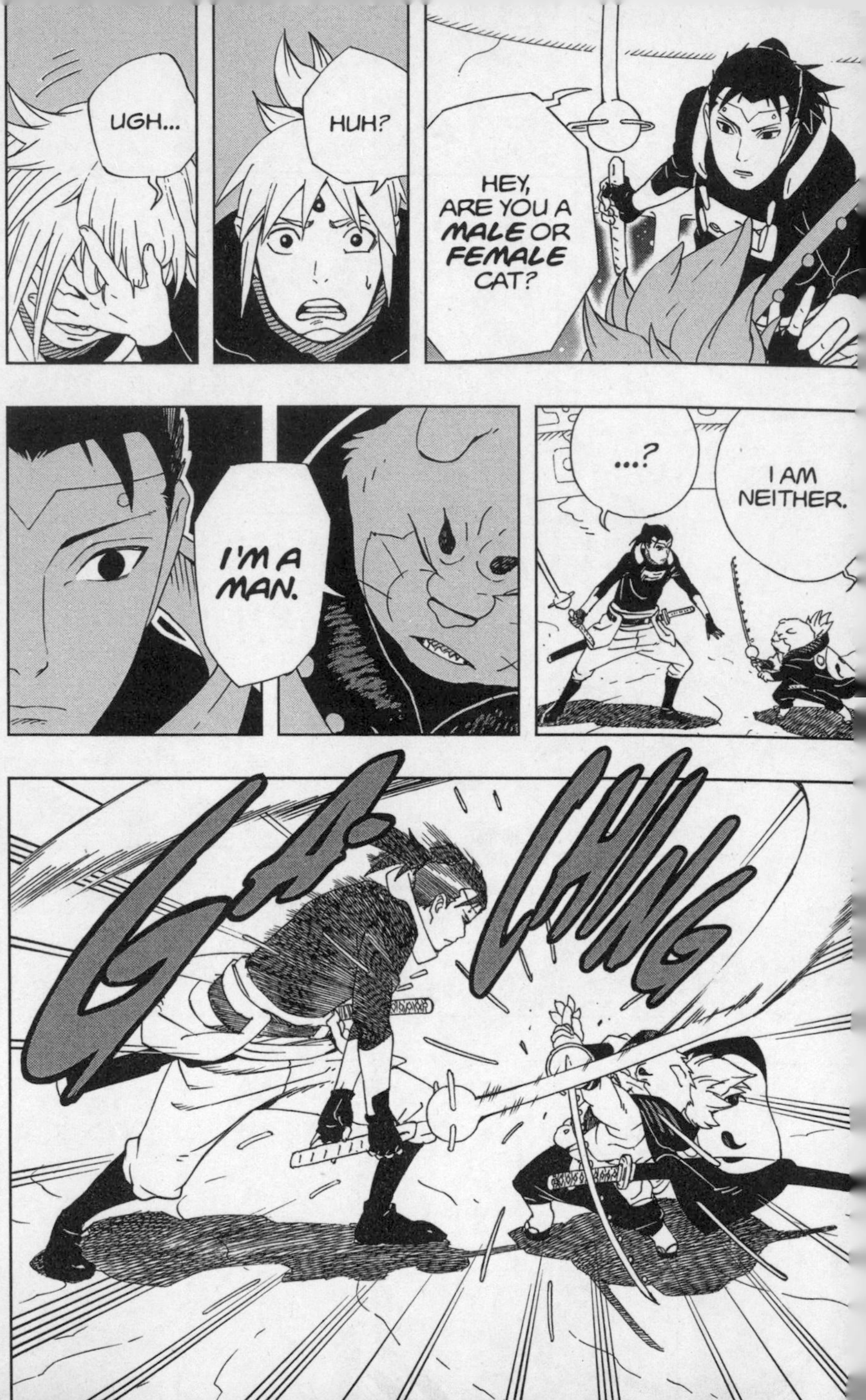
HEY, ARE YOU A MALE OR FEMALE CAT?
HUH?
UGH...
I AM NEITHER.
...?
I'M A MAN.
GA-CHING

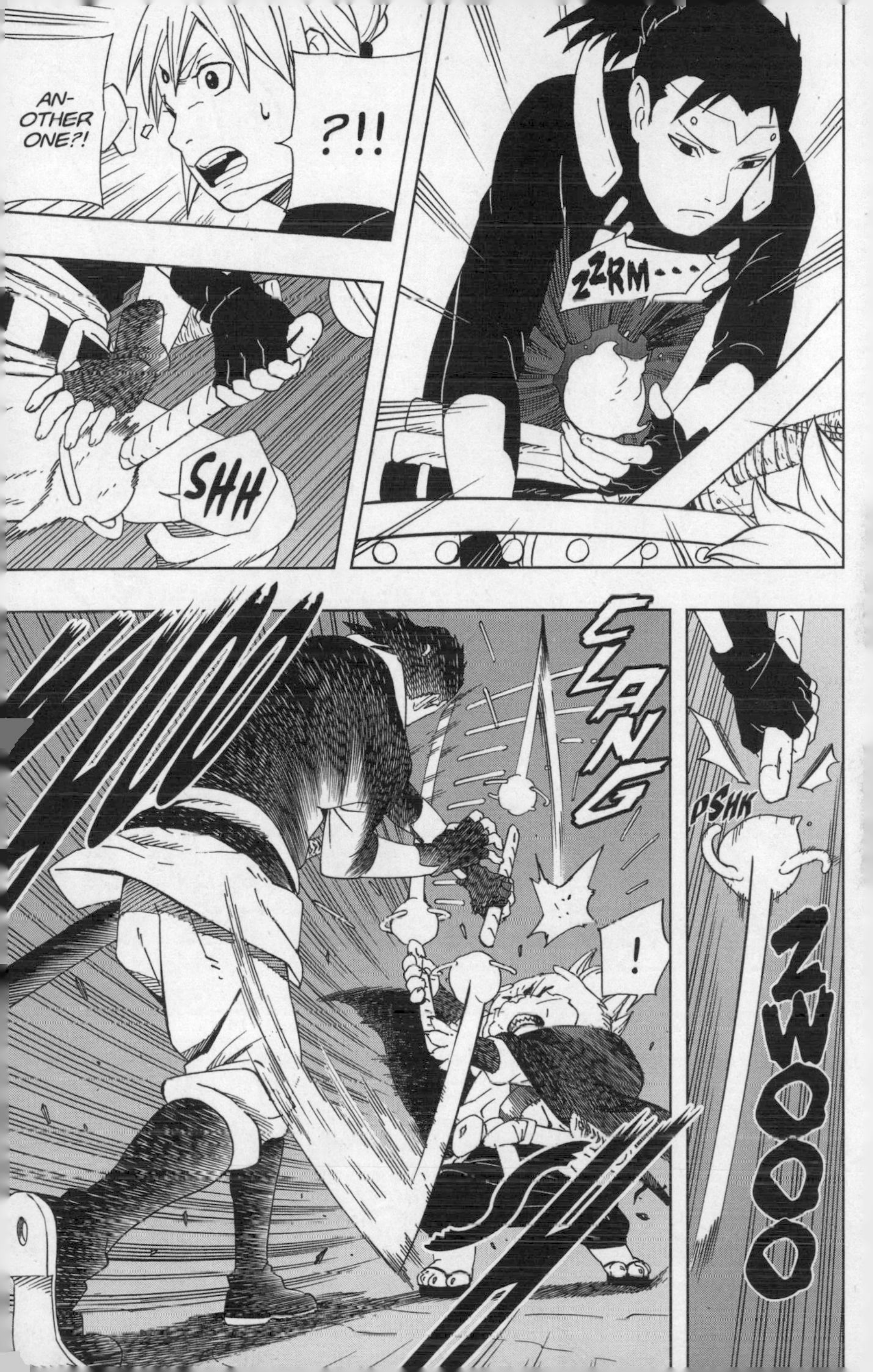
ZZRM...
AN-OTHER ONE?!
?!!
SHH
PSHK
ZWOOO
CLANG
!

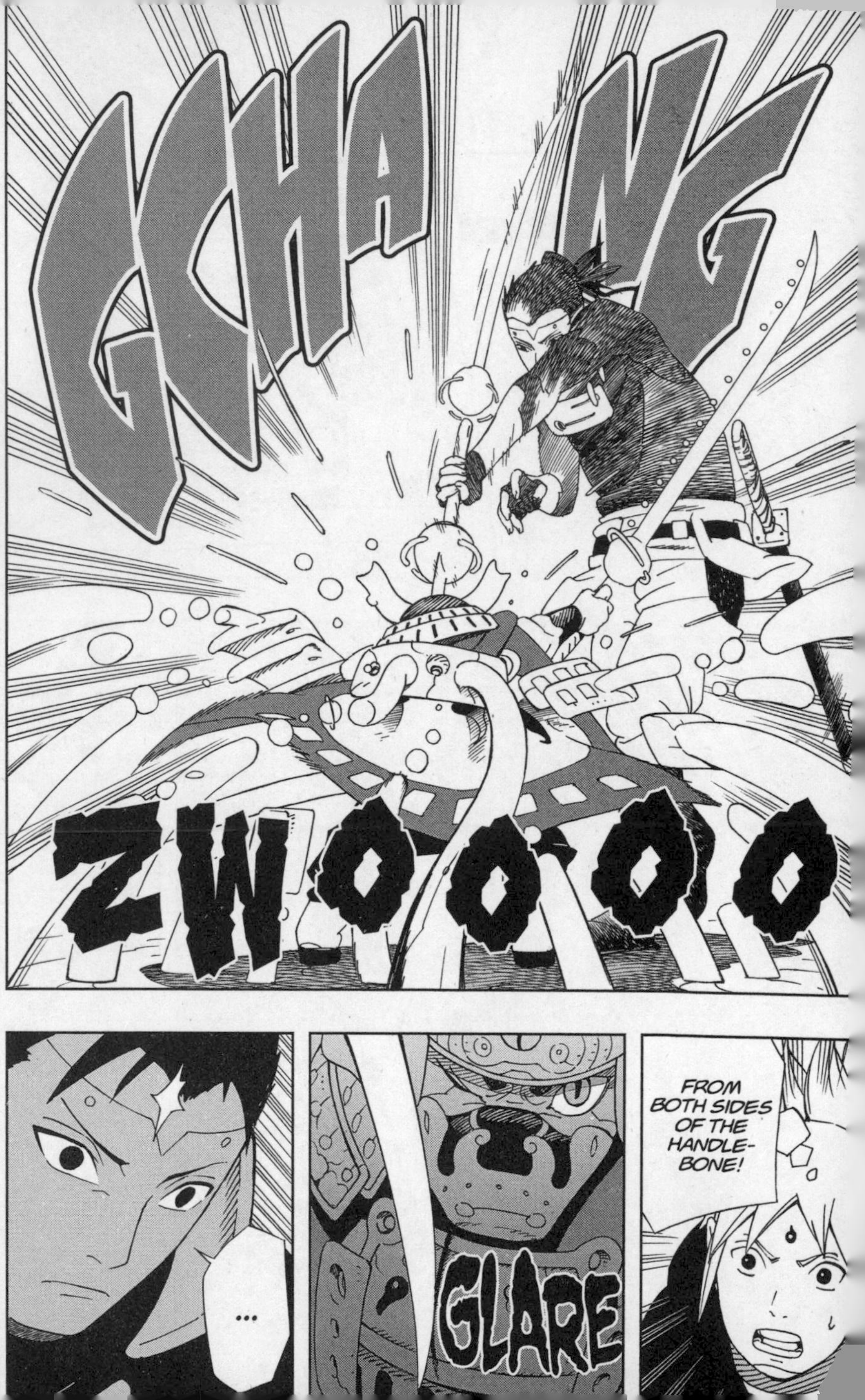
GCHANG
ZWOOOO
FROM BOTH SIDES OF THE HANDLE-BONE!
GLARE
...

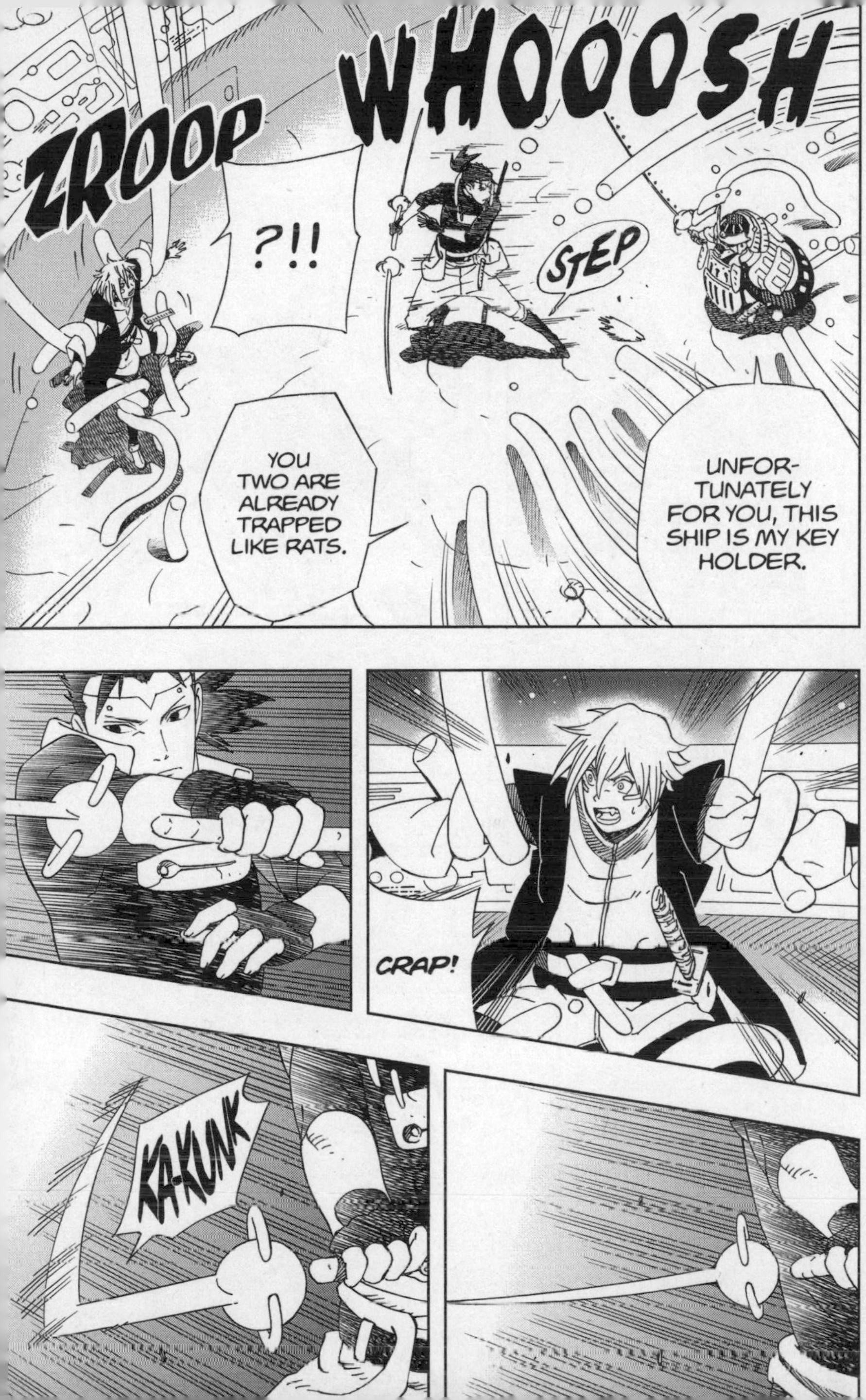
WHOOOSH
STEP
ZROOP
?!!
UNFOR-TUNATELY FOR YOU, THIS SHIP IS MY KEY HOLDER.
YOU TWO ARE ALREADY TRAPPED LIKE RATS.
CRAP!
KA-KUNK

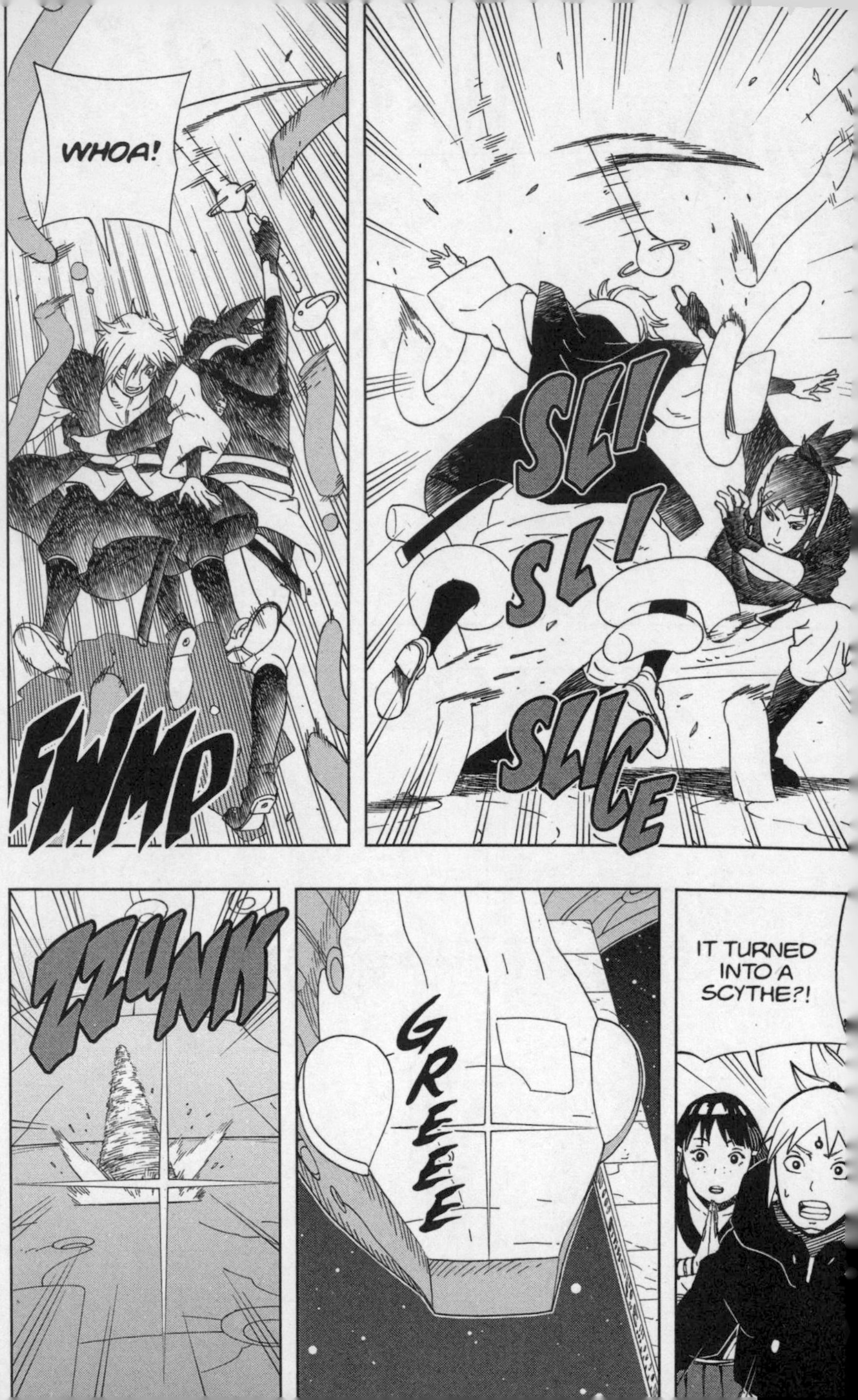
SLI
SLI
SLICE
WHOA!
FWMP
IT TURNED INTO A SCYTHE?!
GREEEE
ZZUNK

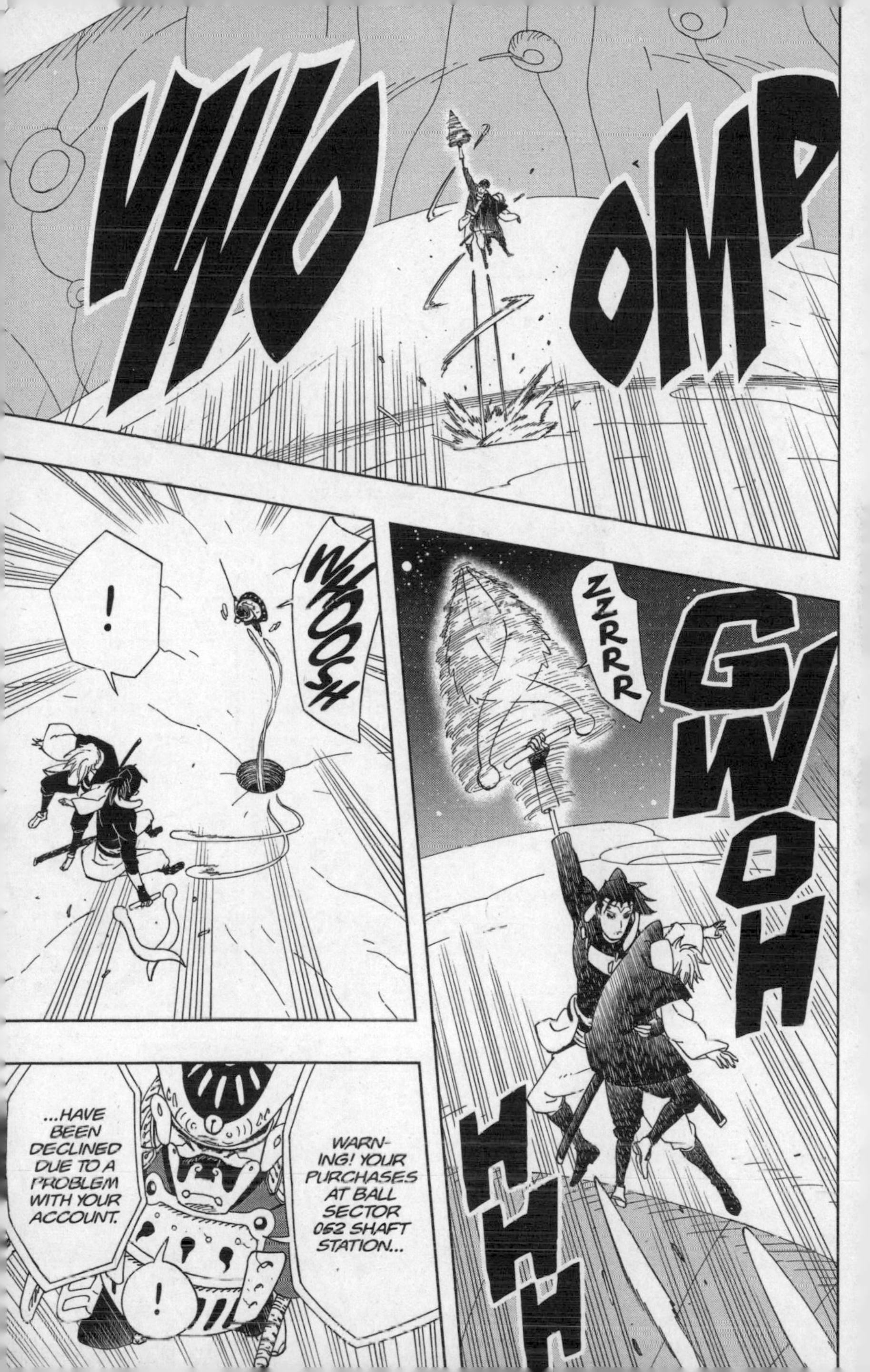
WHOOMP
ZZRRR
GWOOH
HHHH
!
WHOOSH
WARNING! YOUR PURCHASES AT BALL SECTOR 052 SHAFT STATION...
...HAVE BEEN DECLINED DUE TO A PROBLEM WITH YOUR ACCOUNT.
!

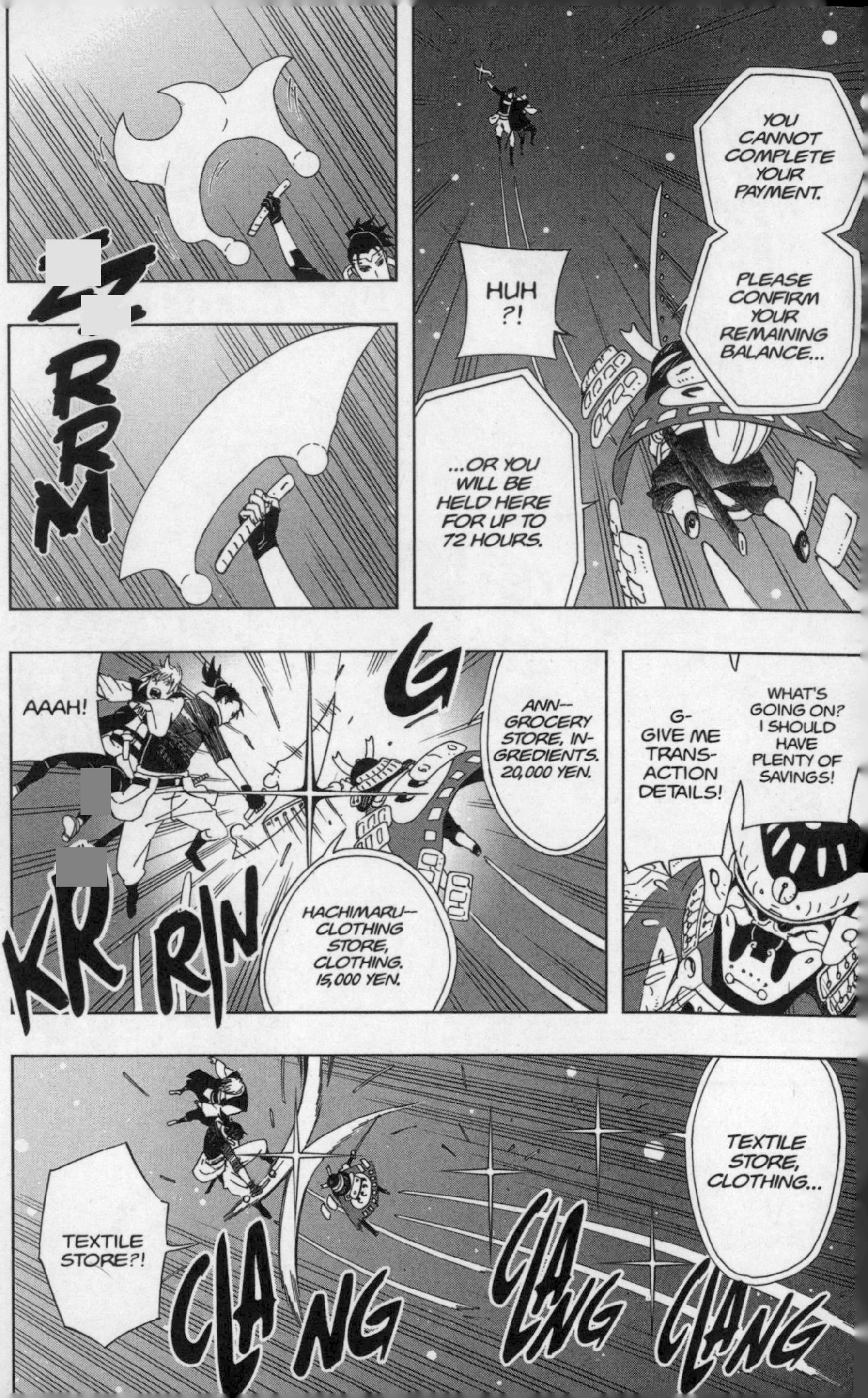
YOU CANNOT COMPLETE YOUR PAYMENT.
PLEASE CONFIRM YOUR REMAINING BALANCE...
HUH ?!
...OR YOU WILL BE HELD HERE FOR UP TO 72 HOURS.
RRM
WHAT'S GOING ON? I SHOULD HAVE PLENTY OF SAVINGS!
G- GIVE ME TRANS- ACTION DETAILS!
ANN-- GROCERY STORE, IN- GREDIENTS. 20,000 YEN.
G
AAAH!
HACHIMARU-- CLOTHING STORE, CLOTHING. 15,000 YEN.
KRRIN
TEXTILE STORE, CLOTHING...
TEXTILE STORE?!
CLANG CLANG CLANG

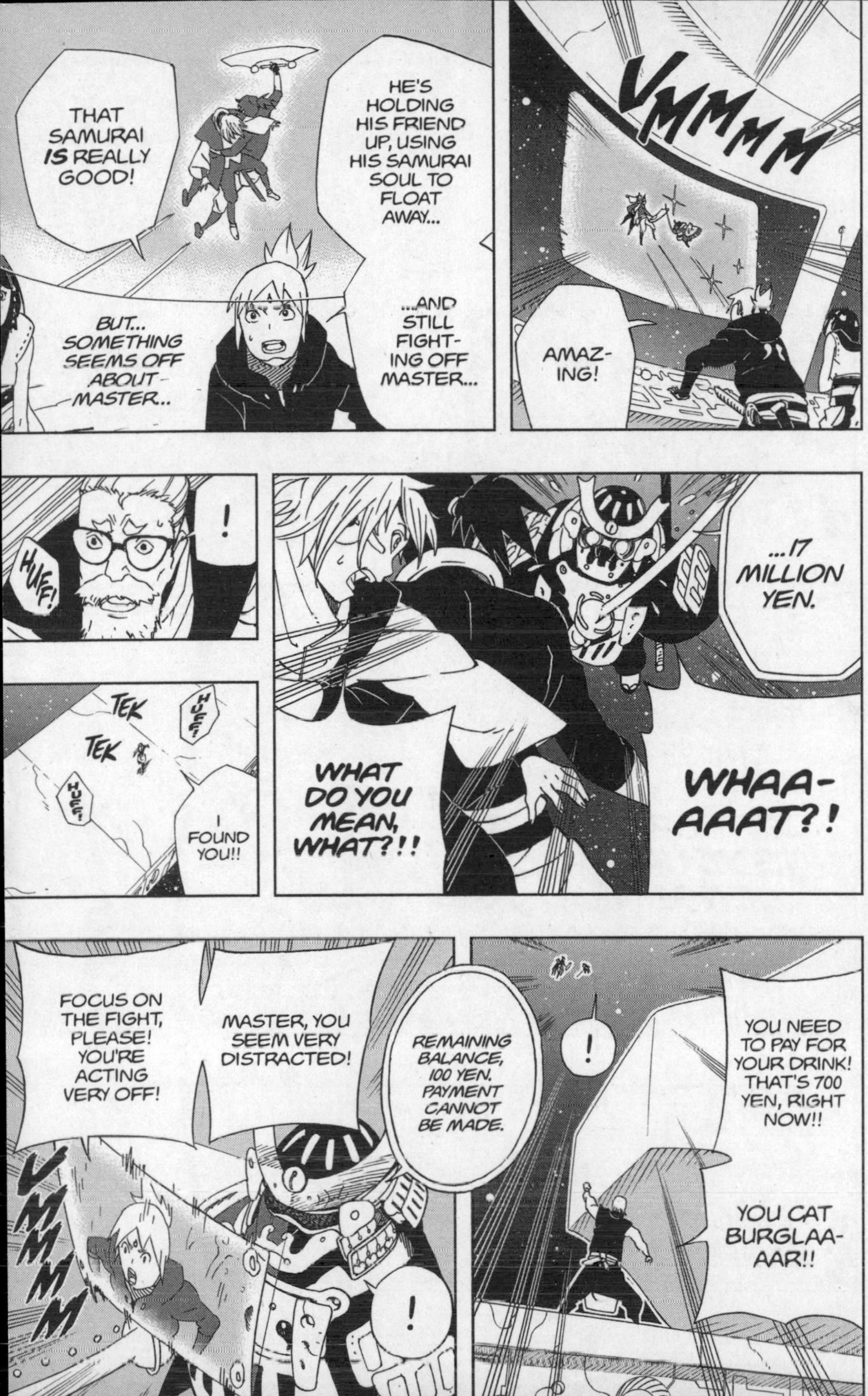
VMMMMM
AMAZ-ING!
HE'S HOLDING HIS FRIEND UP, USING HIS SAMURAI SOUL TO FLOAT AWAY...
THAT SAMURAI IS REALLY GOOD!
...AND STILL FIGHT-ING OFF MASTER...
BUT... SOMETHING SEEMS OFF ABOUT MASTER...
...17 MILLION YEN.
WHAA-AAAT?!
WHAT DO YOU MEAN, WHAT?!!
!
HUFF!
TEK
TEK
HUFF!
HUFF!
I FOUND YOU!!
!
YOU NEED TO PAY FOR YOUR DRINK! THAT'S 700 YEN, RIGHT NOW!!
YOU CAT BURGLAA-AAR!!
REMAINING BALANCE, 100 YEN. PAYMENT CANNOT BE MADE.
MASTER, YOU SEEM VERY DISTRACTED!
FOCUS ON THE FIGHT, PLEASE! YOU'RE ACTING VERY OFF!
!
VMMMMM

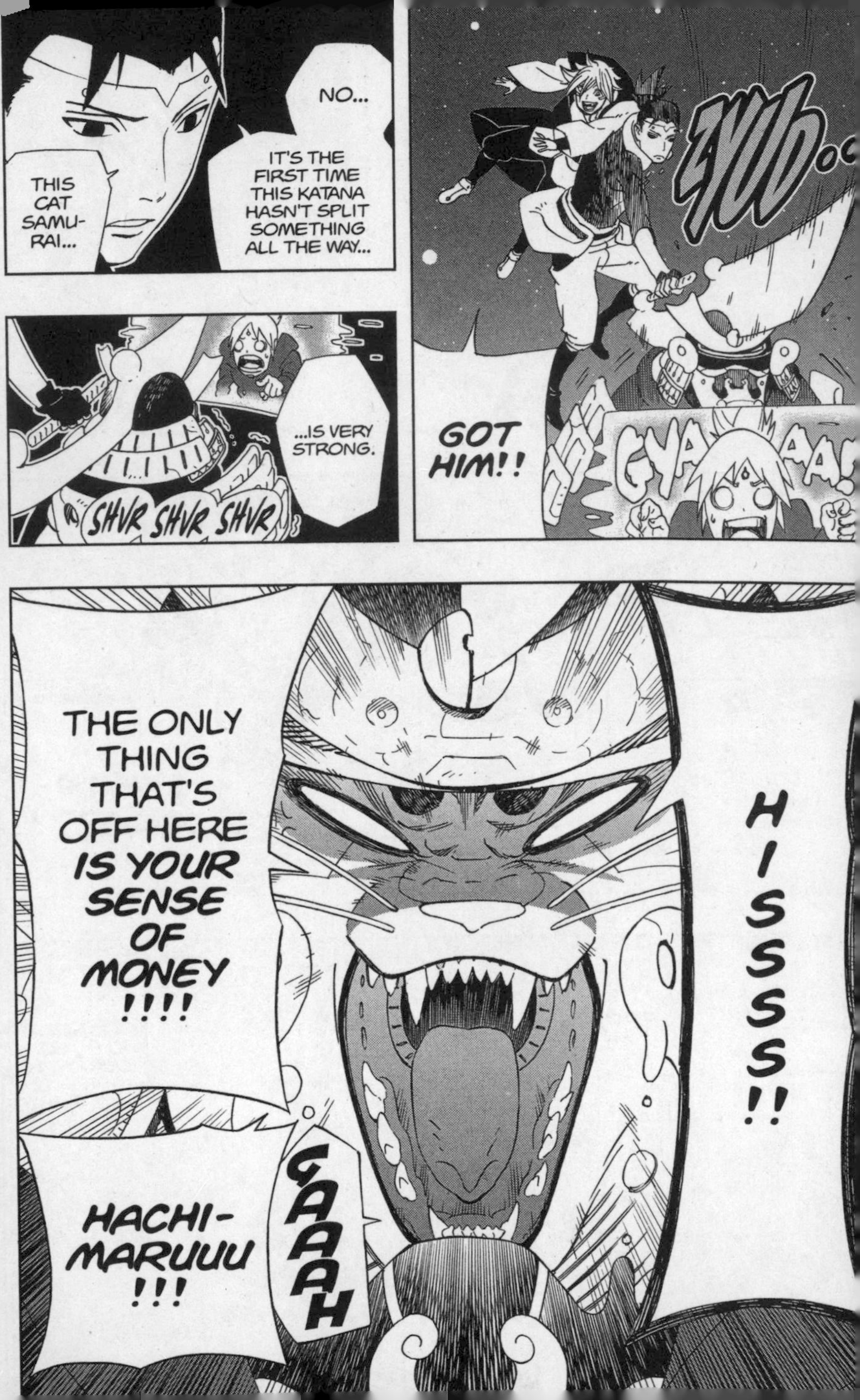
ZYUB..
GOT HIM!!
GYA AA!
NO...
IT'S THE FIRST TIME THIS KATANA HASN'T SPLIT SOMETHING ALL THE WAY...
THIS CAT SAMURAI...
...IS VERY STRONG.
SHVR SHVR SHVR
HISSSS!!
THE ONLY THING THAT'S OFF HERE **IS YOUR SENSE OF MONEY !!!!**
GAAAAH
HACHI-MARUUU !!!

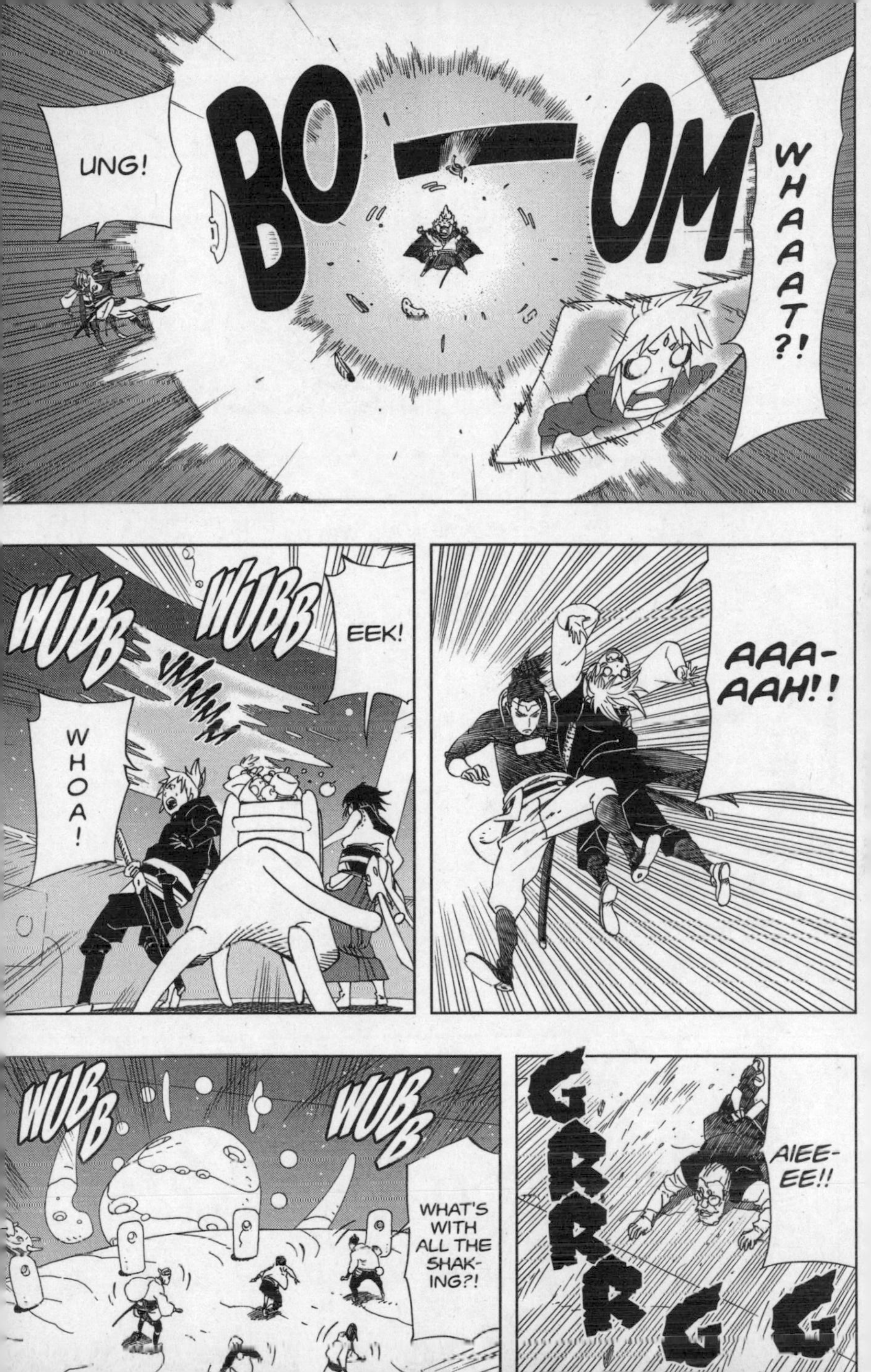
WHAAAAT?!
BO—OM
UNG!
AAA-AAH!!
EEK!
WUBB
WUBB
WHOA!
AIEEE-EE!!
GRRRRGG
WUBB
WUBB
WHAT'S WITH ALL THE SHAK-ING?!

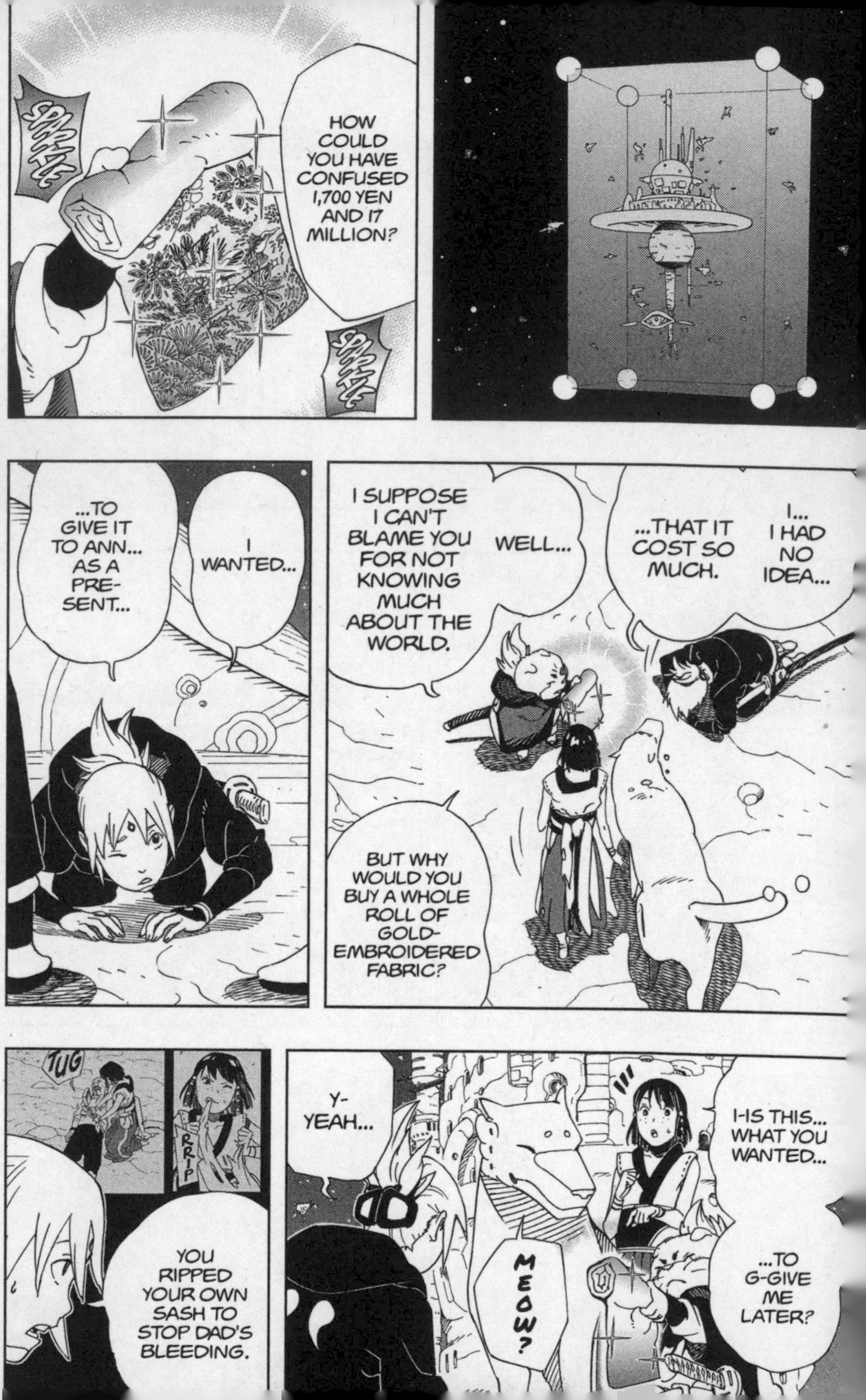
HOW COULD YOU HAVE CONFUSED 1,700 YEN AND 17 MILLION?
SPARKLE
SPARKLE
I... I HAD NO IDEA...
...THAT IT COST SO MUCH.
WELL...
I SUPPOSE I CAN'T BLAME YOU FOR NOT KNOWING MUCH ABOUT THE WORLD.
BUT WHY WOULD YOU BUY A WHOLE ROLL OF GOLD-EMBROIDERED FABRIC?
I WANTED...
...TO GIVE IT TO ANN... AS A PRESENT...
I-IS THIS... WHAT YOU WANTED...
...TO G-GIVE ME LATER?
MEOW?
Y-YEAH...
RRIP
TUG
YOU RIPPED YOUR OWN SASH TO STOP DAD'S BLEEDING.

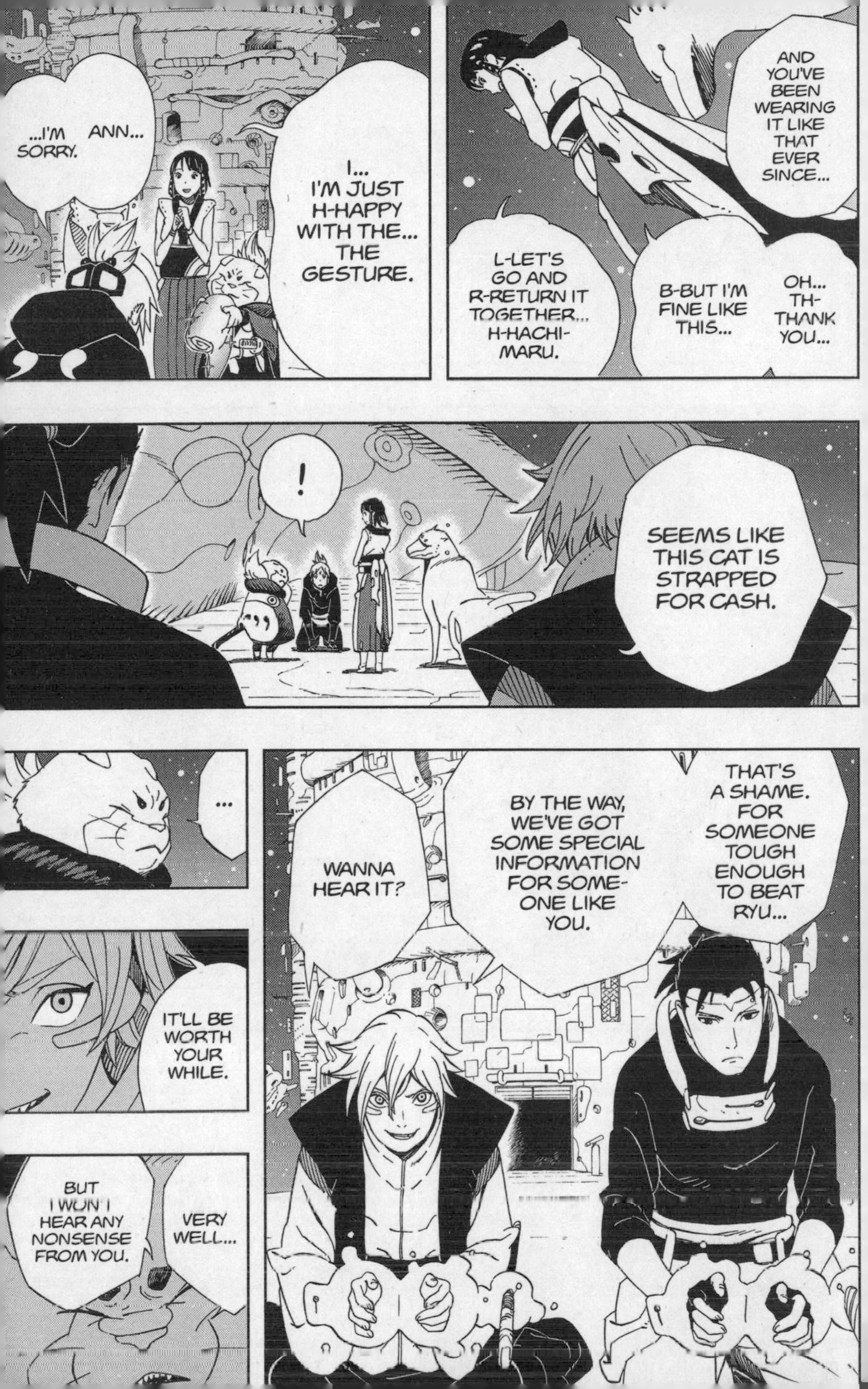
AND YOU'VE BEEN WEARING IT LIKE THAT EVER SINCE...
OH... TH-THANK YOU...
B-BUT I'M FINE LIKE THIS...
L-LET'S GO AND R-RETURN IT TOGETHER... H-HACHI-MARU.
I... I'M JUST H-HAPPY WITH THE... THE GESTURE.
ANN...
...I'M SORRY.
SEEMS LIKE THIS CAT IS STRAPPED FOR CASH.
!
THAT'S A SHAME. FOR SOMEONE TOUGH ENOUGH TO BEAT RYU...
BY THE WAY, WE'VE GOT SOME SPECIAL INFORMATION FOR SOME-ONE LIKE YOU.
WANNA HEAR IT?
...
IT'LL BE WORTH YOUR WHILE.
VERY WELL...
BUT I WON'T HEAR ANY NONSENSE FROM YOU.

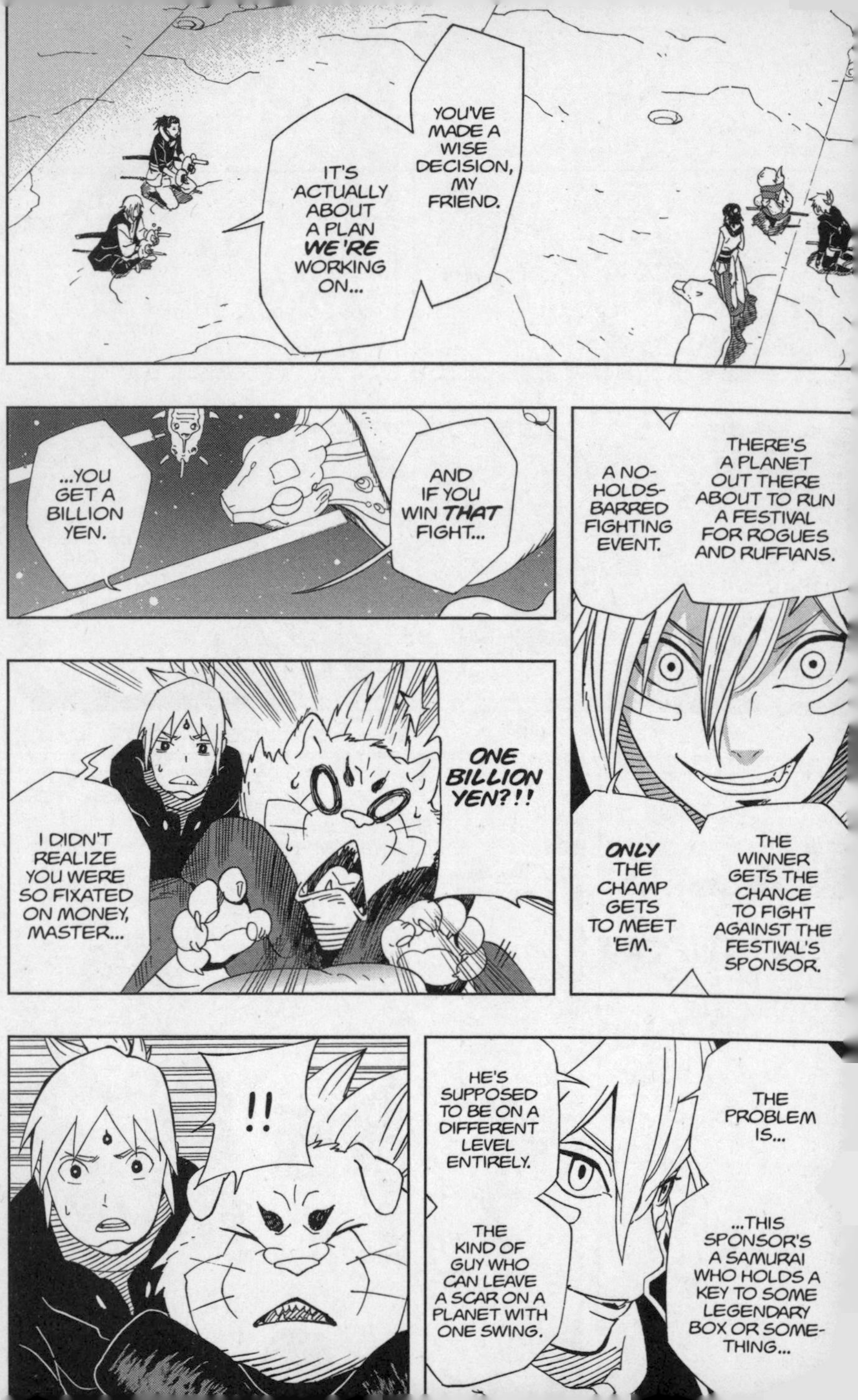
YOU'VE MADE A WISE DECISION, MY FRIEND.
IT'S ACTUALLY ABOUT A PLAN *WE'RE* WORKING ON...
THERE'S A PLANET OUT THERE ABOUT TO RUN A FESTIVAL FOR ROGUES AND RUFFIANS.
A NO-HOLDS-BARRED FIGHTING EVENT.
THE WINNER GETS THE CHANCE TO FIGHT AGAINST THE FESTIVAL'S SPONSOR.
ONLY THE CHAMP GETS TO MEET 'EM.
AND IF YOU WIN *THAT* FIGHT...
...YOU GET A BILLION YEN.
ONE BILLION YEN?!!
I DIDN'T REALIZE YOU WERE SO FIXATED ON MONEY, MASTER...
THE PROBLEM IS...
...THIS SPONSOR'S A SAMURAI WHO HOLDS A KEY TO SOME LEGENDARY BOX OR SOME-THING...
HE'S SUPPOSED TO BE ON A DIFFERENT LEVEL ENTIRELY.
THE KIND OF GUY WHO CAN LEAVE A SCAR ON A PLANET WITH ONE SWING.
!!

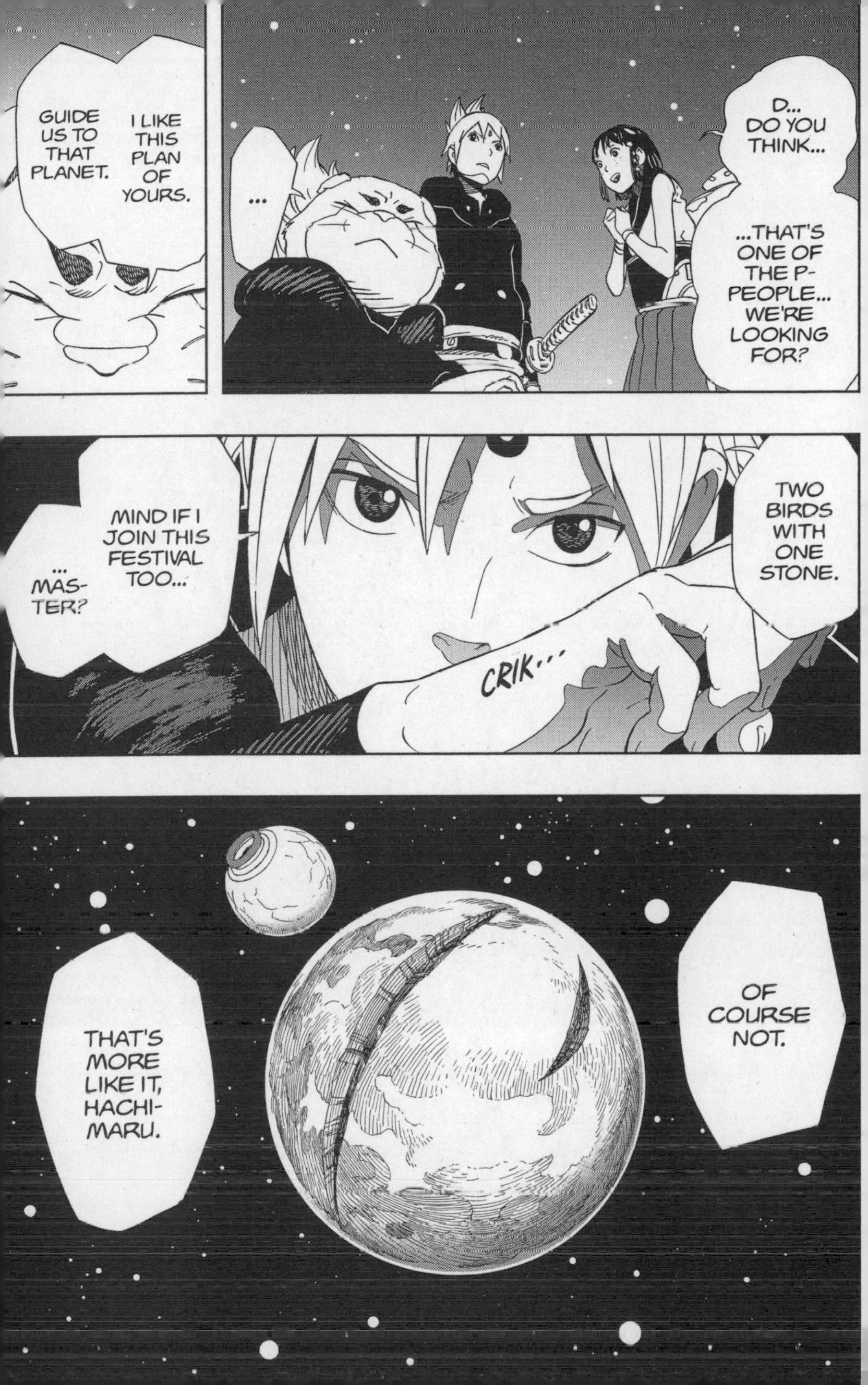
D... DO YOU THINK...
...THAT'S ONE OF THE P-PEOPLE... WE'RE LOOKING FOR?
...
I LIKE THIS PLAN OF YOURS.
GUIDE US TO THAT PLANET.
TWO BIRDS WITH ONE STONE.
CRIK...
MIND IF I JOIN THIS FESTIVAL TOO...
...MASTER?
OF COURSE NOT.
THAT'S MORE LIKE IT, HACHIMARU.

Character Design Sketches: Ata

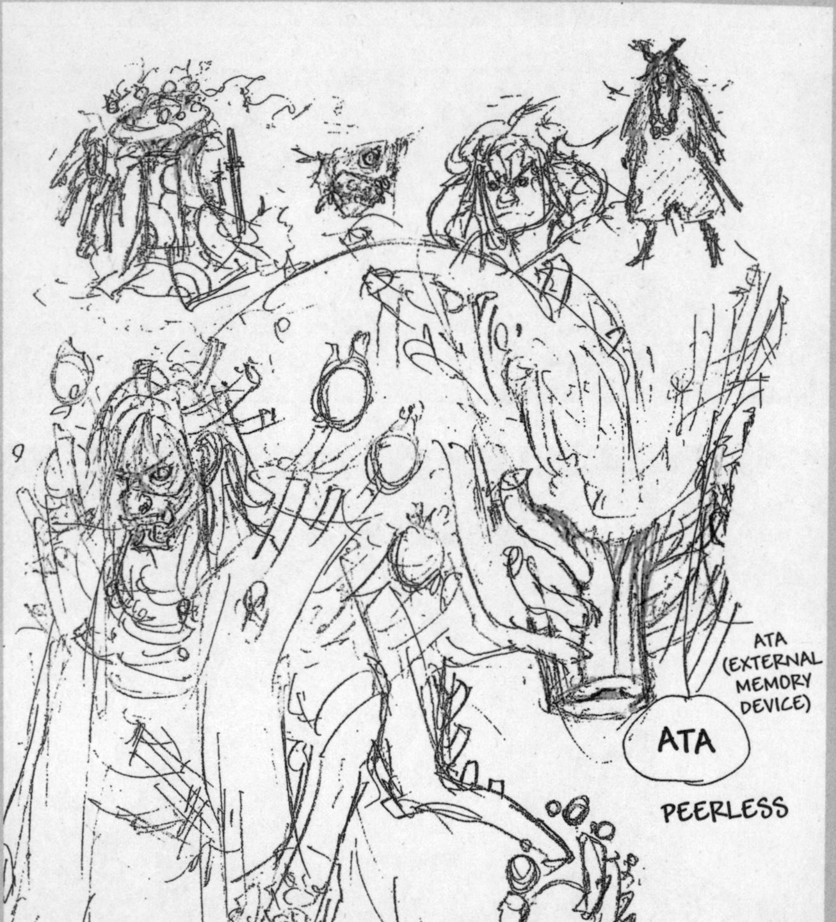
ATA
(EXTERNAL
MEMORY
DEVICE)
ATA
PEERLESS

**CHAPTER 19:
WHATEVER IT TAKES!!!**

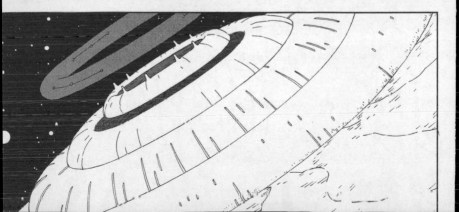

CHAPTER 19: WHATEVER IT TAKES!!!

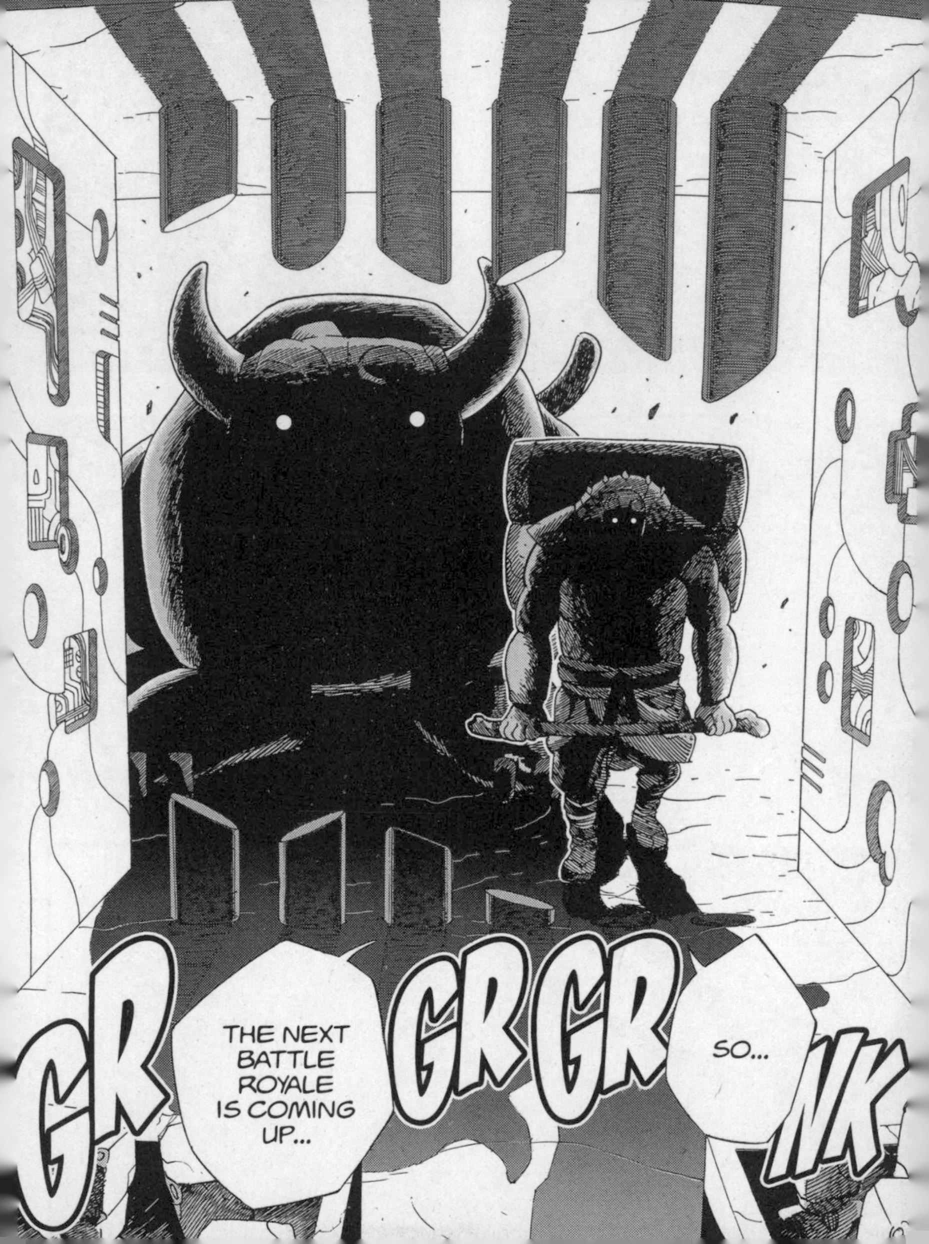
SO...
THE NEXT BATTLE ROYALE IS COMING UP...
GR GR GR NK

WHICH ONE SHALL I TAKE WITH ME?

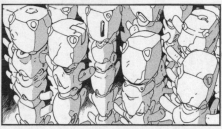

HEY, GUYS!

REMEMBER HOW I WAS NICE ENOUGH TO TELL YOU THE COORDINATES OF THIS PLANET *KENKA* WE'RE HEADING TOWARD?

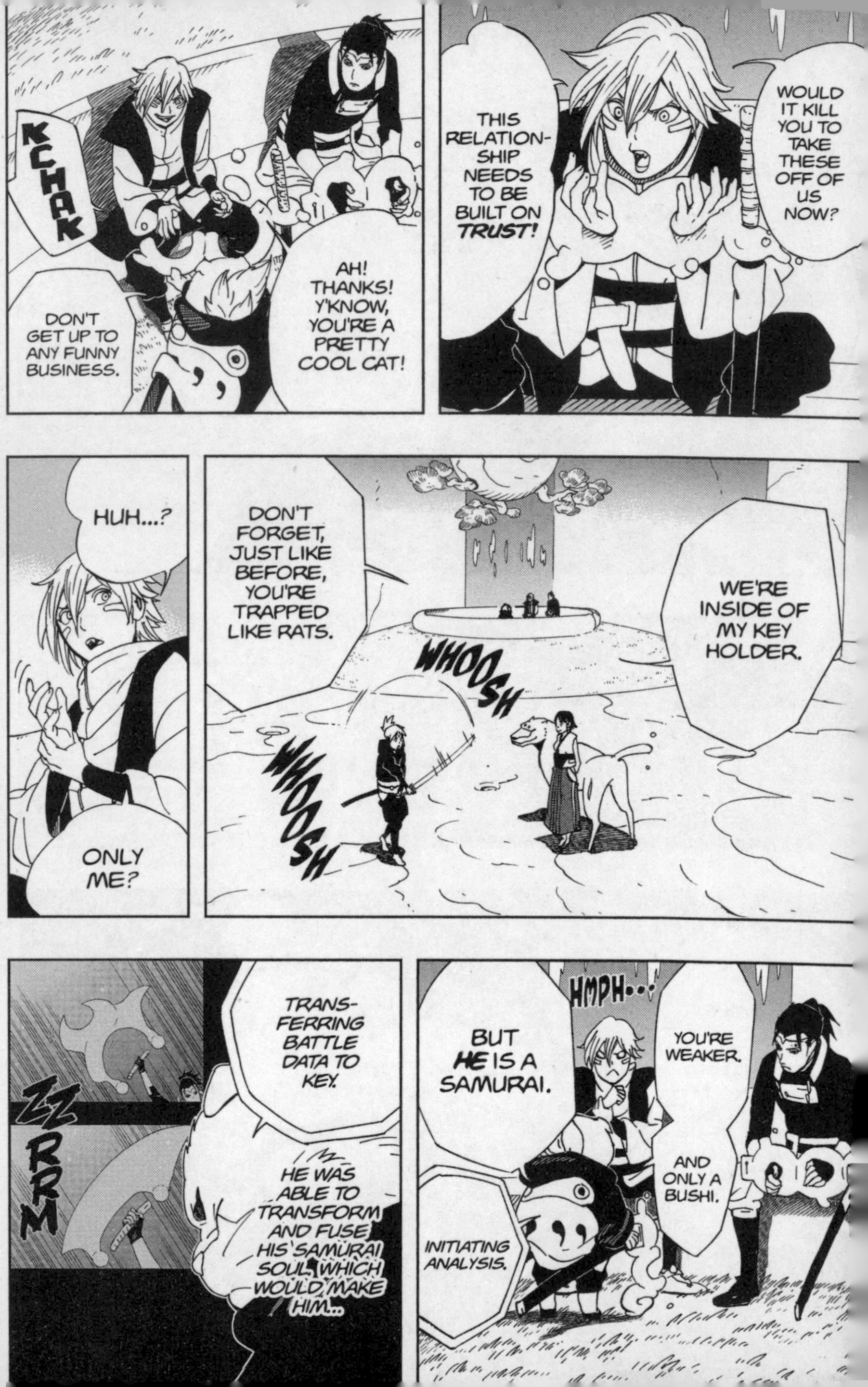
WOULD IT KILL YOU TO TAKE THESE OFF OF US NOW?
THIS RELATIONSHIP NEEDS TO BE BUILT ON TRUST!
KCHAK
AH! THANKS! Y'KNOW, YOU'RE A PRETTY COOL CAT!
DON'T GET UP TO ANY FUNNY BUSINESS.
WE'RE INSIDE OF MY KEY HOLDER.
DON'T FORGET, JUST LIKE BEFORE, YOU'RE TRAPPED LIKE RATS.
WHOOSH
WHOOSH
HUH...?
ONLY ME?
HMPH...
YOU'RE WEAKER.
BUT HE IS A SAMURAI.
AND ONLY A BUSHI.
INITIATING ANALYSIS.
TRANSFERRING BATTLE DATA TO KEY.
HE WAS ABLE TO TRANSFORM AND FUSE HIS SAMURAI SOUL, WHICH WOULD MAKE HIM...
ZZRRM

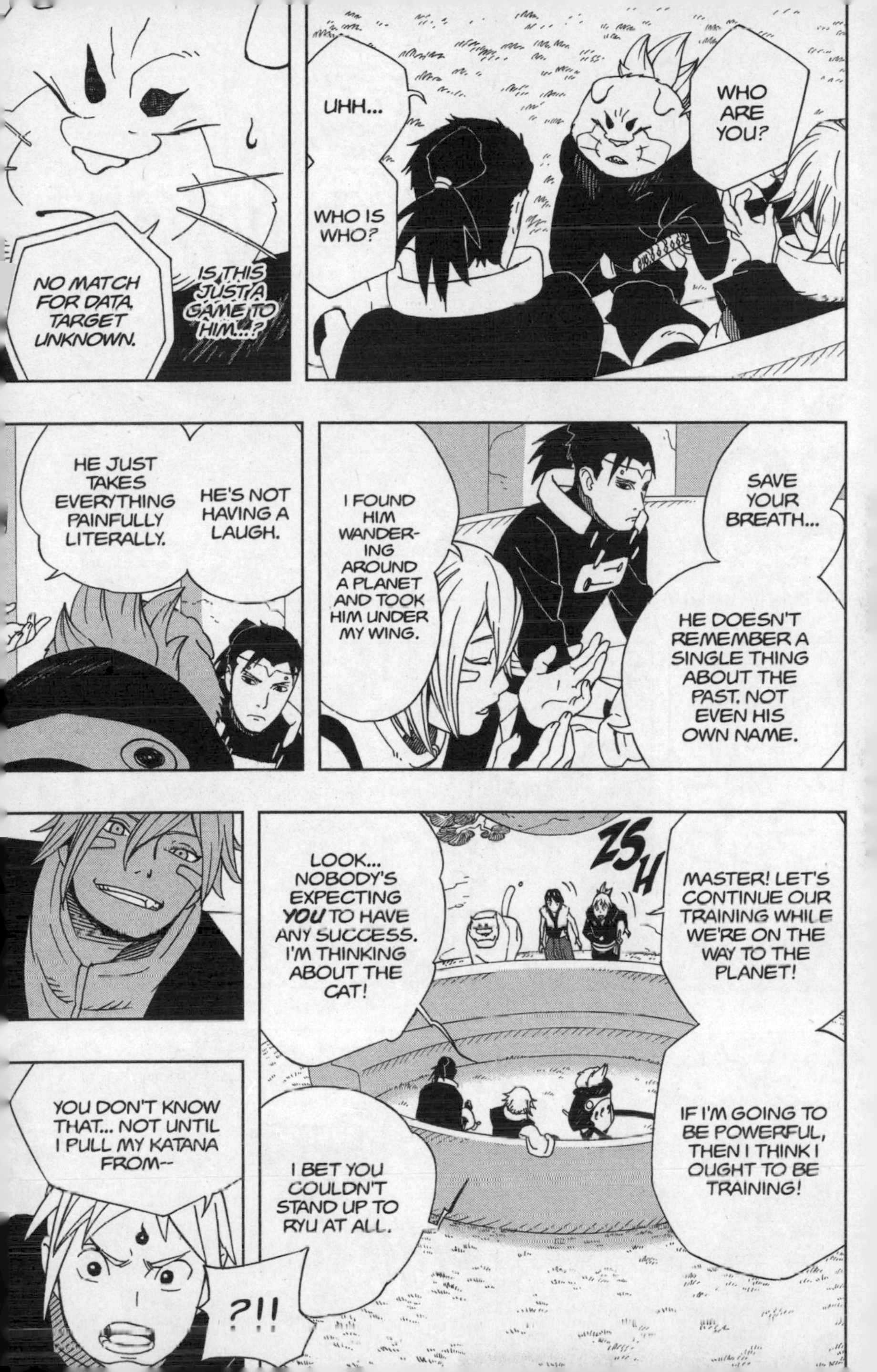
WHO ARE YOU?
UHH...
WHO IS WHO?
IS THIS JUST A GAME TO HIM...?
NO MATCH FOR DATA. TARGET UNKNOWN.
SAVE YOUR BREATH...
I FOUND HIM WANDER-ING AROUND A PLANET AND TOOK HIM UNDER MY WING.
HE DOESN'T REMEMBER A SINGLE THING ABOUT THE PAST. NOT EVEN HIS OWN NAME.
HE'S NOT HAVING A LAUGH.
HE JUST TAKES EVERYTHING PAINFULLY LITERALLY.
ZSH
MASTER! LET'S CONTINUE OUR TRAINING WHILE WE'RE ON THE WAY TO THE PLANET!
LOOK... NOBODY'S EXPECTING YOU TO HAVE ANY SUCCESS. I'M THINKING ABOUT THE CAT!
IF I'M GOING TO BE POWERFUL, THEN I THINK I OUGHT TO BE TRAINING!
I BET YOU COULDN'T STAND UP TO RYU AT ALL.
YOU DON'T KNOW THAT... NOT UNTIL I PULL MY KATANA FROM--
?!!

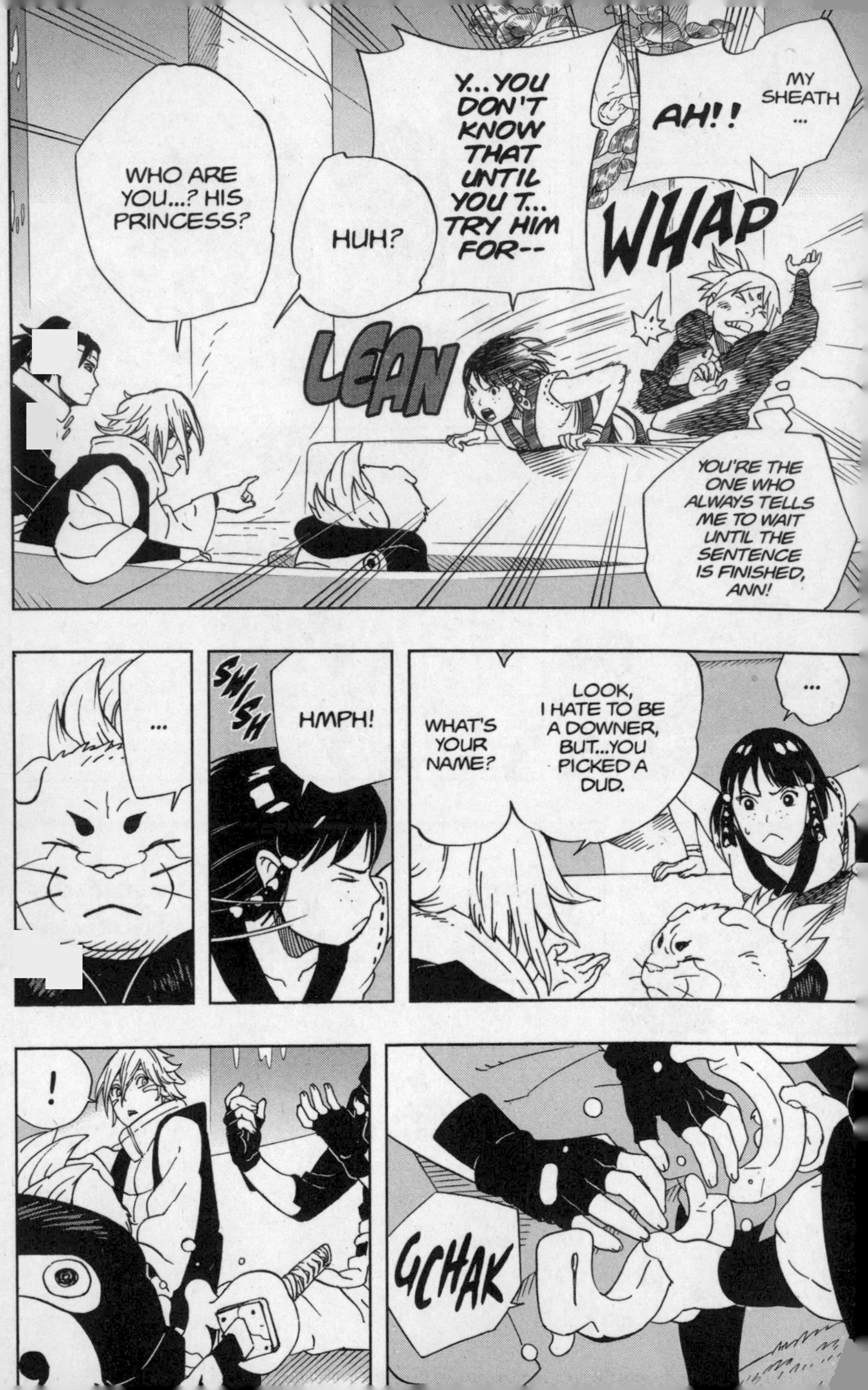
MY SHEATH ...
AH!!
WHAP
Y...YOU DON'T KNOW THAT UNTIL YOU T... TRY HIM FOR--
HUH?
WHO ARE YOU...? HIS PRINCESS?
LEAN
YOU'RE THE ONE WHO ALWAYS TELLS ME TO WAIT UNTIL THE SENTENCE IS FINISHED, ANN!
...
LOOK, I HATE TO BE A DOWNER, BUT...YOU PICKED A DUD.
WHAT'S YOUR NAME?
SWISH
HMPH!
...
GCHAK
!

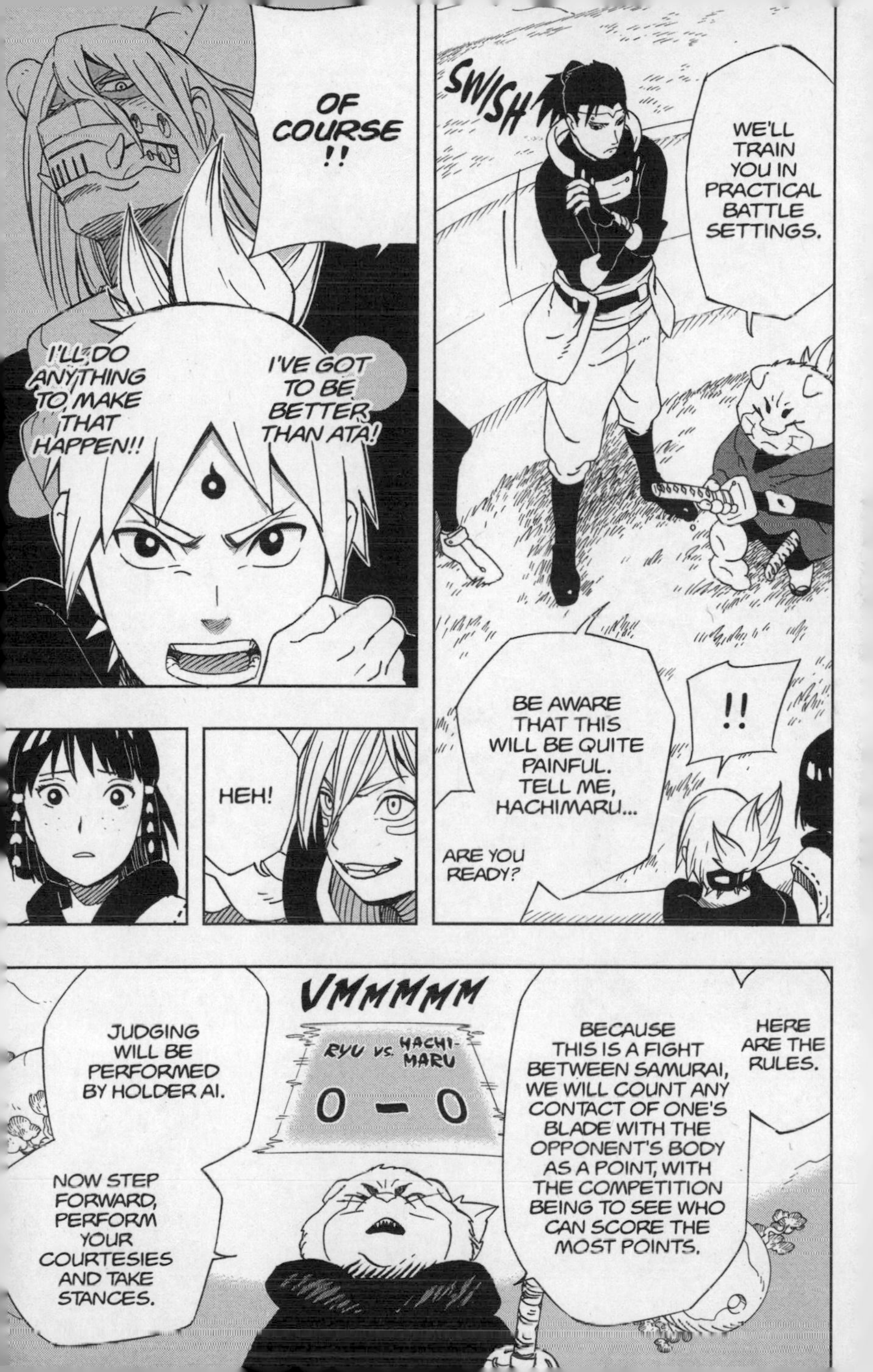
WE'LL TRAIN YOU IN PRACTICAL BATTLE SETTINGS.
SWISH
!!
BE AWARE THAT THIS WILL BE QUITE PAINFUL. TELL ME, HACHIMARU...
ARE YOU READY?
OF COURSE!!
I'VE GOT TO BE BETTER THAN ATA!
I'LL DO ANYTHING TO MAKE THAT HAPPEN!!
HEH!
HERE ARE THE RULES.
BECAUSE THIS IS A FIGHT BETWEEN SAMURAI, WE WILL COUNT ANY CONTACT OF ONE'S BLADE WITH THE OPPONENT'S BODY AS A POINT, WITH THE COMPETITION BEING TO SEE WHO CAN SCORE THE MOST POINTS.
VMMMMM
RYU VS. HACHI-MARU
0 – 0
JUDGING WILL BE PERFORMED BY HOLDER AI.
NOW STEP FORWARD, PERFORM YOUR COURTESIES AND TAKE STANCES.

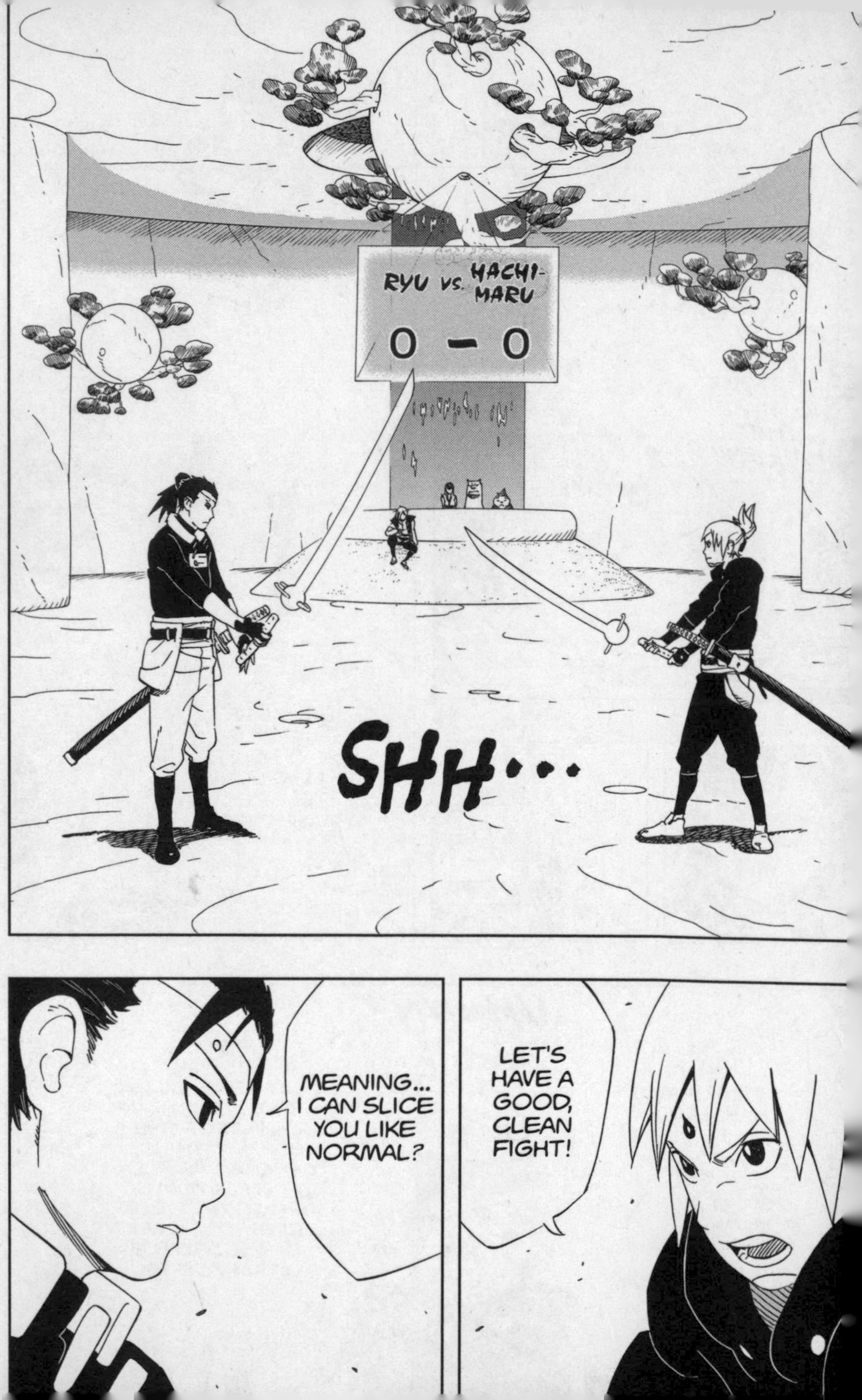
RYU vs. HACHI-MARU
0 – 0
SHH...
LET'S HAVE A GOOD, CLEAN FIGHT!
MEANING... I CAN SLICE YOU LIKE NORMAL?

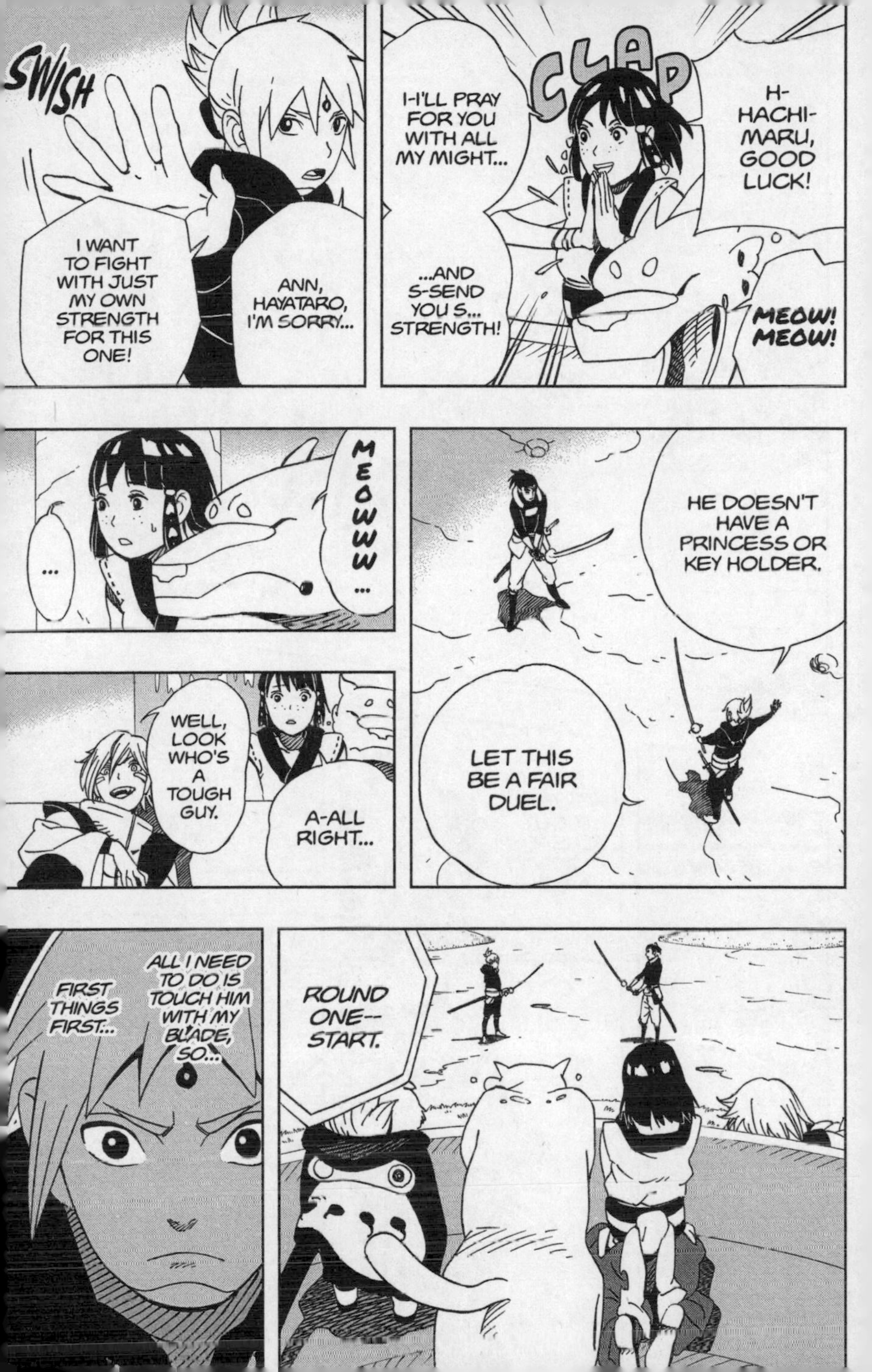
H-HACHIMARU, GOOD LUCK!
CLAP
I-I'LL PRAY FOR YOU WITH ALL MY MIGHT...
...AND S-SEND YOU S... STRENGTH!
MEOW! MEOW!
SWISH
ANN, HAYATARO, I'M SORRY...
I WANT TO FIGHT WITH JUST MY OWN STRENGTH FOR THIS ONE!
HE DOESN'T HAVE A PRINCESS OR KEY HOLDER.
LET THIS BE A FAIR DUEL.
MEOWWW...
...
A-ALL RIGHT...
WELL, LOOK WHO'S A TOUGH GUY.
ROUND ONE--START.
ALL I NEED TO DO IS TOUCH HIM WITH MY BLADE, SO...
FIRST THINGS FIRST...

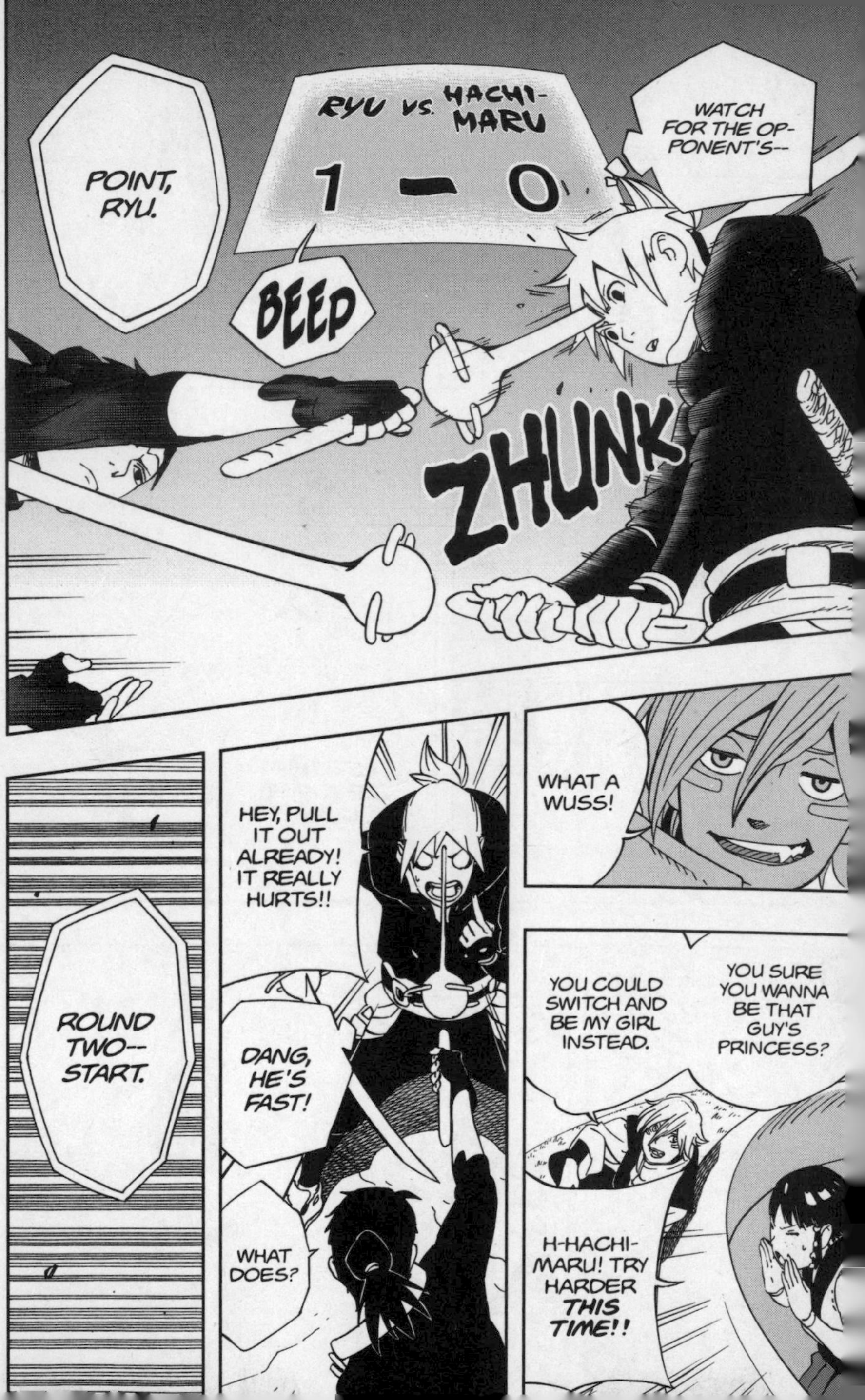
WATCH FOR THE OP-PONENT'S--
RYU VS. HACHI-MARU
1 - 0
ZHUNK
BEEP
POINT, RYU.
WHAT A WUSS!
YOU SURE YOU WANNA BE THAT GUY'S PRINCESS?
YOU COULD SWITCH AND BE MY GIRL INSTEAD.
H-HACHI-MARU! TRY HARDER THIS TIME!!
HEY, PULL IT OUT ALREADY! IT REALLY HURTS!!
DANG, HE'S FAST!
WHAT DOES?
ROUND TWO--START.

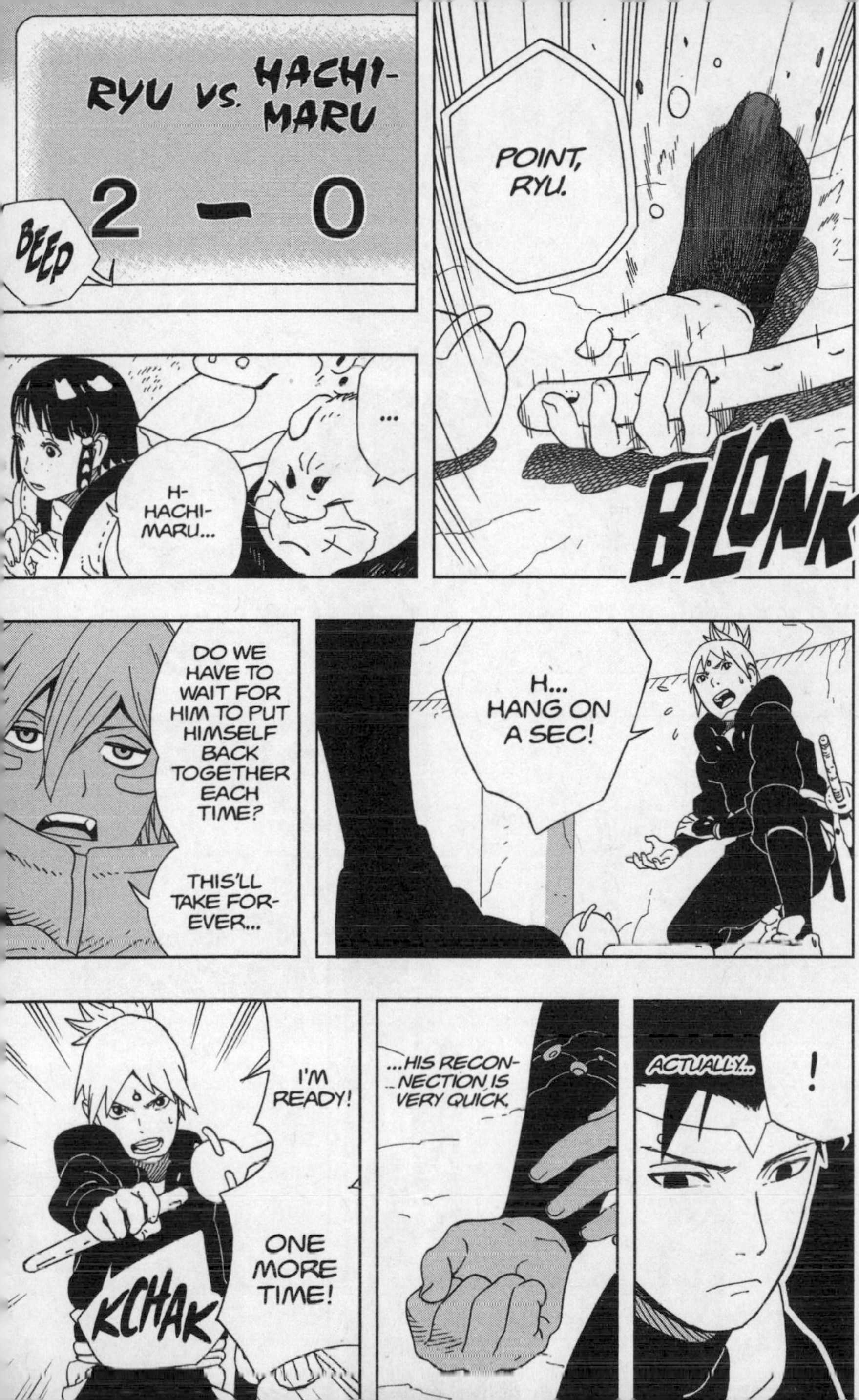
POINT, RYU.
BLONK
RYU VS. HACHI-MARU
2 - 0
BEEP
...
H-HACHI-MARU...
H... HANG ON A SEC!
DO WE HAVE TO WAIT FOR HIM TO PUT HIMSELF BACK TOGETHER EACH TIME?
THIS'LL TAKE FOR-EVER...
!
ACTUALLY...
...HIS RECON-NECTION IS VERY QUICK.
I'M READY!
ONE MORE TIME!
KCHAK

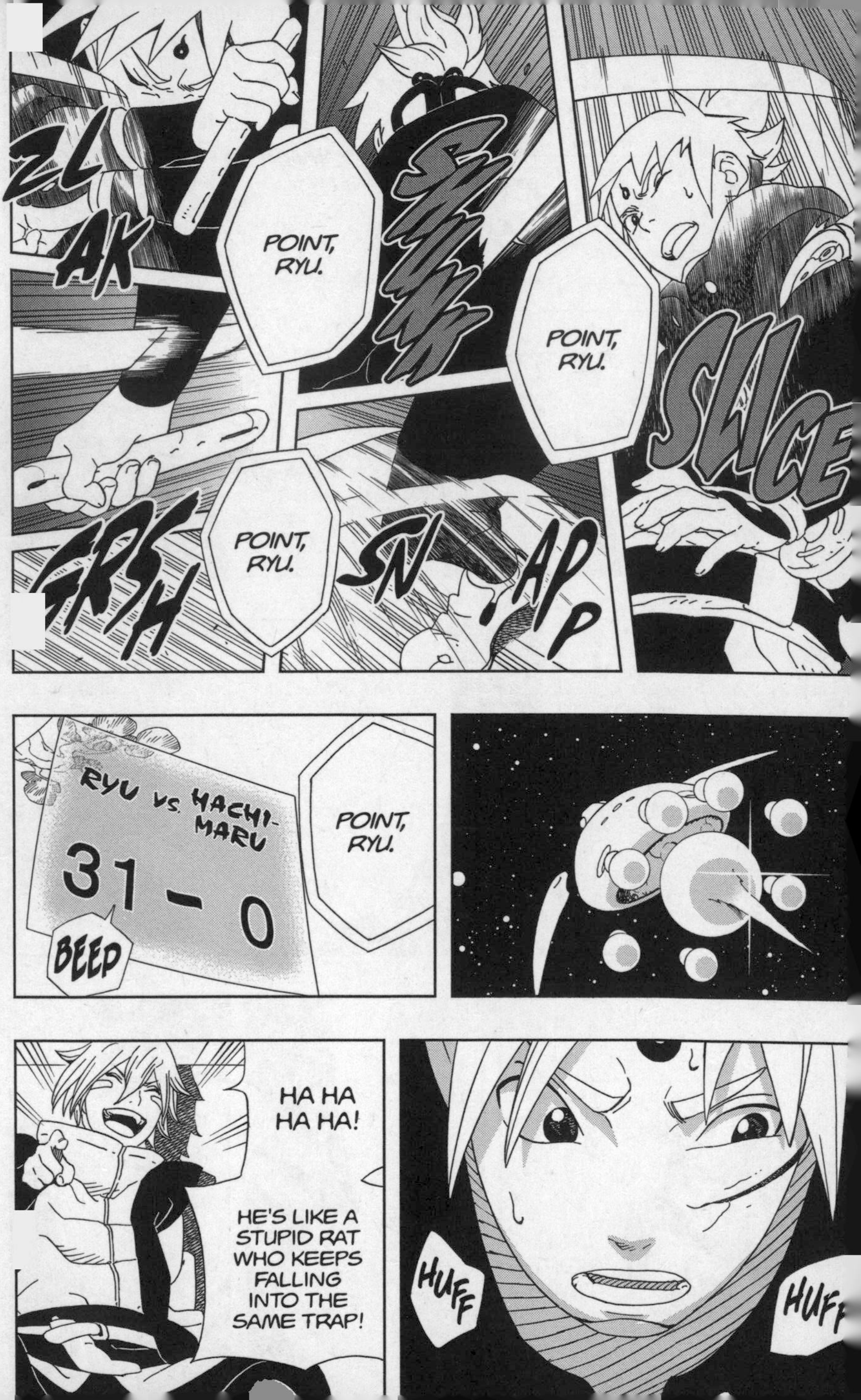
SLICE
POINT, RYU.
POINT, RYU.
SNAP
POINT, RYU.
ZLAK
POINT, RYU.
RYU VS. HACHI-MARU
31 – 0
BEEP
HUFF
HUFF
HA HA HA HA!
HE'S LIKE A STUPID RAT WHO KEEPS FALLING INTO THE SAME TRAP!

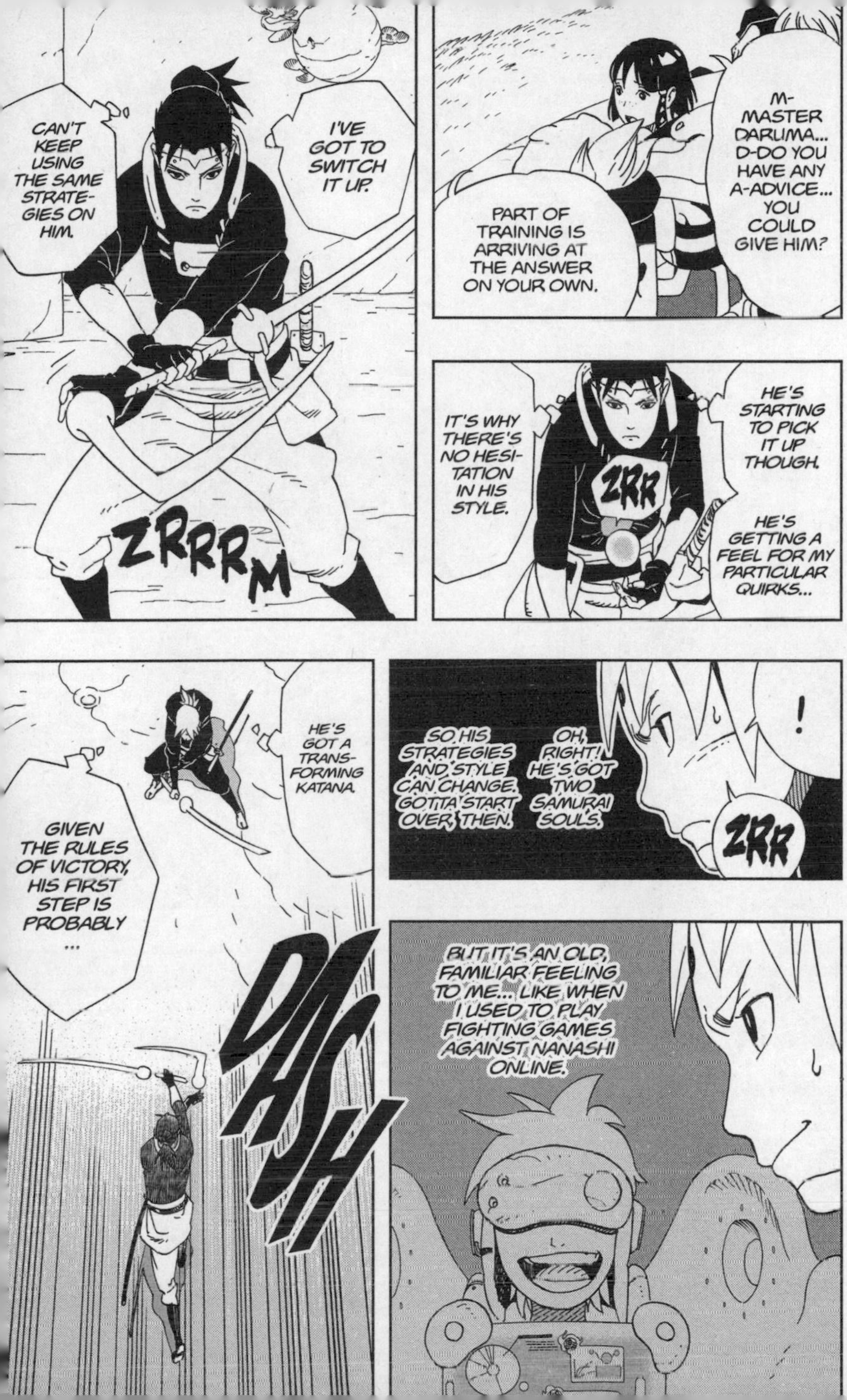
M-MASTER DARUMA... D-DO YOU HAVE ANY A-ADVICE... YOU COULD GIVE HIM?
PART OF TRAINING IS ARRIVING AT THE ANSWER ON YOUR OWN.
HE'S STARTING TO PICK IT UP THOUGH.
HE'S GETTING A FEEL FOR MY PARTICULAR QUIRKS...
ZRR
IT'S WHY THERE'S NO HESITATION IN HIS STYLE.
I'VE GOT TO SWITCH IT UP.
CAN'T KEEP USING THE SAME STRATEGIES ON HIM.
ZRRRRM
!
OH, RIGHT! HE'S GOT TWO SAMURAI SOULS.
SO HIS STRATEGIES AND STYLE CAN CHANGE. GOTTA START OVER, THEN.
ZRR
BUT IT'S AN OLD, FAMILIAR FEELING TO ME... LIKE WHEN I USED TO PLAY FIGHTING GAMES AGAINST NANASHI ONLINE.
HE'S GOT A TRANSFORMING KATANA.
GIVEN THE RULES OF VICTORY, HIS FIRST STEP IS PROBABLY...
DASH

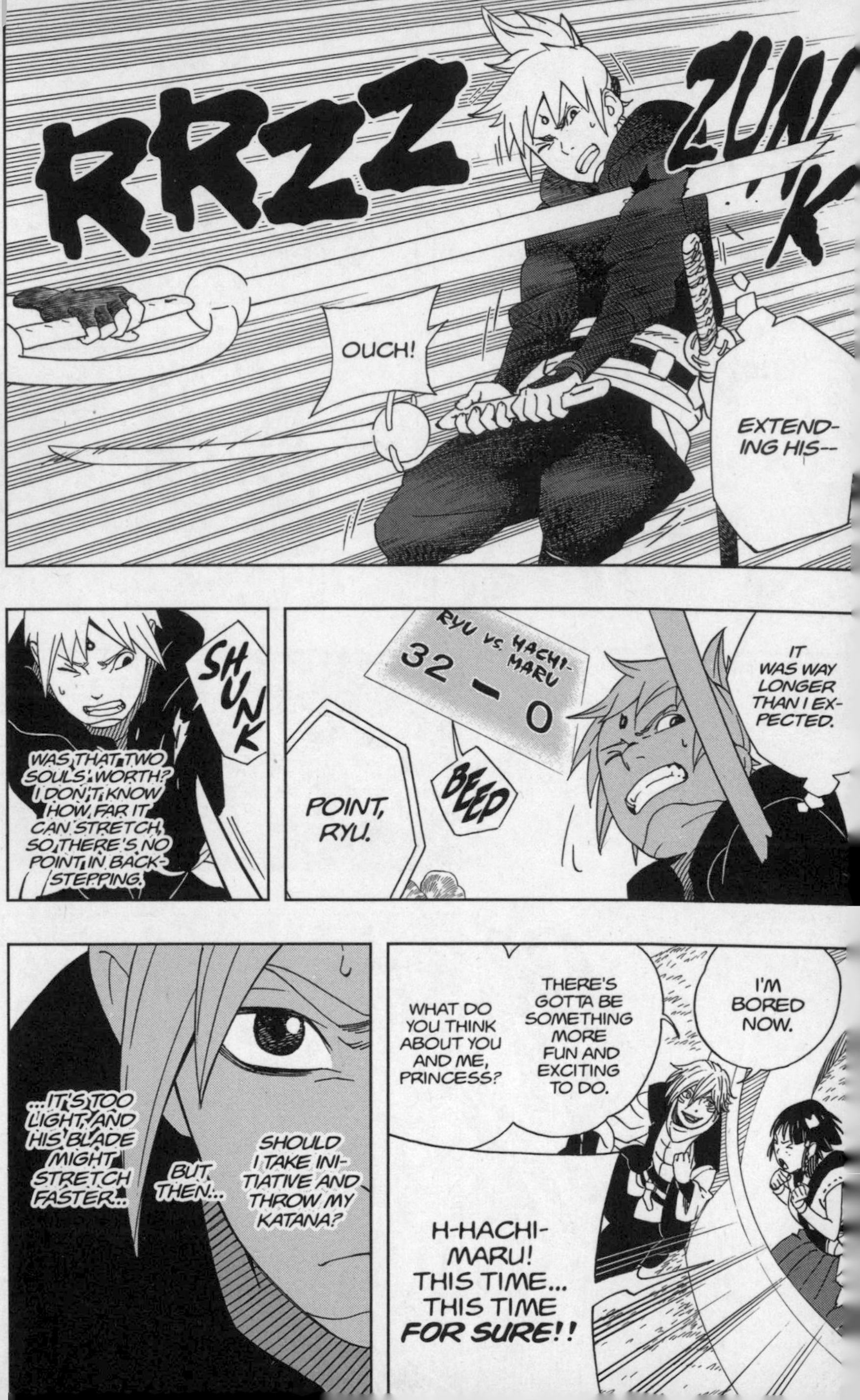
ZUNK
EXTEND-ING HIS--
RRZZ
OUCH!
IT WAS WAY LONGER THAN I EX-PECTED.
RYU VS. HACHI-MARU
32 – 0
BEEP
POINT, RYU.
SHUNK
WAS THAT TWO SOULS' WORTH? I DON'T KNOW HOW FAR IT CAN STRETCH, SO THERE'S NO POINT IN BACK-STEPPING.
I'M BORED NOW.
THERE'S GOTTA BE SOMETHING MORE FUN AND EXCITING TO DO.
WHAT DO YOU THINK ABOUT YOU AND ME, PRINCESS?
H-HACHI-MARU! THIS TIME... THIS TIME **FOR SURE!!**
SHOULD I TAKE INI-TIATIVE AND THROW MY KATANA?
BUT THEN...
...IT'S TOO LIGHT, AND HIS BLADE MIGHT STRETCH FASTER...

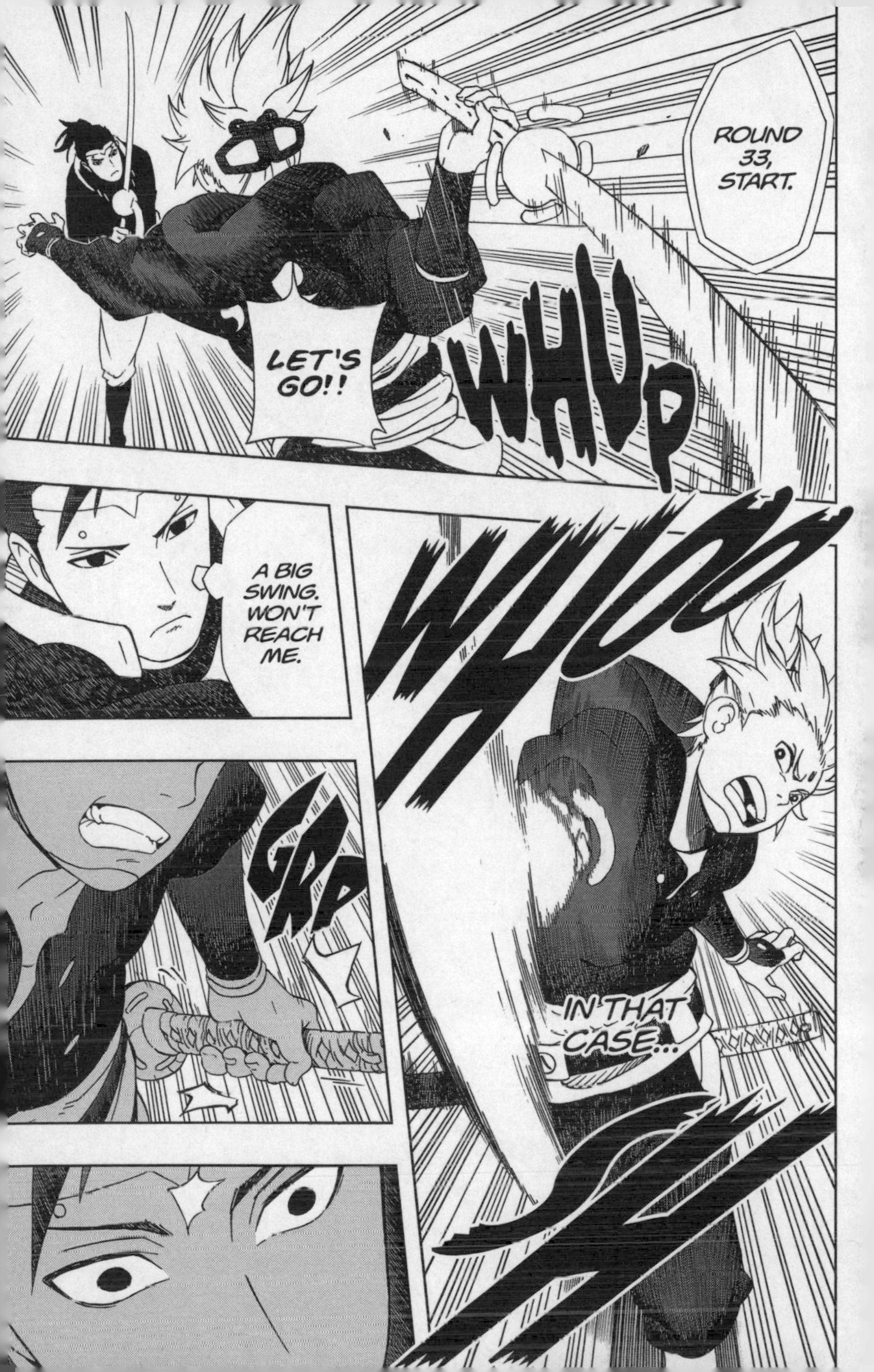
ROUND 33, START.
LET'S GO!!
WHUP
IN THAT CASE...
A BIG SWING. WON'T REACH ME.

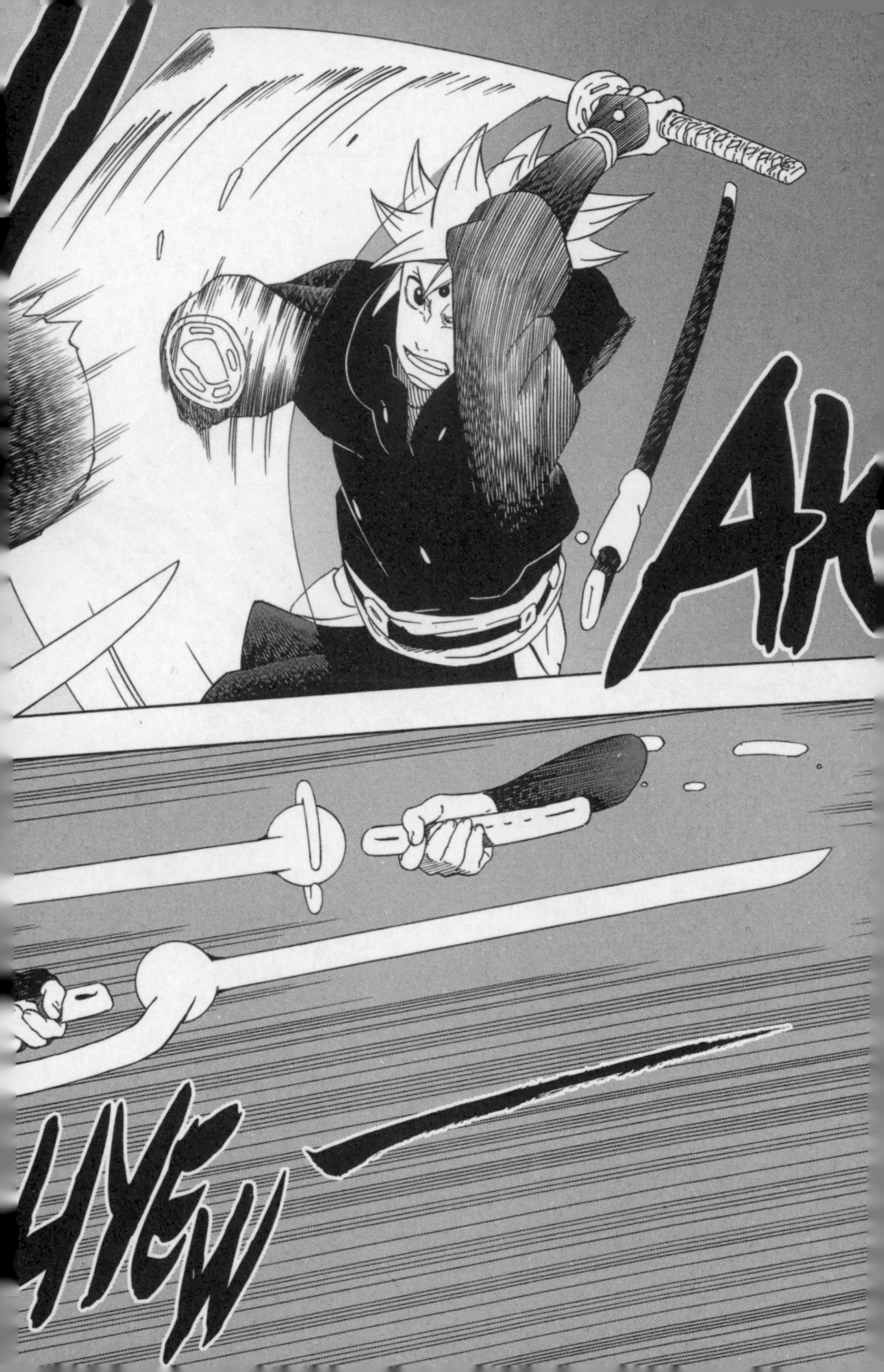
AK
HYEW

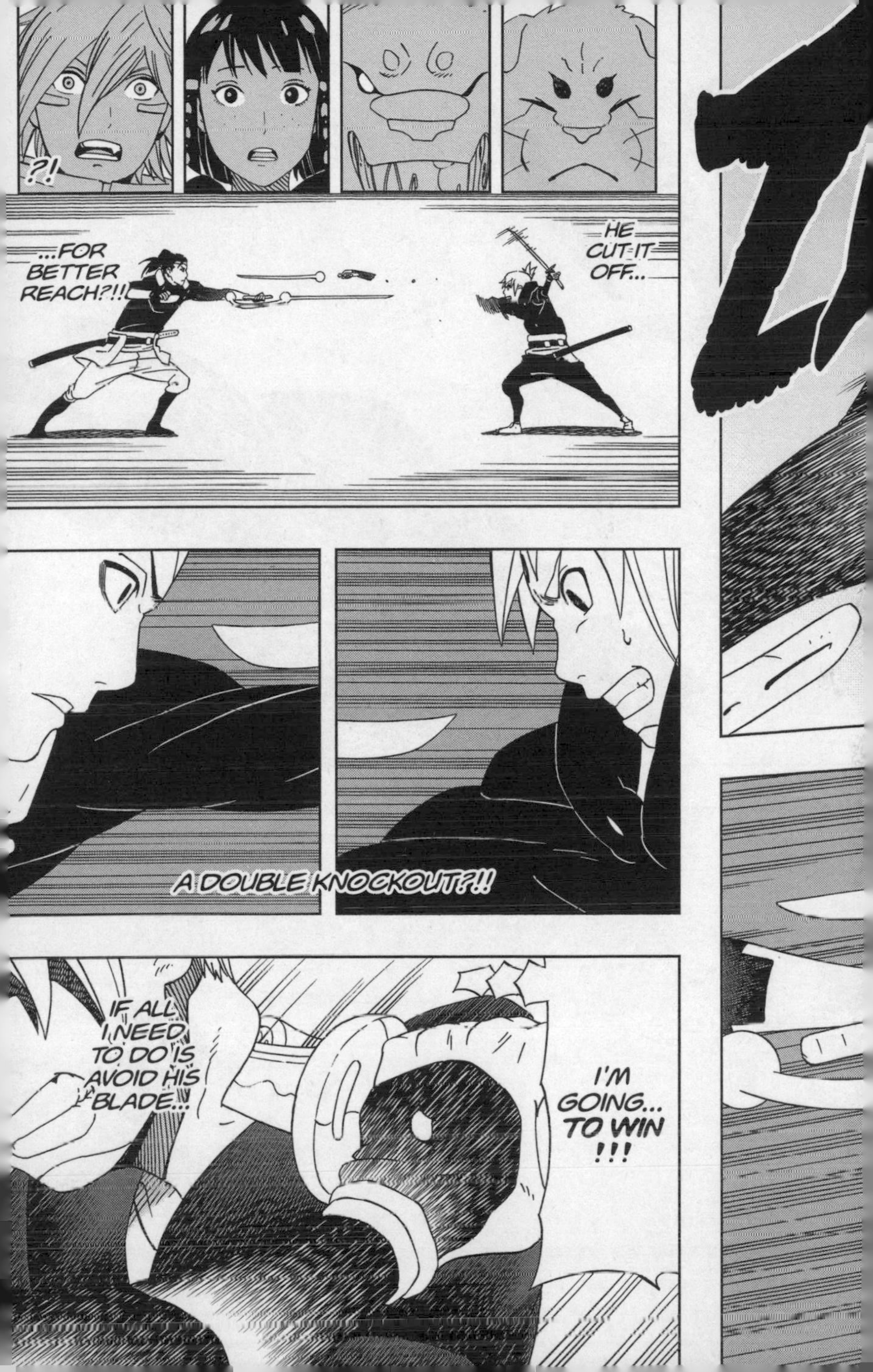
?!
HE CUT IT OFF...
...FOR BETTER REACH?!!
A DOUBLE KNOCKOUT?!!
IF ALL I NEED TO DO IS AVOID HIS BLADE...
I'M GOING... TO WIN !!!

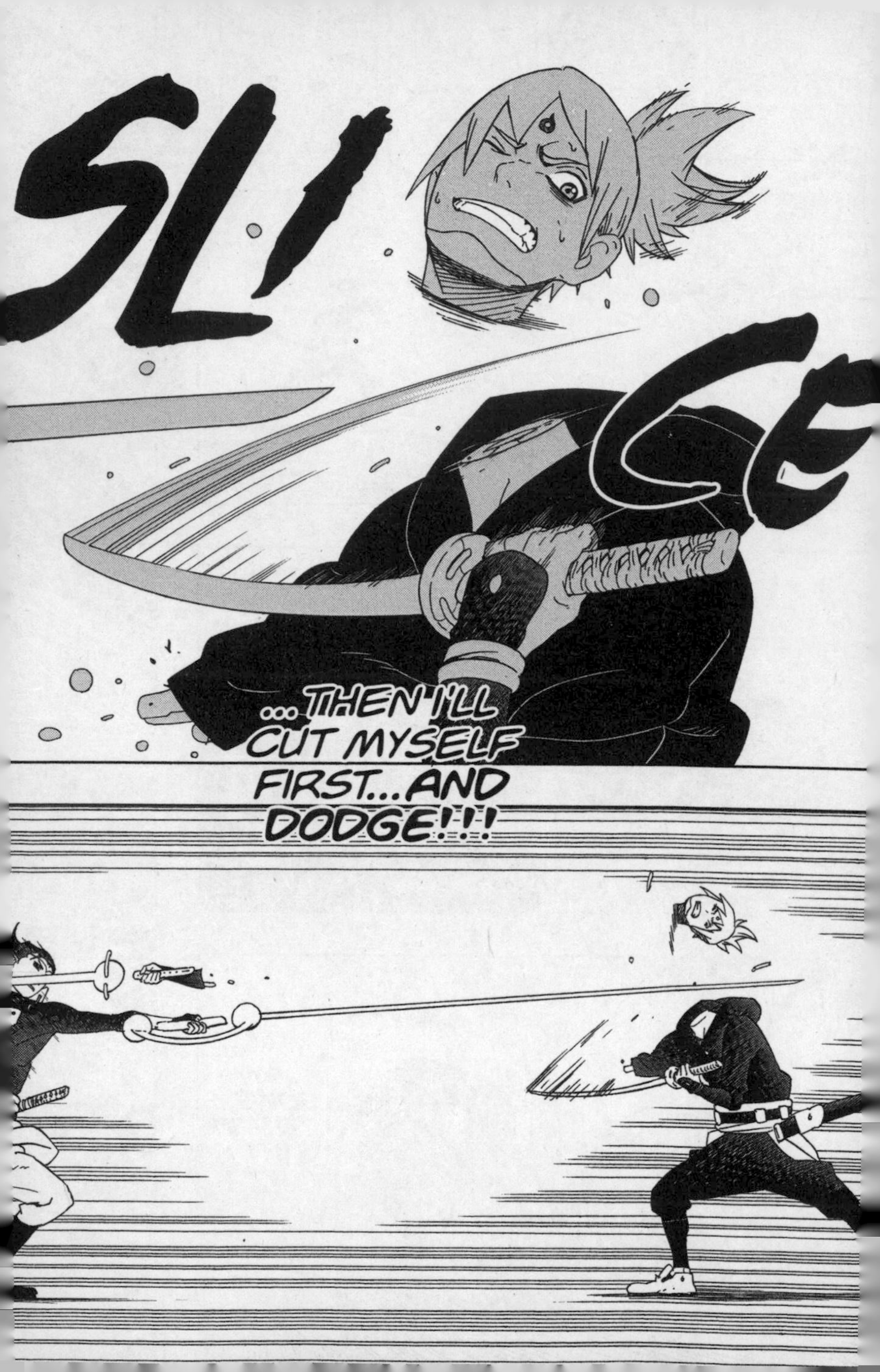
SLICE
...THEN I'LL CUT MYSELF FIRST...AND DODGE!!!

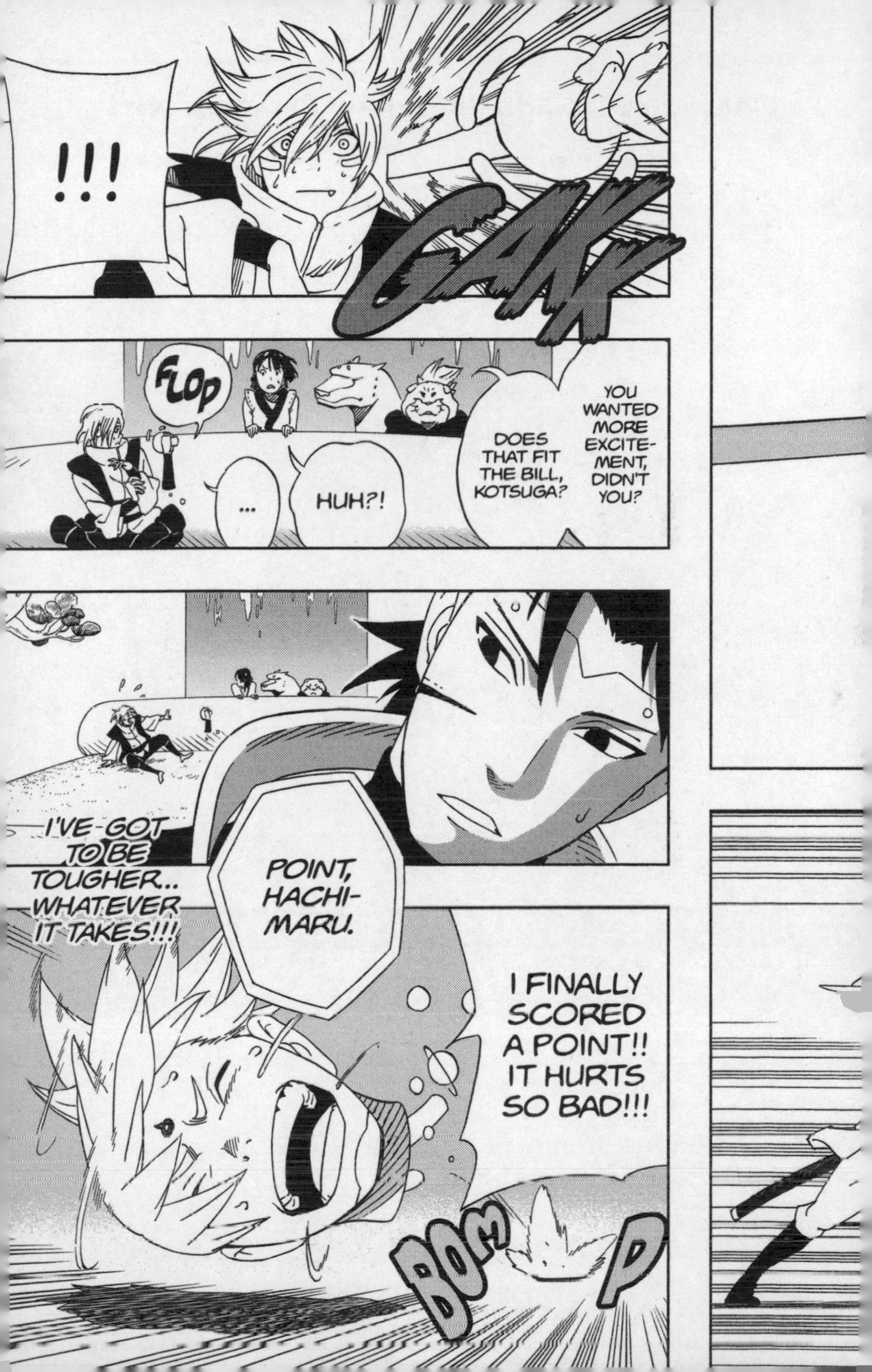
GAK
!!!
YOU WANTED MORE EXCITE-MENT, DIDN'T YOU?
DOES THAT FIT THE BILL, KOTSUGA?
HUH?!
...
FLOP
POINT, HACHI-MARU.
I'VE GOT TO BE TOUGHER... WHATEVER IT TAKES!!!
I FINALLY SCORED A POINT!! IT HURTS SO BAD!!!
BOMP

Character Design Sketches: Princess Niri

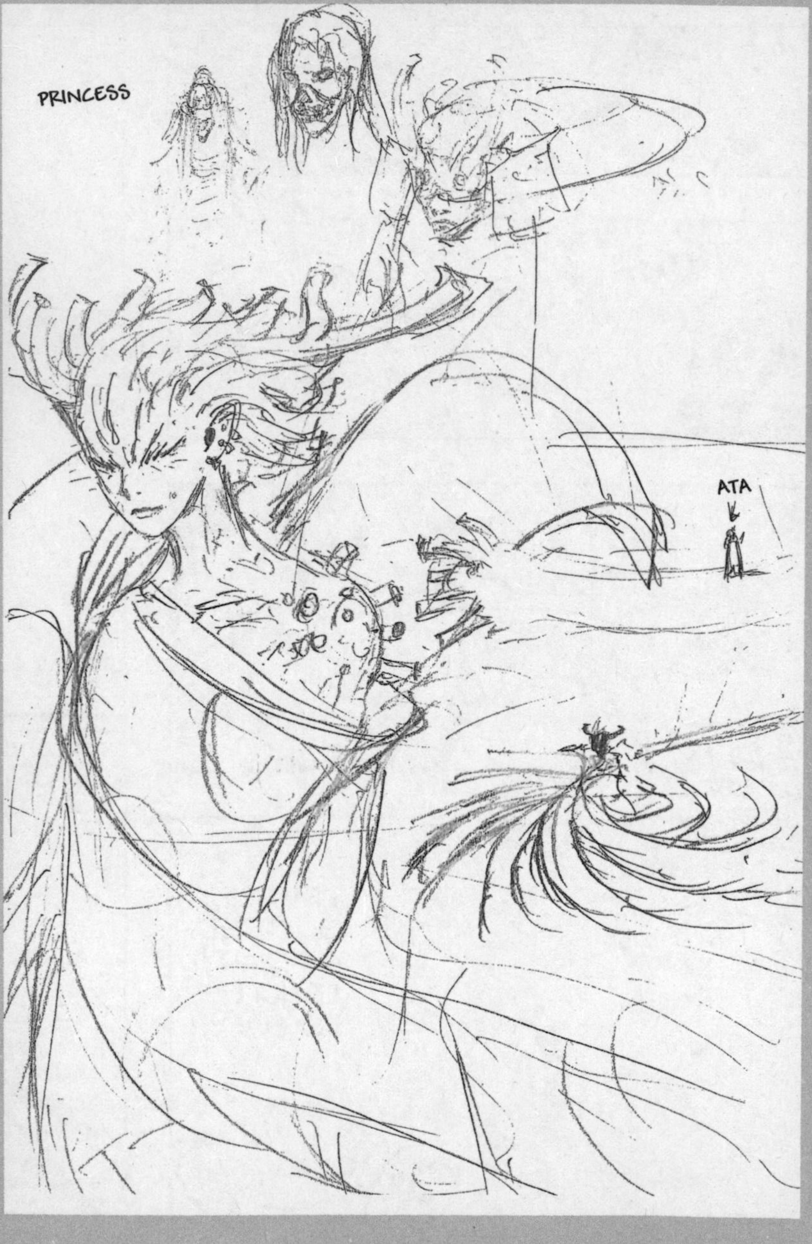

PRINCESS
ATA

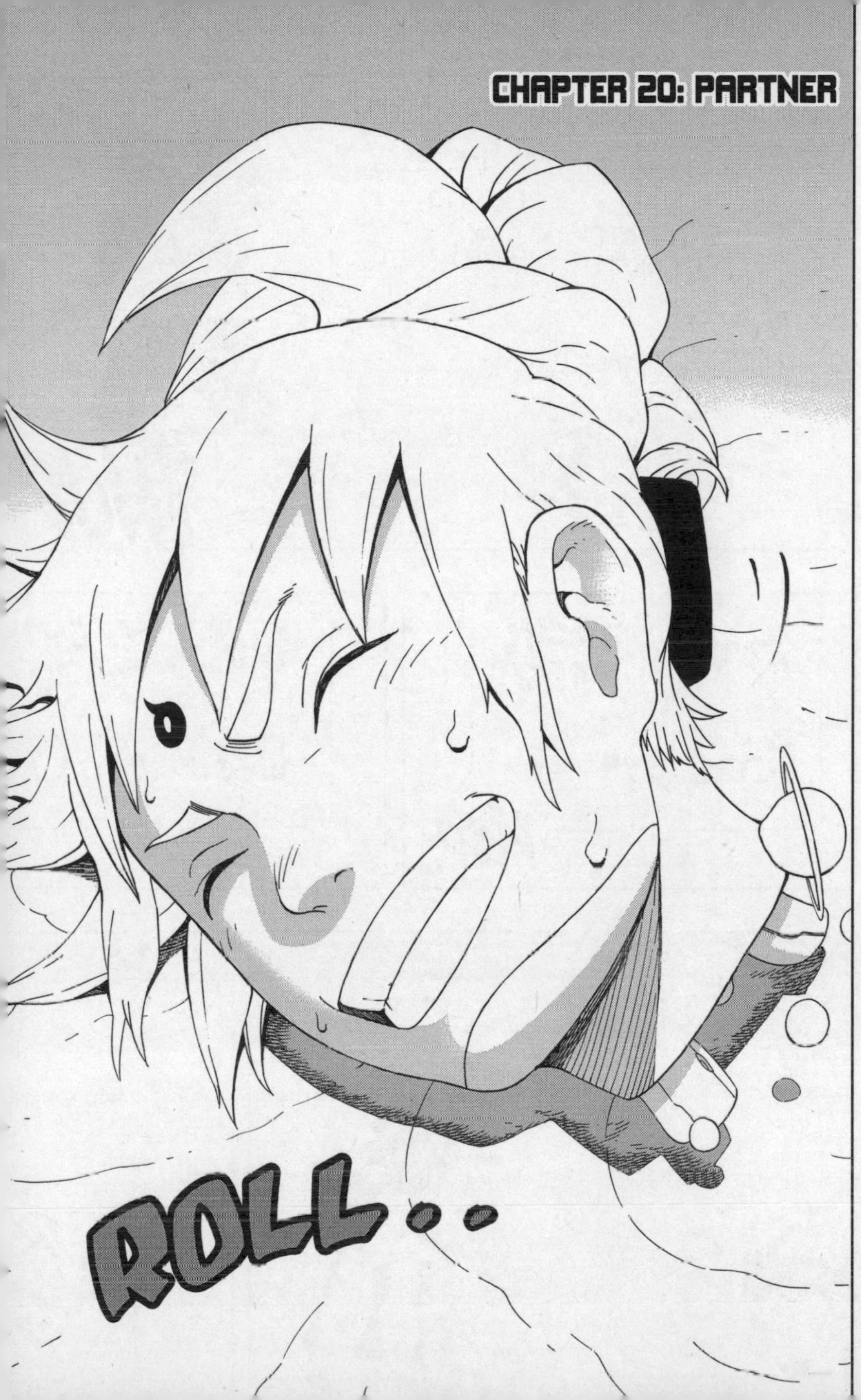
CHAPTER 20: PARTNER
ROLL...

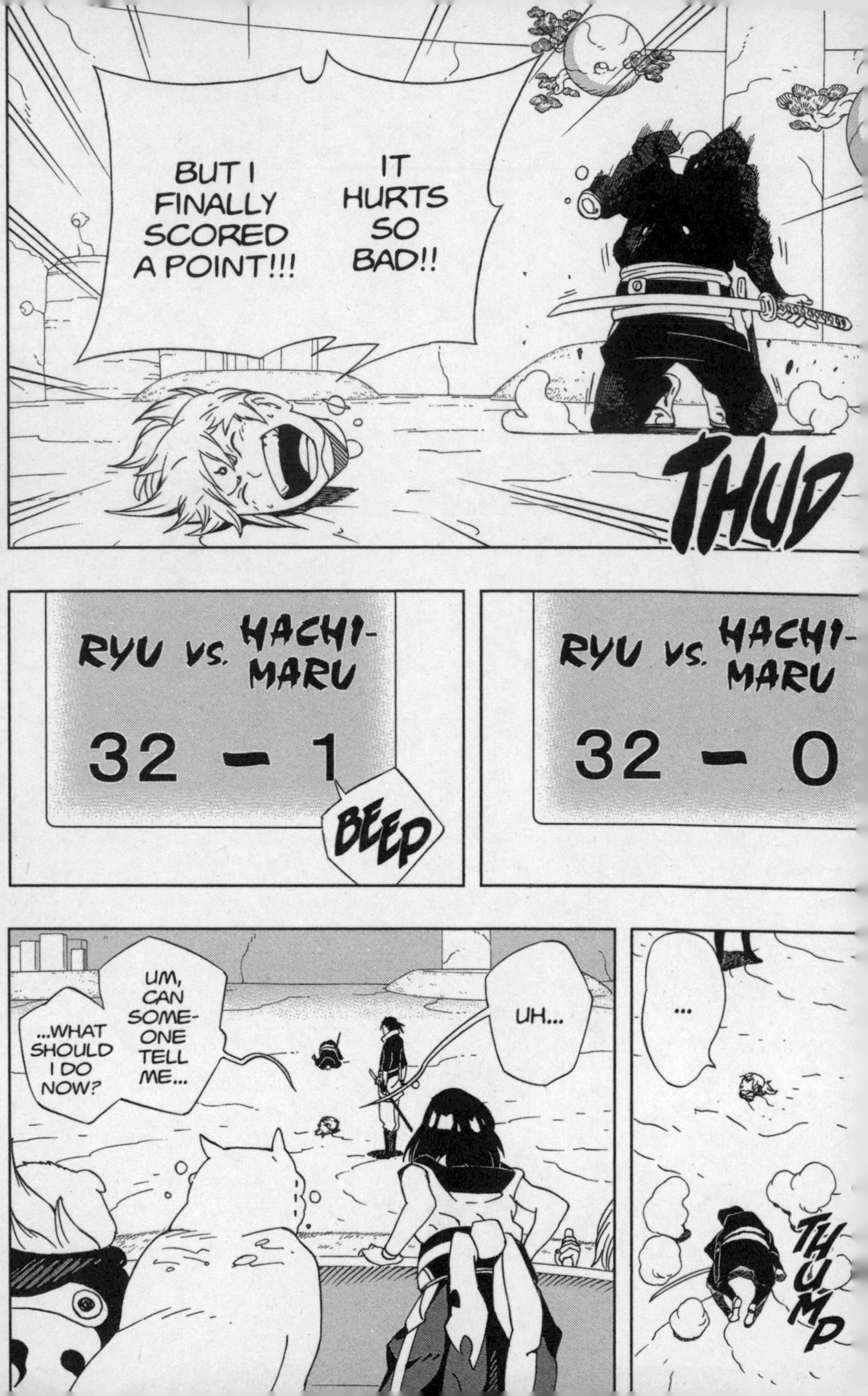
IT HURTS SO BAD!!
BUT I FINALLY SCORED A POINT!!!
THUD
RYU vs. HACHI-MARU
32 - 0
RYU vs. HACHI-MARU
32 - 1
BEEP
...
THUMP
UH...
UM, CAN SOMEONE TELL ME...
...WHAT SHOULD I DO NOW?

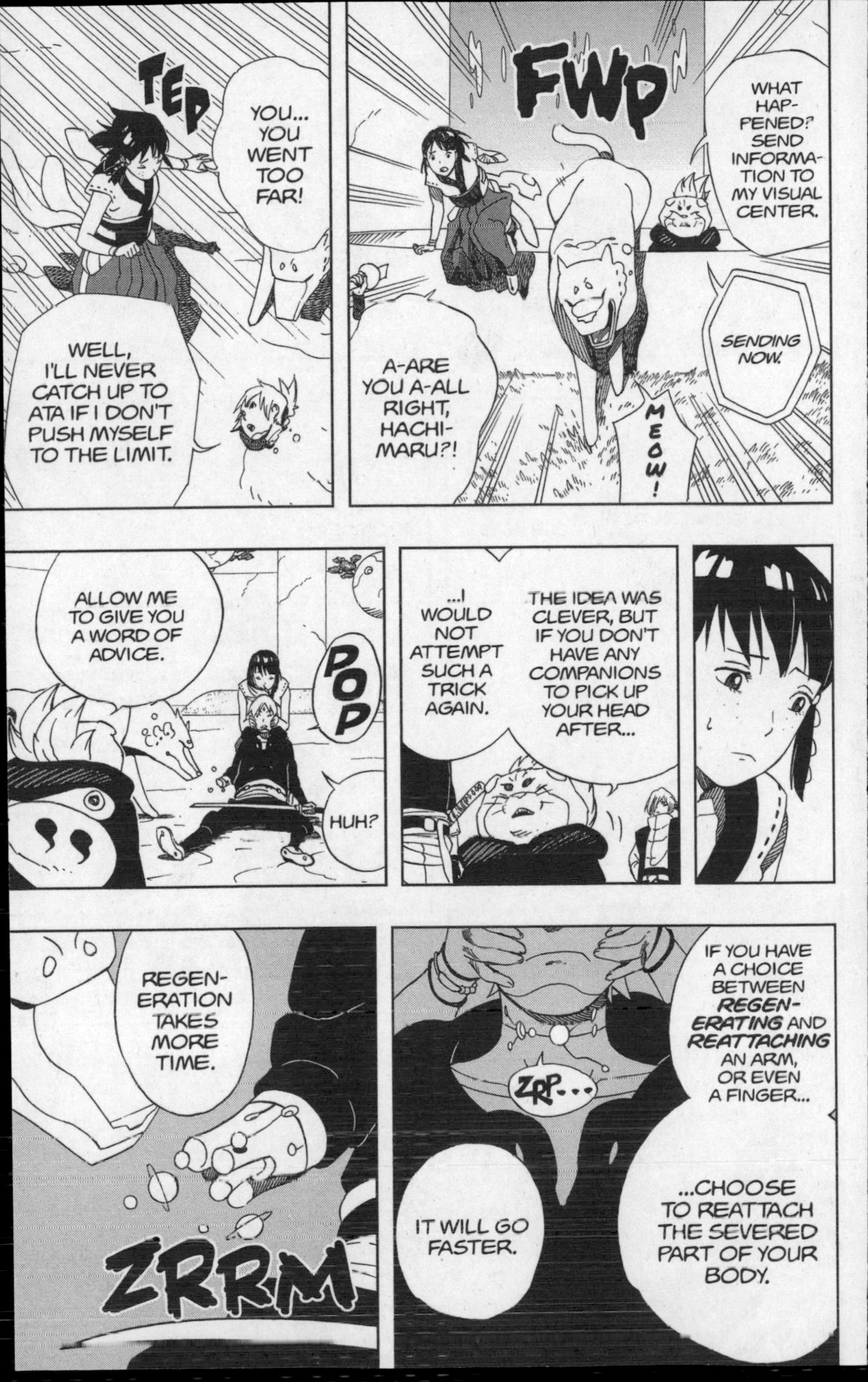
WHAT HAPPENED? SEND INFORMATION TO MY VISUAL CENTER.
FWP
SENDING NOW.
MEOW!
A-ARE YOU A-ALL RIGHT, HACHIMARU?!
TEP
YOU... YOU WENT TOO FAR!
WELL, I'LL NEVER CATCH UP TO ATA IF I DON'T PUSH MYSELF TO THE LIMIT.
THE IDEA WAS CLEVER, BUT IF YOU DON'T HAVE ANY COMPANIONS TO PICK UP YOUR HEAD AFTER...
...I WOULD NOT ATTEMPT SUCH A TRICK AGAIN.
POP
ALLOW ME TO GIVE YOU A WORD OF ADVICE.
HUH?
IF YOU HAVE A CHOICE BETWEEN *REGENERATING* AND *REATTACHING* AN ARM, OR EVEN A FINGER...
ZRP...
...CHOOSE TO REATTACH THE SEVERED PART OF YOUR BODY.
IT WILL GO FASTER.
REGENERATION TAKES MORE TIME.
ZRRM

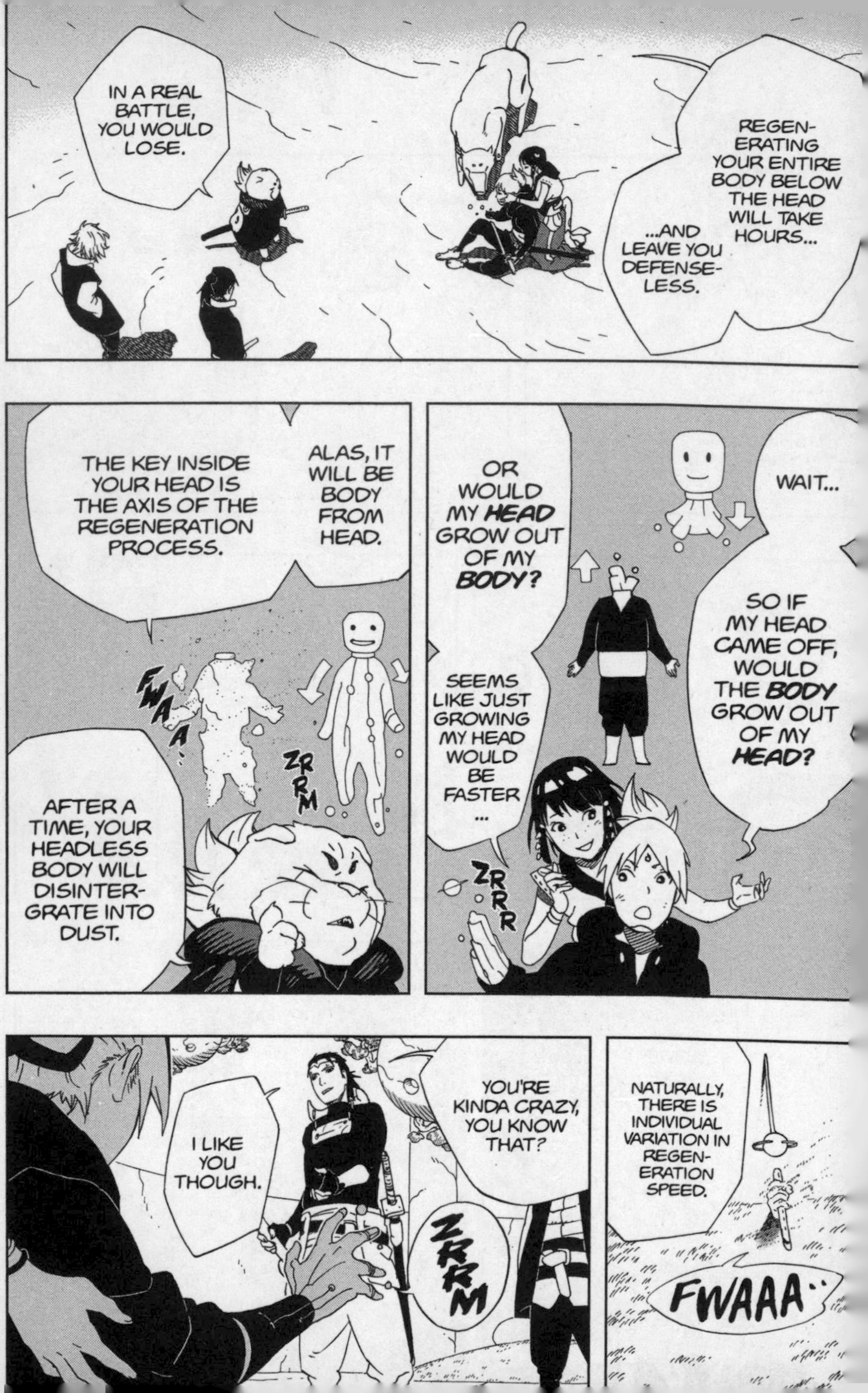
REGEN-ERATING YOUR ENTIRE BODY BELOW THE HEAD WILL TAKE HOURS...
...AND LEAVE YOU DEFENSE-LESS.
IN A REAL BATTLE, YOU WOULD LOSE.
WAIT...
SO IF MY HEAD CAME OFF, WOULD THE BODY GROW OUT OF MY HEAD?
OR WOULD MY HEAD GROW OUT OF MY BODY?
SEEMS LIKE JUST GROWING MY HEAD WOULD BE FASTER ...
ZRRR
ALAS, IT WILL BE BODY FROM HEAD.
THE KEY INSIDE YOUR HEAD IS THE AXIS OF THE REGENERATION PROCESS.
FWAAA
ZRRM
AFTER A TIME, YOUR HEADLESS BODY WILL DISINTERG-RATE INTO DUST.
NATURALLY, THERE IS INDIVIDUAL VARIATION IN REGEN-ERATION SPEED.
FWAAA
YOU'RE KINDA CRAZY, YOU KNOW THAT?
ZRRM
I LIKE YOU THOUGH.

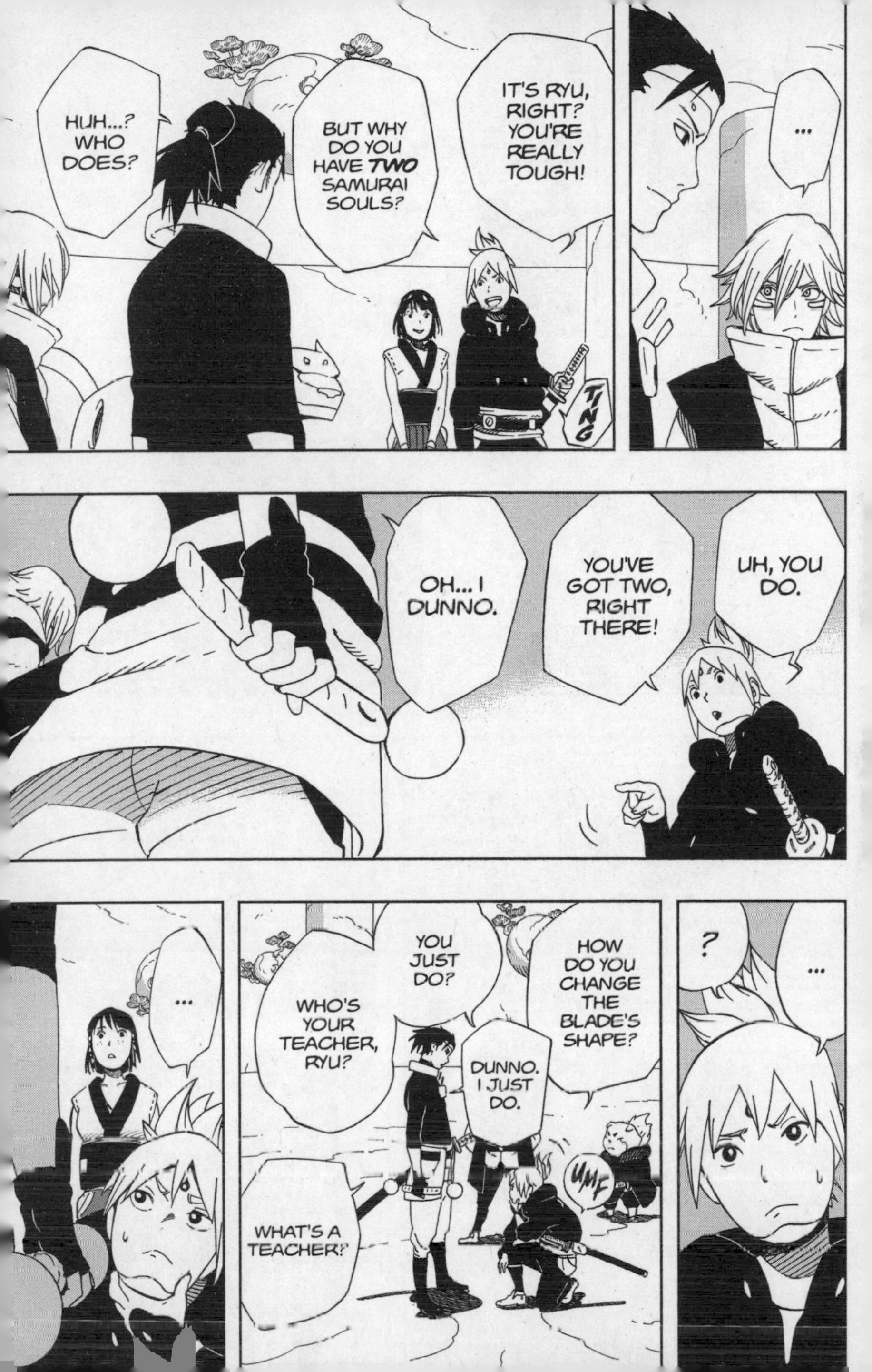
...
IT'S RYU, RIGHT? YOU'RE REALLY TOUGH!
BUT WHY DO YOU HAVE TWO SAMURAI SOULS?
HUH...? WHO DOES?
TING
UH, YOU DO.
YOU'VE GOT TWO, RIGHT THERE!
OH... I DUNNO.
...
?
HOW DO YOU CHANGE THE BLADE'S SHAPE?
DUNNO. I JUST DO.
UMF
YOU JUST DO?
WHO'S YOUR TEACHER, RYU?
WHAT'S A TEACHER?
...

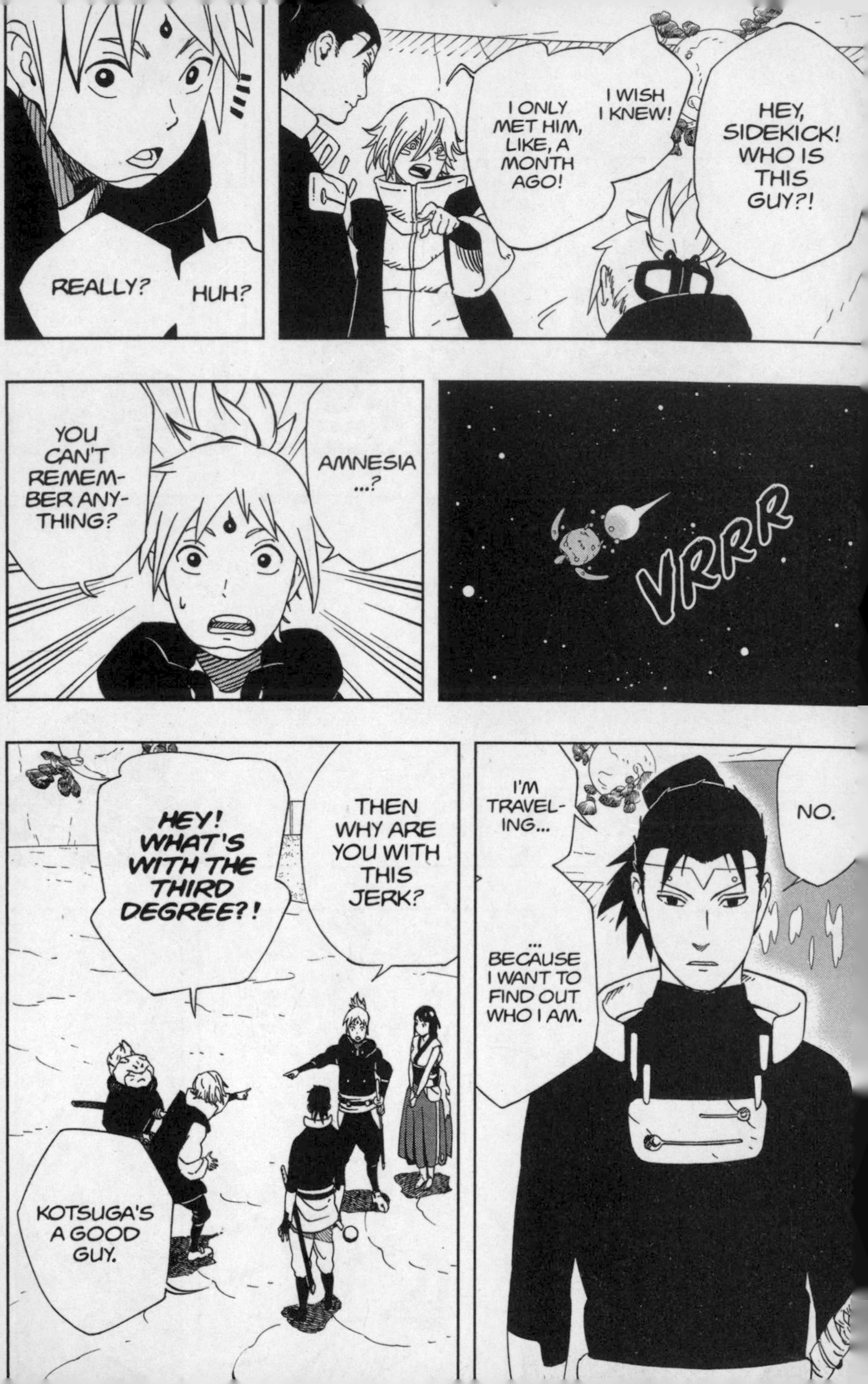
HEY, SIDEKICK! WHO IS THIS GUY?!
I WISH I KNEW!
I ONLY MET HIM, LIKE, A MONTH AGO!
HUH?
REALLY?
VRRR
AMNESIA ...?
YOU CAN'T REMEMBER ANYTHING?
NO.
I'M TRAVELING...
...BECAUSE I WANT TO FIND OUT WHO I AM.
THEN WHY ARE YOU WITH THIS JERK?
HEY! WHAT'S WITH THE THIRD DEGREE?!
KOTSUGA'S A GOOD GUY.

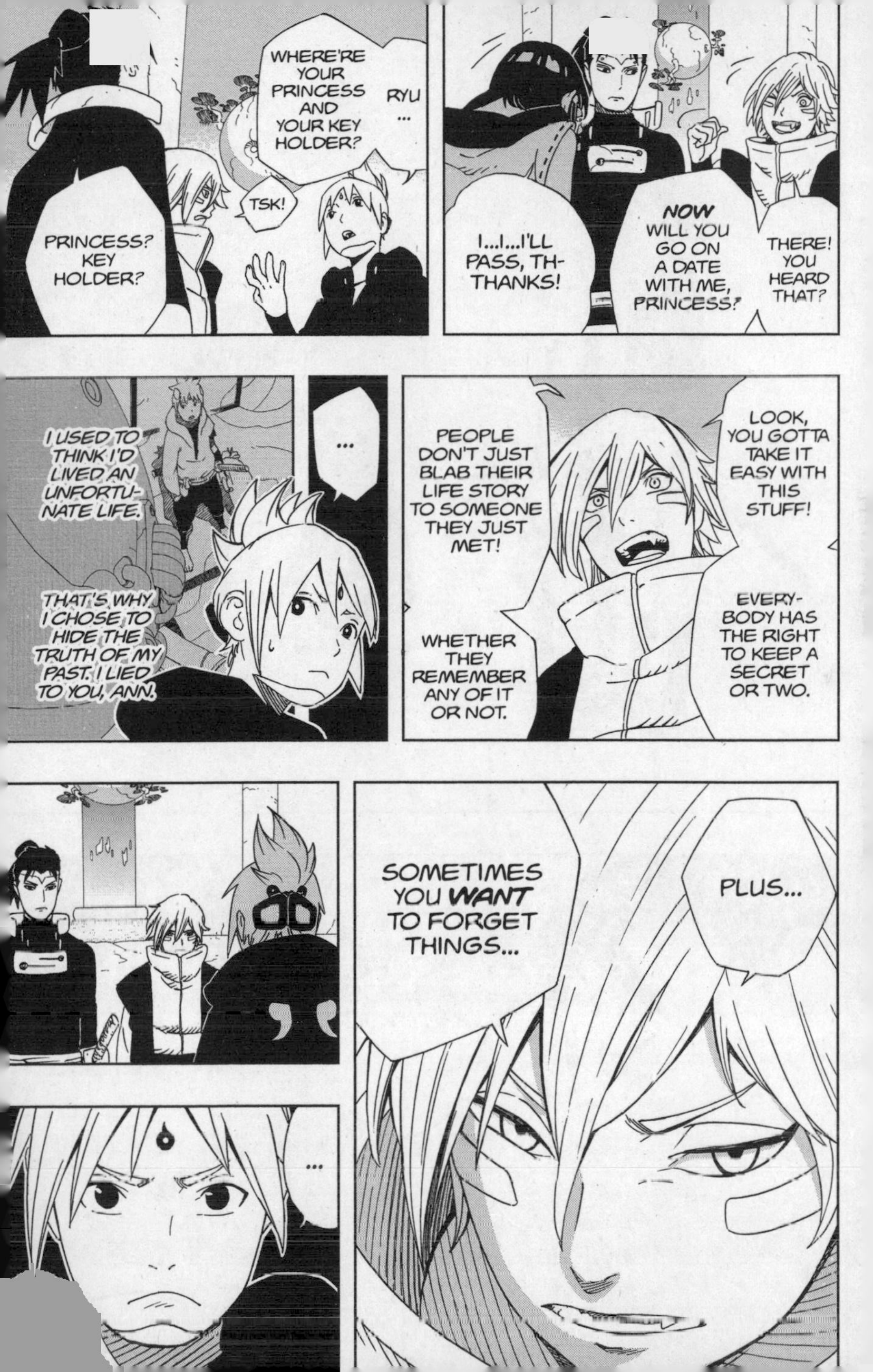
THERE! YOU HEARD THAT?
NOW WILL YOU GO ON A DATE WITH ME, PRINCESS?
I...I...I'LL PASS, TH-THANKS!
WHERE'RE YOUR PRINCESS AND YOUR KEY HOLDER?
RYU ...
TSK!
PRINCESS? KEY HOLDER?
LOOK, YOU GOTTA TAKE IT EASY WITH THIS STUFF!
PEOPLE DON'T JUST BLAB THEIR LIFE STORY TO SOMEONE THEY JUST MET!
EVERY-BODY HAS THE RIGHT TO KEEP A SECRET OR TWO.
WHETHER THEY REMEMBER ANY OF IT OR NOT.
...
I USED TO THINK I'D LIVED AN UNFORTU-NATE LIFE.
THAT'S WHY I CHOSE TO HIDE THE TRUTH OF MY PAST. I LIED TO YOU, ANN.
PLUS...
SOMETIMES YOU *WANT* TO FORGET THINGS...
...

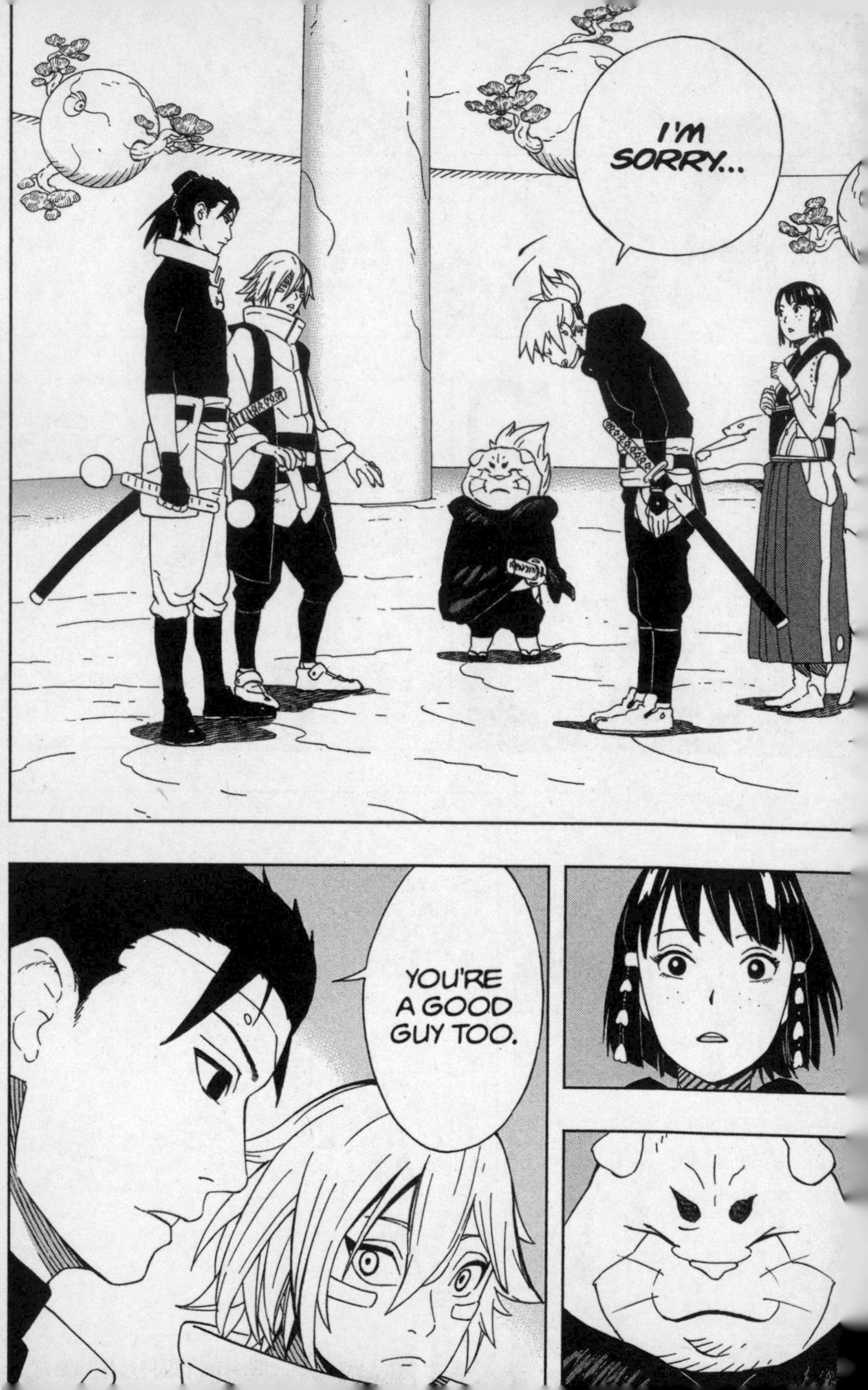
I'M SORRY...
YOU'RE A GOOD GUY TOO.

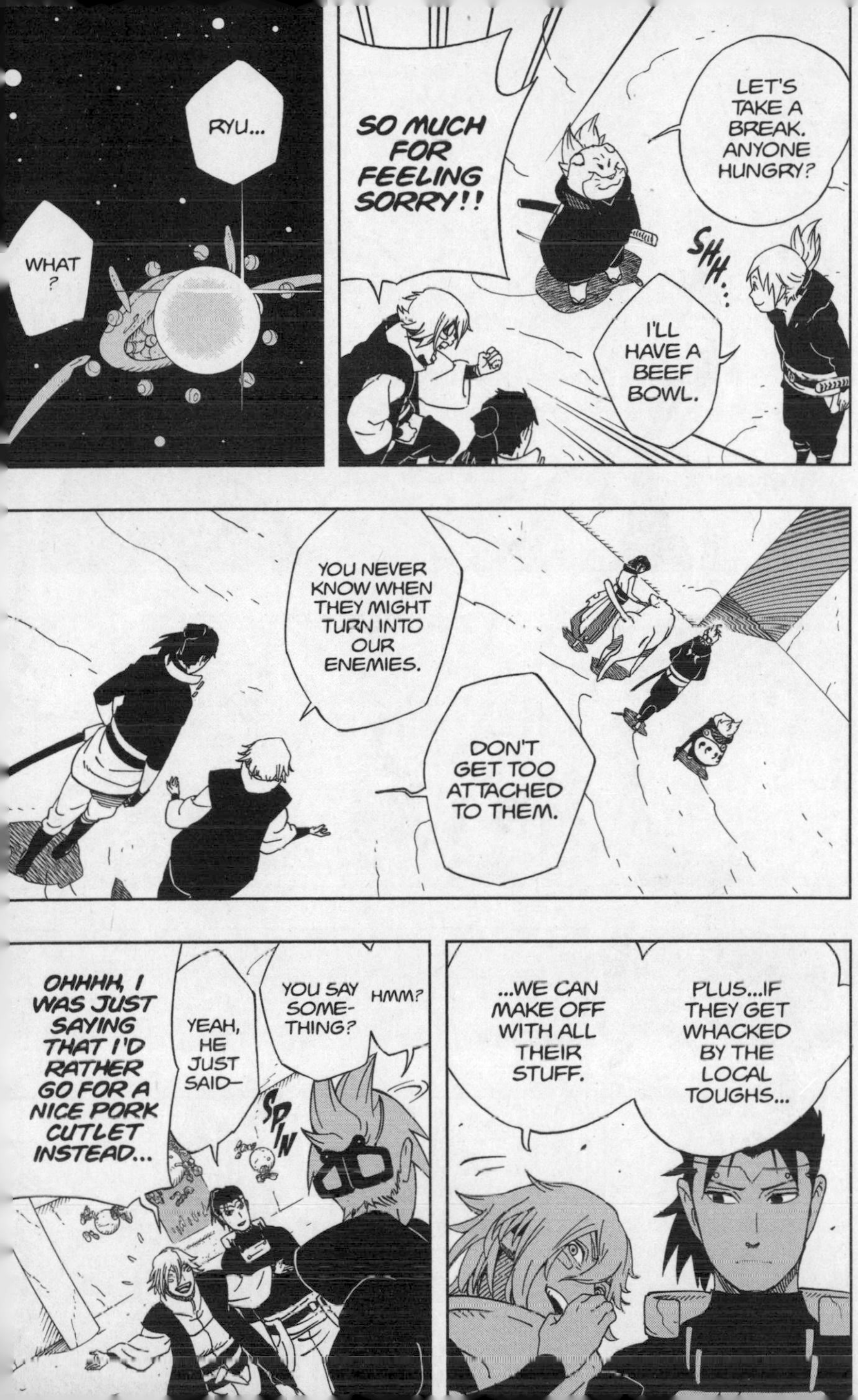
LET'S TAKE A BREAK. ANYONE HUNGRY?
SHH...
I'LL HAVE A BEEF BOWL.
SO MUCH FOR FEELING SORRY!!
RYU...
WHAT?
YOU NEVER KNOW WHEN THEY MIGHT TURN INTO OUR ENEMIES.
DON'T GET TOO ATTACHED TO THEM.
PLUS...IF THEY GET WHACKED BY THE LOCAL TOUGHS...
...WE CAN MAKE OFF WITH ALL THEIR STUFF.
HMM?
YOU SAY SOME-THING?
SPIN
YEAH, HE JUST SAID—
OHHHH, I WAS JUST SAYING THAT I'D RATHER GO FOR A NICE PORK CUTLET INSTEAD...

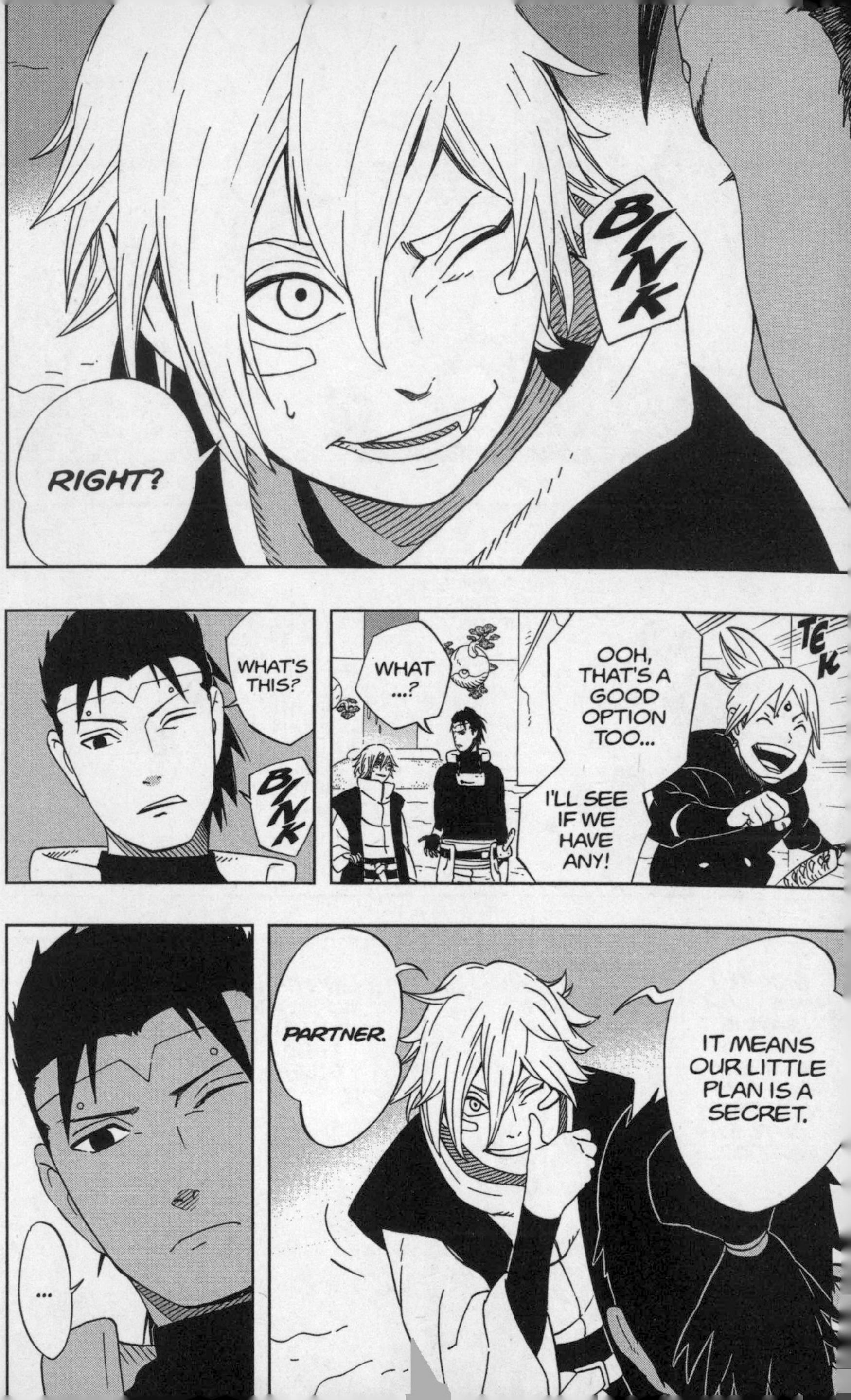
BINK
RIGHT?
TEK
OOH, THAT'S A GOOD OPTION TOO...
I'LL SEE IF WE HAVE ANY!
WHAT ...?
WHAT'S THIS?
BINK
IT MEANS OUR LITTLE PLAN IS A SECRET.
PARTNER.
...

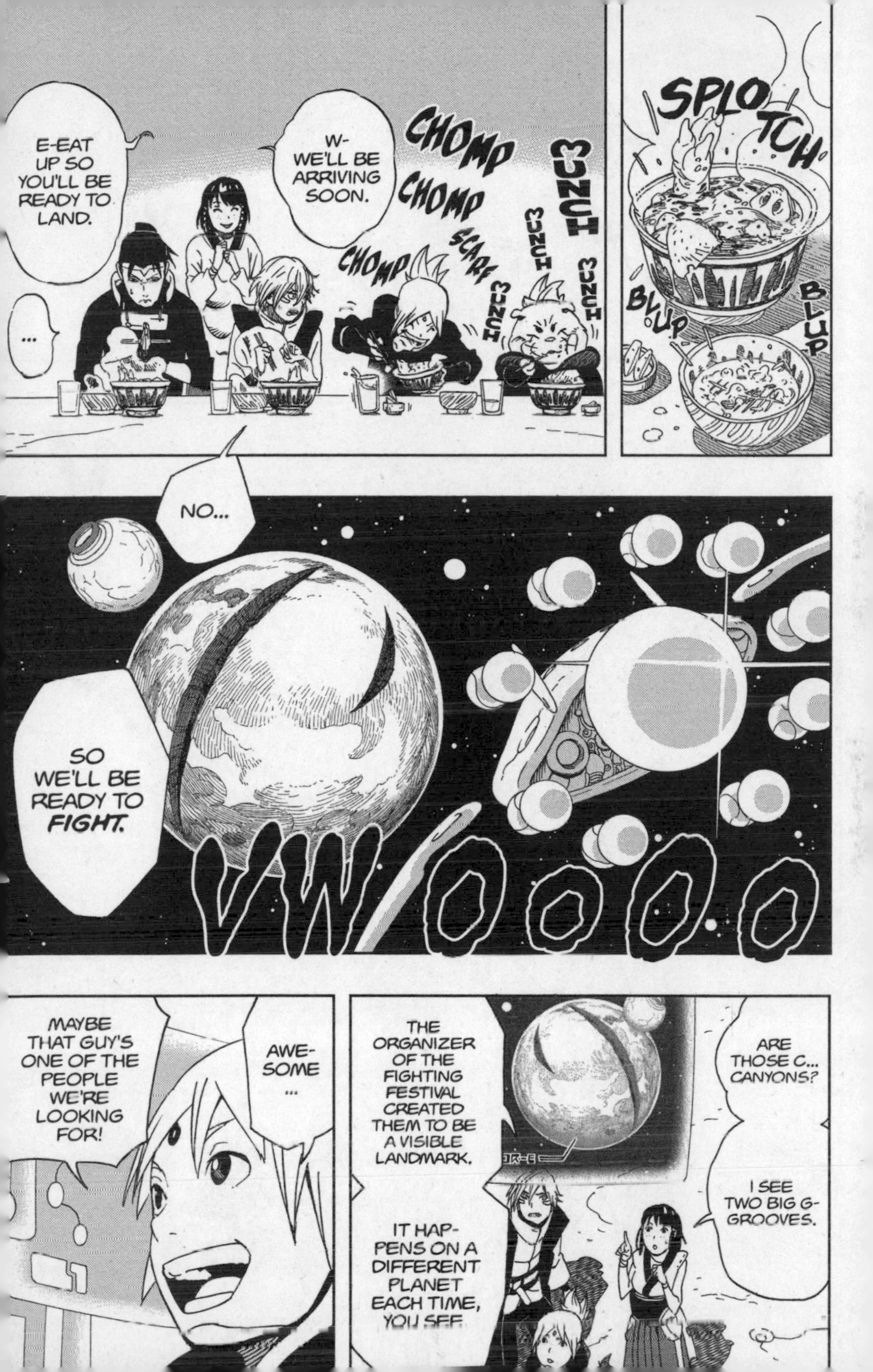

SPLOTCH
BLUP
BLUP
MUNCH
MUNCH
MUNCH
MUNCH
SCARF
CHOMP
CHOMP
CHOMP
W- WE'LL BE ARRIVING SOON.
E-EAT UP SO YOU'LL BE READY TO LAND.
...
NO...
SO WE'LL BE READY TO *FIGHT.*
VWOOOOO
ARE THOSE C... CANYONS?
THE ORGANIZER OF THE FIGHTING FESTIVAL CREATED THEM TO BE A VISIBLE LANDMARK.
I SEE TWO BIG G-GROOVES.
IT HAPPENS ON A DIFFERENT PLANET EACH TIME, YOU SEE.
AWESOME...
MAYBE THAT GUY'S ONE OF THE PEOPLE WE'RE LOOKING FOR!

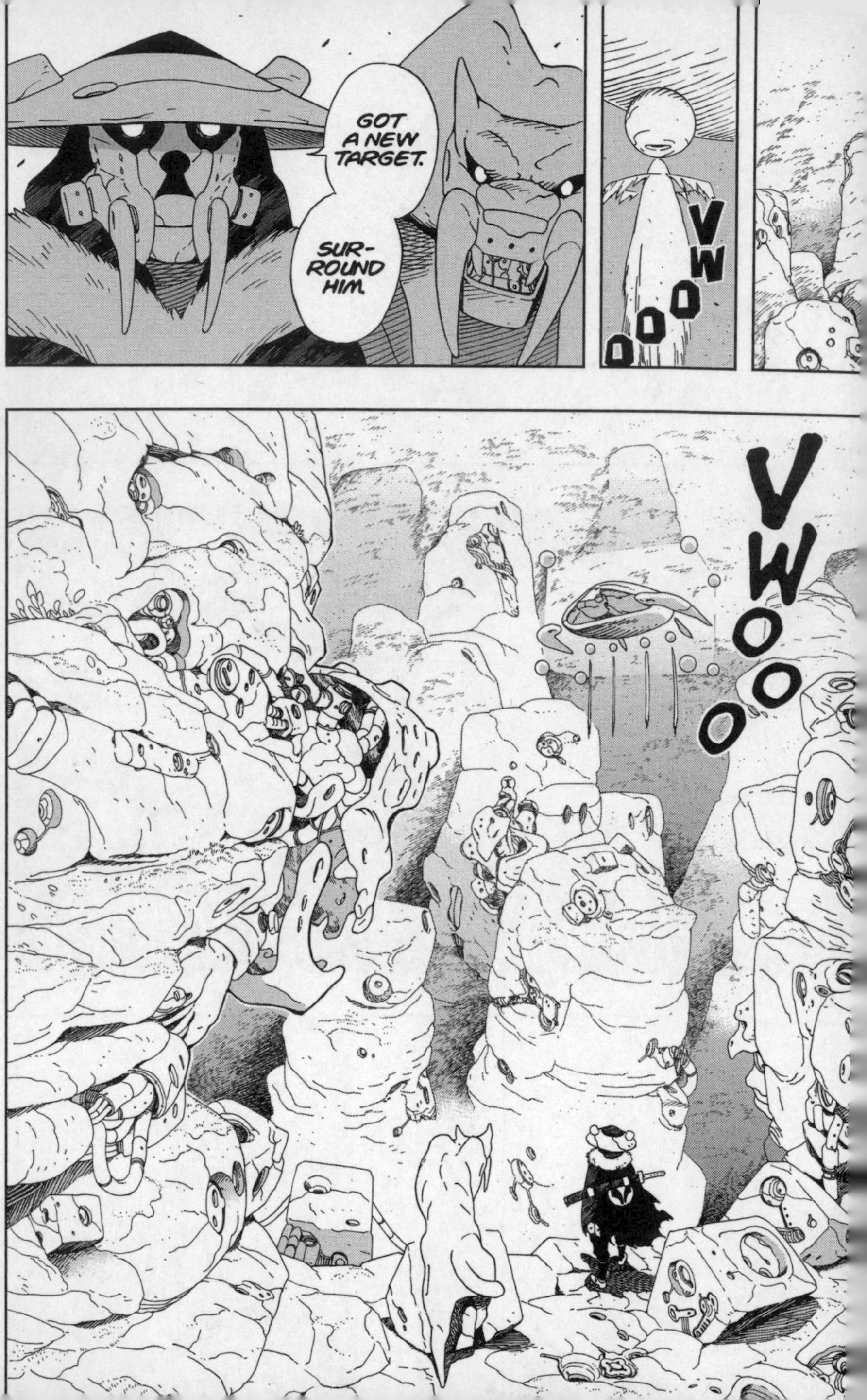
VWOOO
GOT A NEW TARGET.
SUR-ROUND HIM.
VWOOO

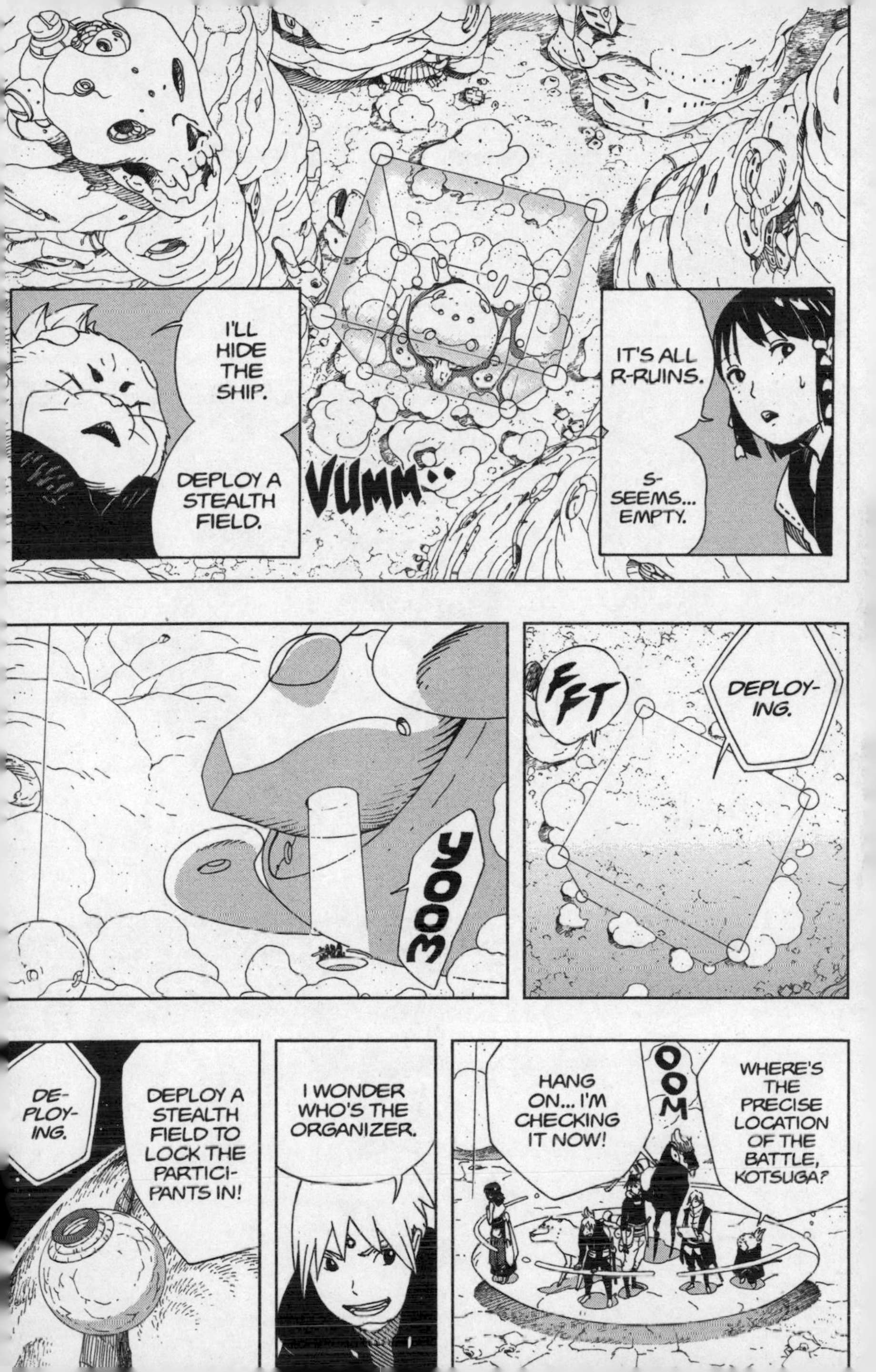
IT'S ALL R-RUINS.
S-SEEMS... EMPTY.
VUMM
I'LL HIDE THE SHIP.
DEPLOY A STEALTH FIELD.
FFT
DEPLOY-ING.
VOOM
WHERE'S THE PRECISE LOCATION OF THE BATTLE, KOTSUGA?
OOM
HANG ON... I'M CHECKING IT NOW!
I WONDER WHO'S THE ORGANIZER.
DEPLOY A STEALTH FIELD TO LOCK THE PARTICI-PANTS IN!
DE-PLOY-ING.

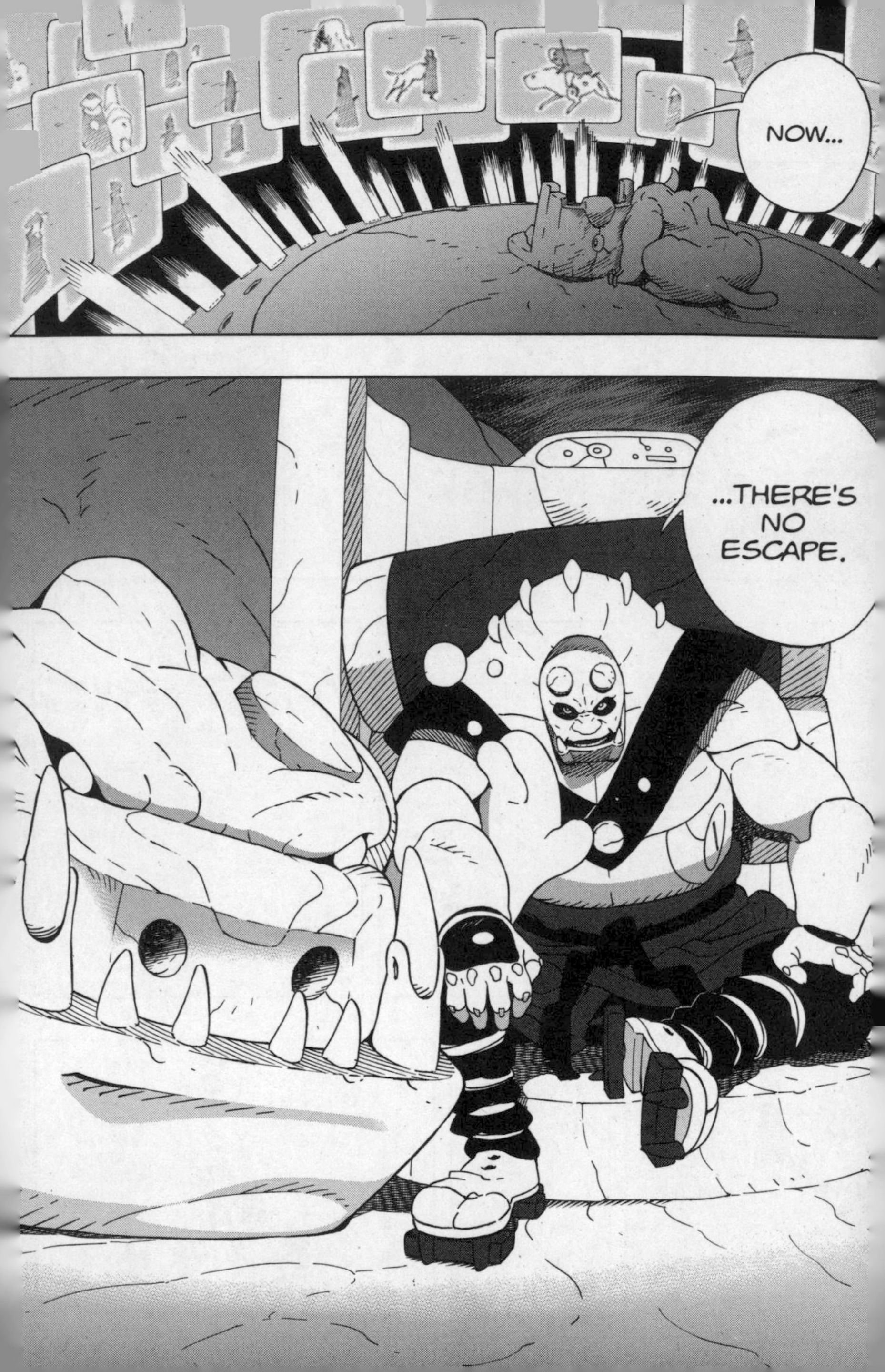
NOW...
...THERE'S NO ESCAPE.

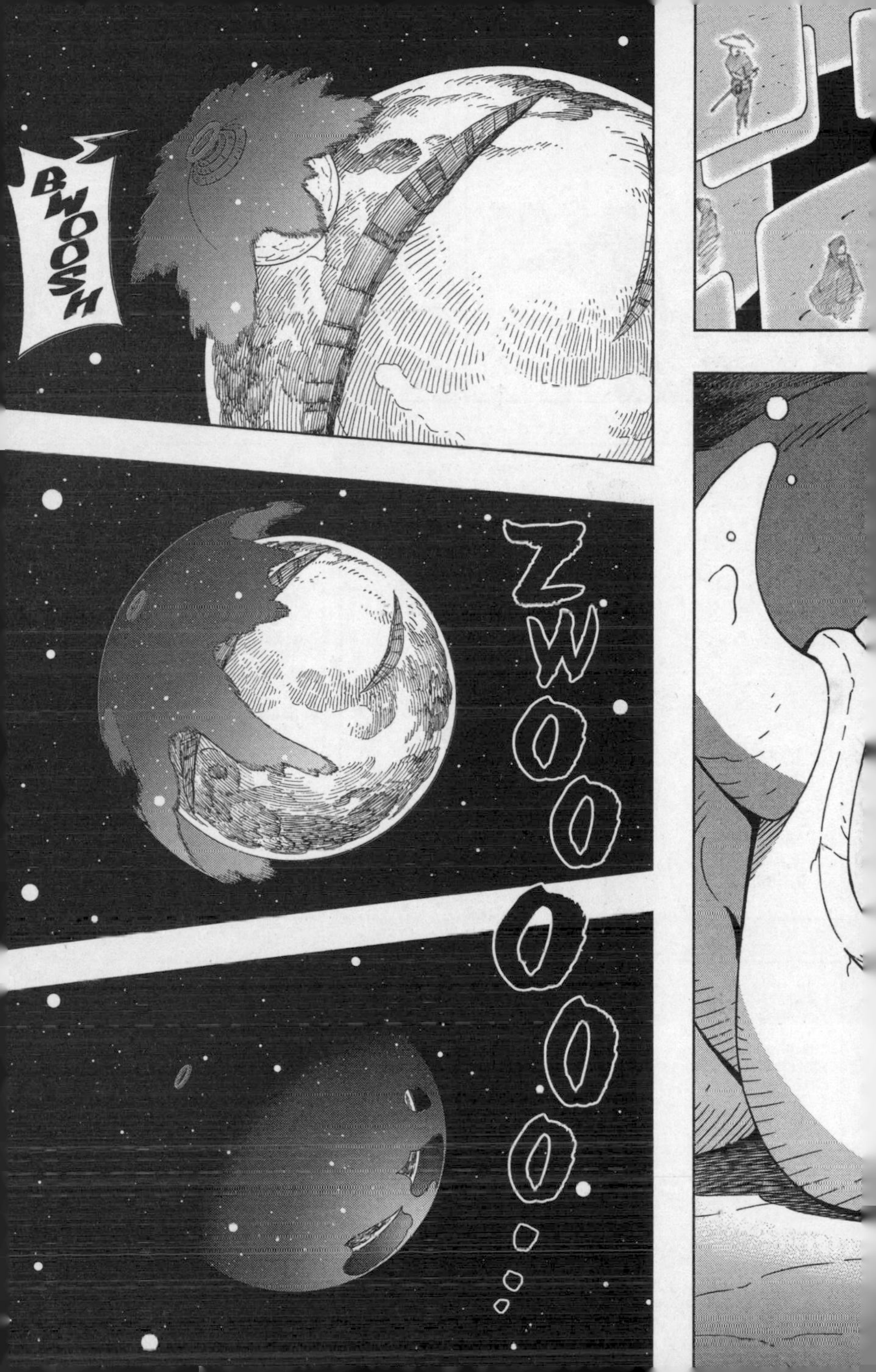
BWOOSH
ZWOOOOOO...

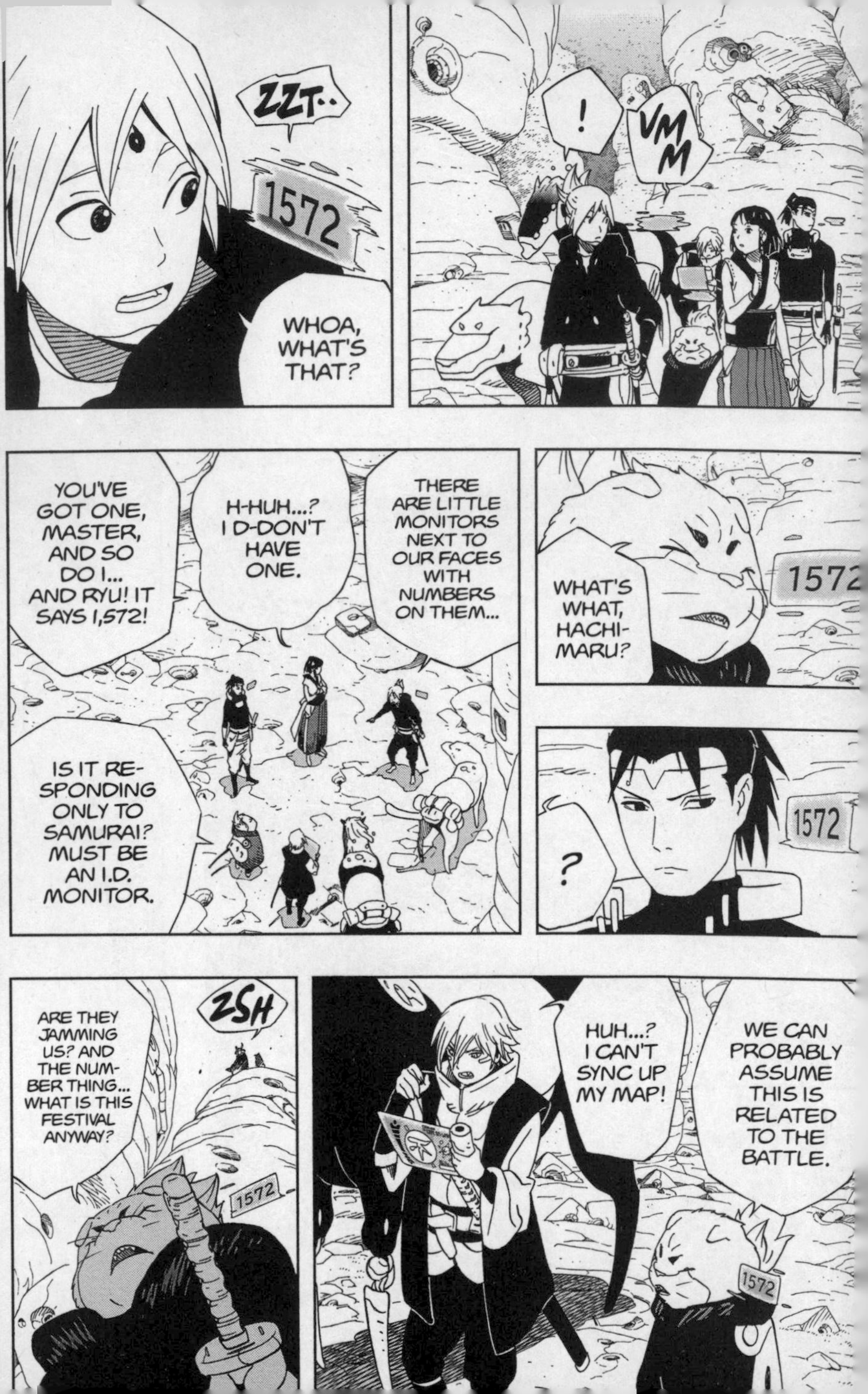
!
VMM
ZZT..
1572
WHOA, WHAT'S THAT?
1572
WHAT'S WHAT, HACHI-MARU?
1572
?
THERE ARE LITTLE MONITORS NEXT TO OUR FACES WITH NUMBERS ON THEM...
H-HUH...? I D-DON'T HAVE ONE.
YOU'VE GOT ONE, MASTER, AND SO DO I... AND RYU! IT SAYS 1,572!
IS IT RE-SPONDING ONLY TO SAMURAI? MUST BE AN I.D. MONITOR.
WE CAN PROBABLY ASSUME THIS IS RELATED TO THE BATTLE.
HUH...? I CAN'T SYNC UP MY MAP!
1572
ZSH
ARE THEY JAMMING US? AND THE NUM-BER THING... WHAT IS THIS FESTIVAL ANYWAY?
1572

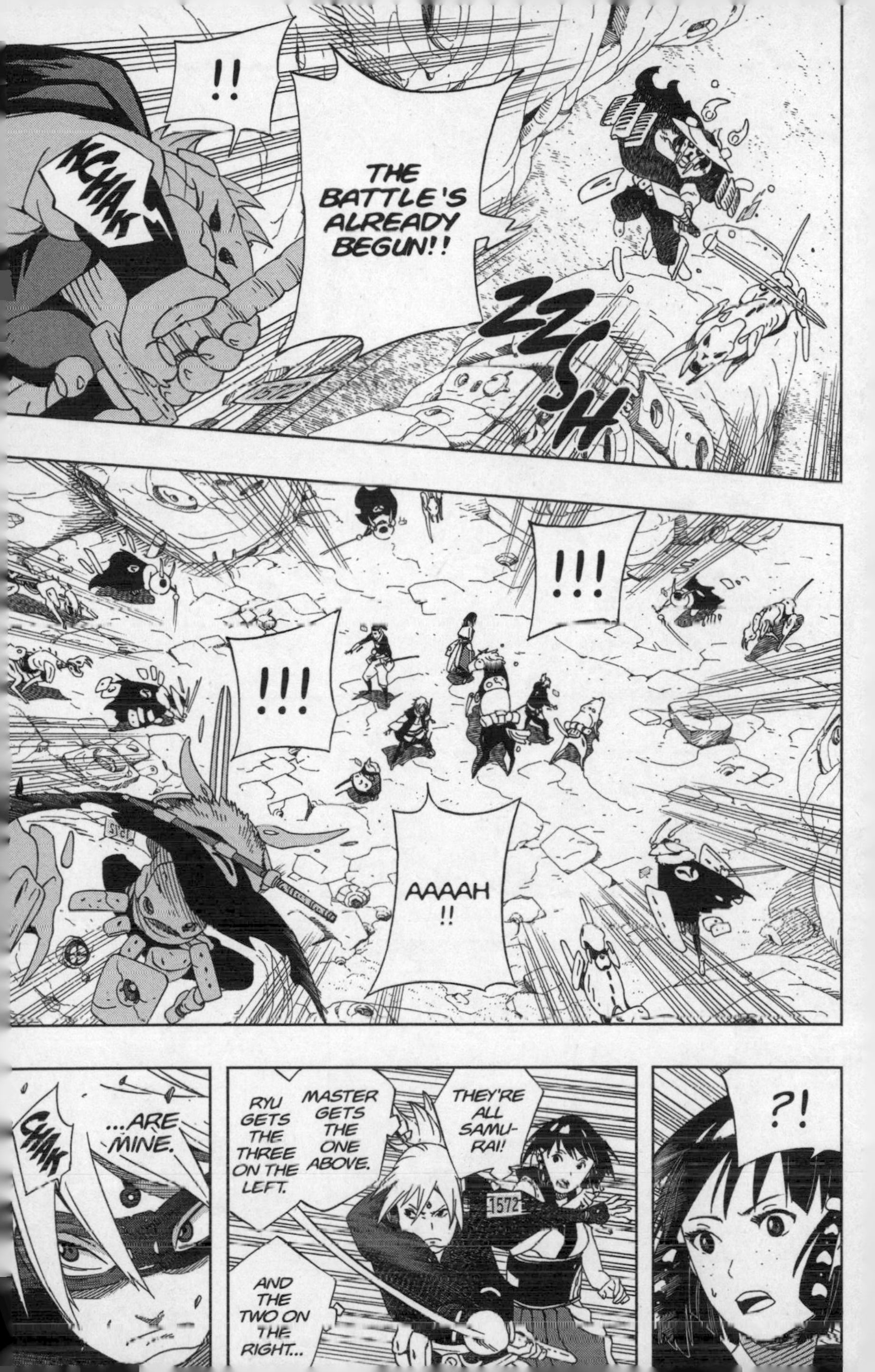
ZZSH
THE BATTLE'S ALREADY BEGUN!!
!!
KCHAK
!!!
!!!
AAAAH !!
?!
THEY'RE ALL SAMURAI!
MASTER GETS THE ONE ABOVE.
RYU GETS THE THREE ON THE LEFT.
1572
AND THE TWO ON THE RIGHT...
...ARE MINE.
CHAK

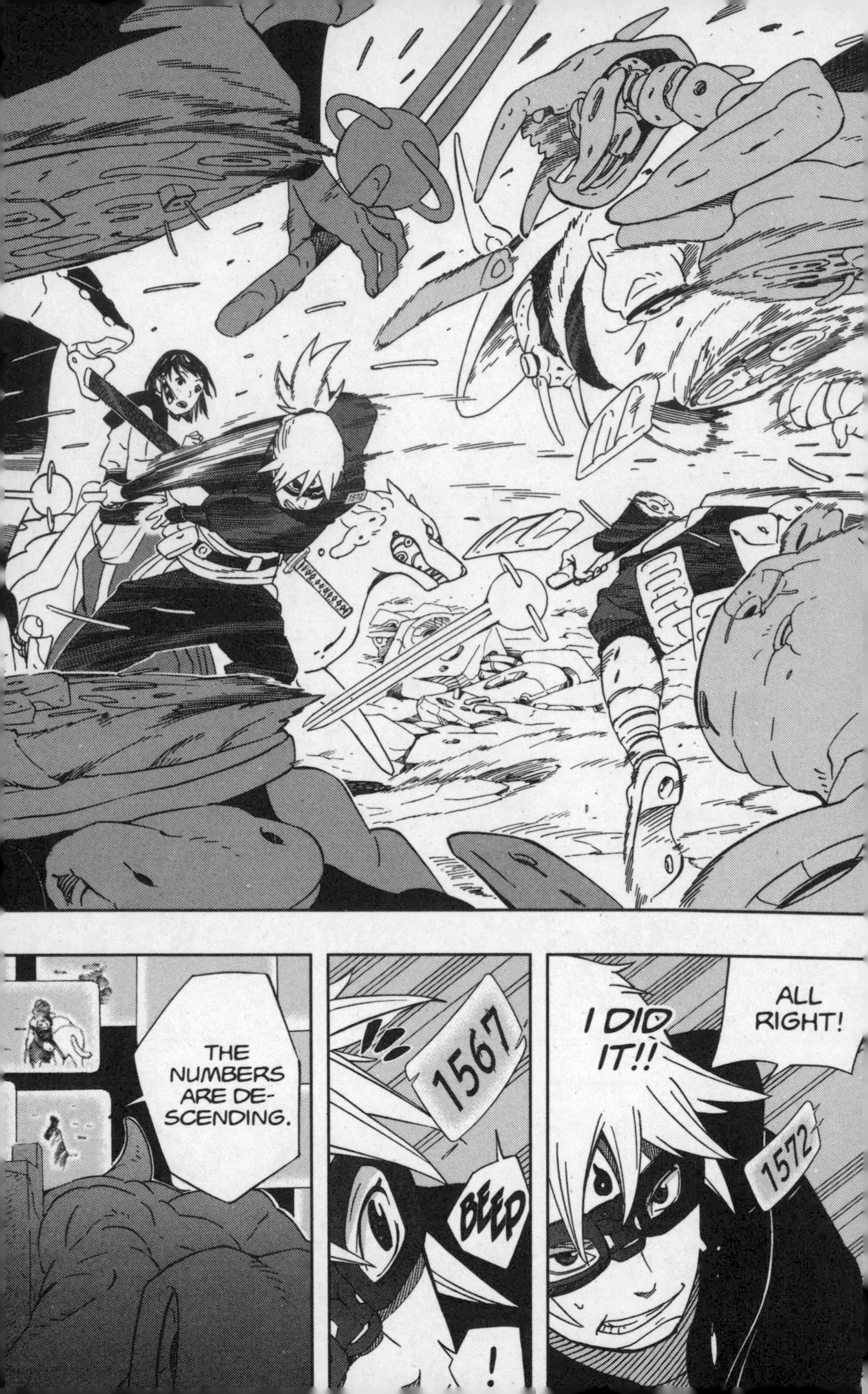
ALL RIGHT!
I DID IT!!
1572
1567
BEEP
!
THE NUMBERS ARE DE-SCENDING.

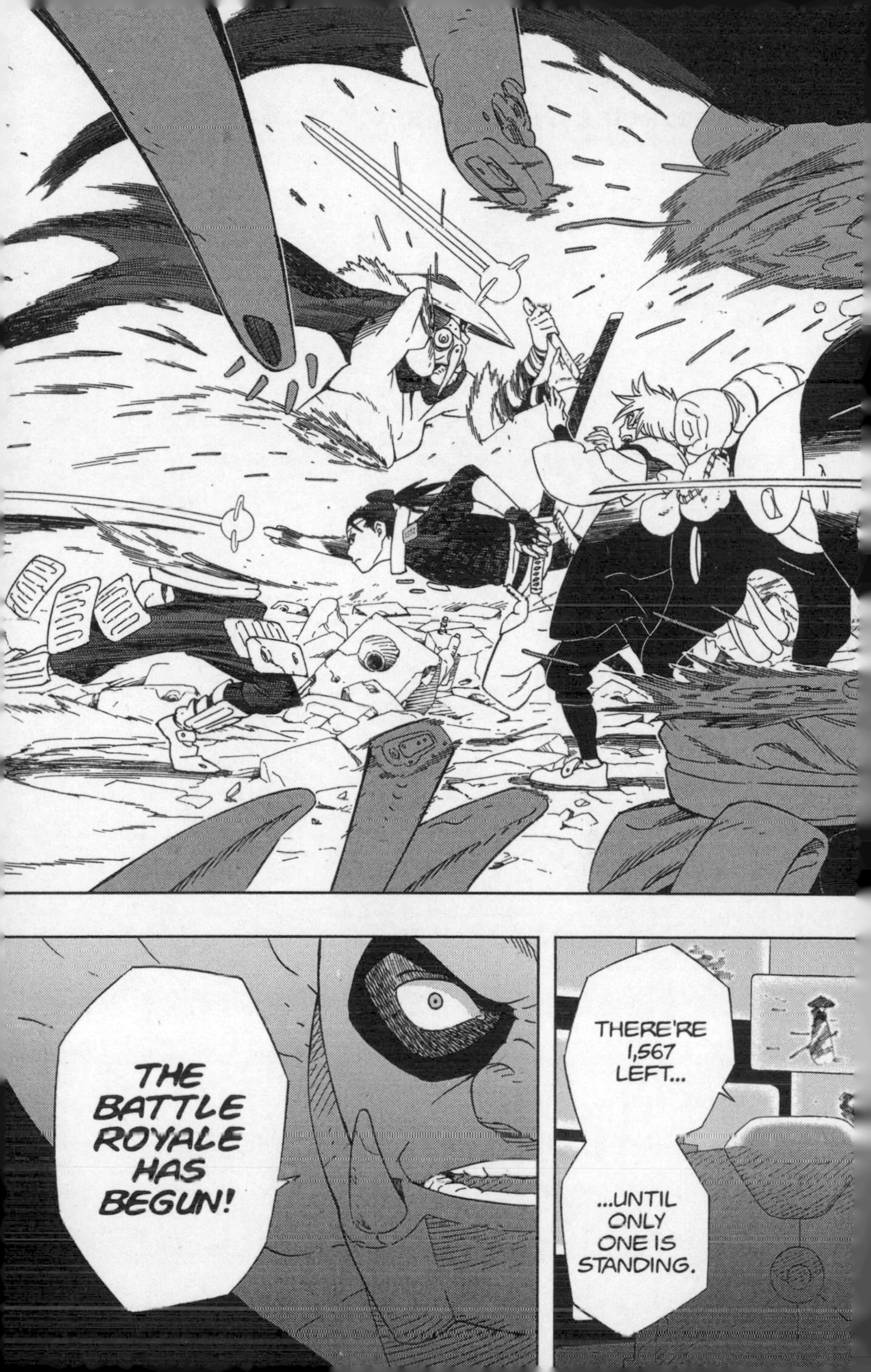
THERE'RE 1,567 LEFT...
...UNTIL ONLY ONE IS STANDING.
THE BATTLE ROYALE HAS BEGUN!

Character Design Sketches: Karura

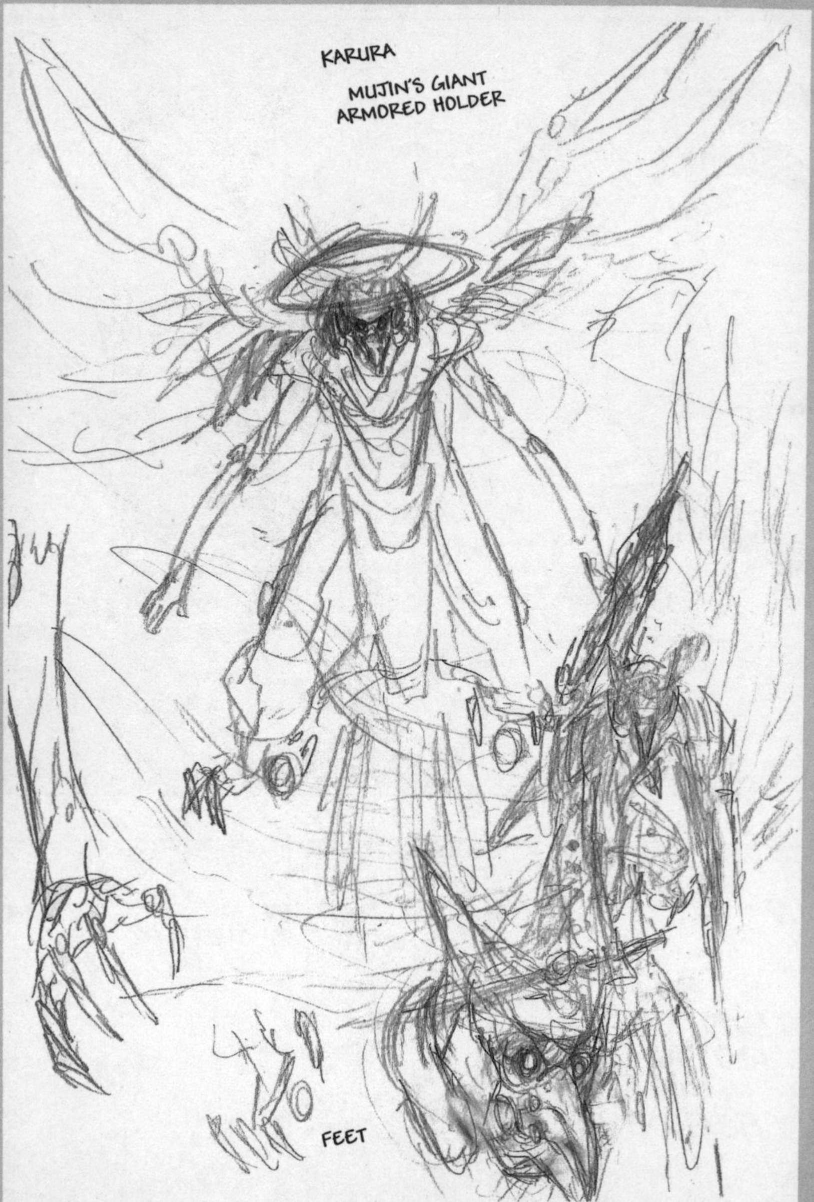
KARURA
MUJIN'S GIANT
ARMORED HOLDER
FEET

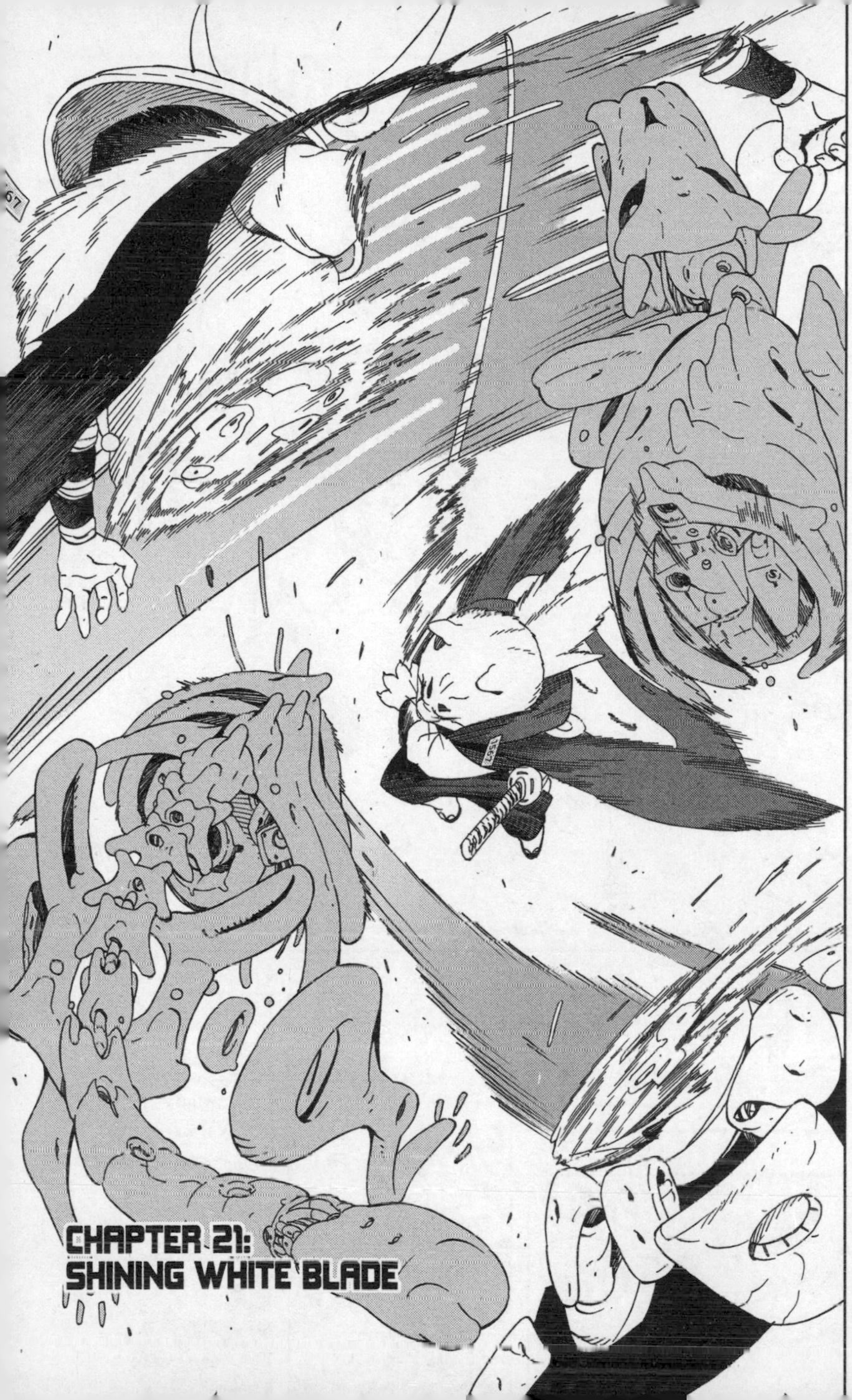
CHAPTER 21:
SHINING WHITE BLADE

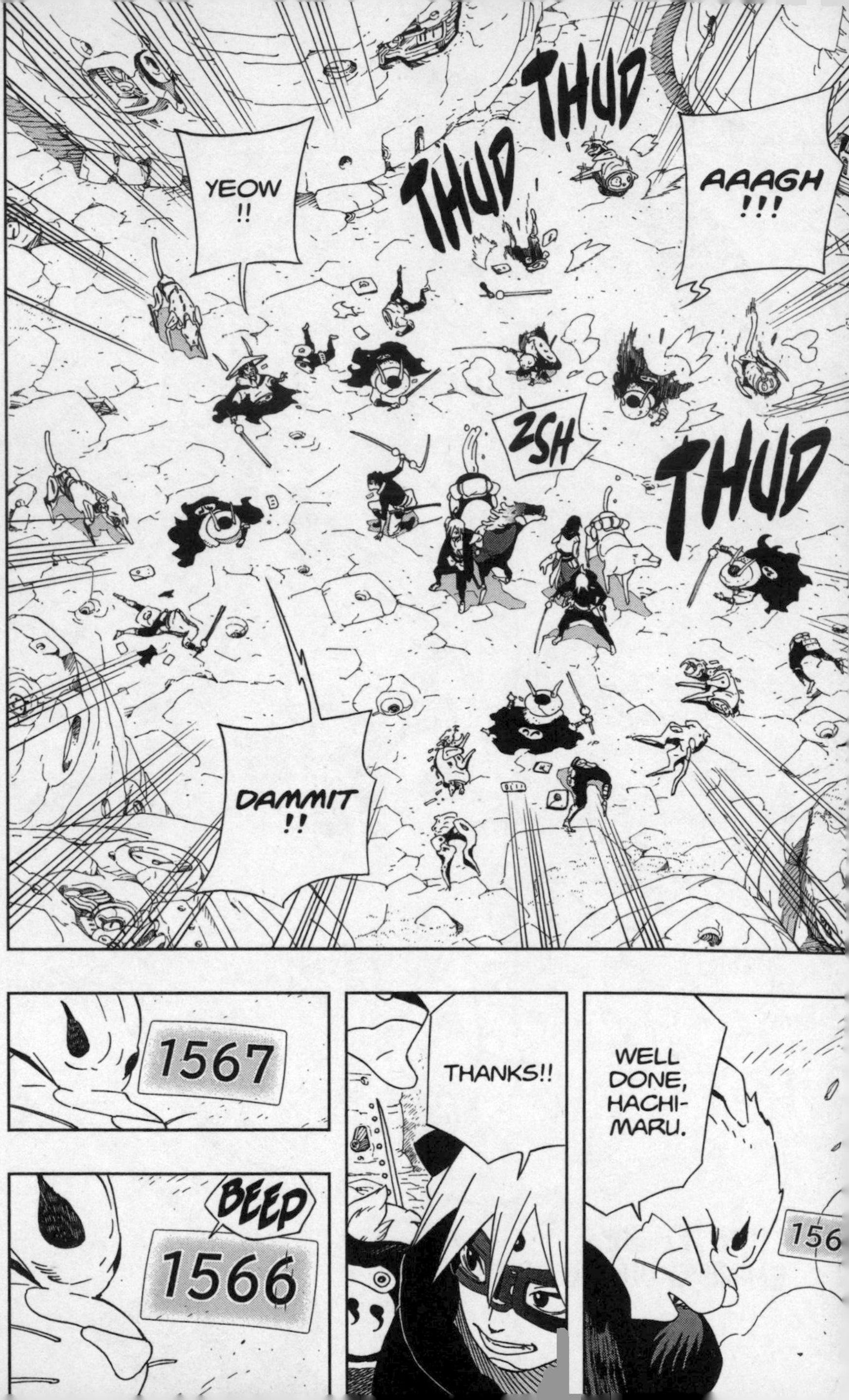
AAAGH !!!
THUD THUD
THUD
YEOW !!
THUD
ZSH
DAMMIT !!
WELL DONE, HACHI-MARU.
156
THANKS!!
1567
BEEP
1566

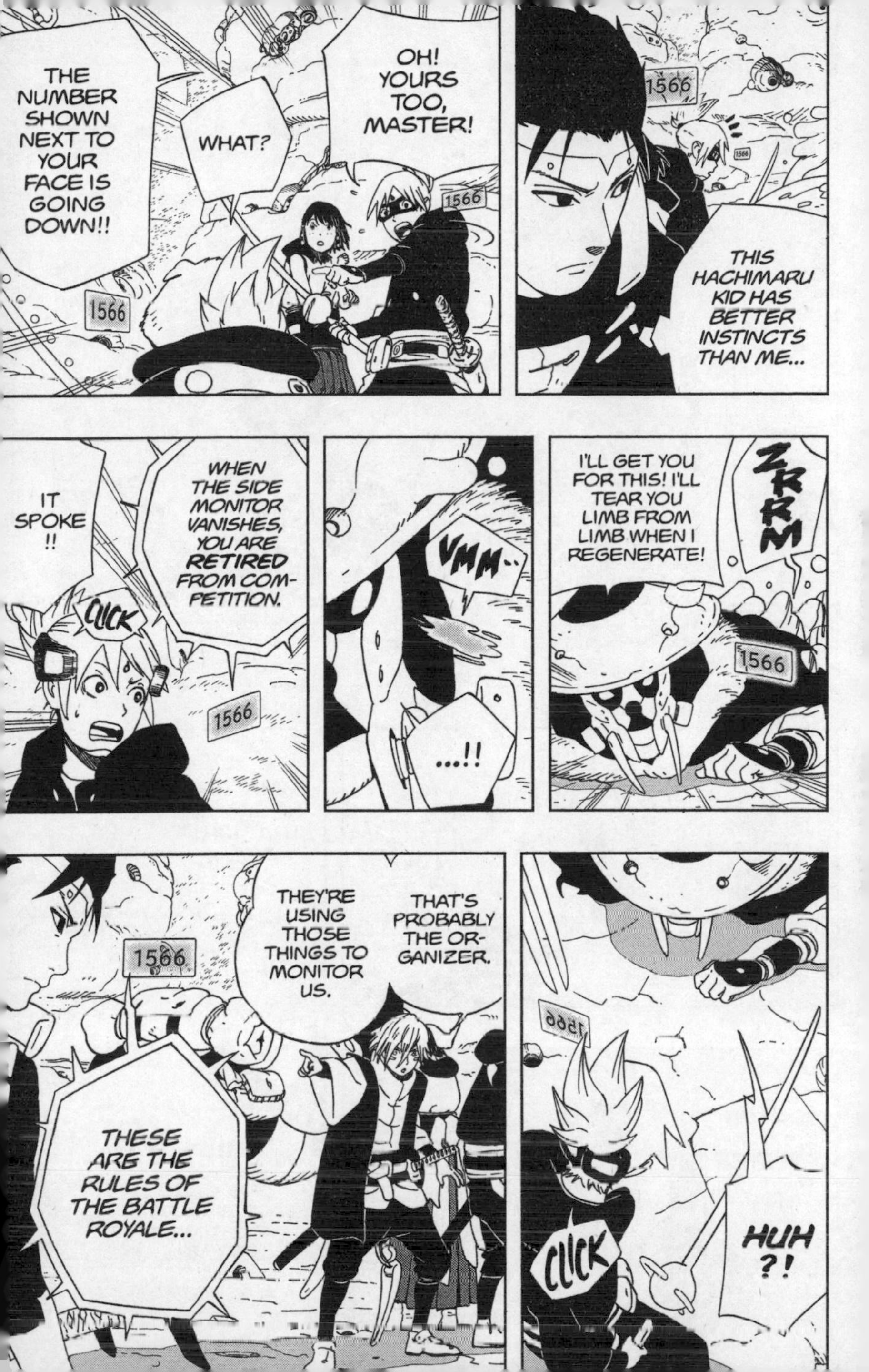
1566
1566
THIS HACHIMARU KID HAS BETTER INSTINCTS THAN ME...
OH! YOURS TOO, MASTER!
1566
WHAT?
THE NUMBER SHOWN NEXT TO YOUR FACE IS GOING DOWN!!
1566
ZRRM
I'LL GET YOU FOR THIS! I'LL TEAR YOU LIMB FROM LIMB WHEN I REGENERATE!
1566
VMM..
...!!
WHEN THE SIDE MONITOR VANISHES, YOU ARE RETIRED FROM COMPETITION.
IT SPOKE !!
CLICK
1566
1566
HUH ?!
CLICK
THAT'S PROBABLY THE ORGANIZER.
THEY'RE USING THOSE THINGS TO MONITOR US.
1566
THESE ARE THE RULES OF THE BATTLE ROYALE...

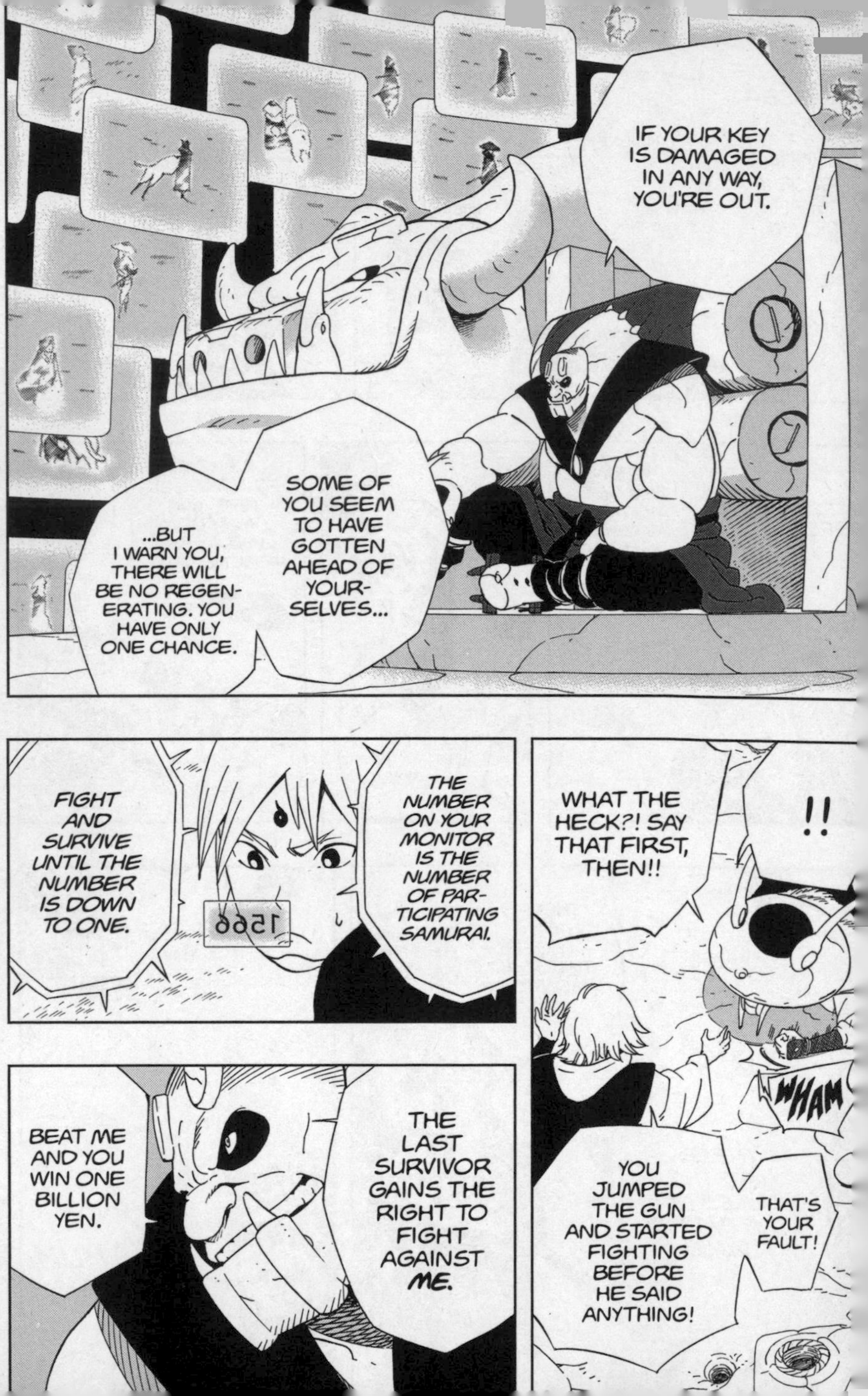
IF YOUR KEY IS DAMAGED IN ANY WAY, YOU'RE OUT.
SOME OF YOU SEEM TO HAVE GOTTEN AHEAD OF YOUR-SELVES...
...BUT I WARN YOU, THERE WILL BE NO REGEN-ERATING. YOU HAVE ONLY ONE CHANCE.
!!
WHAT THE HECK?! SAY THAT FIRST, THEN!!
WHAM
THAT'S YOUR FAULT!
YOU JUMPED THE GUN AND STARTED FIGHTING BEFORE HE SAID ANYTHING!
THE NUMBER ON YOUR MONITOR IS THE NUMBER OF PAR-TICIPATING SAMURAI.
1566
FIGHT AND SURVIVE UNTIL THE NUMBER IS DOWN TO ONE.
THE LAST SURVIVOR GAINS THE RIGHT TO FIGHT AGAINST *ME.*
BEAT ME AND YOU WIN ONE BILLION YEN.

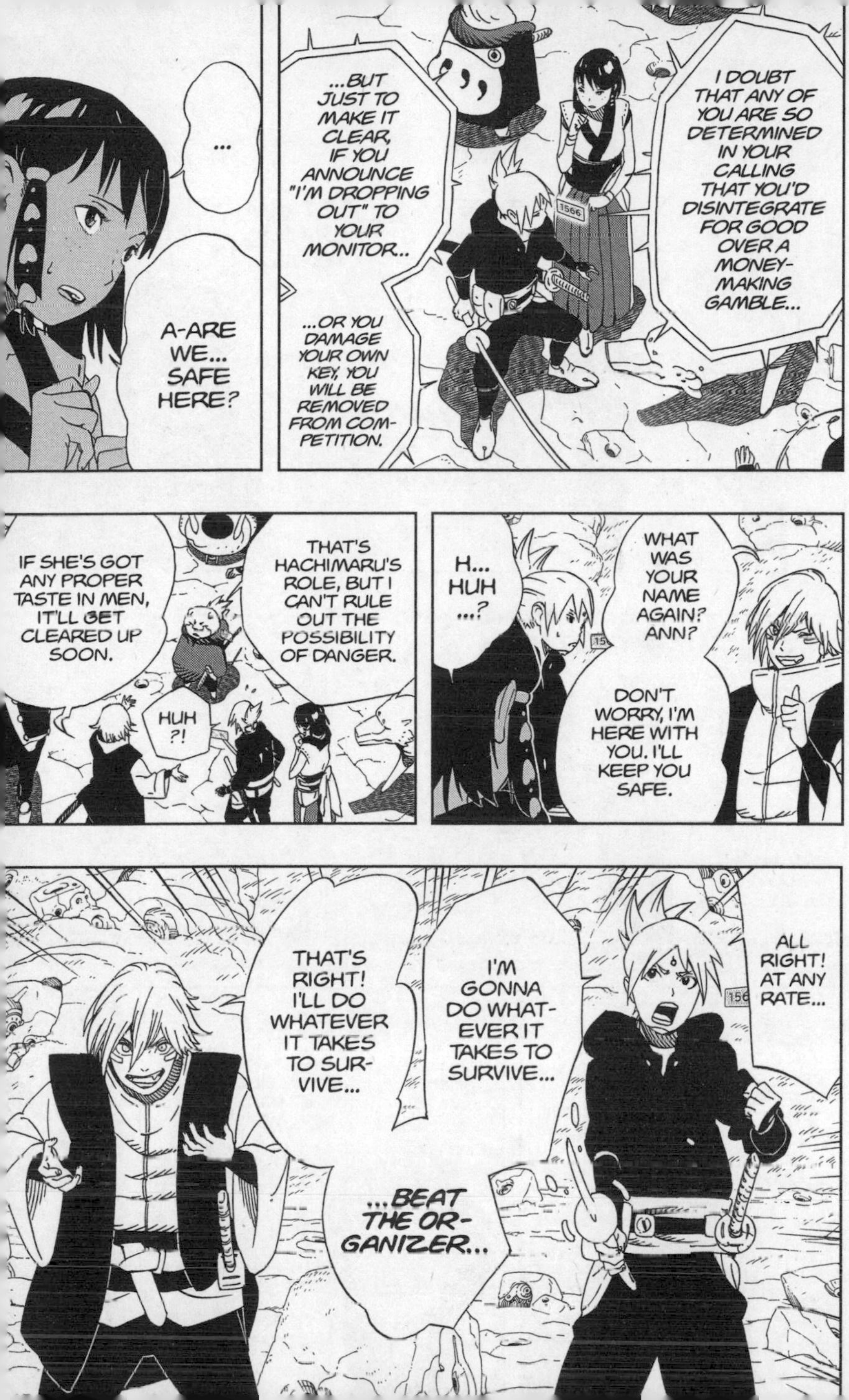
I DOUBT THAT ANY OF YOU ARE SO DETERMINED IN YOUR CALLING THAT YOU'D DISINTEGRATE FOR GOOD OVER A MONEY-MAKING GAMBLE...
...BUT JUST TO MAKE IT CLEAR, IF YOU ANNOUNCE "I'M DROPPING OUT" TO YOUR MONITOR...
...OR YOU DAMAGE YOUR OWN KEY, YOU WILL BE REMOVED FROM COM-PETITION.
1566
...
A-ARE WE... SAFE HERE?
WHAT WAS YOUR NAME AGAIN? ANN?
DON'T WORRY, I'M HERE WITH YOU. I'LL KEEP YOU SAFE.
H... HUH ...?
THAT'S HACHIMARU'S ROLE, BUT I CAN'T RULE OUT THE POSSIBILITY OF DANGER.
IF SHE'S GOT ANY PROPER TASTE IN MEN, IT'LL GET CLEARED UP SOON.
HUH ?!
ALL RIGHT! AT ANY RATE...
I'M GONNA DO WHAT-EVER IT TAKES TO SURVIVE...
THAT'S RIGHT! I'LL DO WHATEVER IT TAKES TO SUR-VIVE...
...BEAT THE OR-GANIZER...

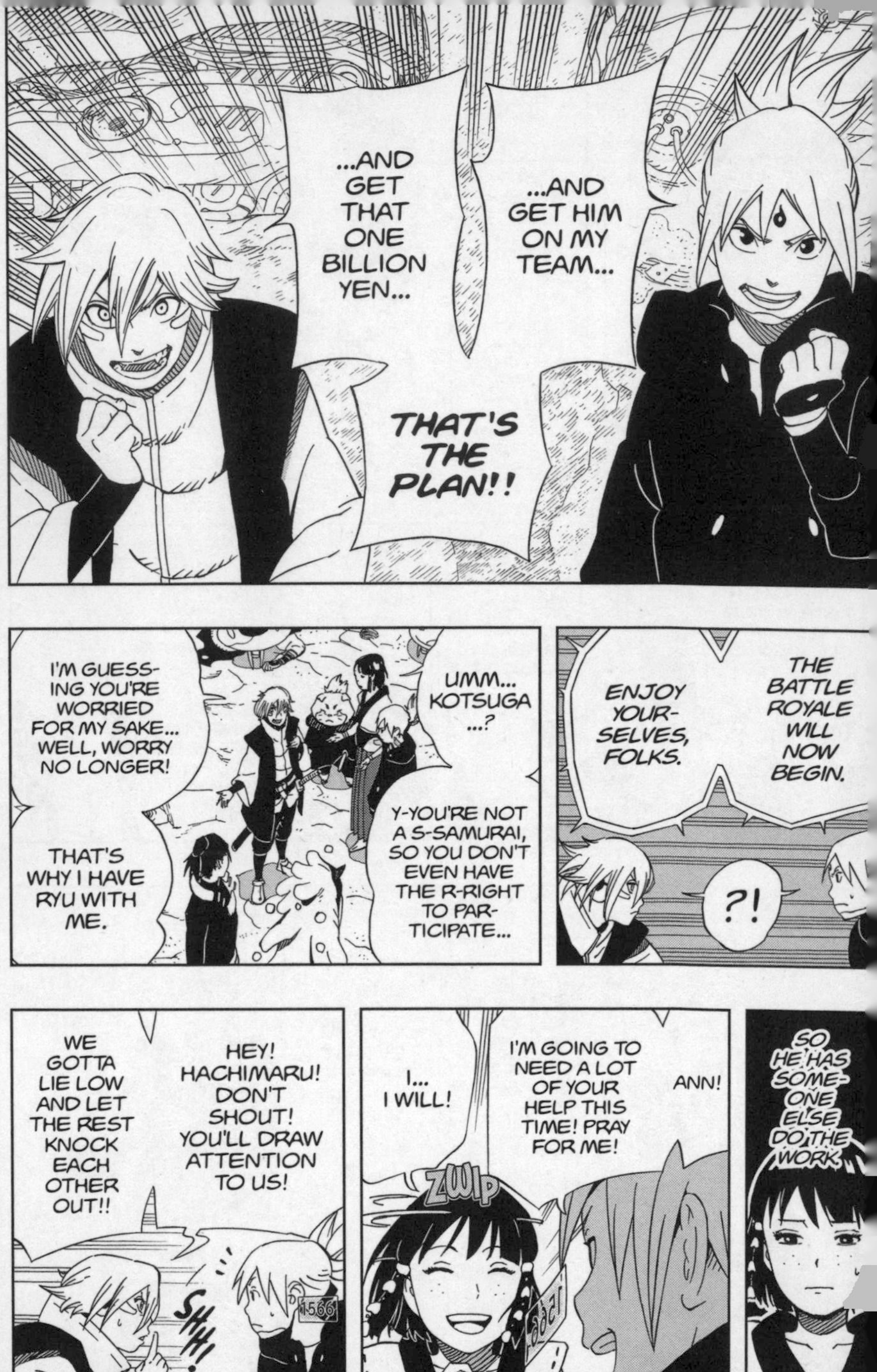
...AND GET HIM ON MY TEAM...
...AND GET THAT ONE BILLION YEN...
THAT'S THE PLAN!!
THE BATTLE ROYALE WILL NOW BEGIN.
ENJOY YOURSELVES, FOLKS.
?!
UMM... KOTSUGA ...?
Y-YOU'RE NOT A S-SAMURAI, SO YOU DON'T EVEN HAVE THE R-RIGHT TO PARTICIPATE...
I'M GUESSING YOU'RE WORRIED FOR MY SAKE... WELL, WORRY NO LONGER!
THAT'S WHY I HAVE RYU WITH ME.
SO HE HAS SOMEONE ELSE DO THE WORK.
ANN!
I'M GOING TO NEED A LOT OF YOUR HELP THIS TIME! PRAY FOR ME!
I... I WILL!
ZWIP
HEY! HACHIMARU! DON'T SHOUT! YOU'LL DRAW ATTENTION TO US!
WE GOTTA LIE LOW AND LET THE REST KNOCK EACH OTHER OUT!!
SHH!!
1566

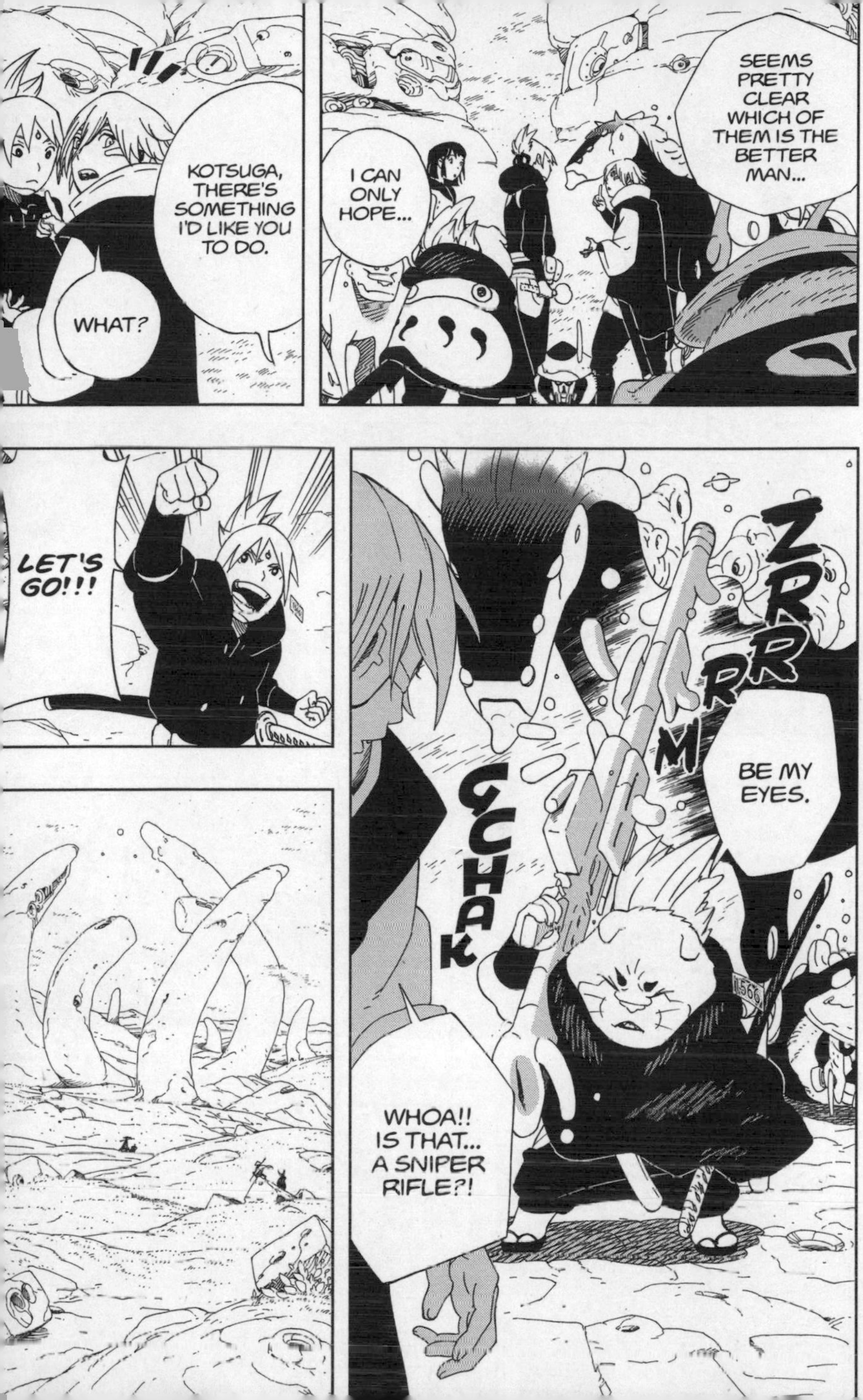
SEEMS PRETTY CLEAR WHICH OF THEM IS THE BETTER MAN...
I CAN ONLY HOPE...
KOTSUGA, THERE'S SOMETHING I'D LIKE YOU TO DO.
WHAT?
ZRRRM
GCHAK
BE MY EYES.
WHOA!! IS THAT... A SNIPER RIFLE?!
LET'S GO!!!

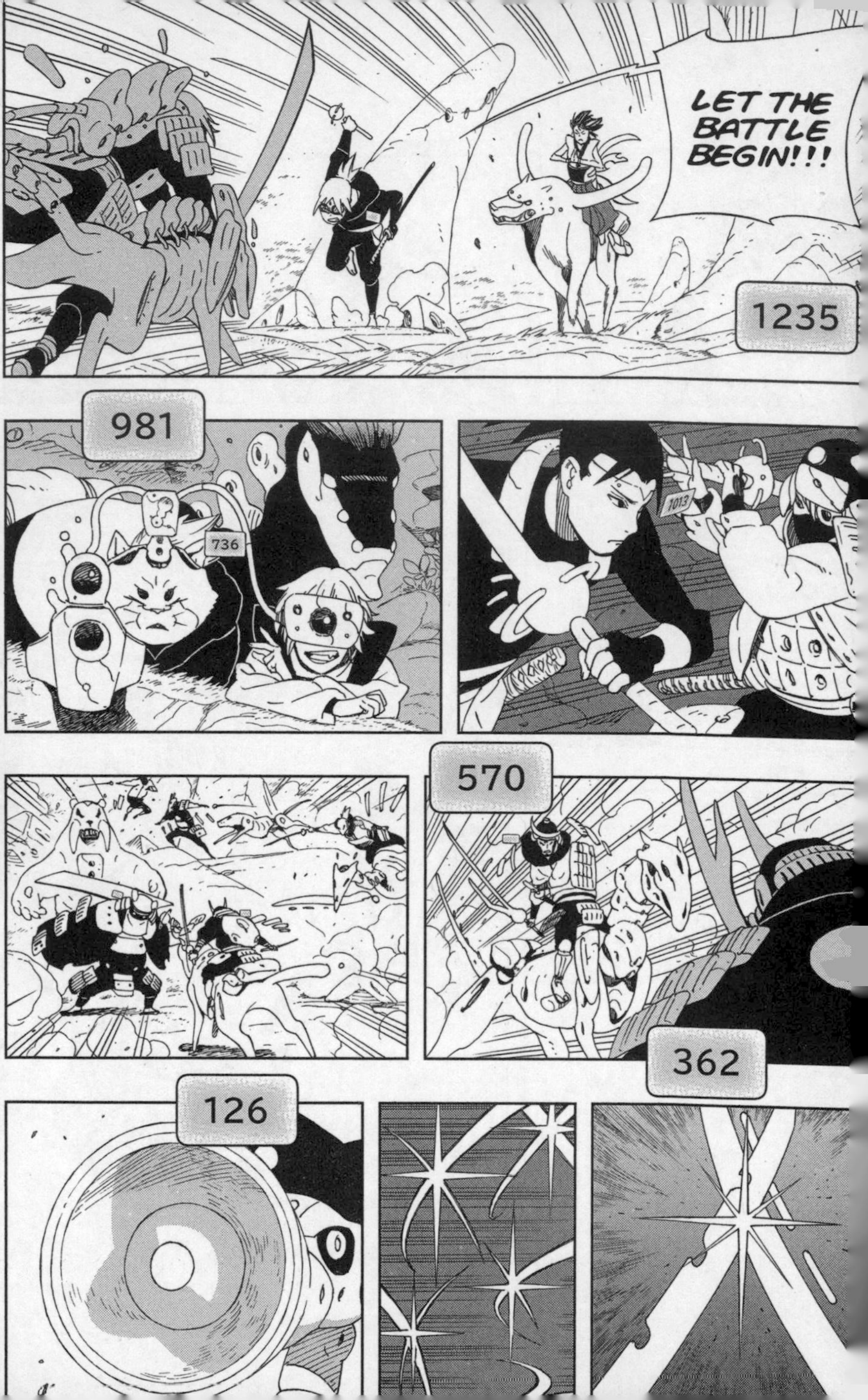
LET THE BATTLE BEGIN!!!
1235
1013
981
736
570
362
126

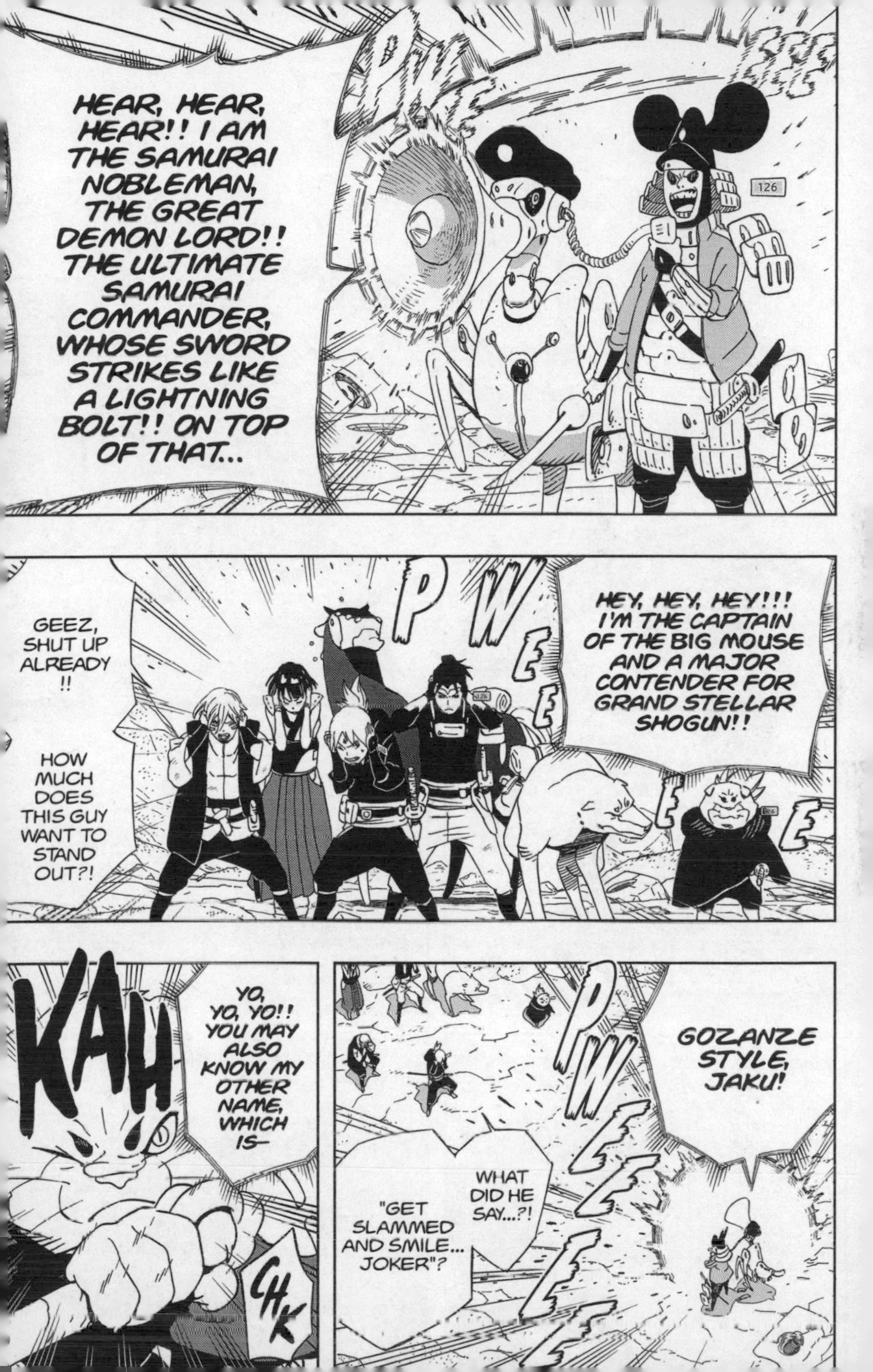

HEAR, HEAR, HEAR!! I AM THE SAMURAI NOBLEMAN, THE GREAT DEMON LORD!! THE ULTIMATE SAMURAI COMMANDER, WHOSE SWORD STRIKES LIKE A LIGHTNING BOLT!! ON TOP OF THAT...
HEY, HEY, HEY!!! I'M THE CAPTAIN OF THE BIG MOUSE AND A MAJOR CONTENDER FOR GRAND STELLAR SHOGUN!!
PWEEEEE
GEEZ, SHUT UP ALREADY!!
HOW MUCH DOES THIS GUY WANT TO STAND OUT?!
GOZANZE STYLE, JAKU!
PWEEEE
WHAT DID HE SAY...?!
"GET SLAMMED AND SMILE... JOKER"?
KAH
YO, YO, YO!! YOU MAY ALSO KNOW MY OTHER NAME, WHICH IS—
CHK

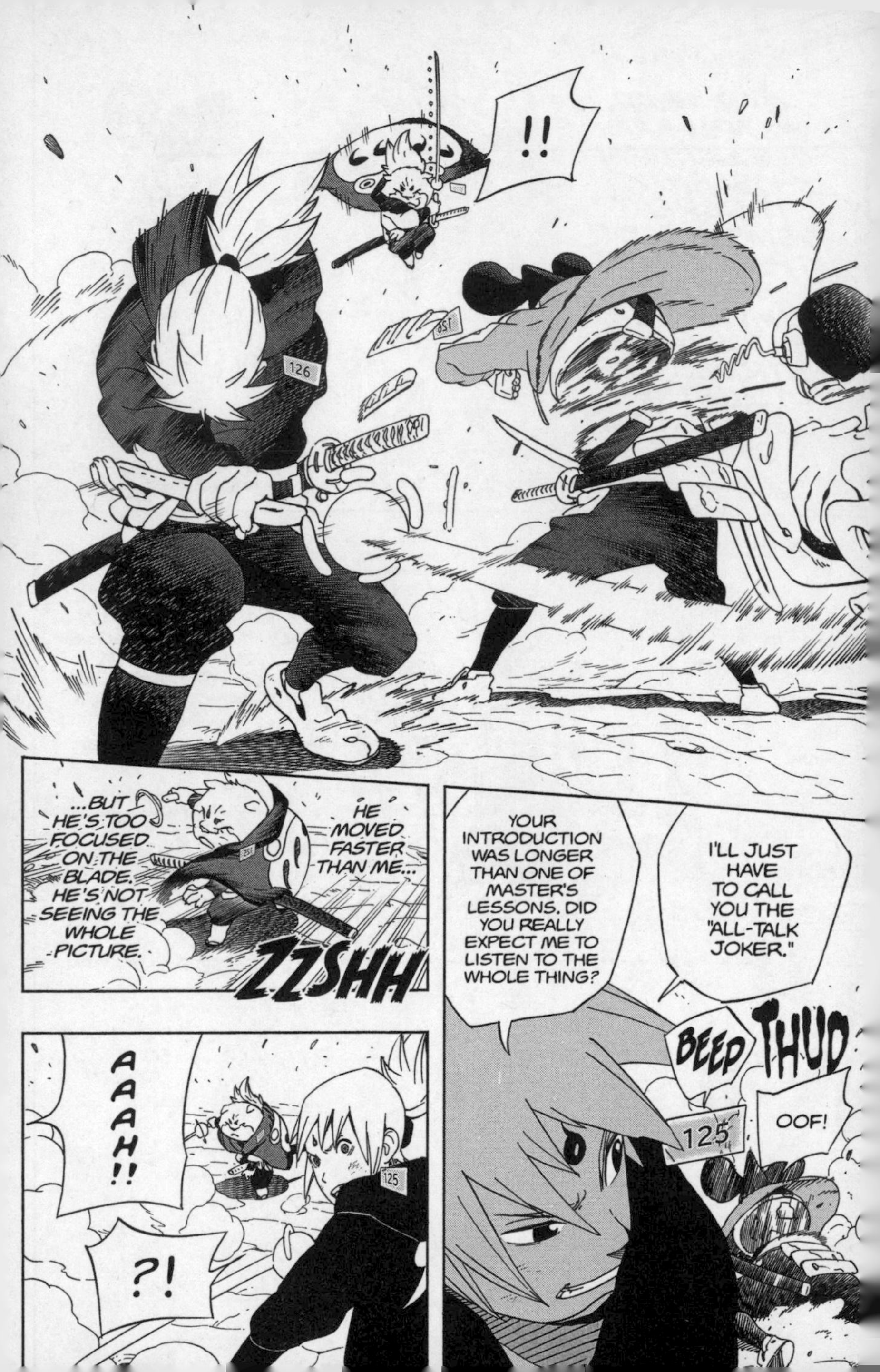
!!
I'LL JUST HAVE TO CALL YOU THE "ALL-TALK JOKER."
YOUR INTRODUCTION WAS LONGER THAN ONE OF MASTER'S LESSONS. DID YOU REALLY EXPECT ME TO LISTEN TO THE WHOLE THING?
THUD
BEEP
OOF!
HE MOVED FASTER THAN ME...
...BUT HE'S TOO FOCUSED ON THE BLADE. HE'S NOT SEEING THE WHOLE PICTURE.
ZZSHH
AAAAH!!
?!

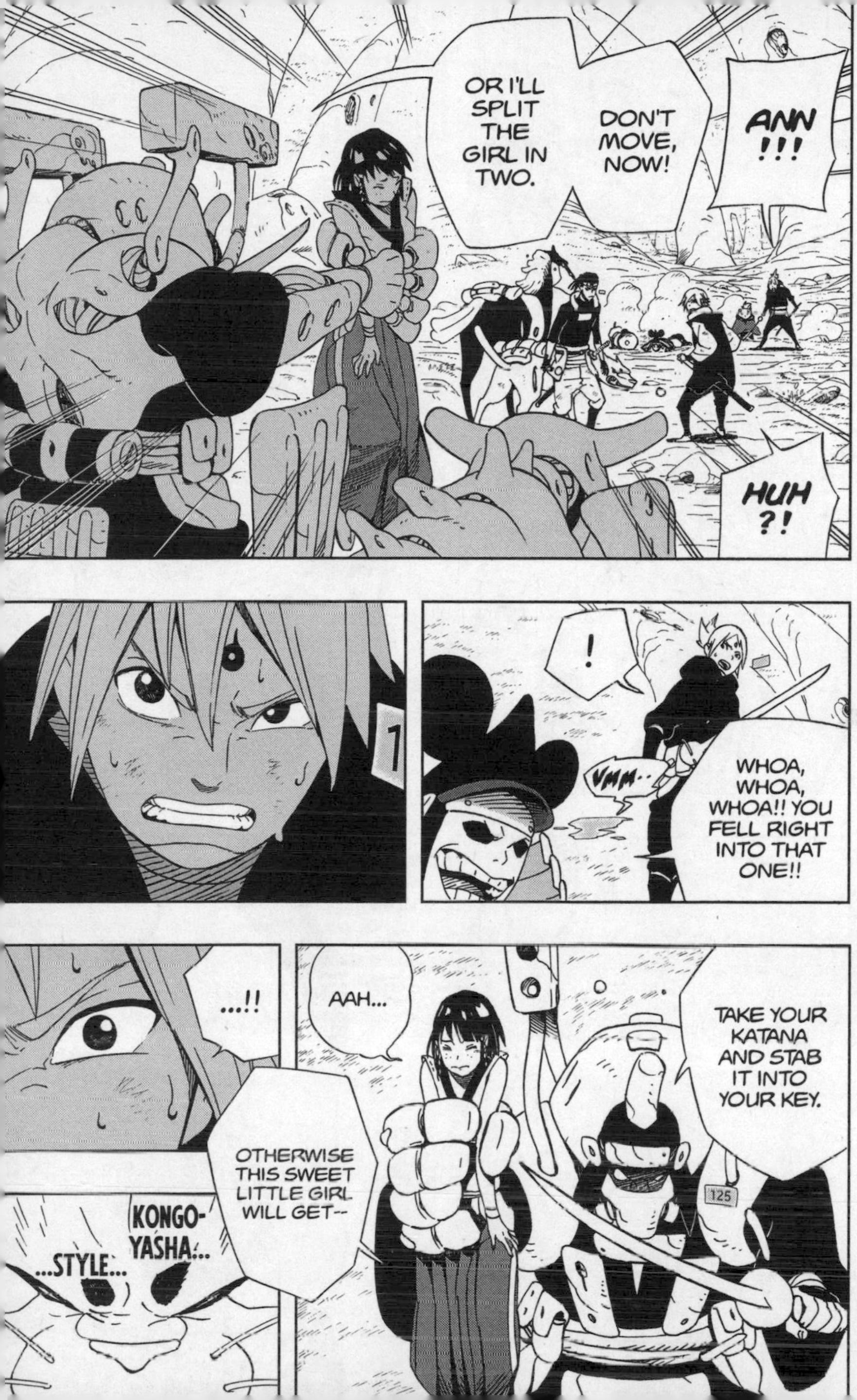
ANN!!!
DON'T MOVE, NOW!
OR I'LL SPLIT THE GIRL IN TWO.
HUH?!
!
WHOA, WHOA, WHOA!! YOU FELL RIGHT INTO THAT ONE!!
UMM..
7
TAKE YOUR KATANA AND STAB IT INTO YOUR KEY.
AAH...
OTHERWISE THIS SWEET LITTLE GIRL WILL GET--
125
...!!
KONGO-YASHA...
...STYLE...

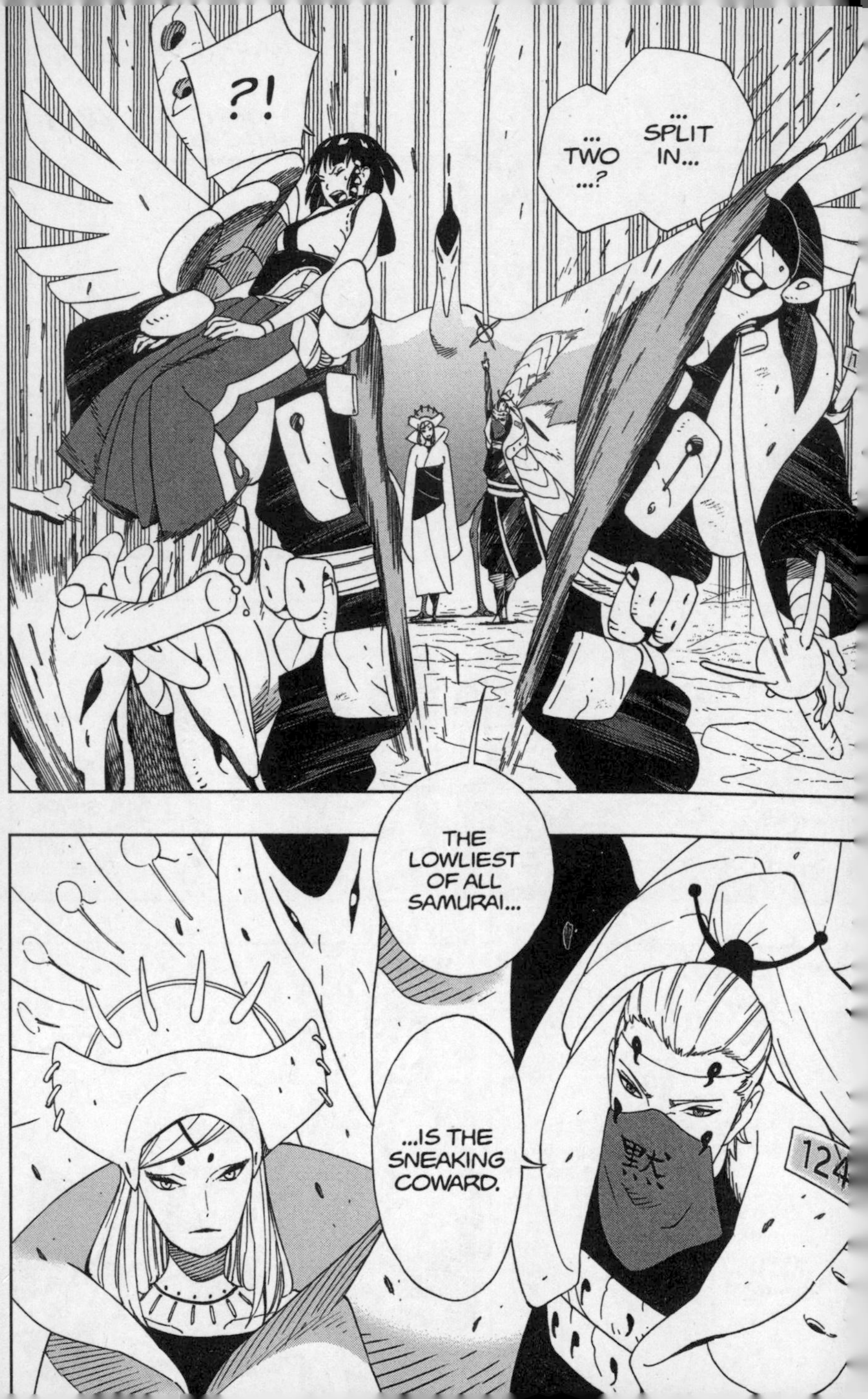
... SPLIT IN... ... TWO ...?
?!
THE LOWLIEST OF ALL SAMURAI...
...IS THE SNEAKING COWARD.
124

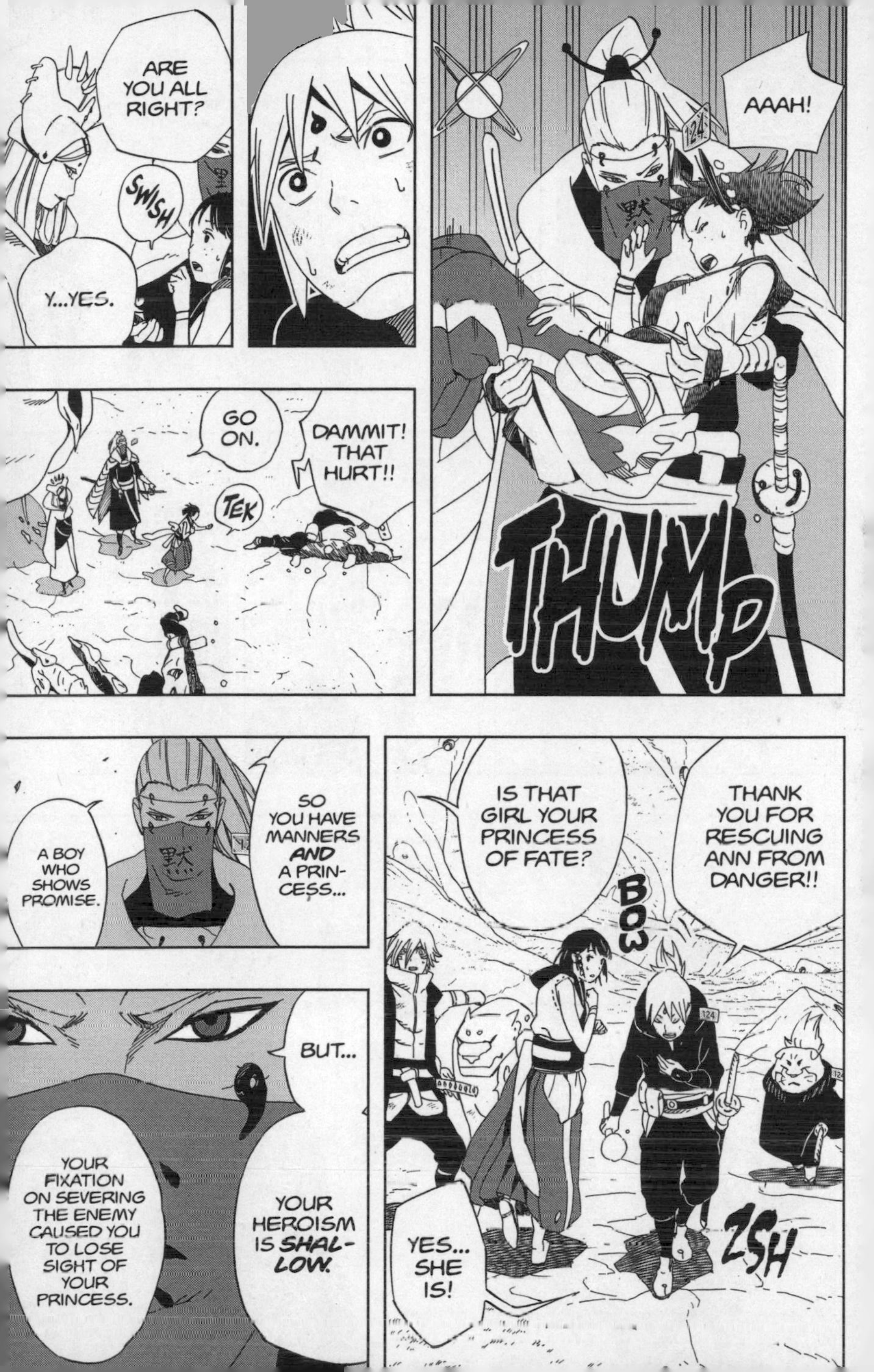
AAAH!
THUMP
ARE YOU ALL RIGHT?
SWISH
Y...YES.
DAMMIT! THAT HURT!!
GO ON.
TEK
THANK YOU FOR RESCUING ANN FROM DANGER!!
IS THAT GIRL YOUR PRINCESS OF FATE?
BOW
ZSH
YES... SHE IS!
SO YOU HAVE MANNERS *AND* A PRINCESS...
A BOY WHO SHOWS PROMISE.
BUT...
YOUR HEROISM IS *SHALLOW.*
YOUR FIXATION ON SEVERING THE ENEMY CAUSED YOU TO LOSE SIGHT OF YOUR PRINCESS.

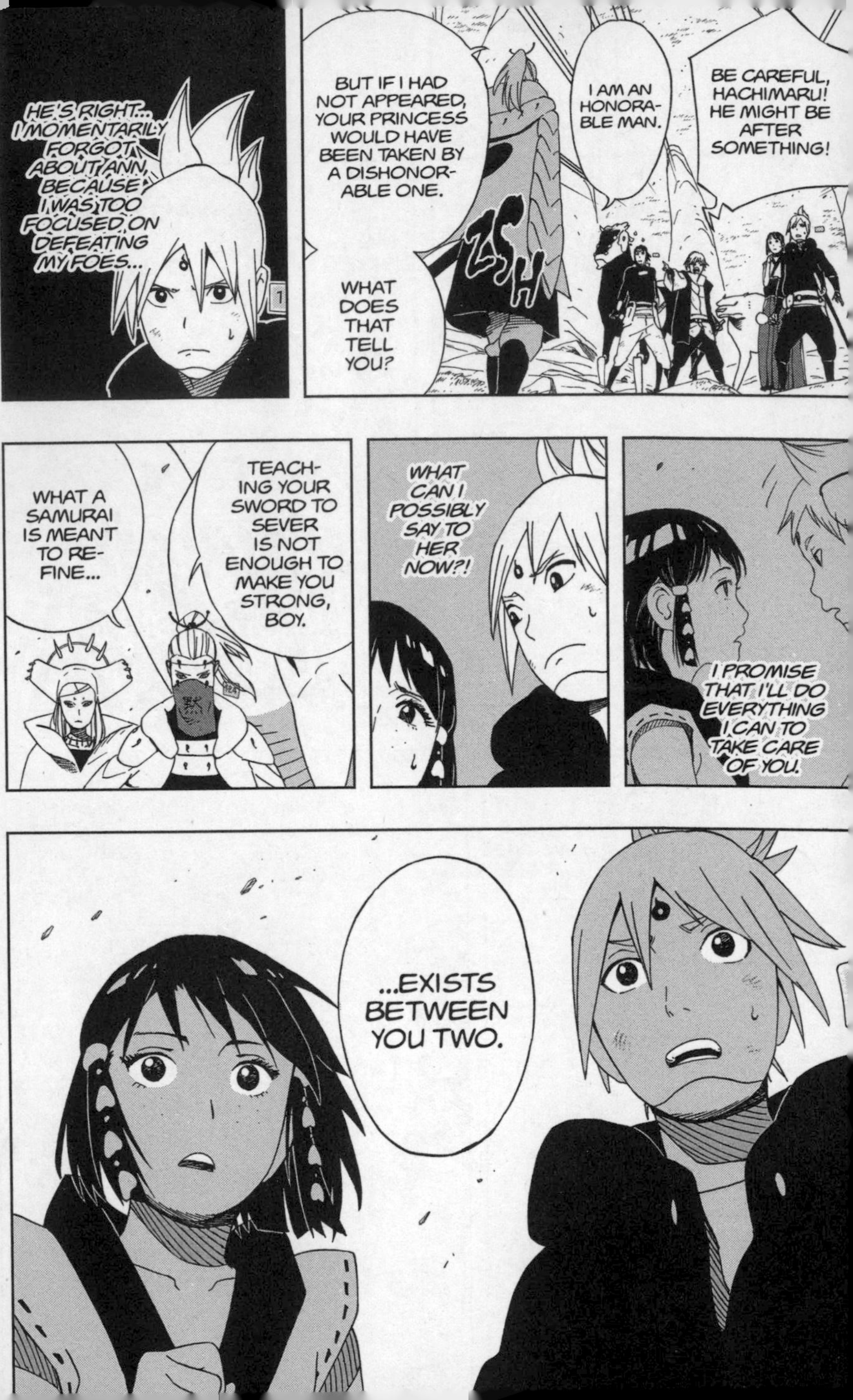
BE CAREFUL, HACHIMARU! HE MIGHT BE AFTER SOMETHING!
I AM AN HONORABLE MAN.
BUT IF I HAD NOT APPEARED, YOUR PRINCESS WOULD HAVE BEEN TAKEN BY A DISHONORABLE ONE.
ZSH
WHAT DOES THAT TELL YOU?
HE'S RIGHT... I MOMENTARILY FORGOT ABOUT ANN, BECAUSE I WAS TOO FOCUSED ON DEFEATING MY FOES...
I PROMISE THAT I'LL DO EVERYTHING I CAN TO TAKE CARE OF YOU.
WHAT CAN I POSSIBLY SAY TO HER NOW?!
TEACHING YOUR SWORD TO SEVER IS NOT ENOUGH TO MAKE YOU STRONG, BOY.
WHAT A SAMURAI IS MEANT TO REFINE...
...EXISTS BETWEEN YOU TWO.

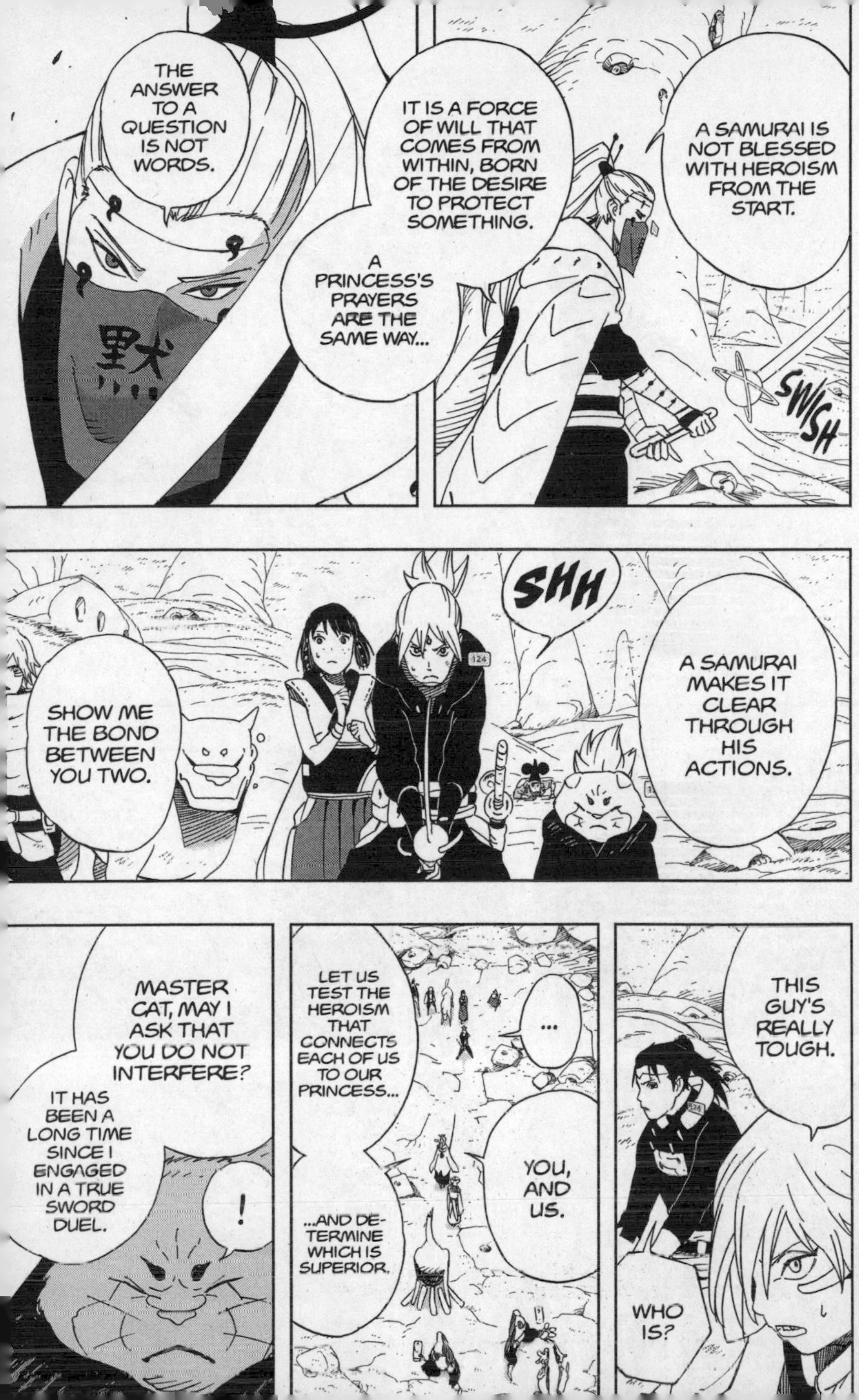
A SAMURAI IS NOT BLESSED WITH HEROISM FROM THE START.
SWISH
IT IS A FORCE OF WILL THAT COMES FROM WITHIN, BORN OF THE DESIRE TO PROTECT SOMETHING.
A PRINCESS'S PRAYERS ARE THE SAME WAY...
THE ANSWER TO A QUESTION IS NOT WORDS.
SHH
A SAMURAI MAKES IT CLEAR THROUGH HIS ACTIONS.
SHOW ME THE BOND BETWEEN YOU TWO.
THIS GUY'S REALLY TOUGH.
WHO IS?
...
LET US TEST THE HEROISM THAT CONNECTS EACH OF US TO OUR PRINCESS...
YOU, AND US.
...AND DE-TERMINE WHICH IS SUPERIOR.
MASTER CAT, MAY I ASK THAT YOU DO NOT INTERFERE?
IT HAS BEEN A LONG TIME SINCE I ENGAGED IN A TRUE SWORD DUEL.
!

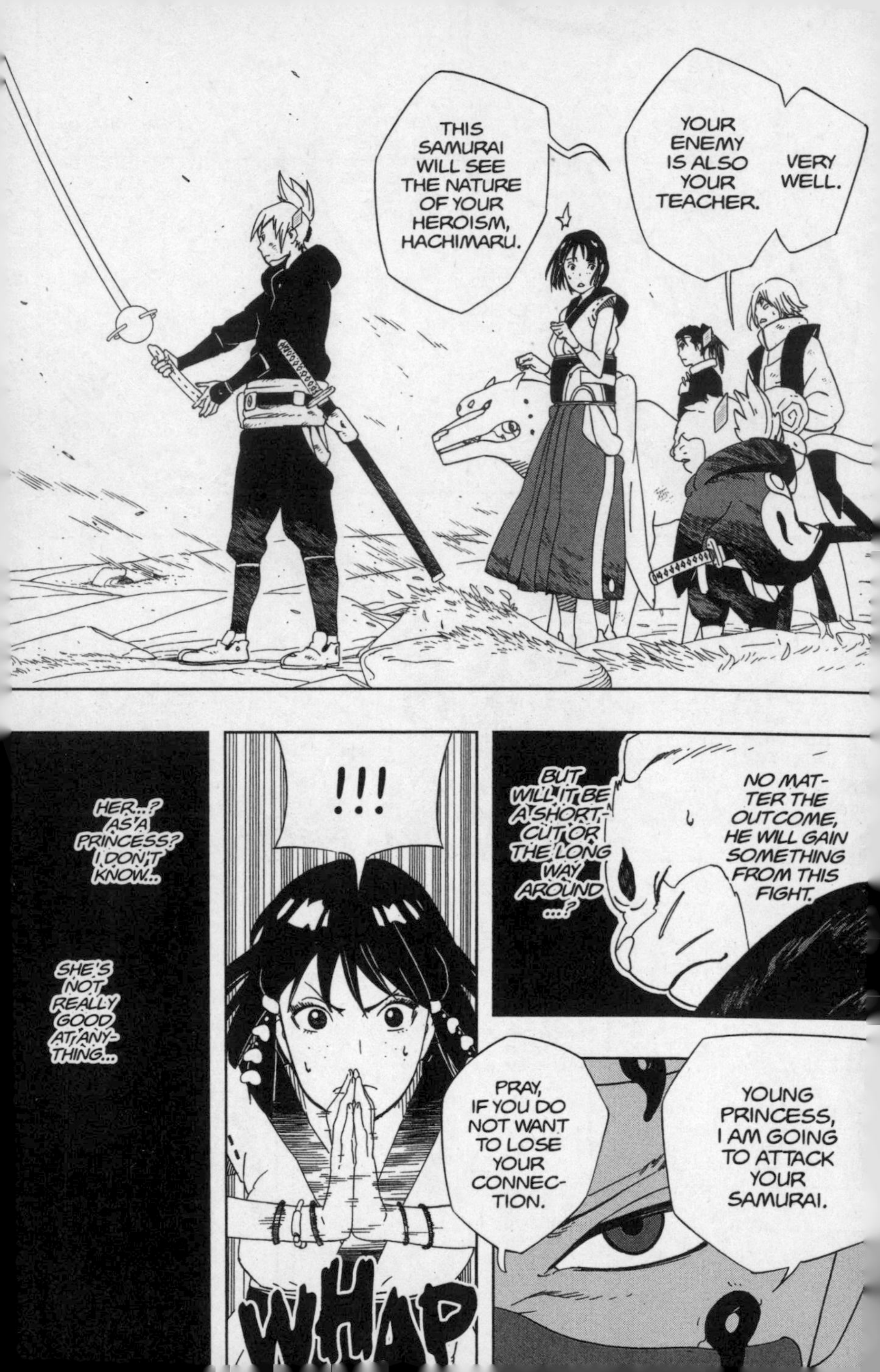
VERY WELL.
YOUR ENEMY IS ALSO YOUR TEACHER.
THIS SAMURAI WILL SEE THE NATURE OF YOUR HEROISM, HACHIMARU.
NO MATTER THE OUTCOME, HE WILL GAIN SOMETHING FROM THIS FIGHT.
BUT WILL IT BE A SHORTCUT OR THE LONG WAY AROUND ...?
YOUNG PRINCESS, I AM GOING TO ATTACK YOUR SAMURAI.
PRAY, IF YOU DO NOT WANT TO LOSE YOUR CONNECTION.
!!!
WHAP
HER...? AS A PRINCESS? I DON'T KNOW...
SHE'S NOT REALLY GOOD AT ANYTHING...

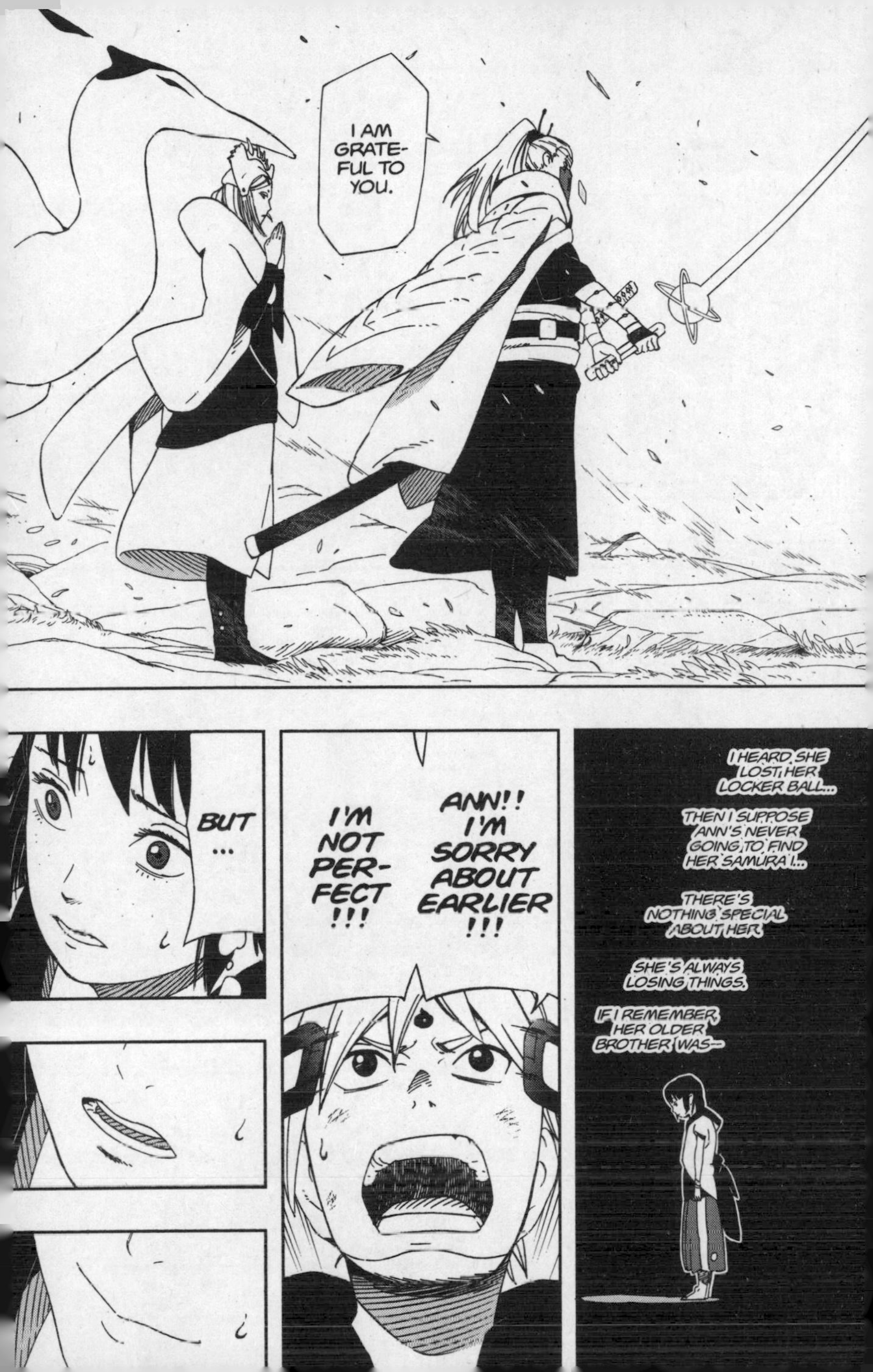
I AM GRATE-FUL TO YOU.
I HEARD SHE LOST HER LOCKER BALL...
THEN I SUPPOSE ANN'S NEVER GOING TO FIND HER SAMURAI...
THERE'S NOTHING SPECIAL ABOUT HER.
SHE'S ALWAYS LOSING THINGS.
IF I REMEMBER, HER OLDER BROTHER WAS--
ANN!! I'M SORRY ABOUT EARLIER!!!
I'M NOT PER-FECT!!!
BUT...

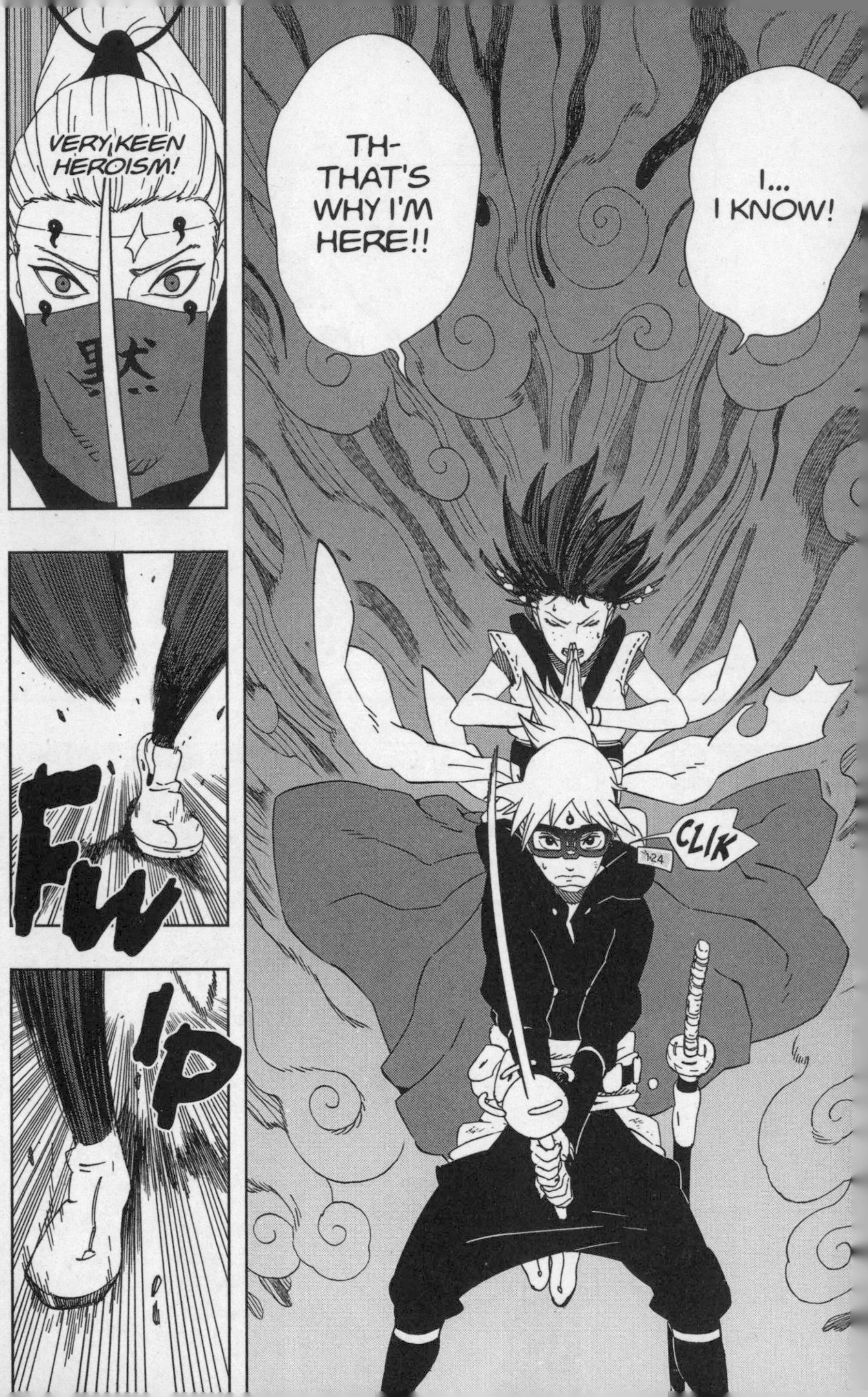
I... I KNOW!
TH- THAT'S WHY I'M HERE!!
CLIK
VERY KEEN HEROISM!
FW
IP

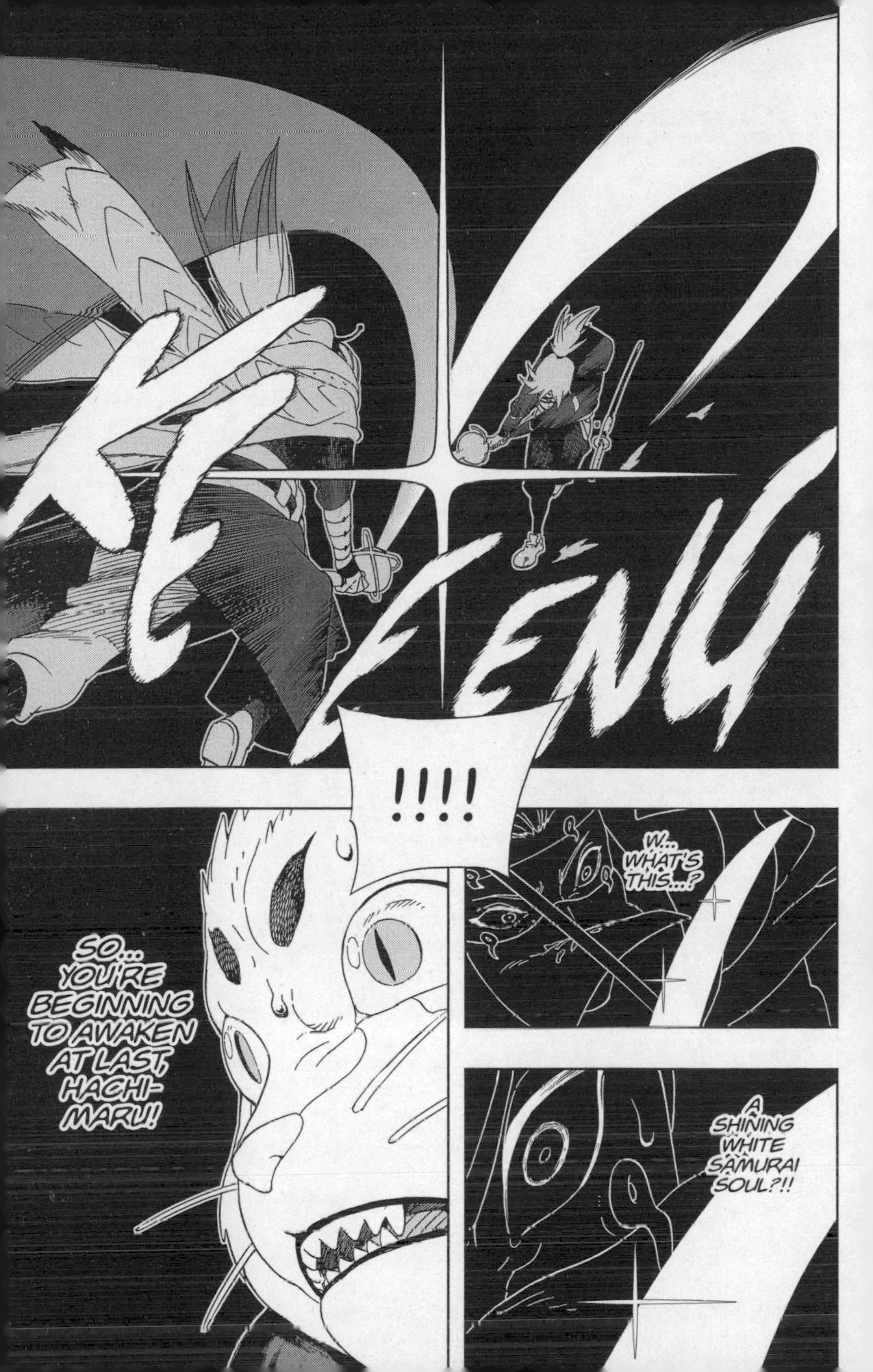
!!!!
W... WHAT'S THIS...?
A SHINING WHITE SAMURAI SOUL?!!
SO... YOU'RE BEGINNING TO AWAKEN AT LAST, HACHI-MARU!

Character Design Sketches: Hachimaru

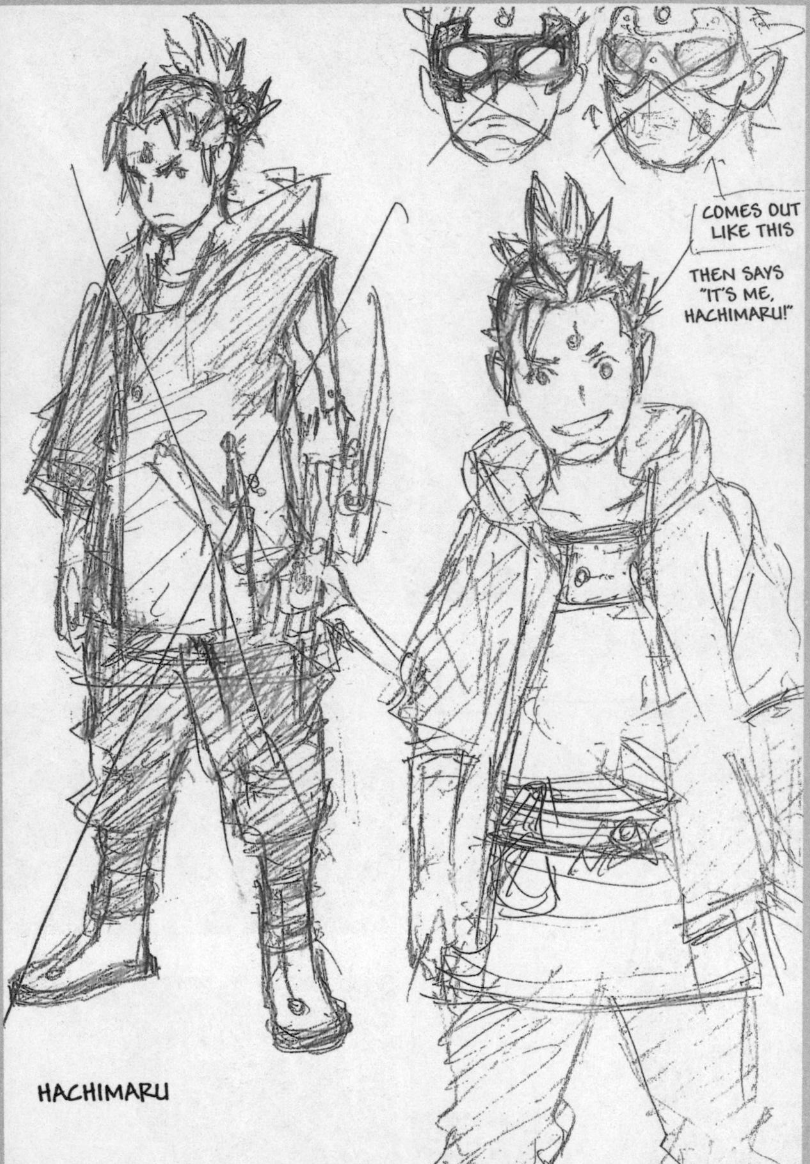
COMES OUT LIKE THIS
THEN SAYS "IT'S ME, HACHIMARU!"
HACHIMARU

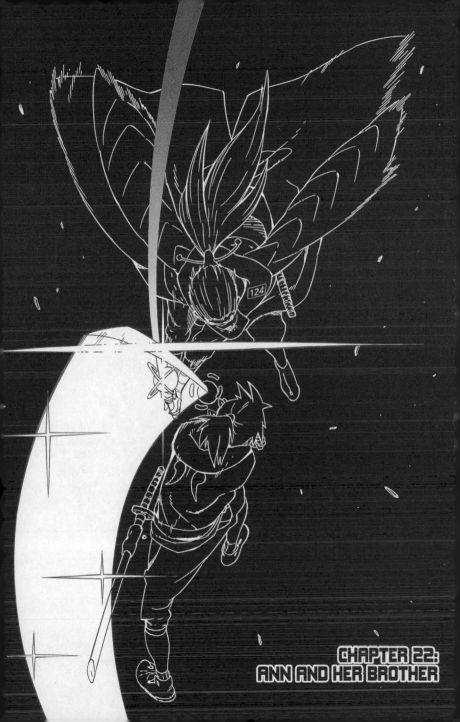

CHAPTER 22:
ANN AND HER BROTHER

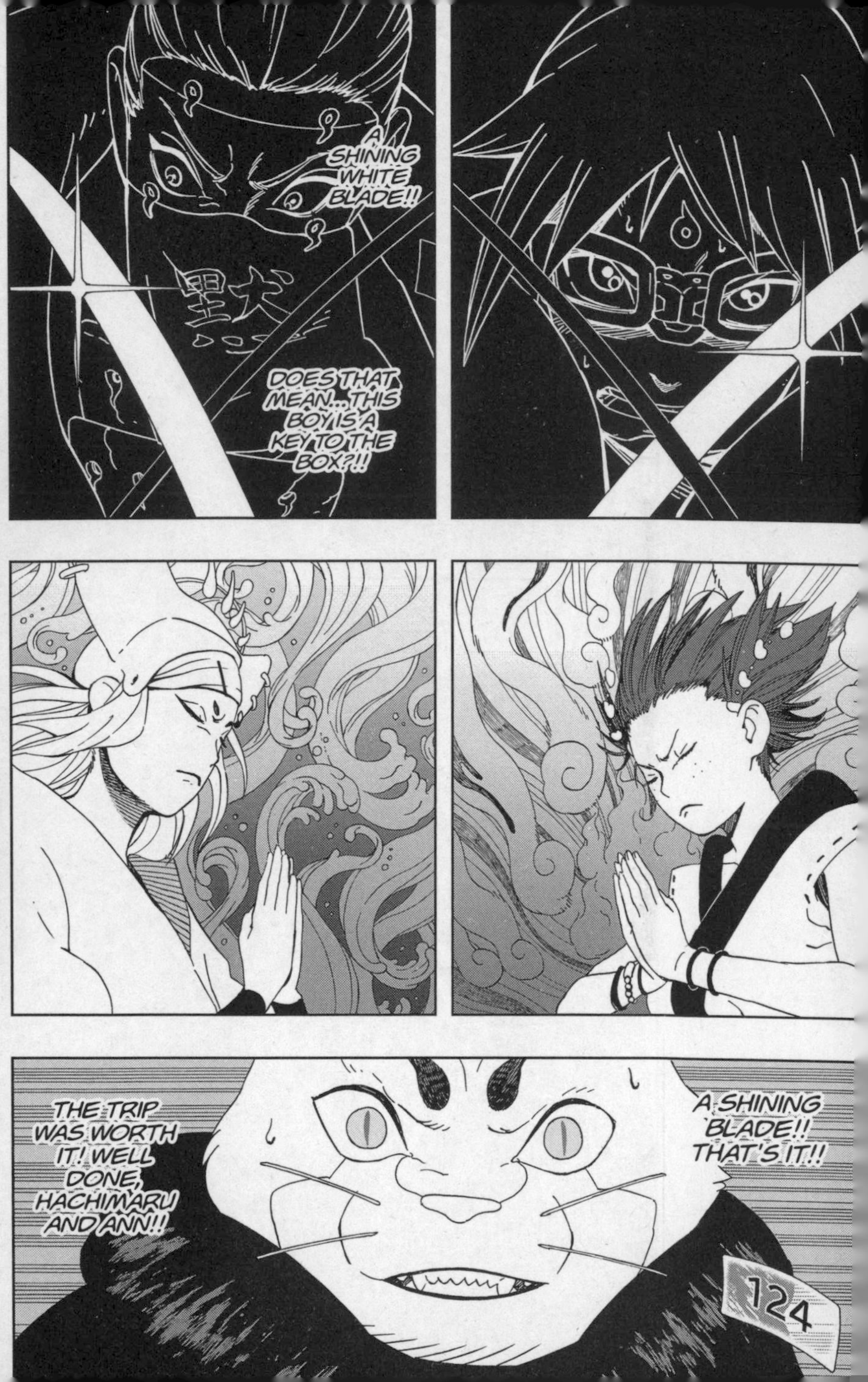
A SHINING WHITE BLADE!!
DOES THAT MEAN... THIS BOY IS A KEY TO THE BOX?!!
A SHINING BLADE!! THAT'S IT!!
THE TRIP WAS WORTH IT! WELL DONE, HACHIMARU AND ANN!!

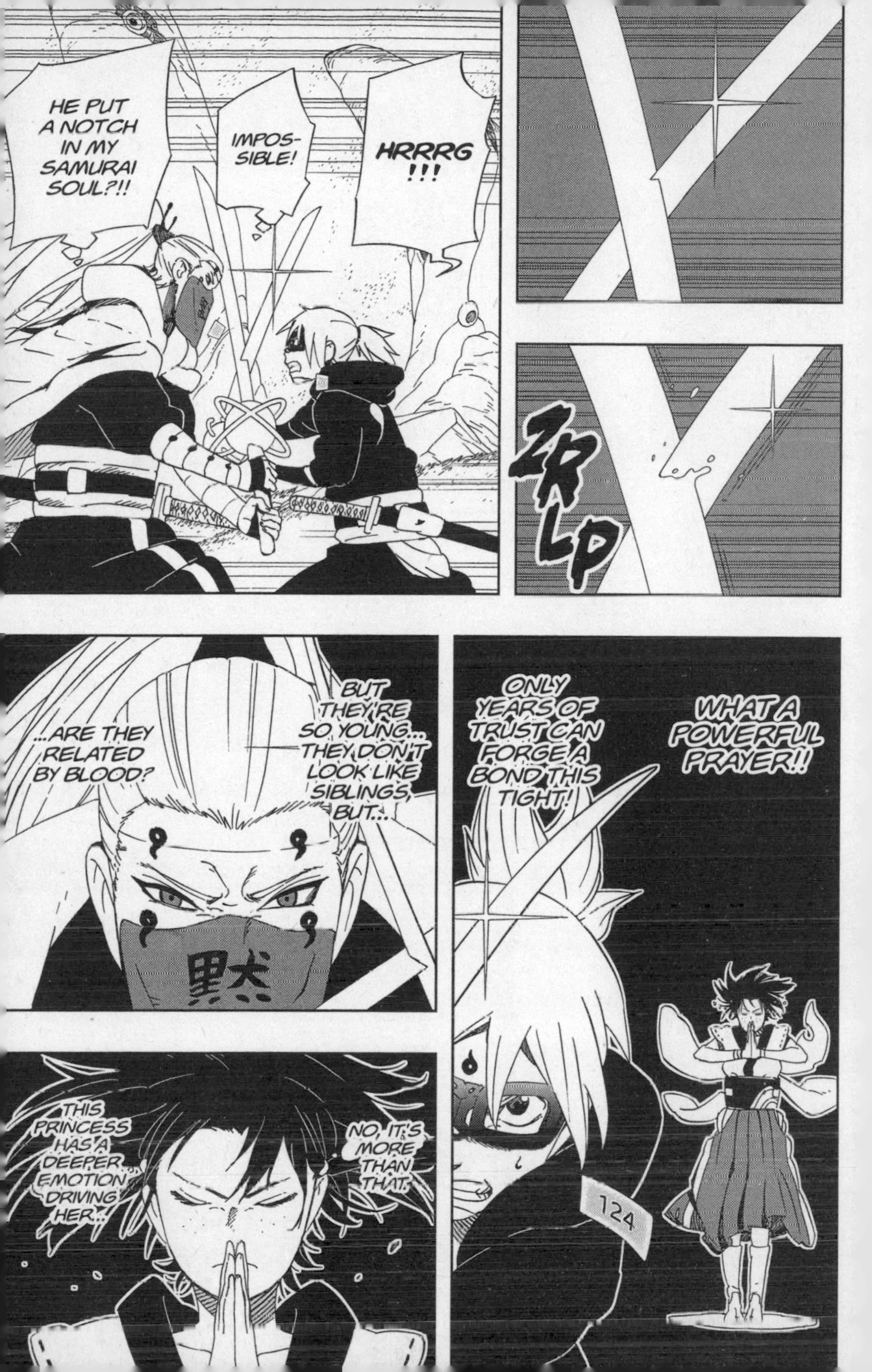
ZR
LP
HRRRG!!!
IMPOSSIBLE!
HE PUT A NOTCH IN MY SAMURAI SOUL?!!
WHAT A POWERFUL PRAYER!!
ONLY YEARS OF TRUST CAN FORGE A BOND THIS TIGHT!
124
BUT THEY'RE SO YOUNG... THEY DON'T LOOK LIKE SIBLINGS, BUT...
...ARE THEY RELATED BY BLOOD?
NO, IT'S MORE THAN THAT.
THIS PRINCESS HAS A DEEPER EMOTION DRIVING HER...

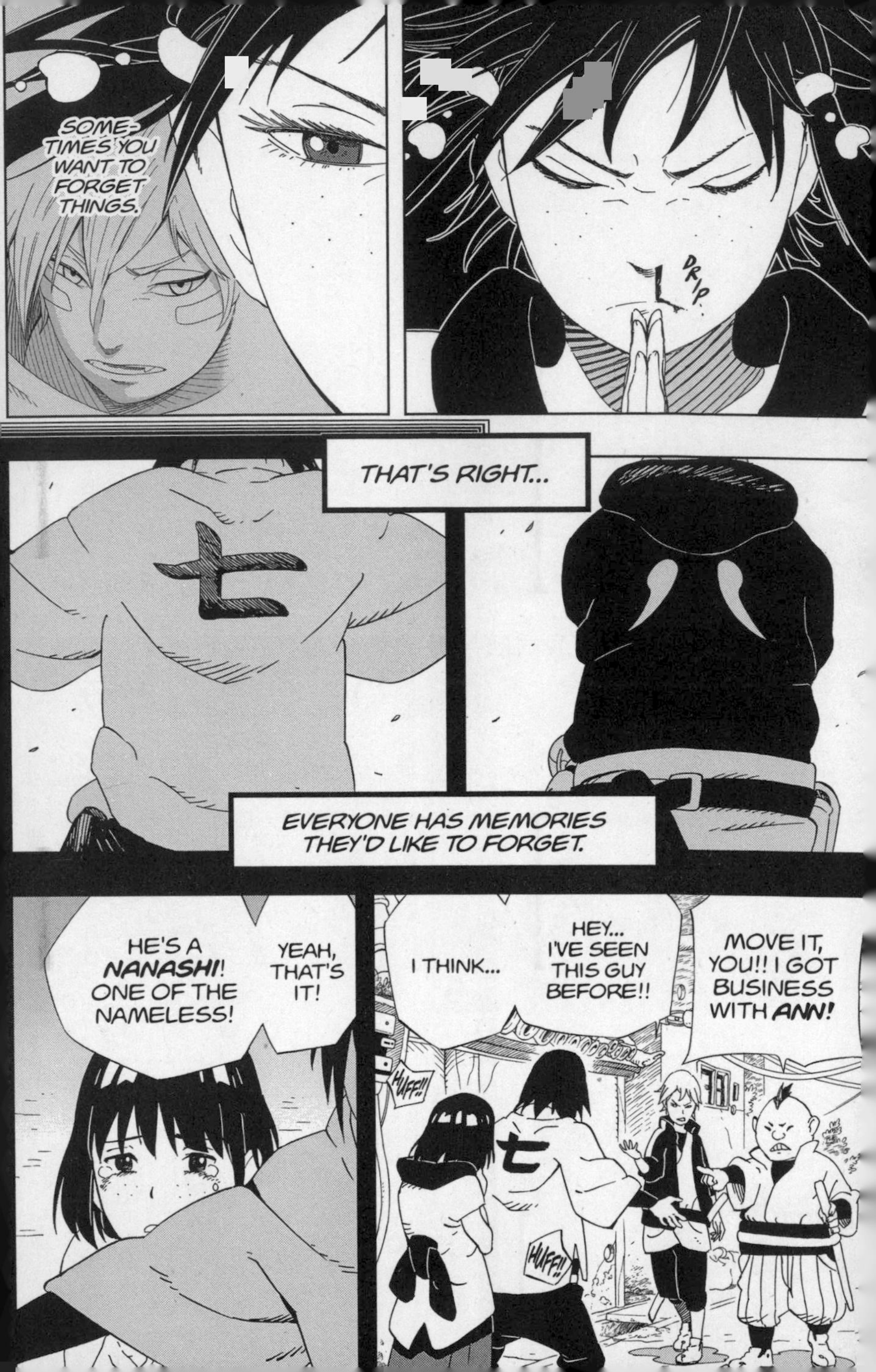
DRIP
SOME-TIMES YOU WANT TO FORGET THINGS.
THAT'S RIGHT...
EVERYONE HAS MEMORIES THEY'D LIKE TO FORGET.
MOVE IT, YOU!! I GOT BUSINESS WITH **ANN**!
HEY... I'VE SEEN THIS GUY BEFORE!!
I THINK...
HUFF!!
HUFF!!
YEAH, THAT'S IT!
HE'S A ***NANASHI***! ONE OF THE NAMELESS!

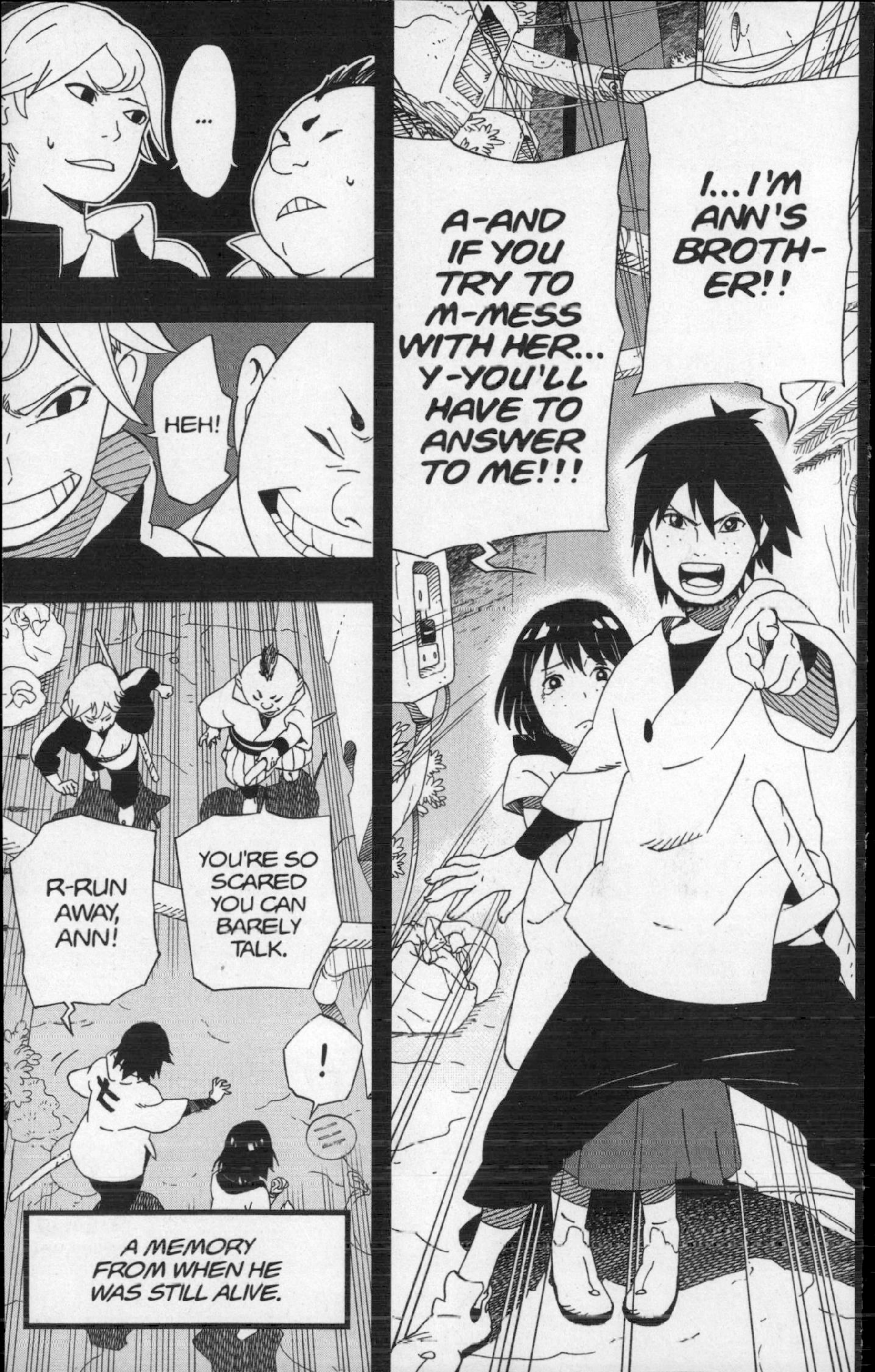
I...I'M ANN'S BROTH-ER!!
A-AND IF YOU TRY TO M-MESS WITH HER... Y-YOU'LL HAVE TO ANSWER TO ME!!!
...
HEH!
YOU'RE SO SCARED YOU CAN BARELY TALK.
R-RUN AWAY, ANN!
!
A MEMORY FROM WHEN HE WAS STILL ALIVE.

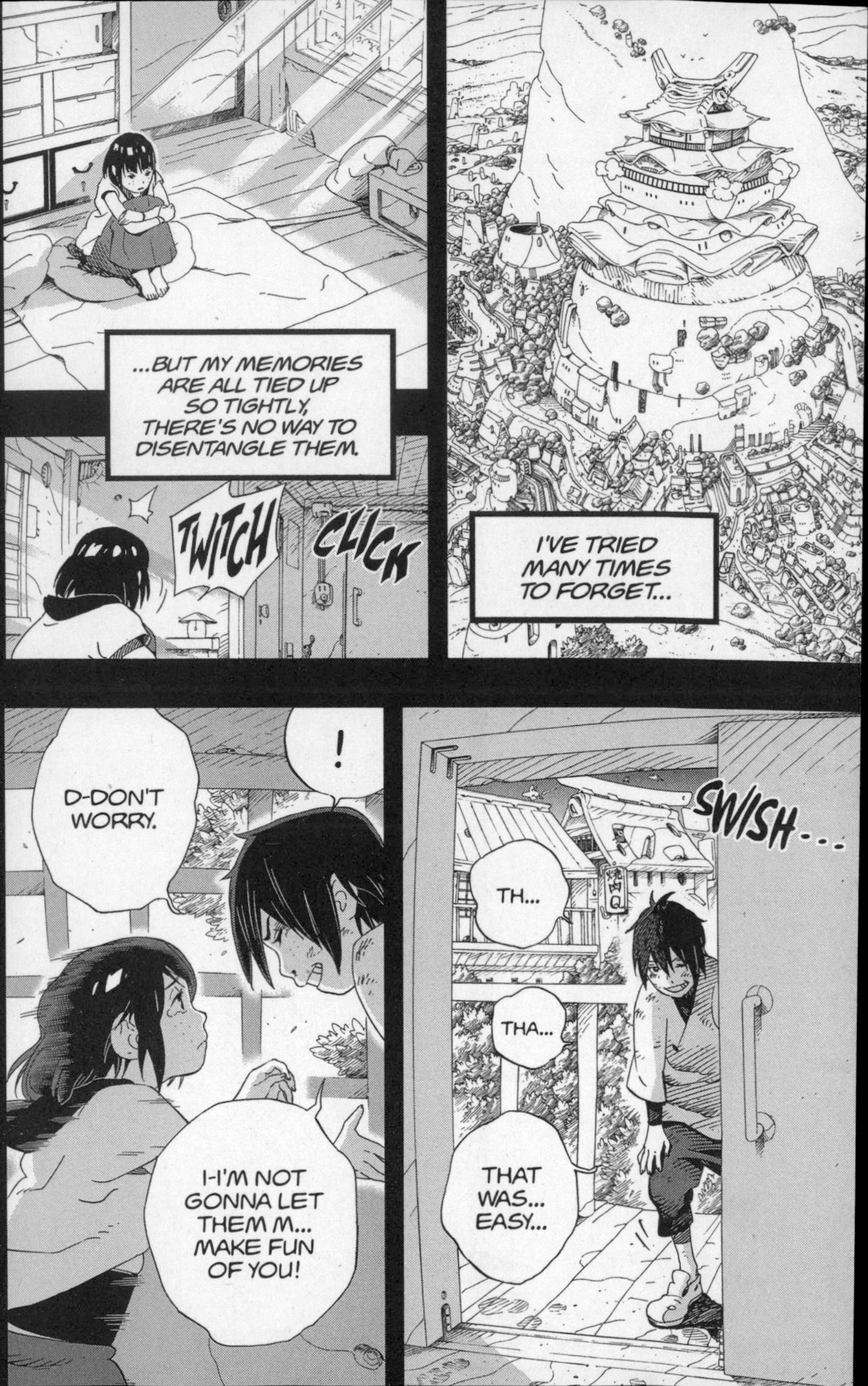
I'VE TRIED MANY TIMES TO FORGET...
...BUT MY MEMORIES ARE ALL TIED UP SO TIGHTLY, THERE'S NO WAY TO DISENTANGLE THEM.
CLICK
TWITCH
SWISH...
TH...
THA...
THAT WAS... EASY...
!
D-DON'T WORRY.
I-I'M NOT GONNA LET THEM M... MAKE FUN OF YOU!

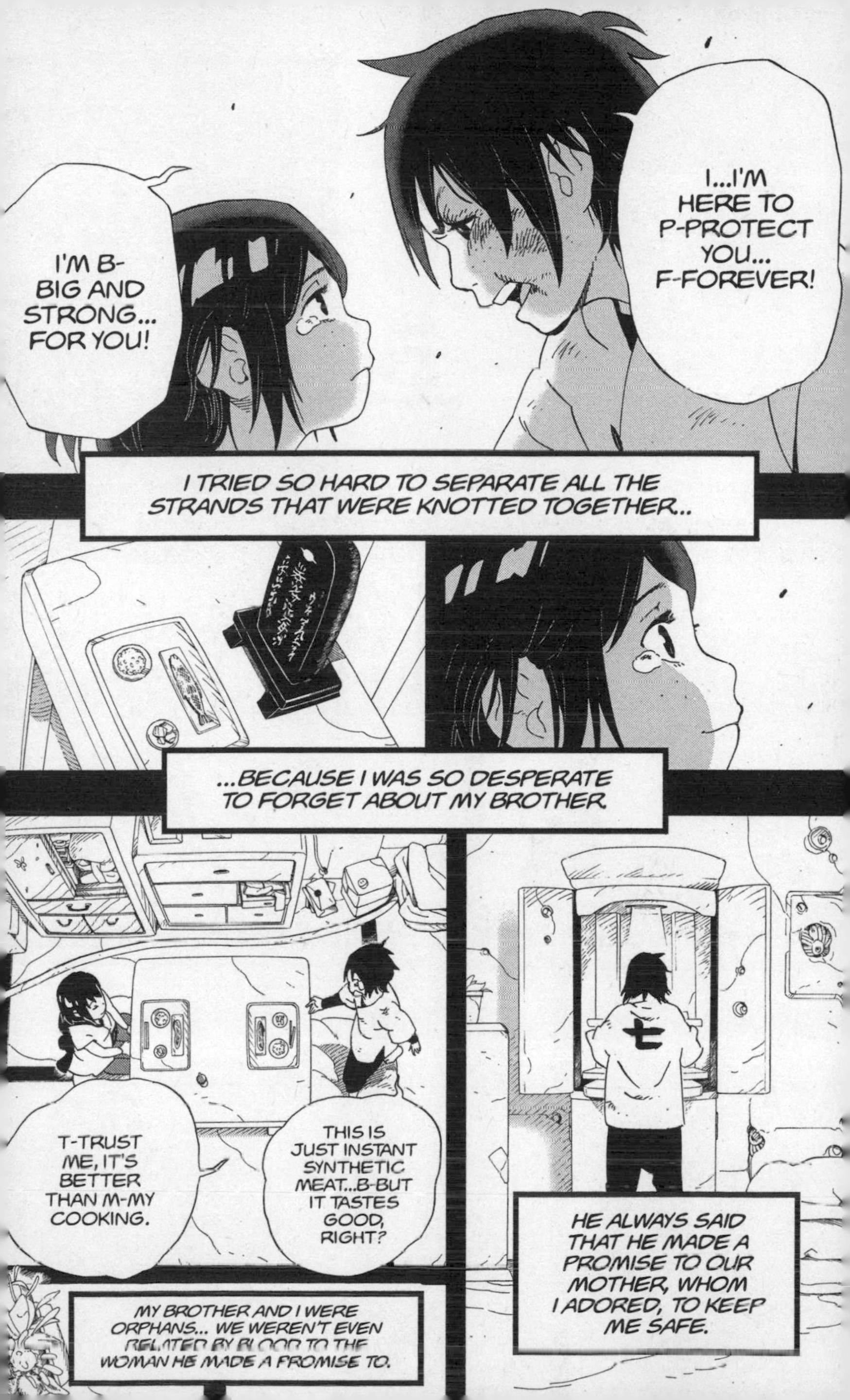
I...I'M HERE TO P-PROTECT YOU... F-FOREVER!
I'M B- BIG AND STRONG... FOR YOU!
I TRIED SO HARD TO SEPARATE ALL THE STRANDS THAT WERE KNOTTED TOGETHER...
...BECAUSE I WAS SO DESPERATE TO FORGET ABOUT MY BROTHER.
HE ALWAYS SAID THAT HE MADE A PROMISE TO OUR MOTHER, WHOM I ADORED, TO KEEP ME SAFE.
THIS IS JUST INSTANT SYNTHETIC MEAT...B-BUT IT TASTES GOOD, RIGHT?
T-TRUST ME, IT'S BETTER THAN M-MY COOKING.
MY BROTHER AND I WERE ORPHANS... WE WEREN'T EVEN RELATED BY BLOOD TO THE WOMAN HE MADE A PROMISE TO.

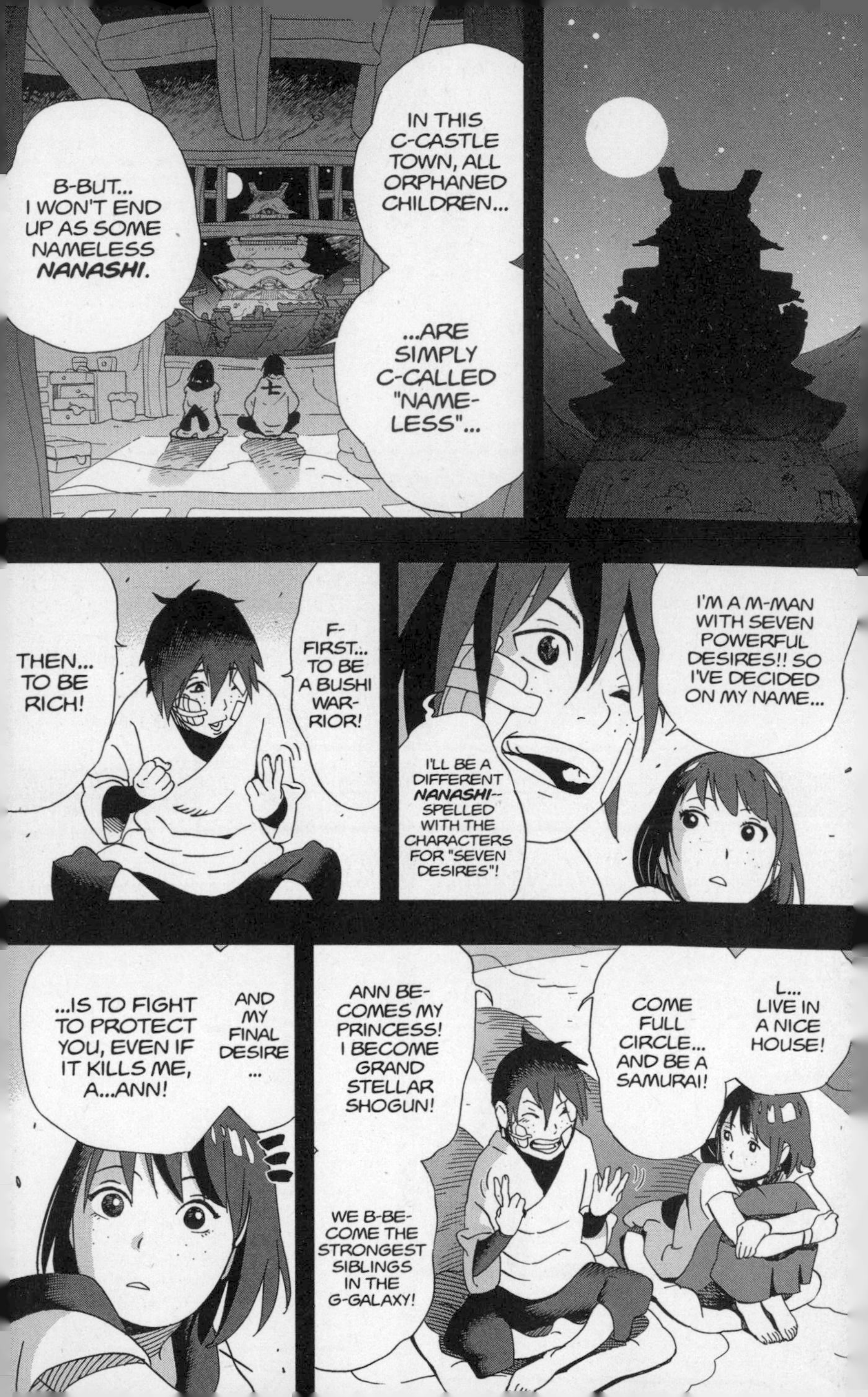
IN THIS C-CASTLE TOWN, ALL ORPHANED CHILDREN...
...ARE SIMPLY C-CALLED "NAMELESS"...
B-BUT... I WON'T END UP AS SOME NAMELESS NANASHI.
I'M A M-MAN WITH SEVEN POWERFUL DESIRES!! SO I'VE DECIDED ON MY NAME...
I'LL BE A DIFFERENT NANASHI--SPELLED WITH THE CHARACTERS FOR "SEVEN DESIRES"!
F-FIRST... TO BE A BUSHI WARRIOR!
THEN... TO BE RICH!
L... LIVE IN A NICE HOUSE!
COME FULL CIRCLE... AND BE A SAMURAI!
ANN BECOMES MY PRINCESS! I BECOME GRAND STELLAR SHOGUN!
WE B-BECOME THE STRONGEST SIBLINGS IN THE G-GALAXY!
AND MY FINAL DESIRE...
...IS TO FIGHT TO PROTECT YOU, EVEN IF IT KILLS ME, A...ANN!

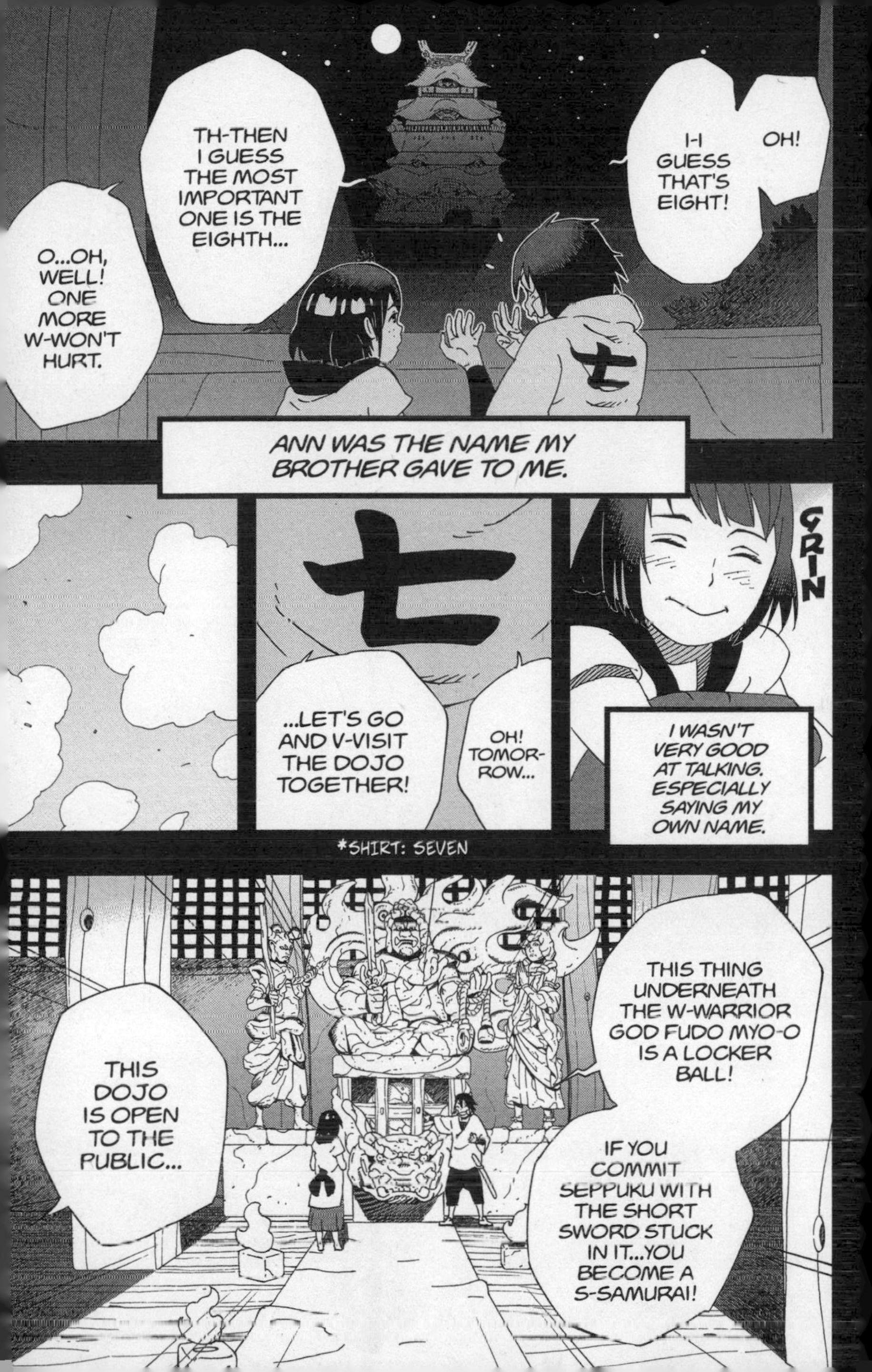
OH!
I-I GUESS THAT'S EIGHT!
TH-THEN I GUESS THE MOST IMPORTANT ONE IS THE EIGHTH...
O...OH, WELL! ONE MORE W-WON'T HURT.
ANN WAS THE NAME MY BROTHER GAVE TO ME.
GRIN
I WASN'T VERY GOOD AT TALKING. ESPECIALLY SAYING MY OWN NAME.
OH! TOMORROW...
...LET'S GO AND V-VISIT THE DOJO TOGETHER!
*SHIRT: SEVEN
THIS THING UNDERNEATH THE W-WARRIOR GOD FUDO MYO-O IS A LOCKER BALL!
IF YOU COMMIT SEPPUKU WITH THE SHORT SWORD STUCK IN IT...YOU BECOME A S-SAMURAI!
THIS DOJO IS OPEN TO THE PUBLIC...

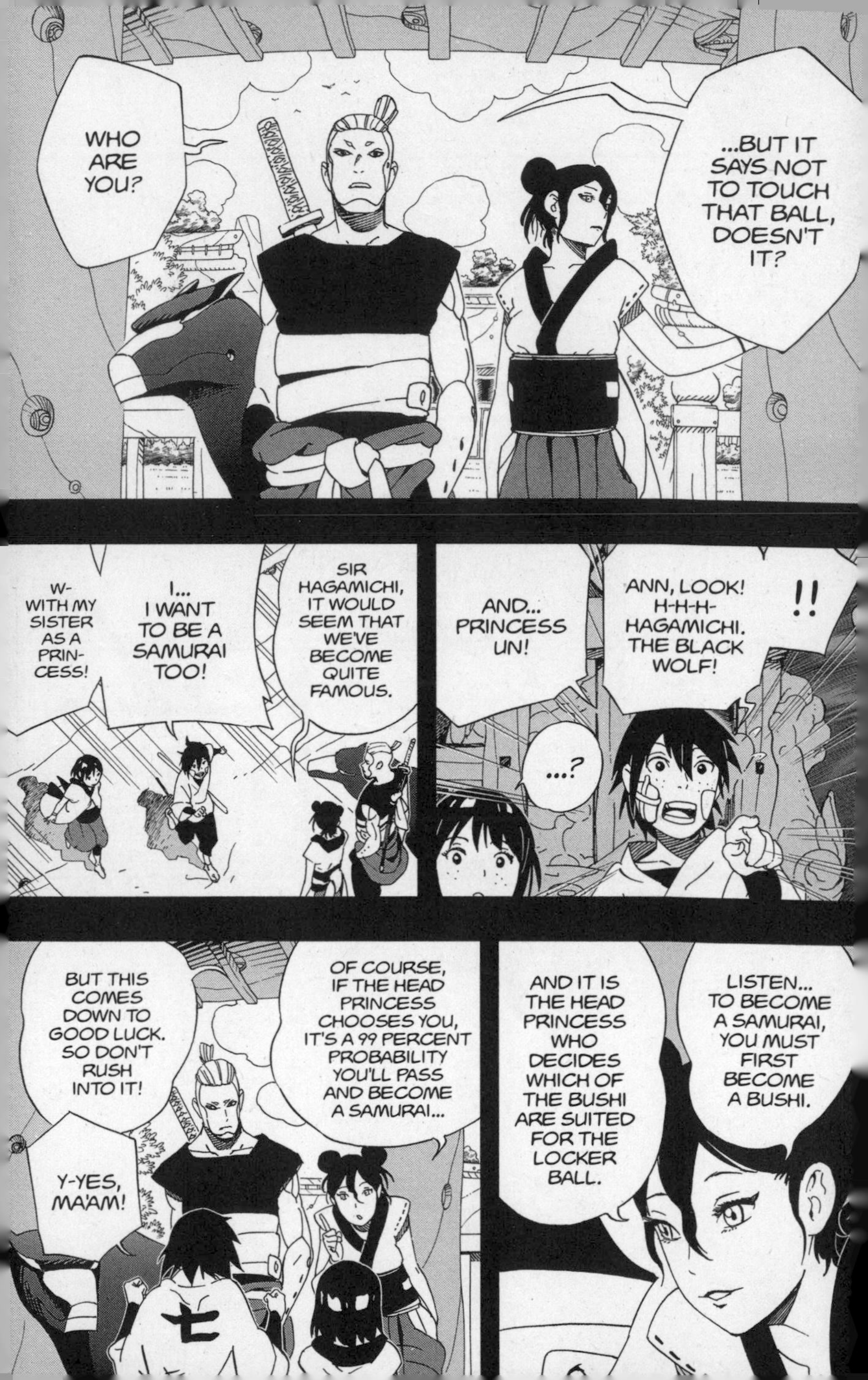
...BUT IT SAYS NOT TO TOUCH THAT BALL, DOESN'T IT?
WHO ARE YOU?
!!
ANN, LOOK! H-H-H-HAGAMICHI. THE BLACK WOLF!
AND... PRINCESS UN!
...?
SIR HAGAMICHI, IT WOULD SEEM THAT WE'VE BECOME QUITE FAMOUS.
I... I WANT TO BE A SAMURAI TOO!
W-WITH MY SISTER AS A PRINCESS!
LISTEN... TO BECOME A SAMURAI, YOU MUST FIRST BECOME A BUSHI.
AND IT IS THE HEAD PRINCESS WHO DECIDES WHICH OF THE BUSHI ARE SUITED FOR THE LOCKER BALL.
OF COURSE, IF THE HEAD PRINCESS CHOOSES YOU, IT'S A 99 PERCENT PROBABILITY YOU'LL PASS AND BECOME A SAMURAI...
BUT THIS COMES DOWN TO GOOD LUCK. SO DON'T RUSH INTO IT!
Y-YES, MA'AM!

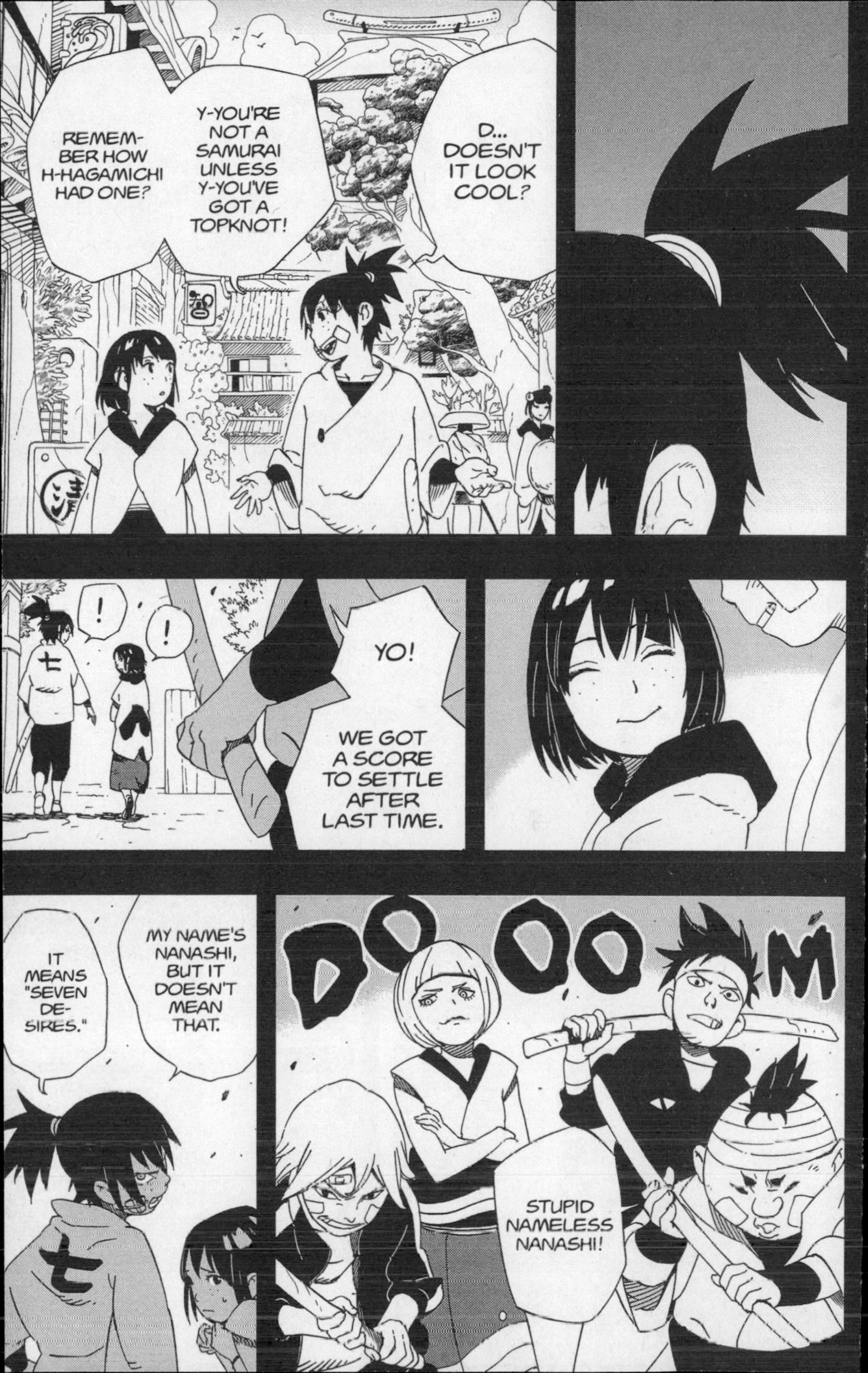
D... DOESN'T IT LOOK COOL?
Y-YOU'RE NOT A SAMURAI UNLESS Y-YOU'VE GOT A TOPKNOT!
REMEM-BER HOW H-HAGAMICHI HAD ONE?
YO!
WE GOT A SCORE TO SETTLE AFTER LAST TIME.
!
!
DOOOM
STUPID NAMELESS NANASHI!
MY NAME'S NANASHI, BUT IT DOESN'T MEAN THAT.
IT MEANS "SEVEN DE-SIRES."

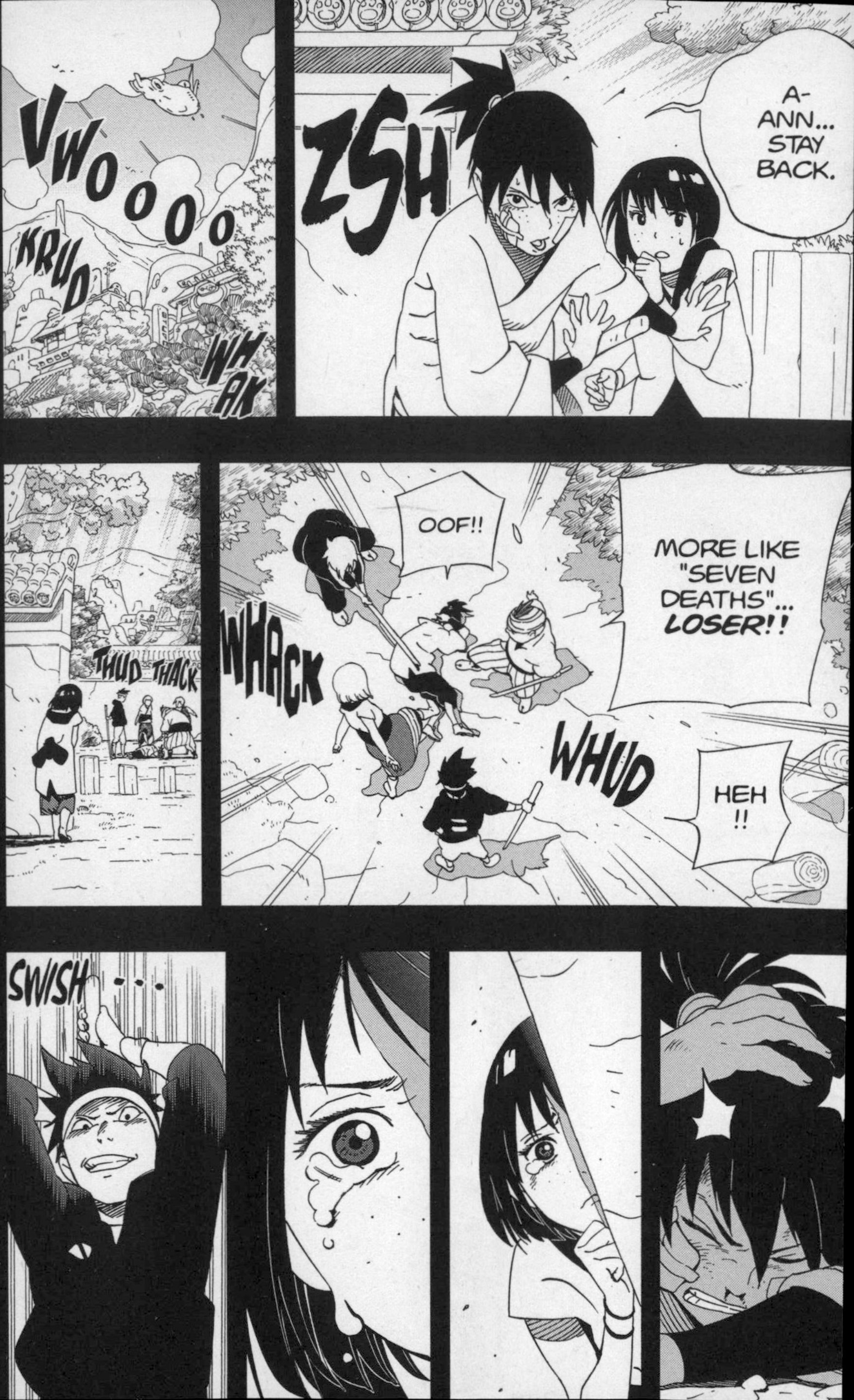
A-
ANN... STAY BACK.
ZSH
VWOOOOO
KRUD
WHAK
MORE LIKE "SEVEN DEATHS"... LOSER!!
OOF!!
HEH !!
WHUD
WHACK
THUD THACK
SWISH
...

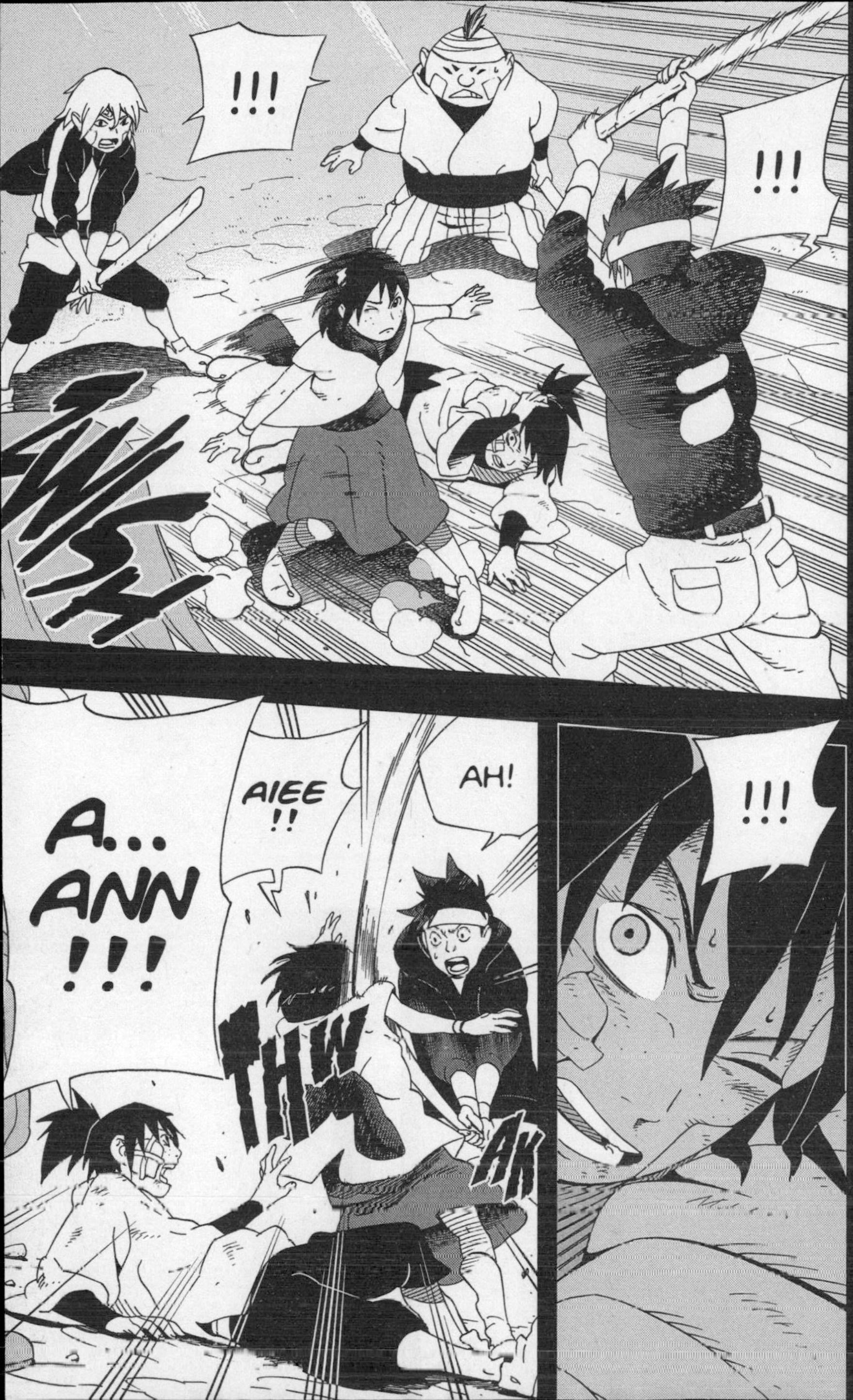
!!!
!!!
SWISH
!!!
AH!
AIEE !!
A... ANN !!!
THWAK

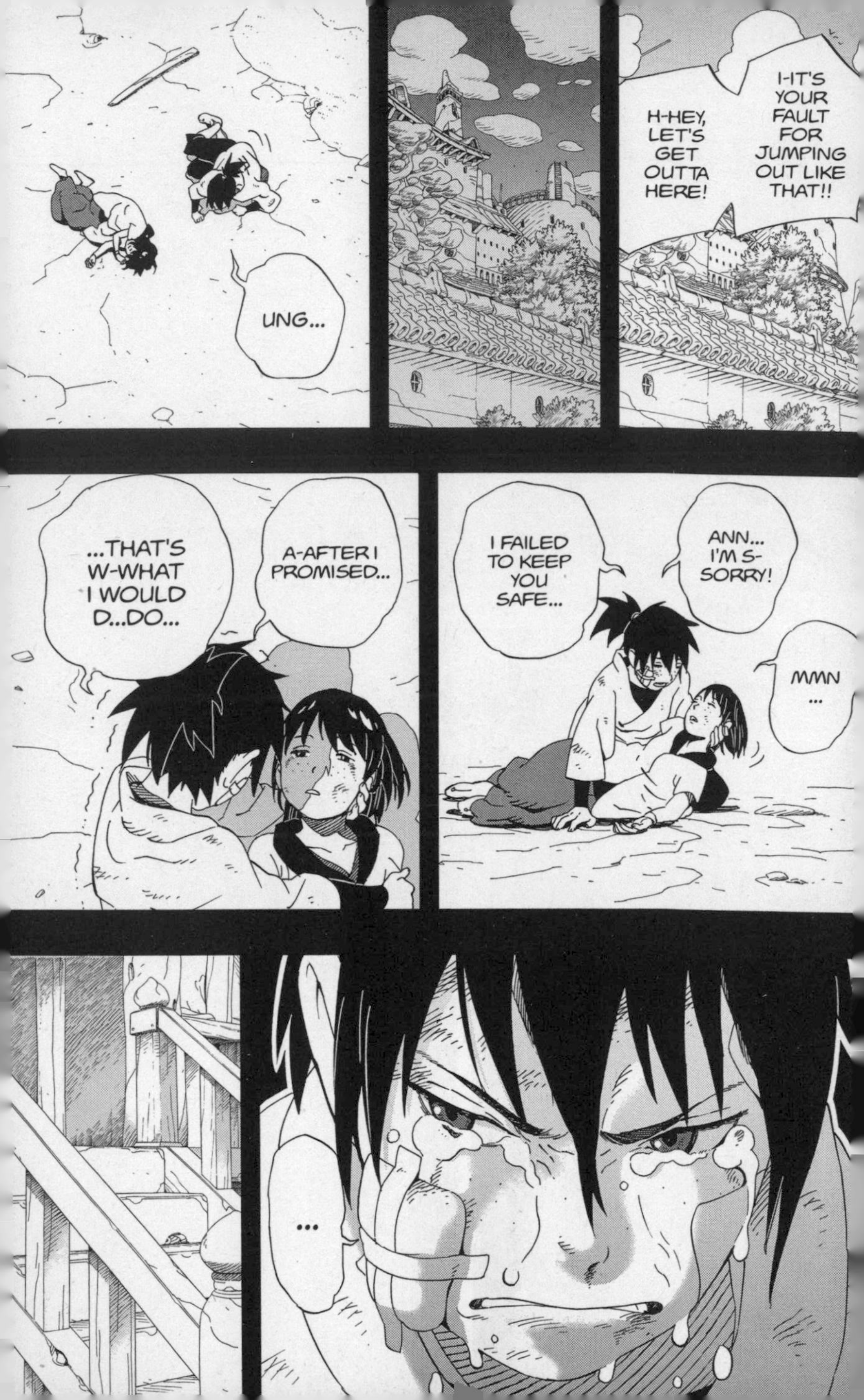
I-IT'S YOUR FAULT FOR JUMPING OUT LIKE THAT!!
H-HEY, LET'S GET OUTTA HERE!
UNG...
ANN... I'M S-SORRY!
I FAILED TO KEEP YOU SAFE...
MMN ...
A-AFTER I PROMISED...
...THAT'S W-WHAT I WOULD D...DO...
...

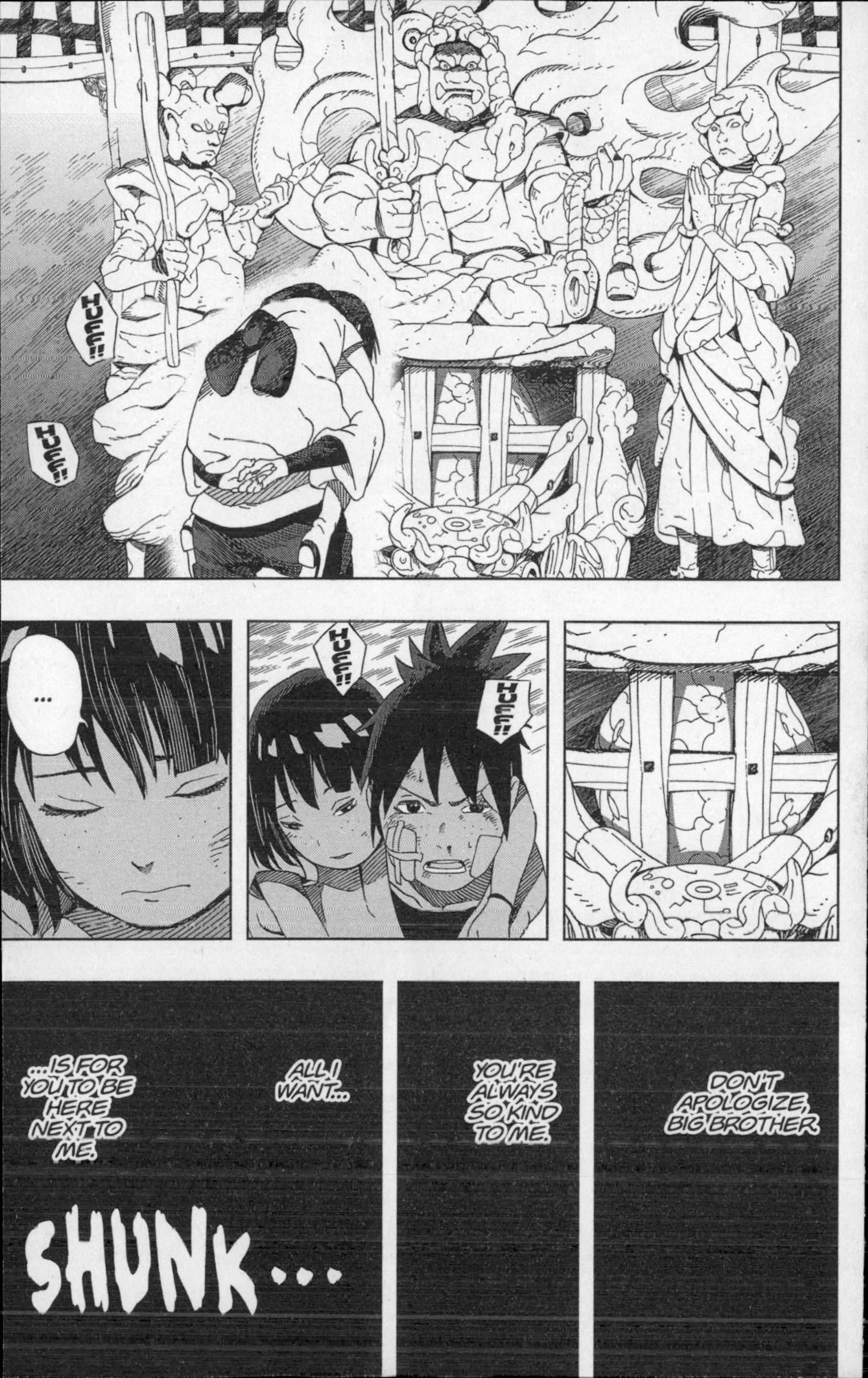
HUFF!!
HUFF!!
HUFF!!
HUFF!!
...
DON'T APOLOGIZE, BIG BROTHER.
YOU'RE ALWAYS SO KIND TO ME.
ALL I WANT...
...IS FOR YOU TO BE HERE NEXT TO ME.
SHUNK...

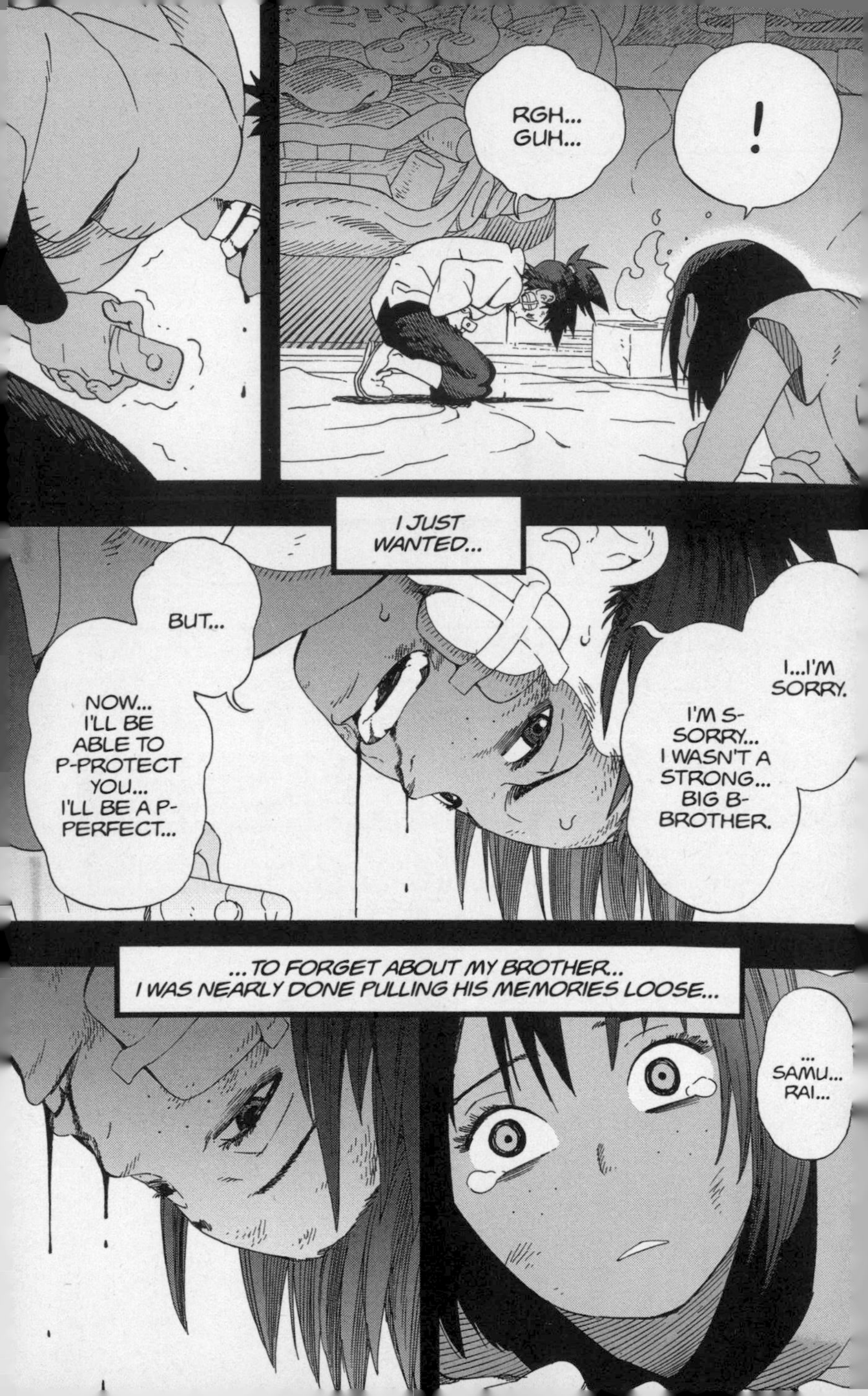
!
RGH... GUH...
I JUST WANTED...
I...I'M SORRY.
I'M S-SORRY... I WASN'T A STRONG... BIG B-BROTHER.
BUT...
NOW... I'LL BE ABLE TO P-PROTECT YOU... I'LL BE A P-PERFECT...
...TO FORGET ABOUT MY BROTHER... I WAS NEARLY DONE PULLING HIS MEMORIES LOOSE...
... SAMU... RAI...

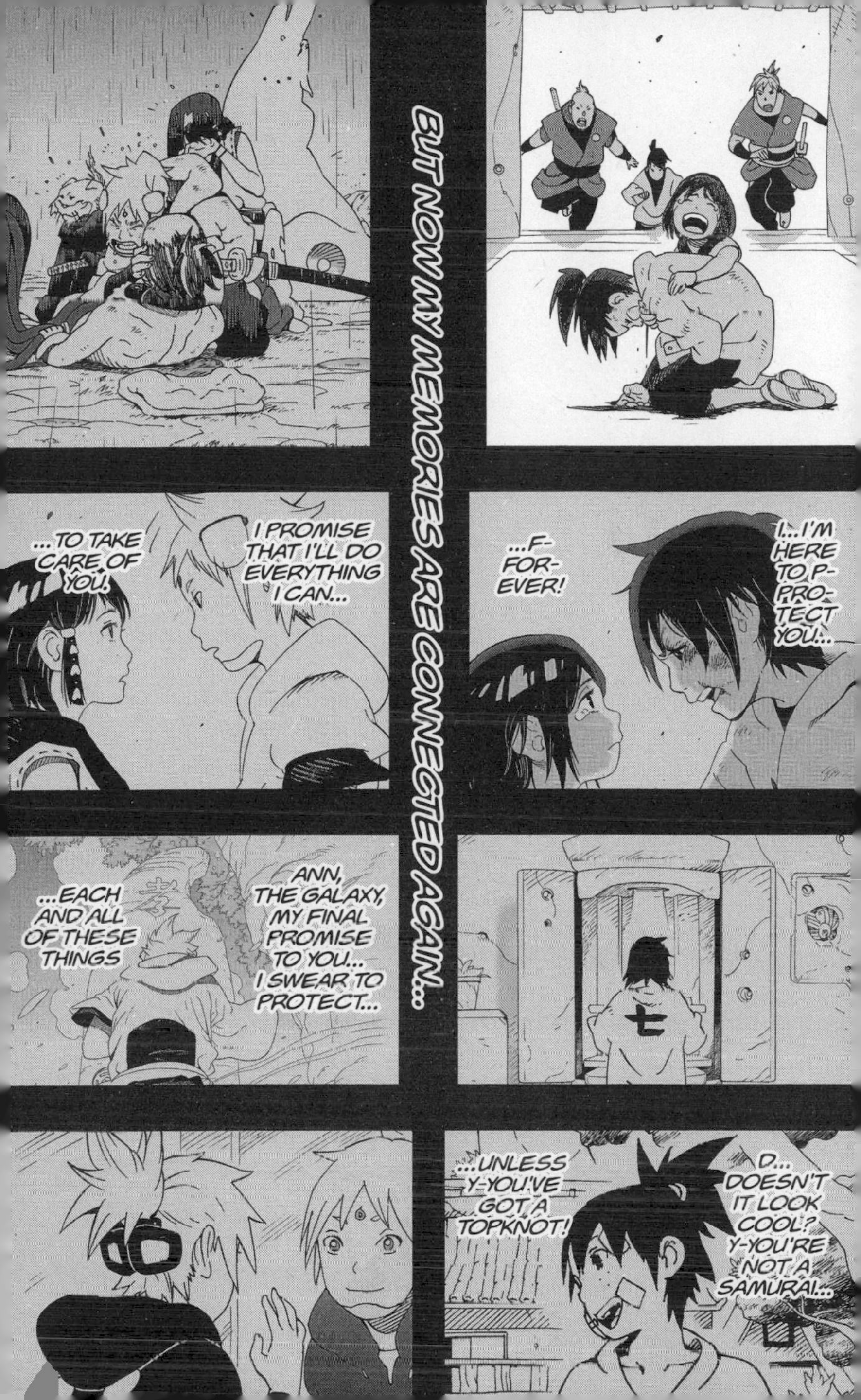
BUT NOW MY MEMORIES ARE CONNECTED AGAIN...
I...I'M HERE TO P-PRO-TECT YOU...
...F-FOR-EVER!
I PROMISE THAT I'LL DO EVERYTHING I CAN...
...TO TAKE CARE OF YOU.
ANN, THE GALAXY, MY FINAL PROMISE TO YOU... I SWEAR TO PROTECT...
...EACH AND ALL OF THESE THINGS
D... DOESN'T IT LOOK COOL? Y-YOU'RE NOT A SAMURAI...
...UNLESS Y-YOU'VE GOT A TOPKNOT!

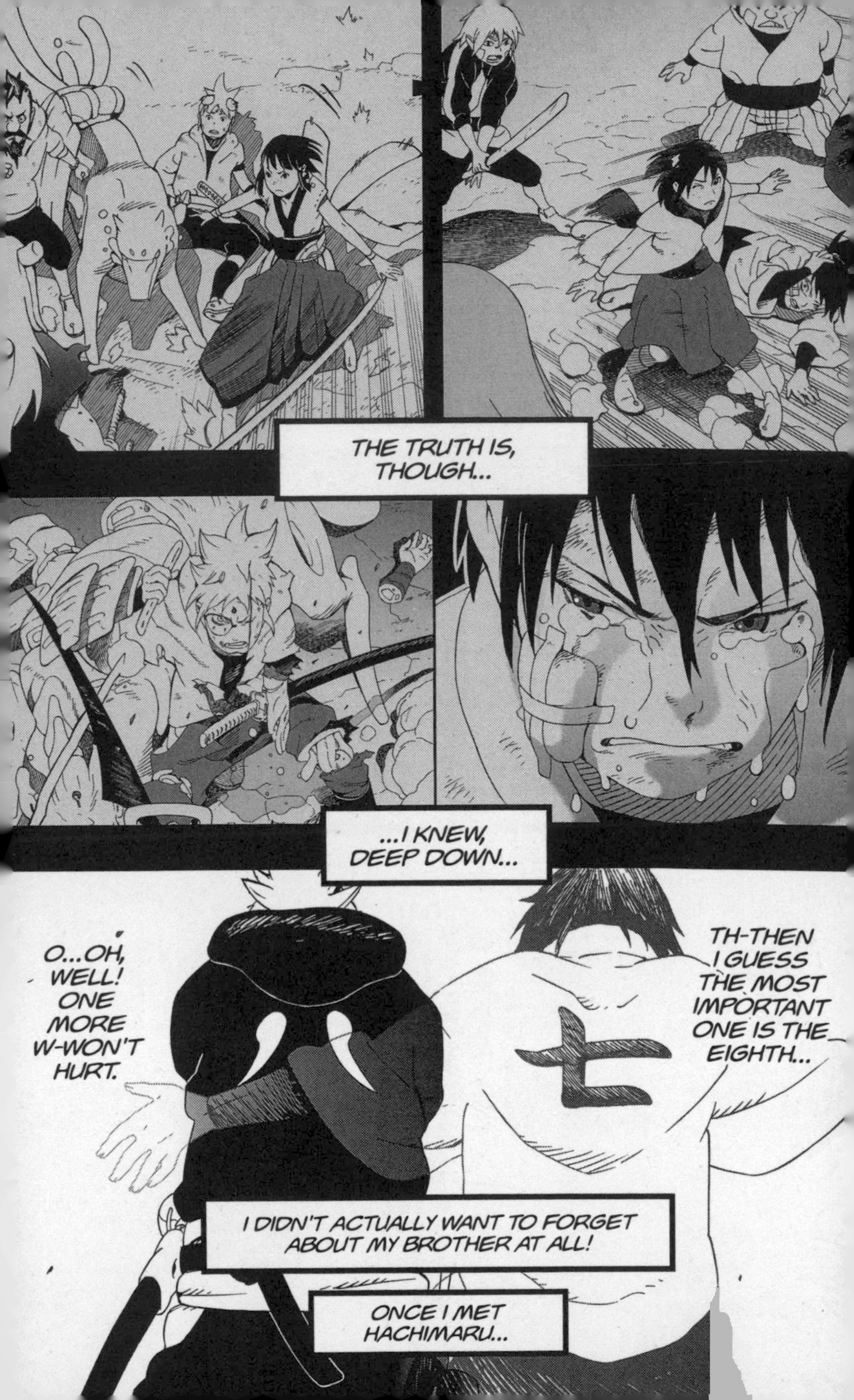
THE TRUTH IS, THOUGH...
...I KNEW, DEEP DOWN...
TH-THEN I GUESS THE MOST IMPORTANT ONE IS THE EIGHTH...
O...OH, WELL! ONE MORE W-WON'T HURT.
I DIDN'T ACTUALLY WANT TO FORGET ABOUT MY BROTHER AT ALL!
ONCE I MET HACHIMARU...

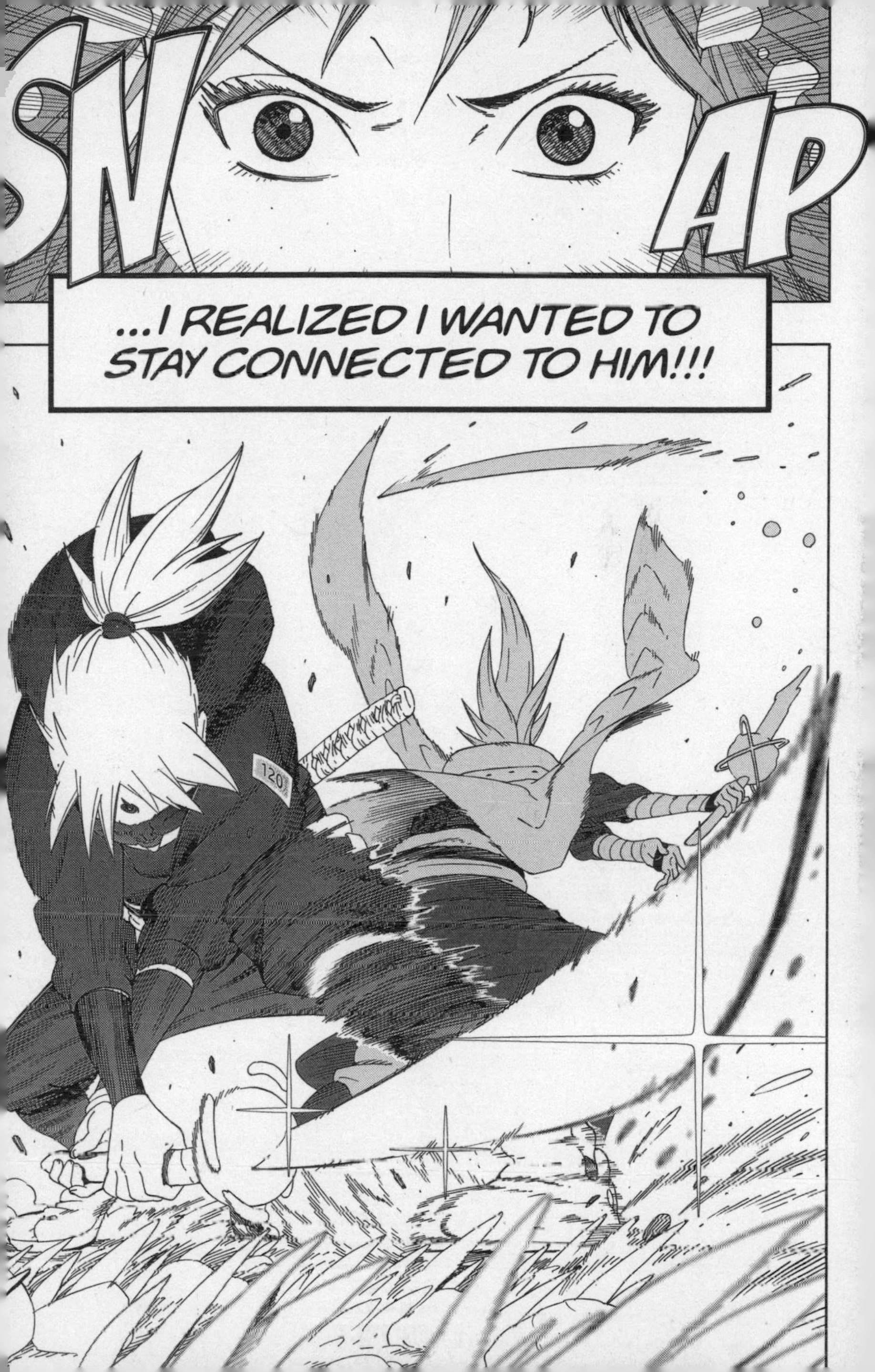
SNAP
...I REALIZED I WANTED TO STAY CONNECTED TO HIM!!!
120

Character Design Sketches: Kotsuga & Ryu

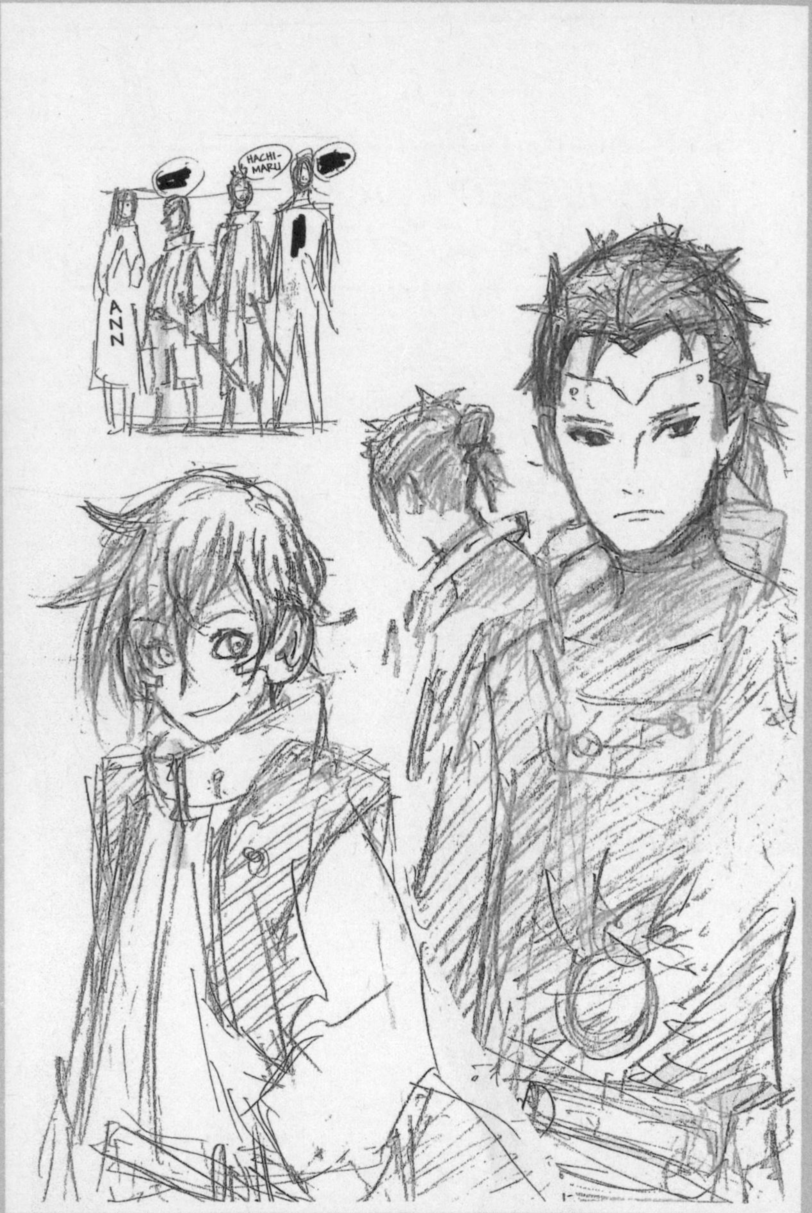
[redacted]
HACHI-MARU
[redacted]
ANN

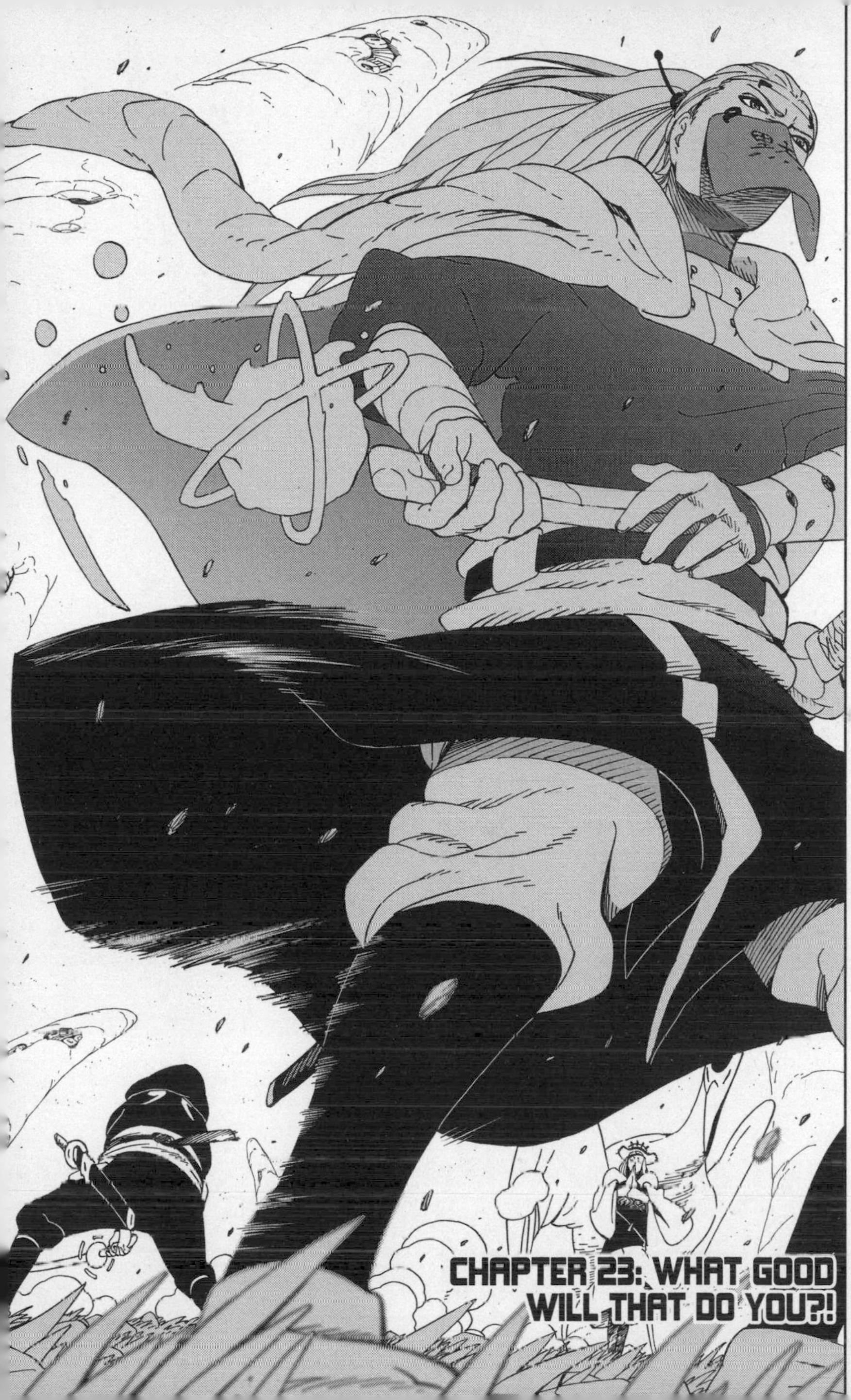
CHAPTER 23: WHAT GOOD WILL THAT DO YOU?!

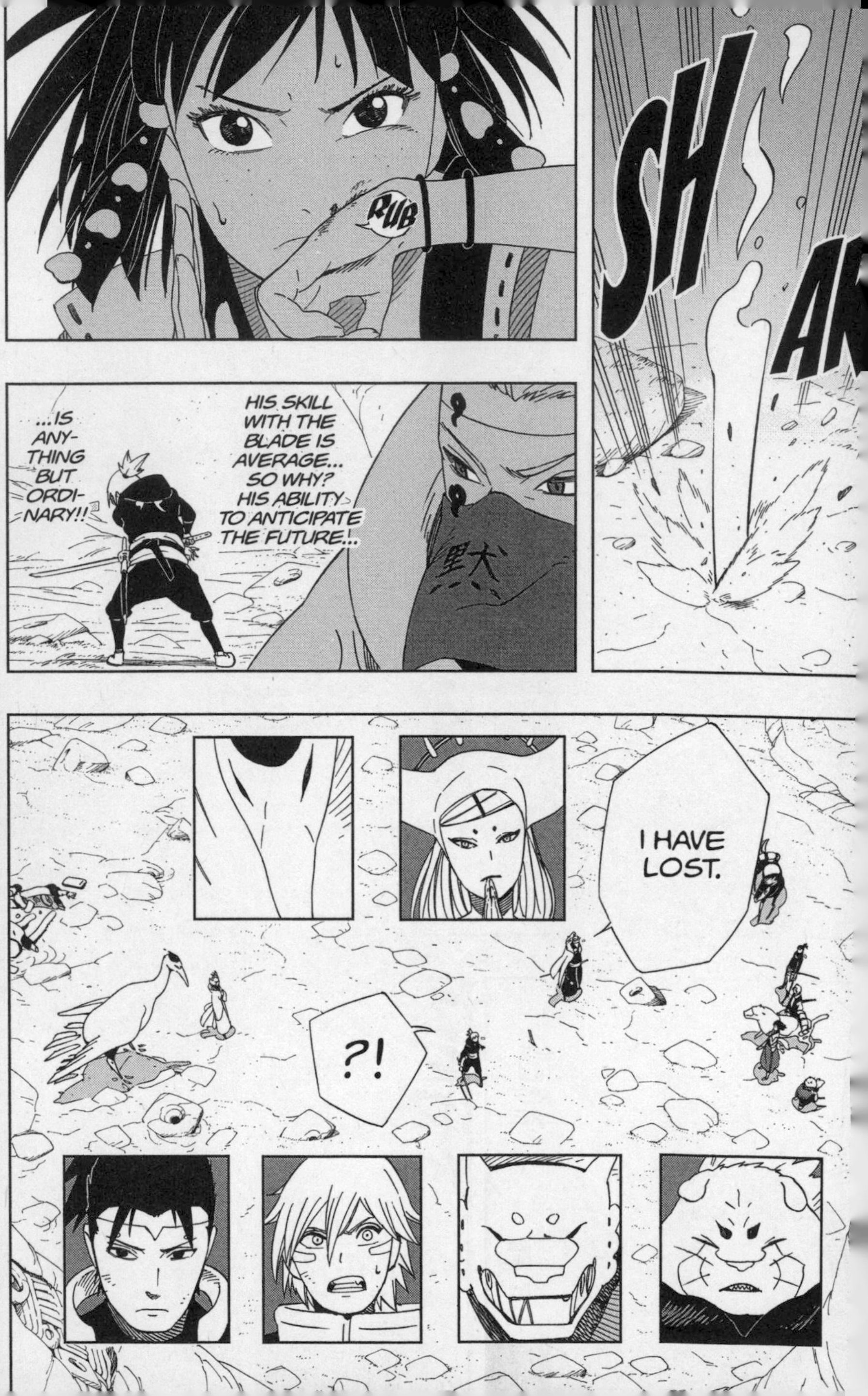
SHAK
RUB
HIS SKILL WITH THE BLADE IS AVERAGE... SO WHY? HIS ABILITY TO ANTICIPATE THE FUTURE...
...IS ANYTHING BUT ORDINARY!!
I HAVE LOST.
?!

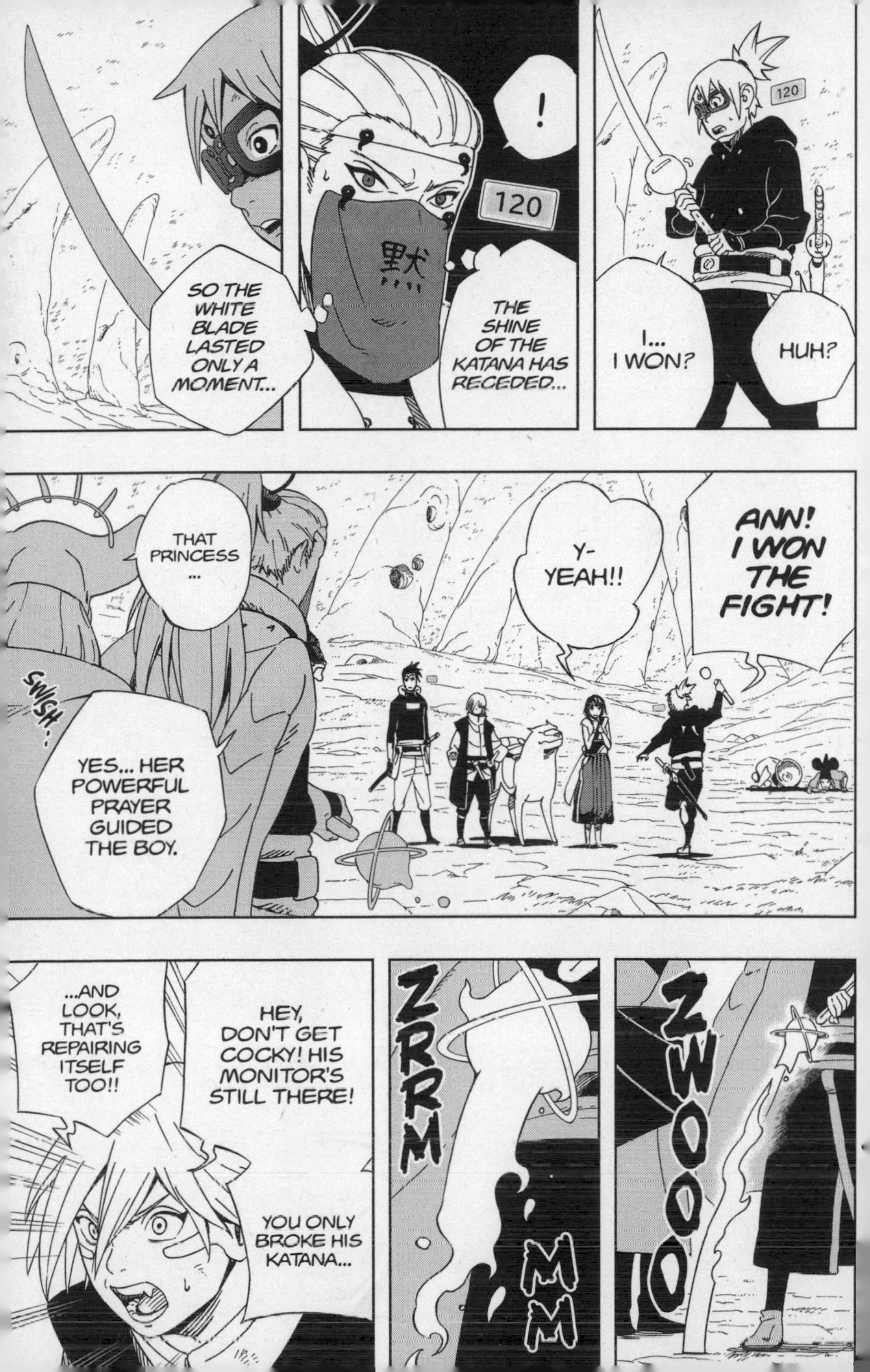
HUH?
I... I WON?
120
!
120
THE SHINE OF THE KATANA HAS RECEDED...
SO THE WHITE BLADE LASTED ONLY A MOMENT...
ANN! I WON THE FIGHT!
Y- YEAH!!
THAT PRINCESS ...
SWISH.
YES... HER POWERFUL PRAYER GUIDED THE BOY.
ZWOOOO
ZRRM
MMM
HEY, DON'T GET COCKY! HIS MONITOR'S STILL THERE!
YOU ONLY BROKE HIS KATANA...
...AND LOOK, THAT'S REPAIRING ITSELF TOO!!

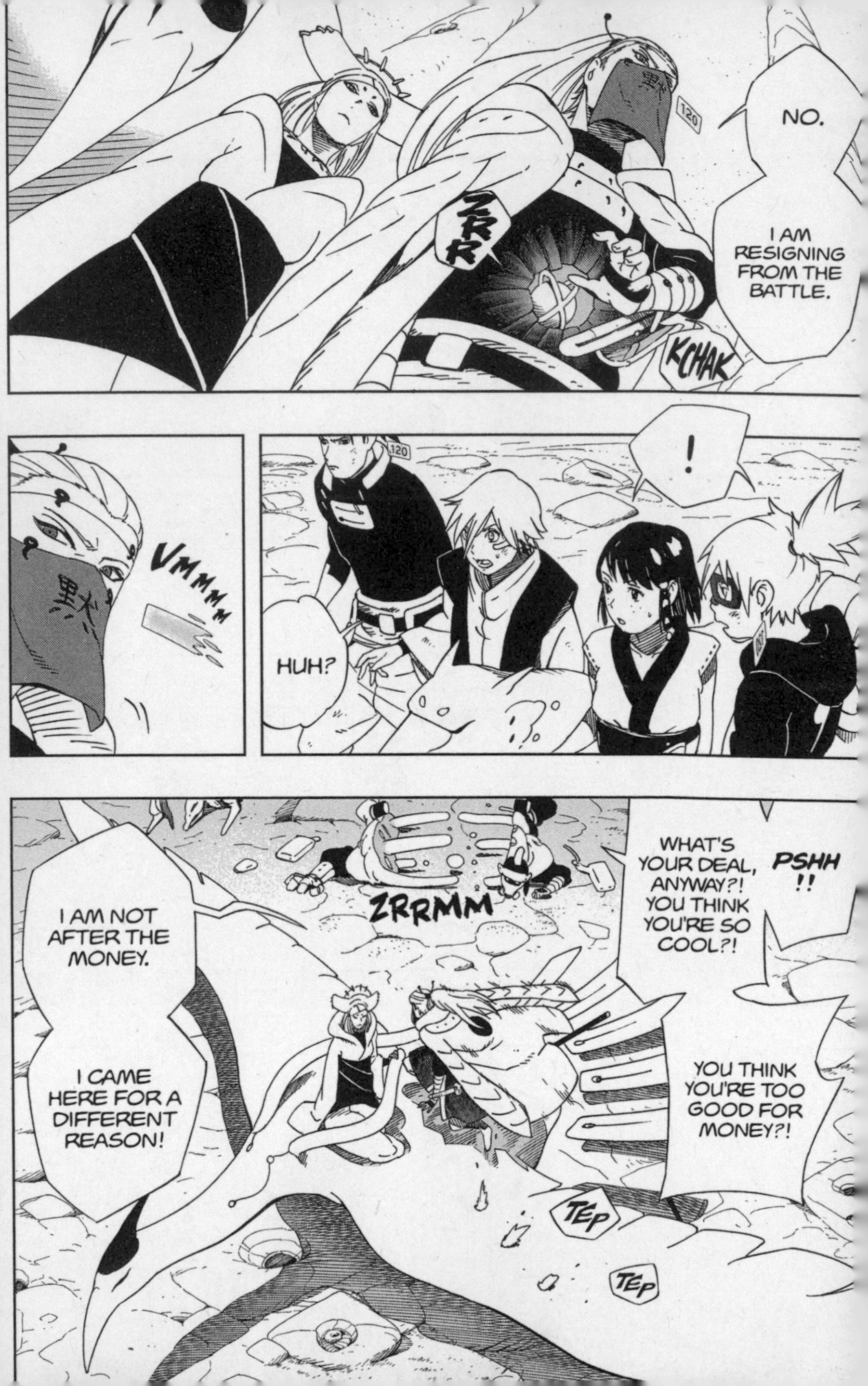
NO.
I AM RESIGNING FROM THE BATTLE.
ZRRR
KCHAK
!
HUH?
VMMMM
PSHH!!
WHAT'S YOUR DEAL, ANYWAY?! YOU THINK YOU'RE SO COOL?!
ZRRMM
I AM NOT AFTER THE MONEY.
YOU THINK YOU'RE TOO GOOD FOR MONEY?!
I CAME HERE FOR A DIFFERENT REASON!
TEP
TEP

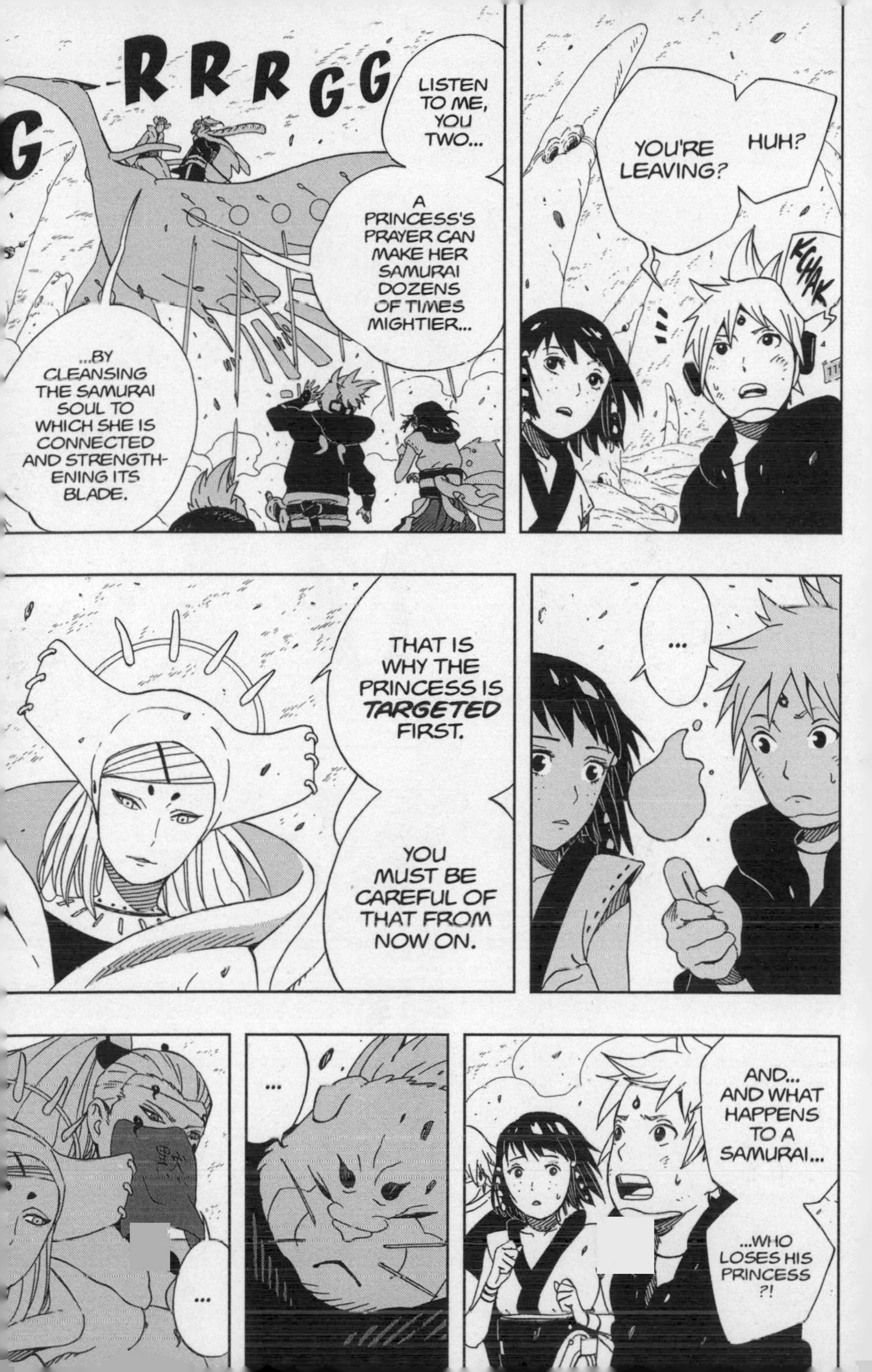
HUH?
YOU'RE LEAVING?
KCHAK
GRRRGG
LISTEN TO ME, YOU TWO...
A PRINCESS'S PRAYER CAN MAKE HER SAMURAI DOZENS OF TIMES MIGHTIER...
...BY CLEANSING THE SAMURAI SOUL TO WHICH SHE IS CONNECTED AND STRENGTHENING ITS BLADE.
...
THAT IS WHY THE PRINCESS IS *TARGETED* FIRST.
YOU MUST BE CAREFUL OF THAT FROM NOW ON.
AND... AND WHAT HAPPENS TO A SAMURAI...
...WHO LOSES HIS PRINCESS ?!
...
...

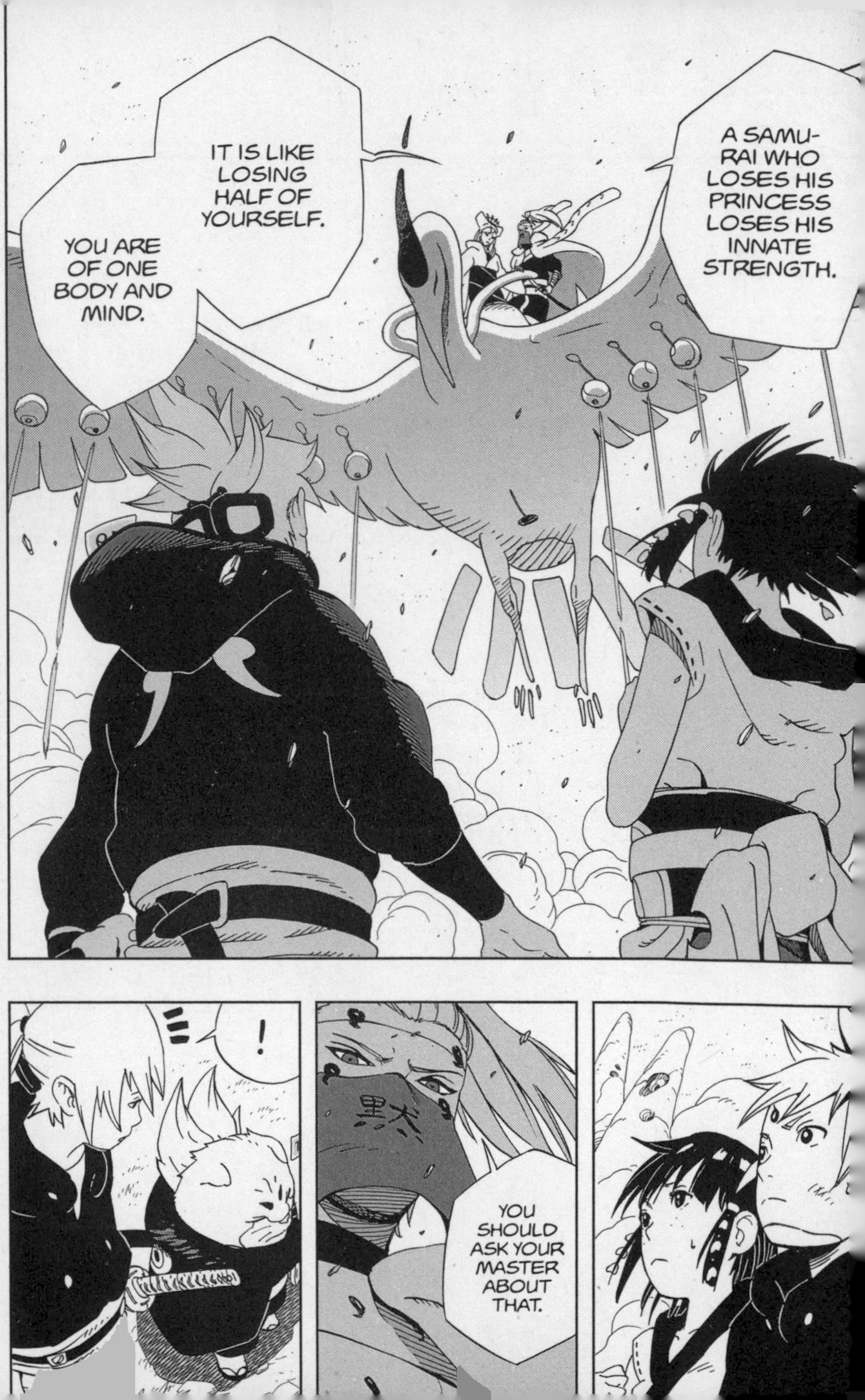
A SAMURAI WHO LOSES HIS PRINCESS LOSES HIS INNATE STRENGTH.
IT IS LIKE LOSING HALF OF YOURSELF.
YOU ARE OF ONE BODY AND MIND.
YOU SHOULD ASK YOUR MASTER ABOUT THAT.
!

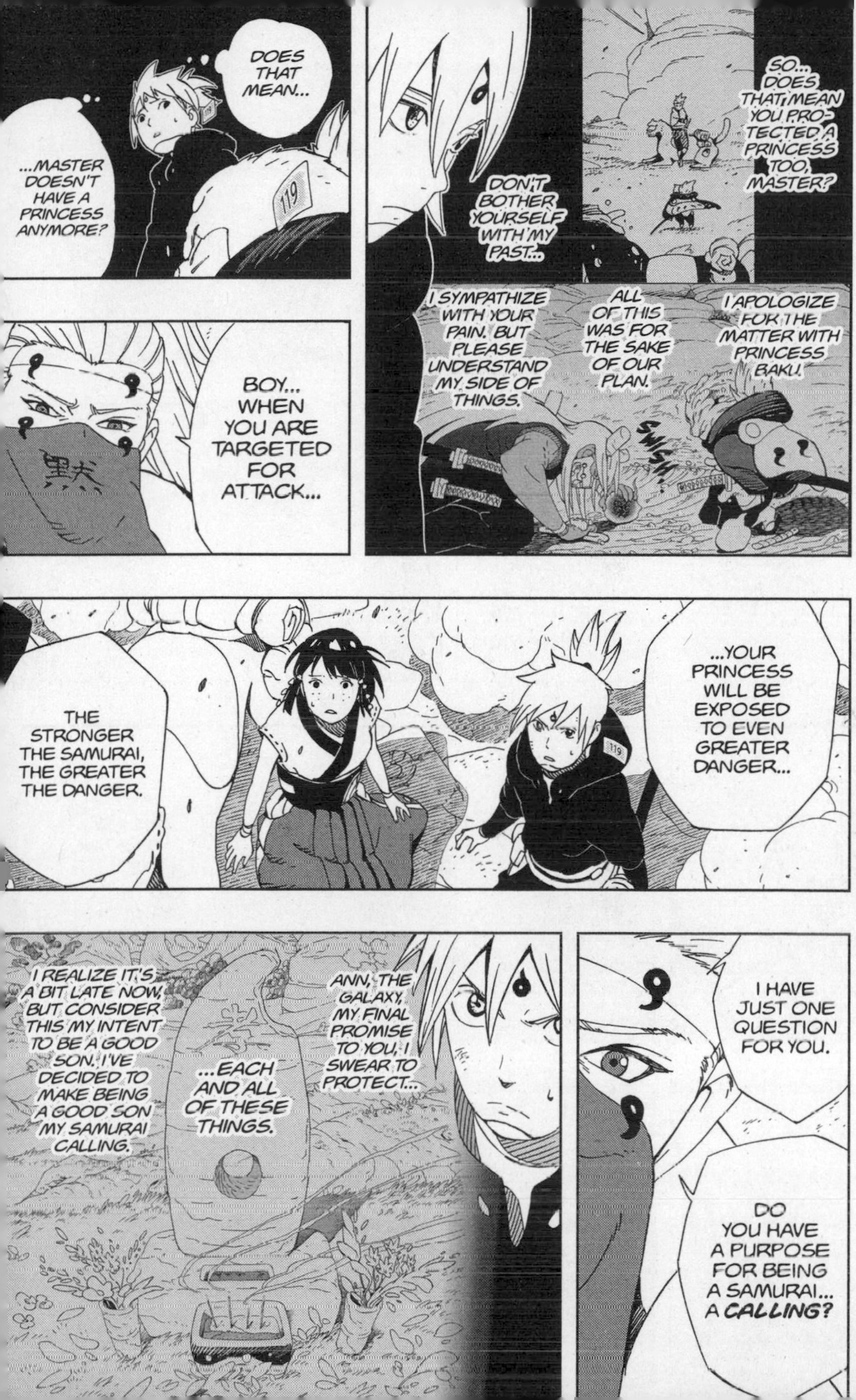
SO... DOES THAT MEAN YOU PROTECTED A PRINCESS TOO, MASTER?
DON'T BOTHER YOURSELF WITH MY PAST...
DOES THAT MEAN...
...MASTER DOESN'T HAVE A PRINCESS ANYMORE?
I APOLOGIZE FOR THE MATTER WITH PRINCESS BAKU.
ALL OF THIS WAS FOR THE SAKE OF OUR PLAN.
I SYMPATHIZE WITH YOUR PAIN. BUT PLEASE UNDERSTAND MY SIDE OF THINGS.
SWISH
BOY... WHEN YOU ARE TARGETED FOR ATTACK...
...YOUR PRINCESS WILL BE EXPOSED TO EVEN GREATER DANGER...
THE STRONGER THE SAMURAI, THE GREATER THE DANGER.
I HAVE JUST ONE QUESTION FOR YOU.
DO YOU HAVE A PURPOSE FOR BEING A SAMURAI... A CALLING?
ANN, THE GALAXY, MY FINAL PROMISE TO YOU, I SWEAR TO PROTECT...
...EACH AND ALL OF THESE THINGS.
I REALIZE IT'S A BIT LATE NOW, BUT CONSIDER THIS MY INTENT TO BE A GOOD SON. I'VE DECIDED TO MAKE BEING A GOOD SON MY SAMURAI CALLING.

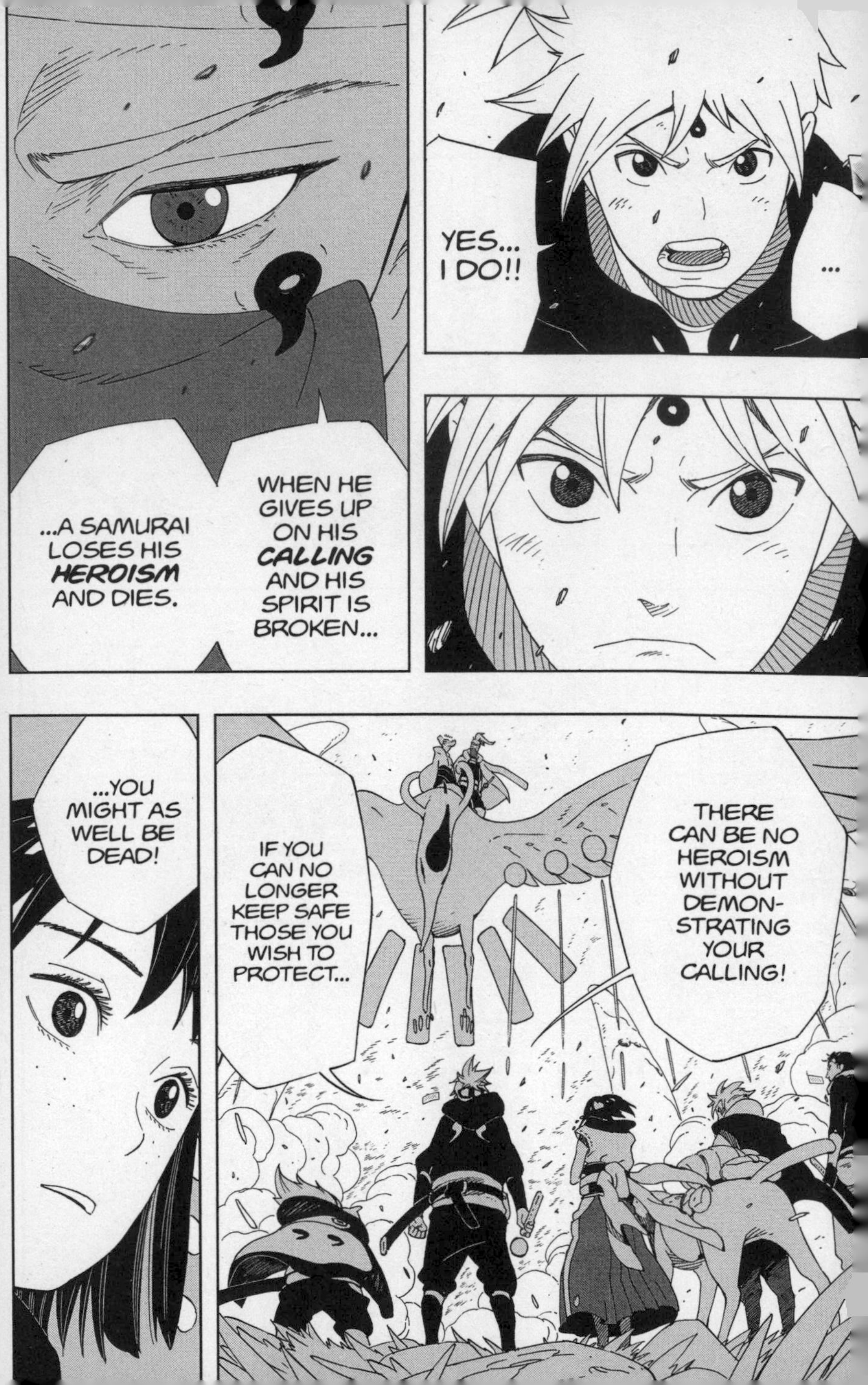
...
YES... I DO!!
WHEN HE GIVES UP ON HIS *CALLING* AND HIS SPIRIT IS BROKEN...
...A SAMURAI LOSES HIS *HEROISM* AND DIES.
THERE CAN BE NO HEROISM WITHOUT DEMON-STRATING YOUR CALLING!
IF YOU CAN NO LONGER KEEP SAFE THOSE YOU WISH TO PROTECT...
...YOU MIGHT AS WELL BE DEAD!

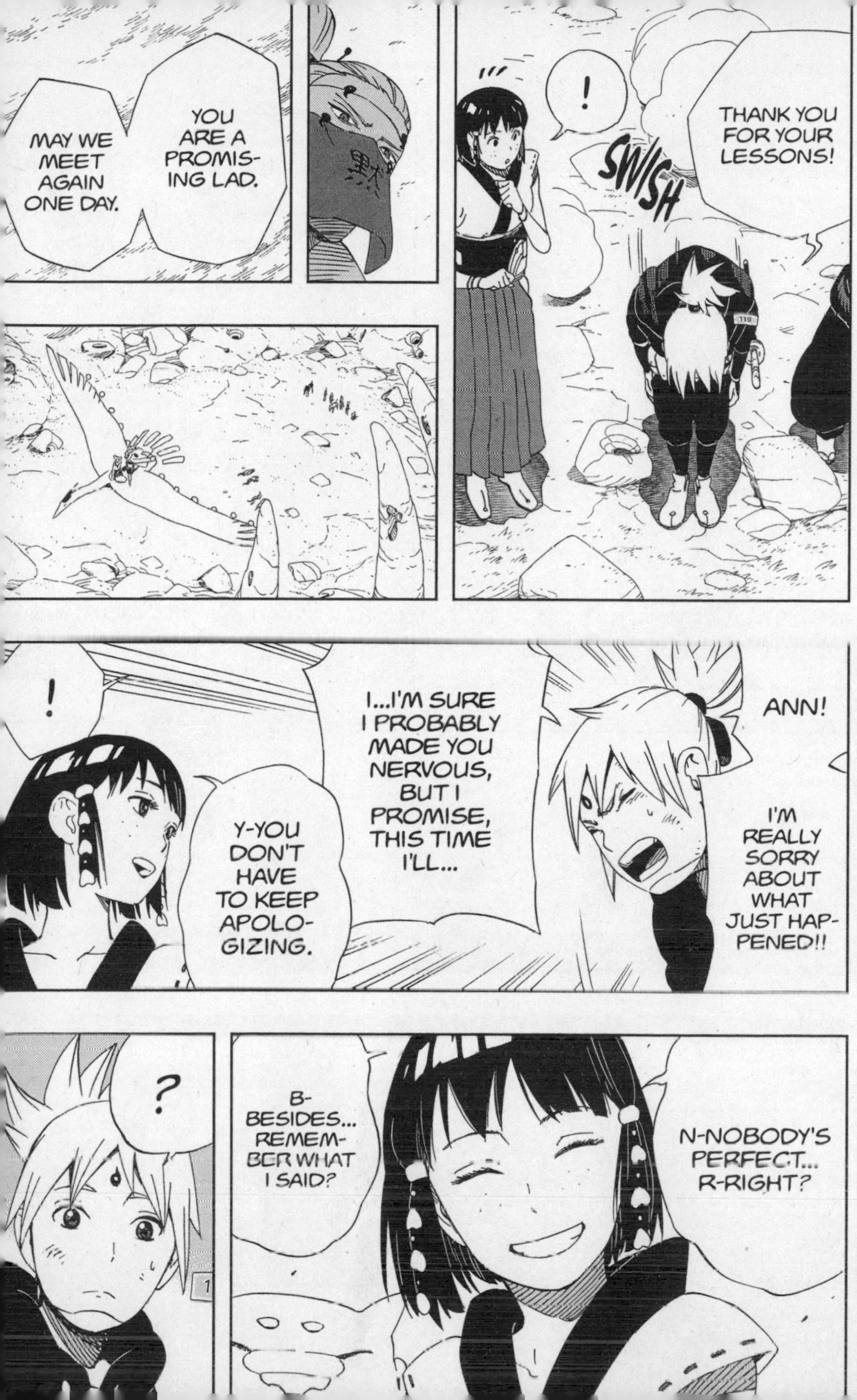
THANK YOU FOR YOUR LESSONS!
SWISH
!
YOU ARE A PROMISING LAD.
MAY WE MEET AGAIN ONE DAY.
ANN!
I'M REALLY SORRY ABOUT WHAT JUST HAPPENED!!
I...I'M SURE I PROBABLY MADE YOU NERVOUS, BUT I PROMISE, THIS TIME I'LL...
!
Y-YOU DON'T HAVE TO KEEP APOLOGIZING.
N-NOBODY'S PERFECT... R-RIGHT?
B-BESIDES... REMEMBER WHAT I SAID?
?

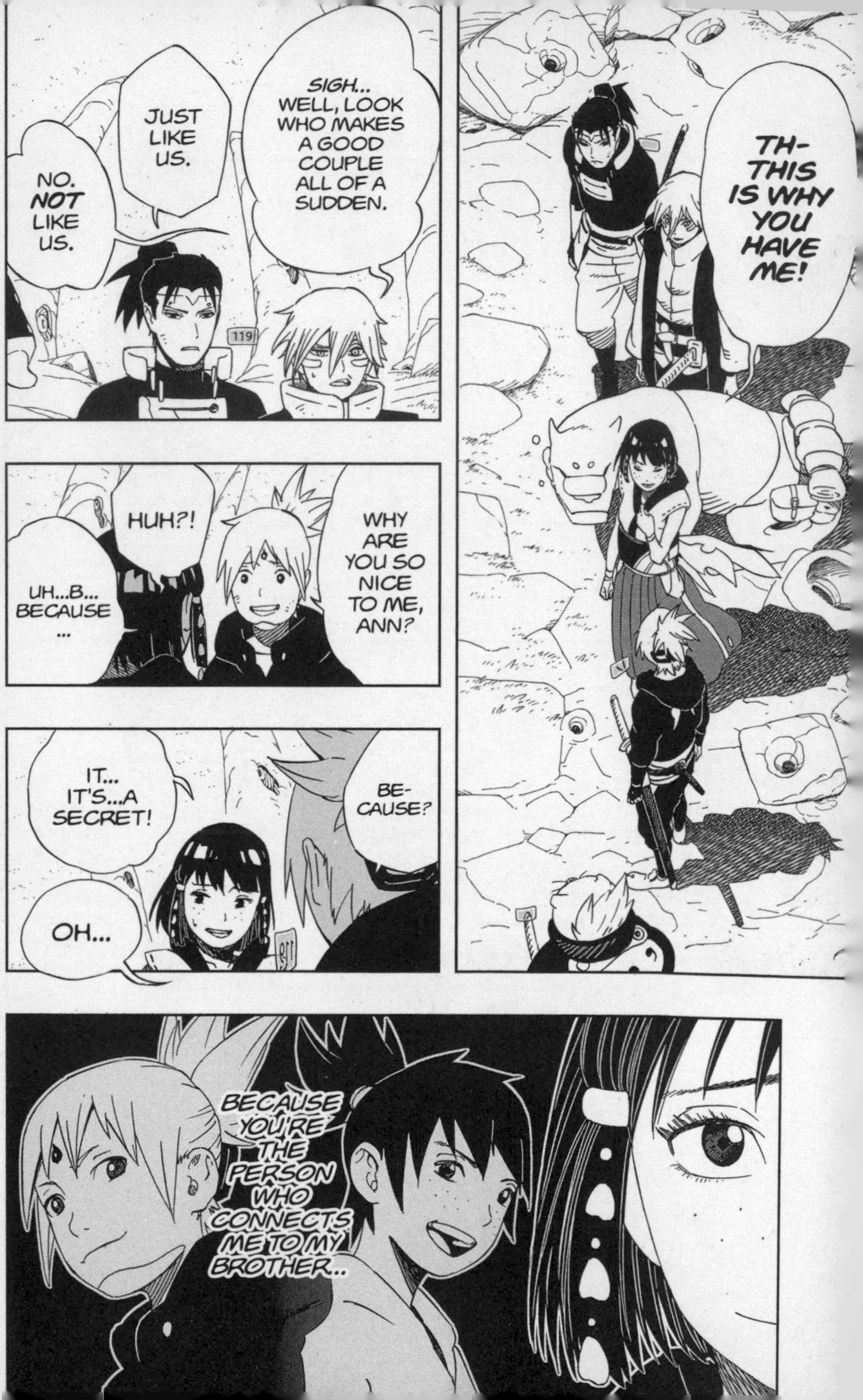
TH- THIS IS WHY YOU HAVE ME!
SIGH... WELL, LOOK WHO MAKES A GOOD COUPLE ALL OF A SUDDEN.
JUST LIKE US.
NO. NOT LIKE US.
WHY ARE YOU SO NICE TO ME, ANN?
HUH?!
UH...B... BECAUSE ...
BE- CAUSE?
IT... IT'S...A SECRET!
OH...
BECAUSE YOU'RE THE PERSON WHO CONNECTS ME TO MY BROTHER...

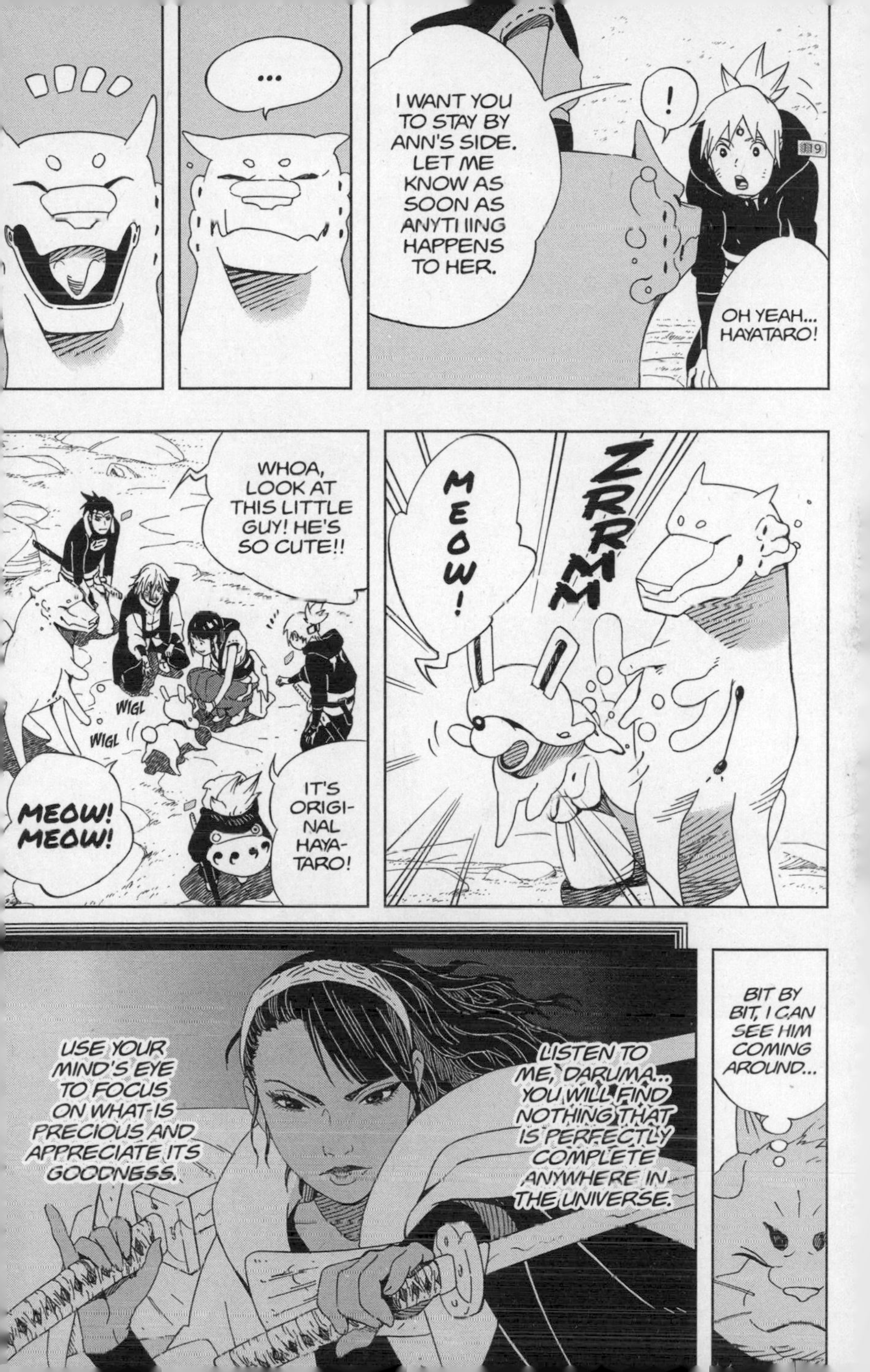
I WANT YOU TO STAY BY ANN'S SIDE. LET ME KNOW AS SOON AS ANYTHING HAPPENS TO HER.
!
OH YEAH... HAYATARO!
...
ZRRMM
MEOW!
WHOA, LOOK AT THIS LITTLE GUY! HE'S SO CUTE!!
IT'S ORIGINAL HAYATARO!
WIGL
WIGL
MEOW! MEOW!
BIT BY BIT, I CAN SEE HIM COMING AROUND...
LISTEN TO ME, DARUMA... YOU WILL FIND NOTHING THAT IS PERFECTLY COMPLETE ANYWHERE IN THE UNIVERSE.
USE YOUR MIND'S EYE TO FOCUS ON WHAT IS PRECIOUS AND APPRECIATE ITS GOODNESS.

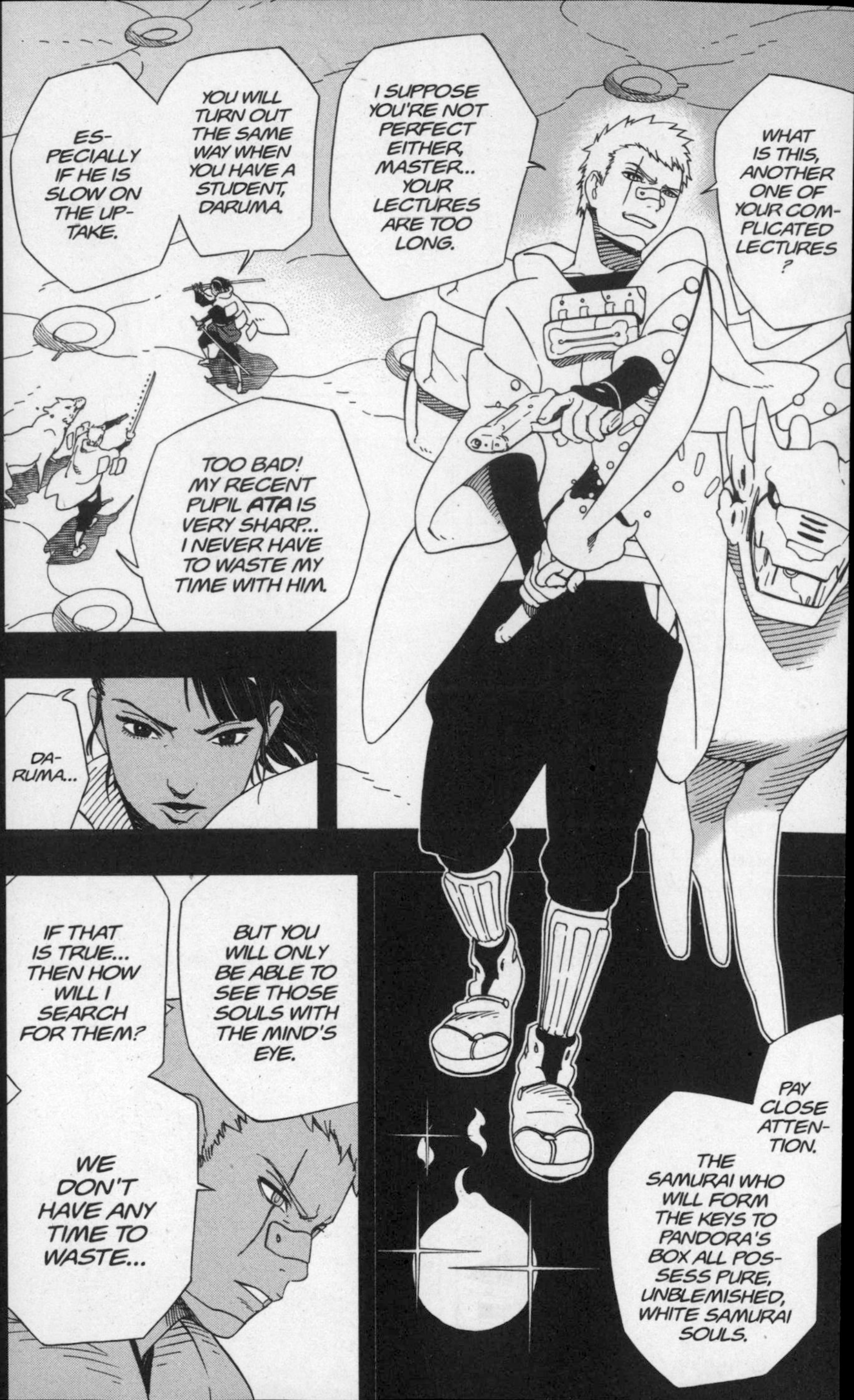
WHAT IS THIS, ANOTHER ONE OF YOUR COMPLICATED LECTURES?
I SUPPOSE YOU'RE NOT PERFECT EITHER, MASTER... YOUR LECTURES ARE TOO LONG.
YOU WILL TURN OUT THE SAME WAY WHEN YOU HAVE A STUDENT, DARUMA.
ESPECIALLY IF HE IS SLOW ON THE UPTAKE.
TOO BAD! MY RECENT PUPIL ATA IS VERY SHARP... I NEVER HAVE TO WASTE MY TIME WITH HIM.
DARUMA...
PAY CLOSE ATTENTION.
THE SAMURAI WHO WILL FORM THE KEYS TO PANDORA'S BOX ALL POSSESS PURE, UNBLEMISHED, WHITE SAMURAI SOULS.
IF THAT IS TRUE... THEN HOW WILL I SEARCH FOR THEM?
BUT YOU WILL ONLY BE ABLE TO SEE THOSE SOULS WITH THE MIND'S EYE.
WE DON'T HAVE ANY TIME TO WASTE...

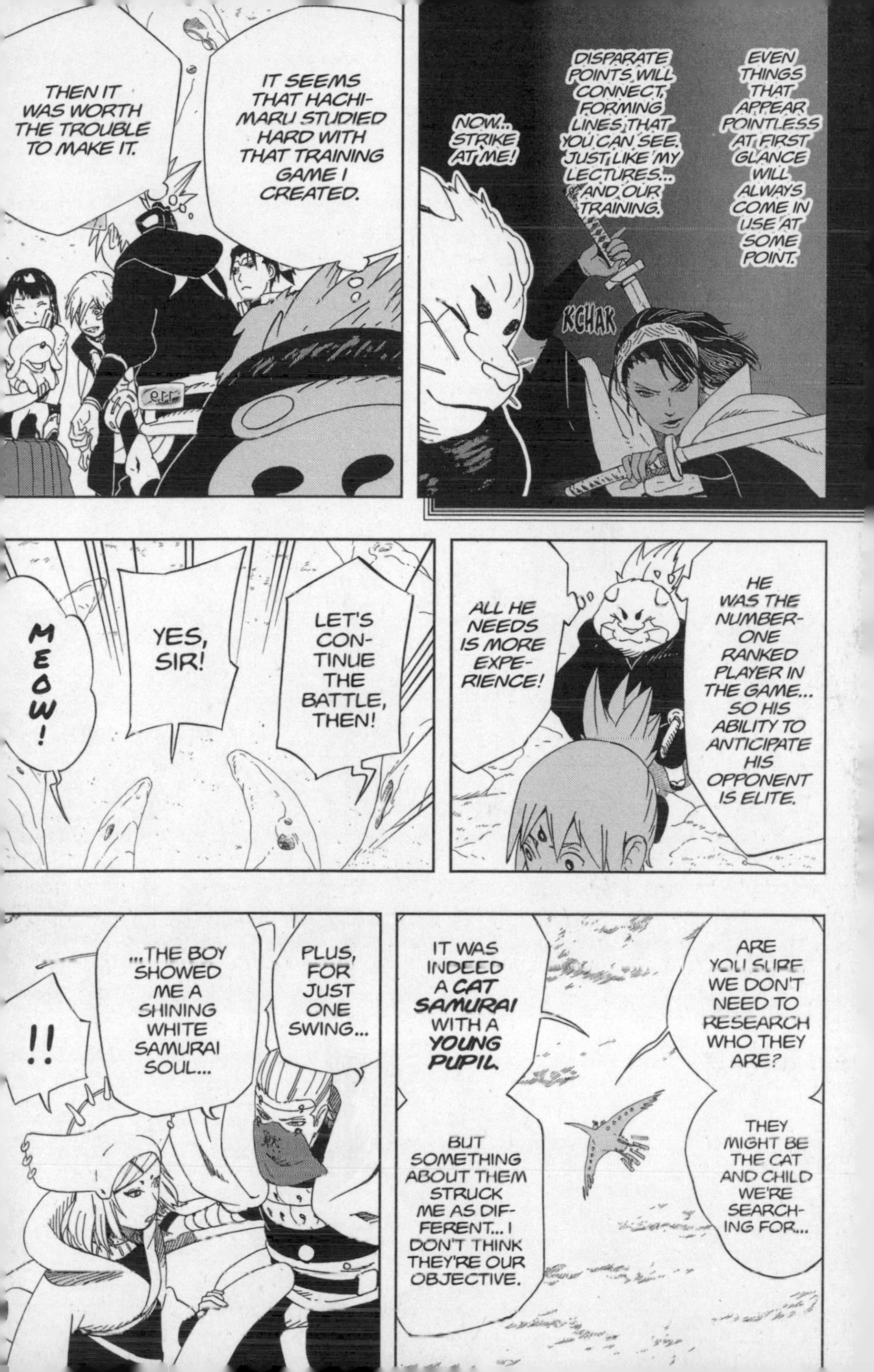
EVEN THINGS THAT APPEAR POINTLESS AT FIRST GLANCE WILL ALWAYS COME IN USE AT SOME POINT.
DISPARATE POINTS WILL CONNECT, FORMING LINES THAT YOU CAN SEE. JUST LIKE MY LECTURES... AND OUR TRAINING.
NOW... STRIKE AT ME!
KCHAK
IT SEEMS THAT HACHI-MARU STUDIED HARD WITH THAT TRAINING GAME I CREATED.
THEN IT WAS WORTH THE TROUBLE TO MAKE IT.
HE WAS THE NUMBER-ONE RANKED PLAYER IN THE GAME... SO HIS ABILITY TO ANTICIPATE HIS OPPONENT IS ELITE.
ALL HE NEEDS IS MORE EXPE-RIENCE!
LET'S CON-TINUE THE BATTLE, THEN!
YES, SIR!
MEOW!
ARE YOU SURE WE DON'T NEED TO RESEARCH WHO THEY ARE?
IT WAS INDEED A **CAT SAMURAI** WITH A **YOUNG PUPIL.**
THEY MIGHT BE THE CAT AND CHILD WE'RE SEARCH-ING FOR...
BUT SOMETHING ABOUT THEM STRUCK ME AS DIF-FERENT... I DON'T THINK THEY'RE OUR OBJECTIVE.
PLUS, FOR JUST ONE SWING...
...THE BOY SHOWED ME A SHINING WHITE SAMURAI SOUL...
!!

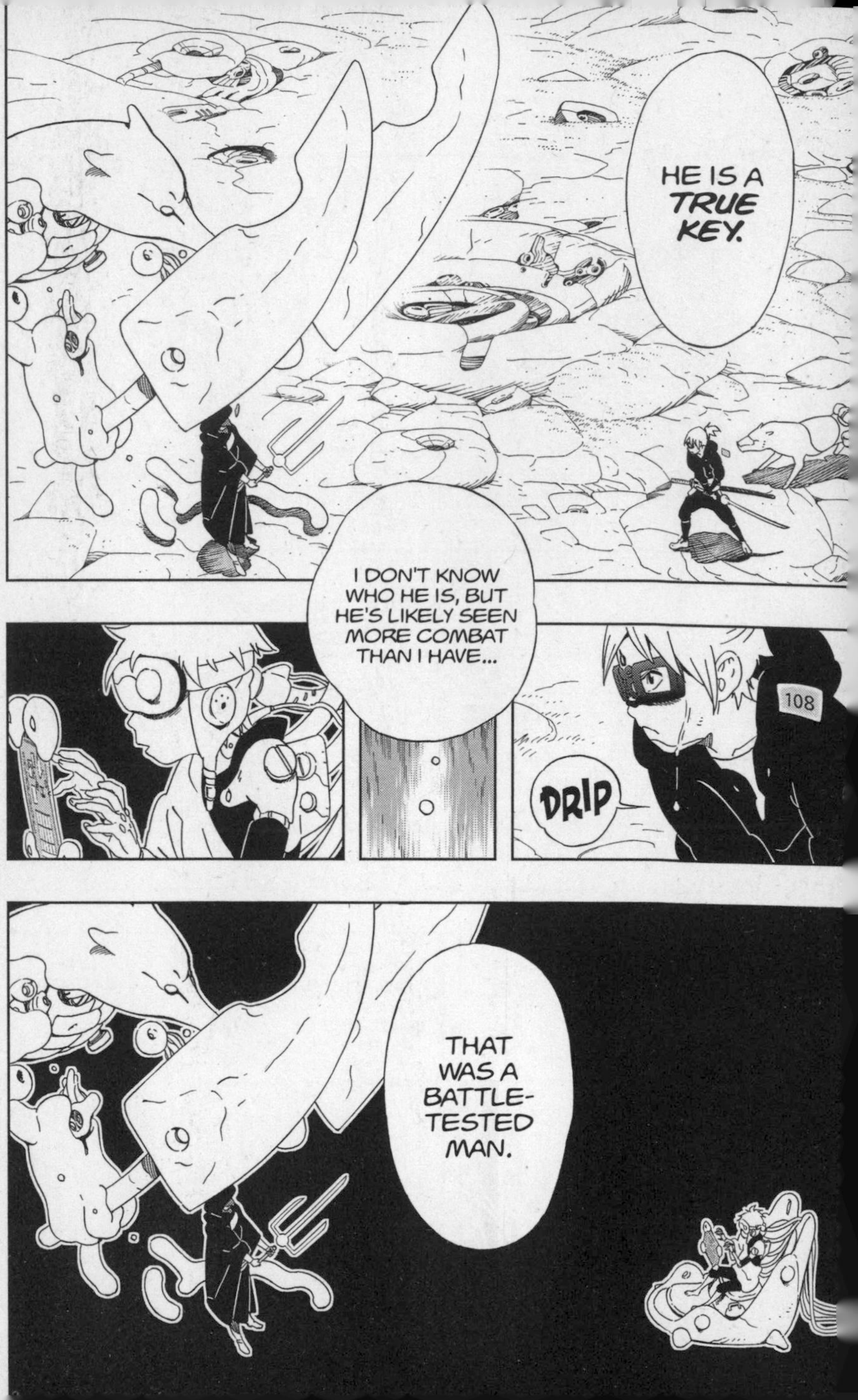
HE IS A TRUE KEY.
108
DRIP
I DON'T KNOW WHO HE IS, BUT HE'S LIKELY SEEN MORE COMBAT THAN I HAVE...
THAT WAS A BATTLE-TESTED MAN.

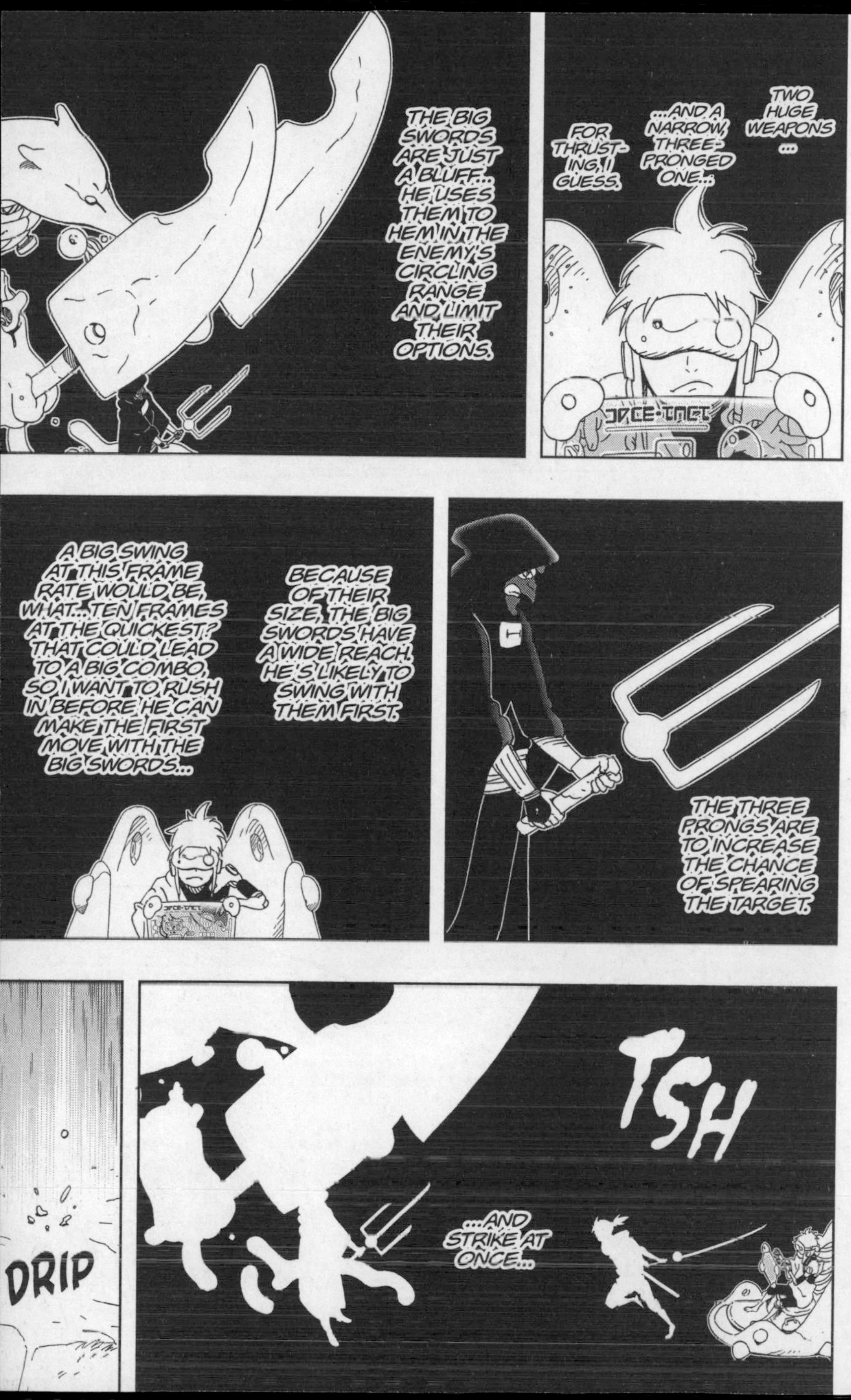
TWO HUGE WEAPONS...
...AND A NARROW, THREE-PRONGED ONE...
FOR THRUSTING, I GUESS.
THE BIG SWORDS ARE JUST A BLUFF... HE USES THEM TO HEM IN THE ENEMY'S CIRCLING RANGE AND LIMIT THEIR OPTIONS.
THE THREE PRONGS ARE TO INCREASE THE CHANCE OF SPEARING THE TARGET.
BECAUSE OF THEIR SIZE, THE BIG SWORDS HAVE A WIDE REACH. HE'S LIKELY TO SWING WITH THEM FIRST.
A BIG SWING AT THIS FRAME RATE WOULD BE, WHAT... TEN FRAMES AT THE QUICKEST? THAT COULD LEAD TO A BIG COMBO, SO I WANT TO RUSH IN BEFORE HE CAN MAKE THE FIRST MOVE WITH THE BIG SWORDS...
TSH
...AND STRIKE AT ONCE...
DRIP

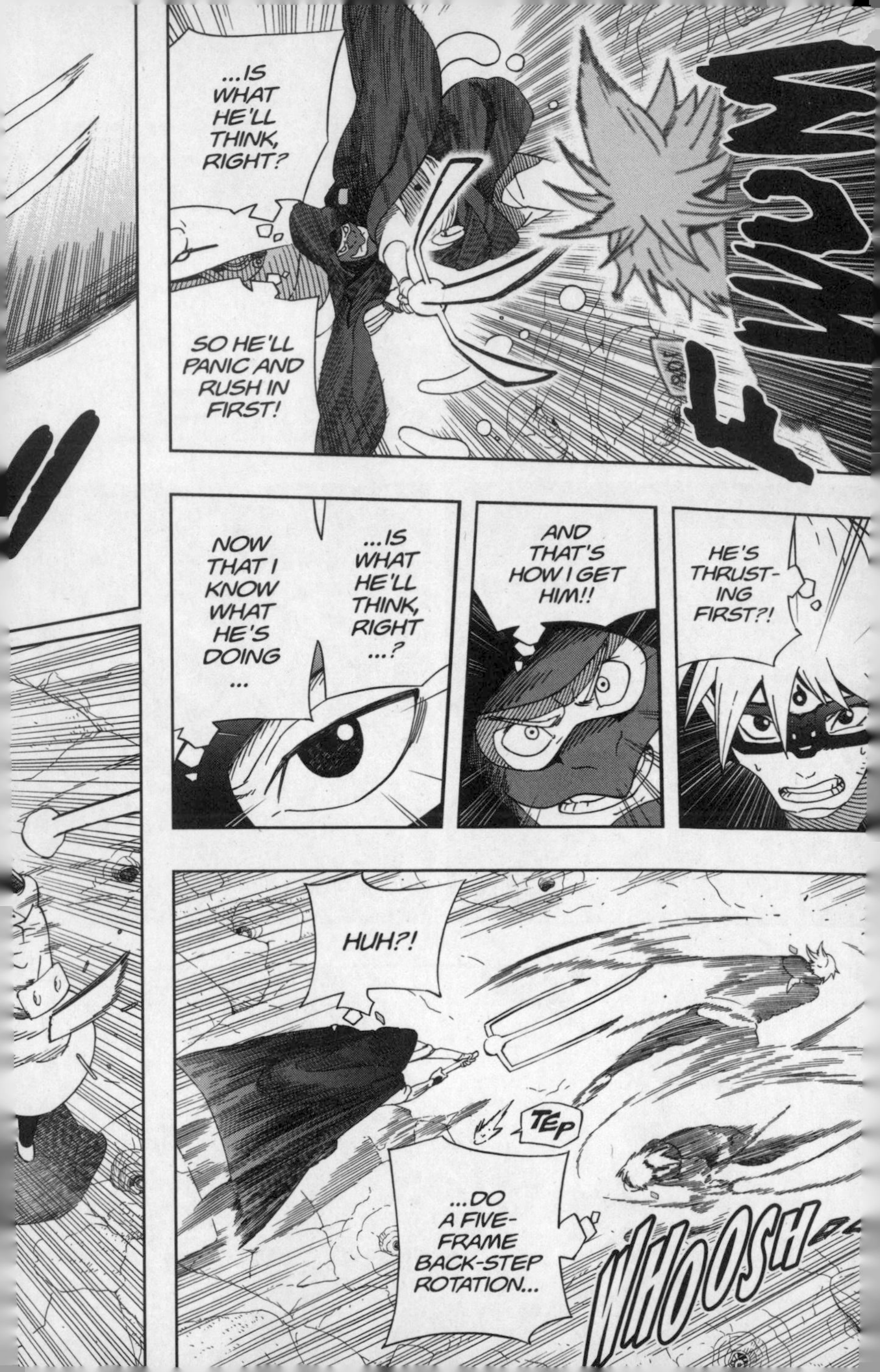
...IS WHAT HE'LL THINK, RIGHT?
SO HE'LL PANIC AND RUSH IN FIRST!
HE'S THRUST-ING FIRST?!
AND THAT'S HOW I GET HIM!!
...IS WHAT HE'LL THINK, RIGHT ...?
NOW THAT I KNOW WHAT HE'S DOING ...
HUH?!
TEP
...DO A FIVE-FRAME BACK-STEP ROTATION...
WHOOSH

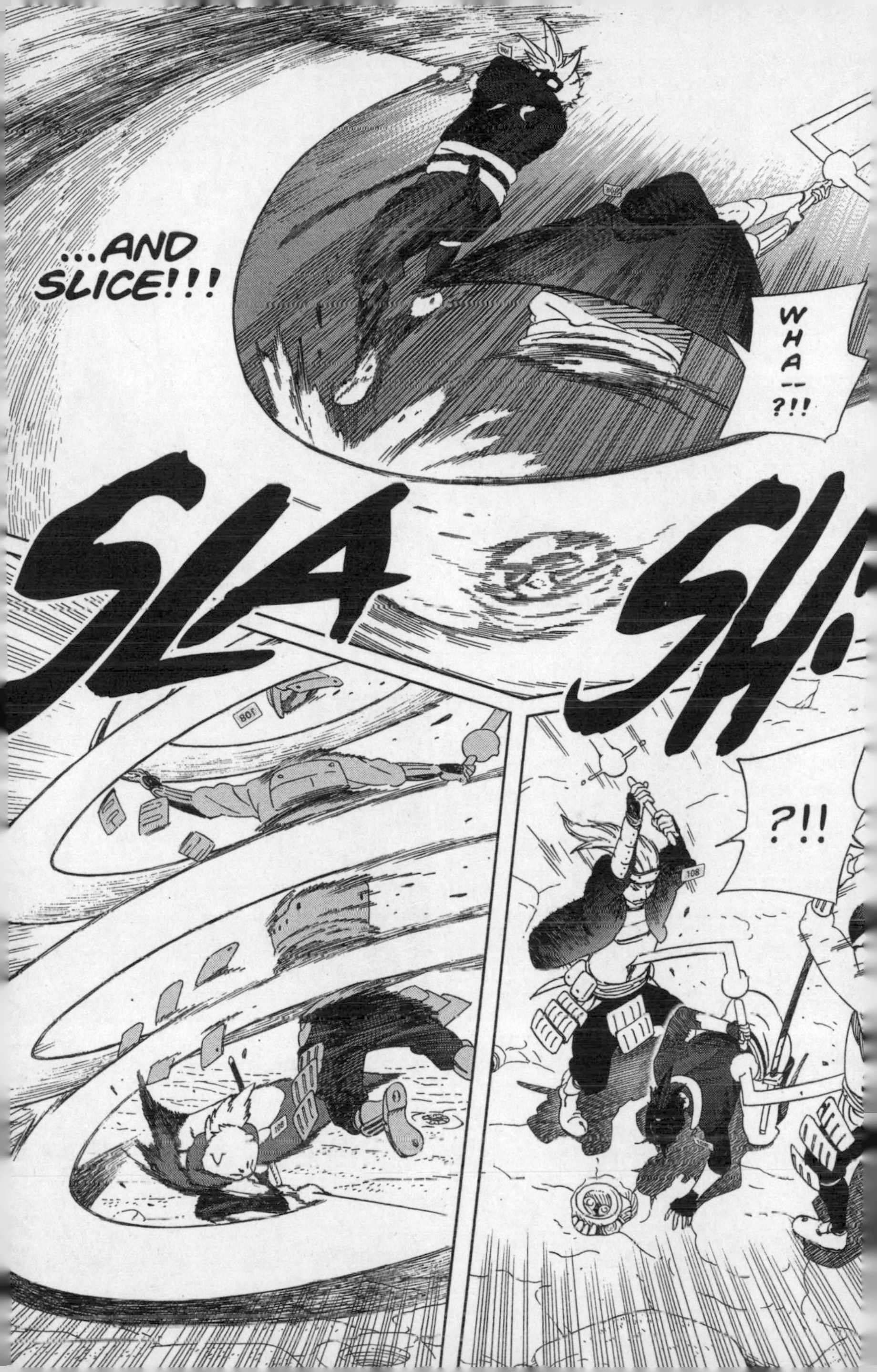
WHA--?!!
...AND SLICE!!!
SLA
SH
?!!

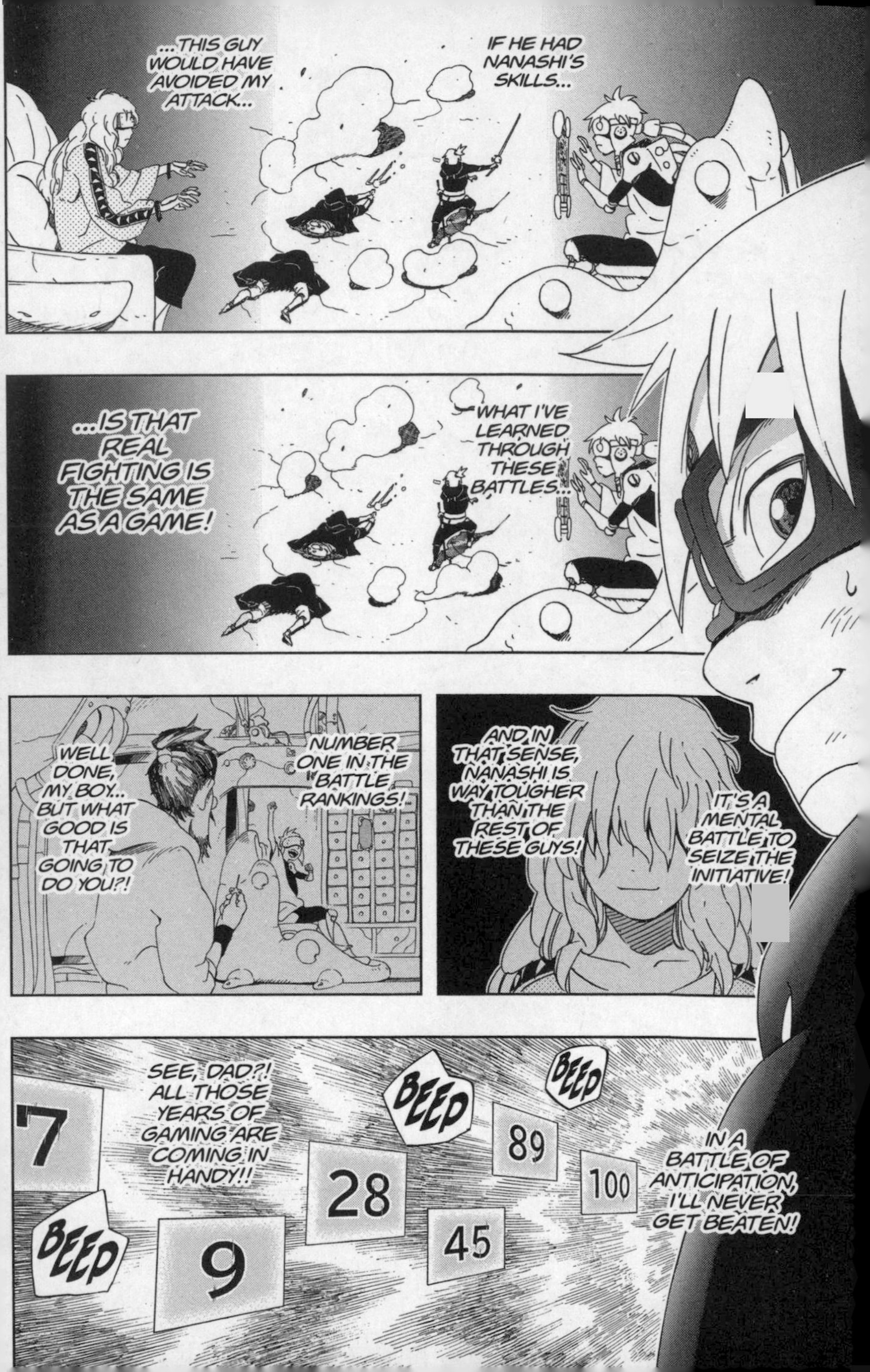
IF HE HAD NANASHI'S SKILLS...
...THIS GUY WOULD HAVE AVOIDED MY ATTACK...
WHAT I'VE LEARNED THROUGH THESE BATTLES...
...IS THAT REAL FIGHTING IS THE SAME AS A GAME!
AND IN THAT SENSE, NANASHI IS WAY TOUGHER THAN THE REST OF THESE GUYS!
IT'S A MENTAL BATTLE TO SEIZE THE INITIATIVE!
NUMBER ONE IN THE BATTLE RANKINGS!
WELL DONE, MY BOY... BUT WHAT GOOD IS THAT GOING TO DO YOU?!
IN A BATTLE OF ANTICIPATION, I'LL NEVER GET BEATEN!
BEEP
BEEP
SEE, DAD?! ALL THOSE YEARS OF GAMING ARE COMING IN HANDY!!
BEEP
100
89
45
28
9
7

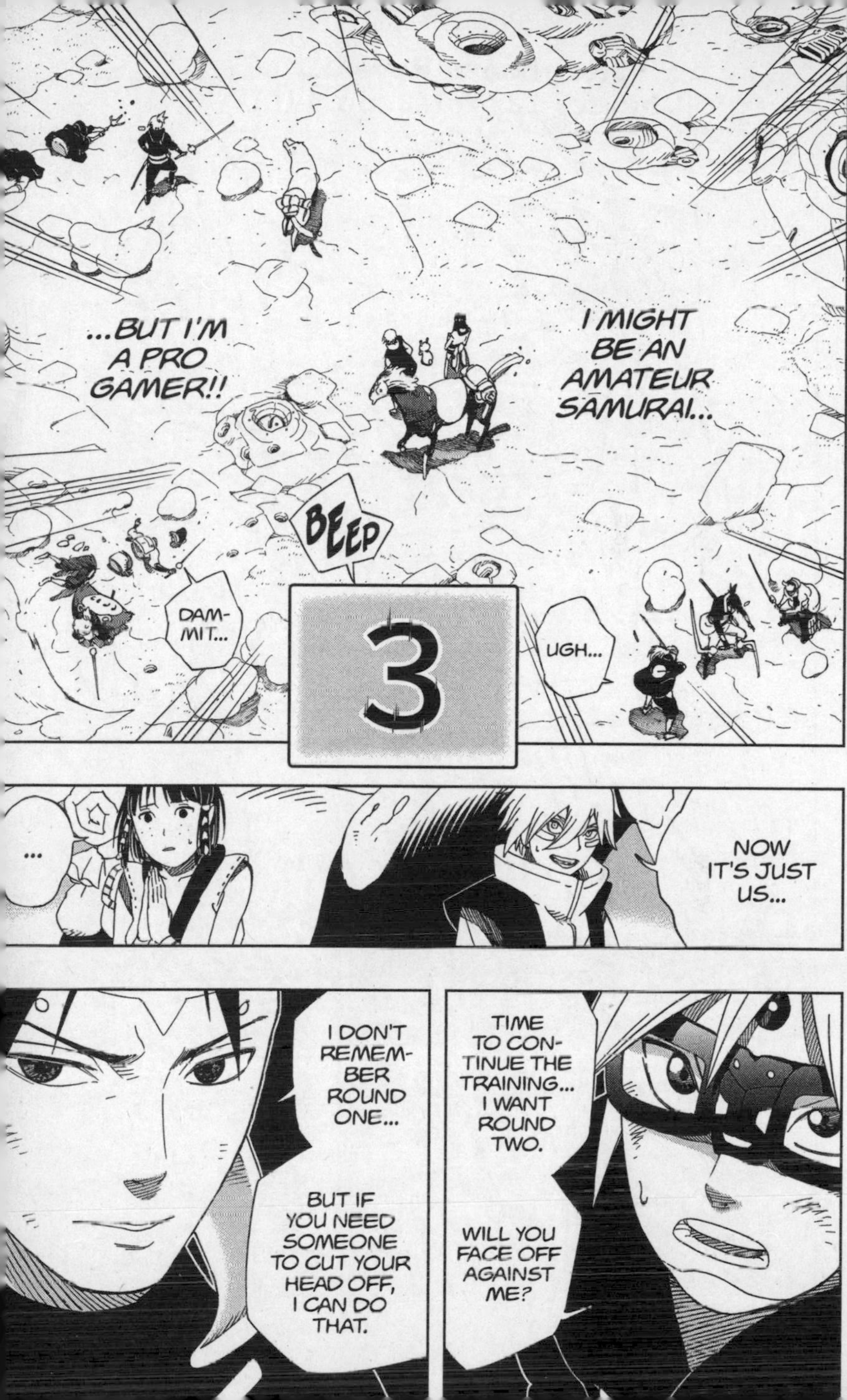
I MIGHT BE AN AMATEUR SAMURAI...
...BUT I'M A PRO GAMER!!
BEEP
3
UGH...
DAM-MIT...
NOW IT'S JUST US...
...
TIME TO CON-TINUE THE TRAINING... I WANT ROUND TWO.
WILL YOU FACE OFF AGAINST ME?
I DON'T REMEM-BER ROUND ONE...
BUT IF YOU NEED SOMEONE TO CUT YOUR HEAD OFF, I CAN DO THAT.

Storyboard Reveal!
Chapter 12 (Vol. 2, pg. 116)

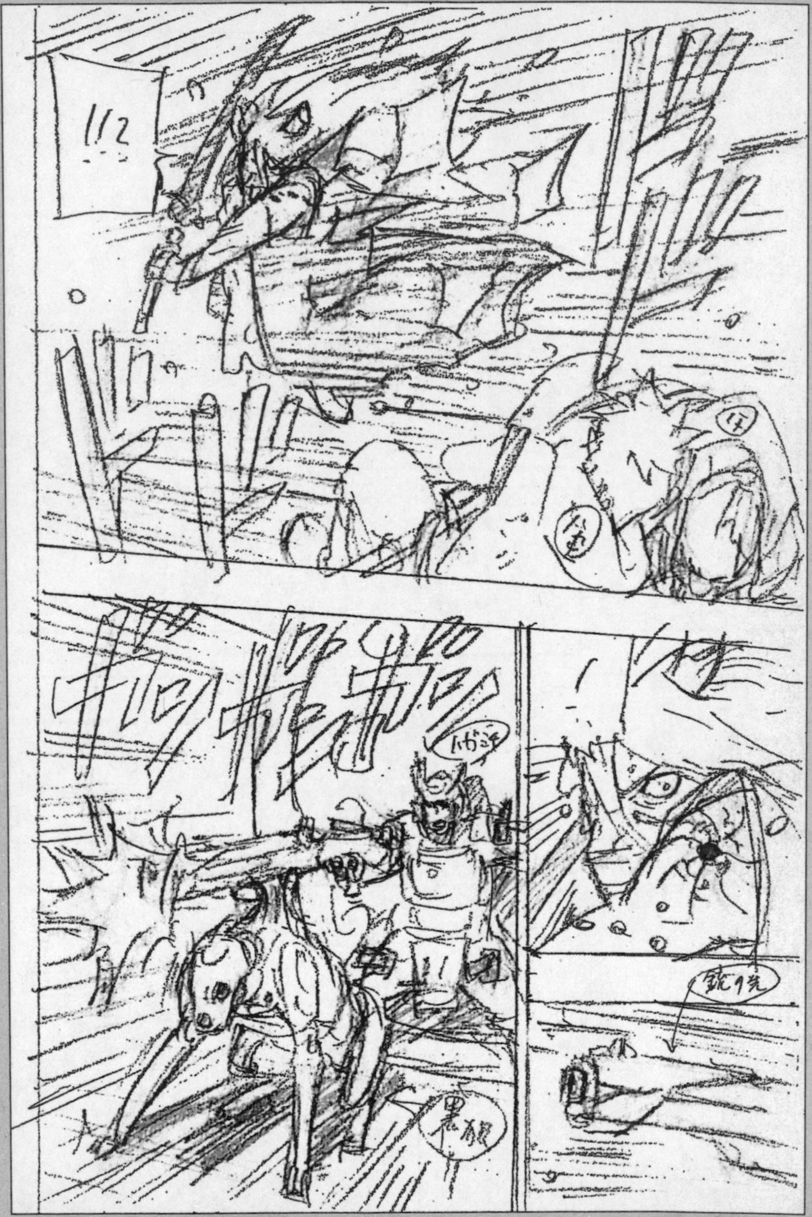

CHAPTER 24: HACHIMARU VS. RYU, REMATCH!!

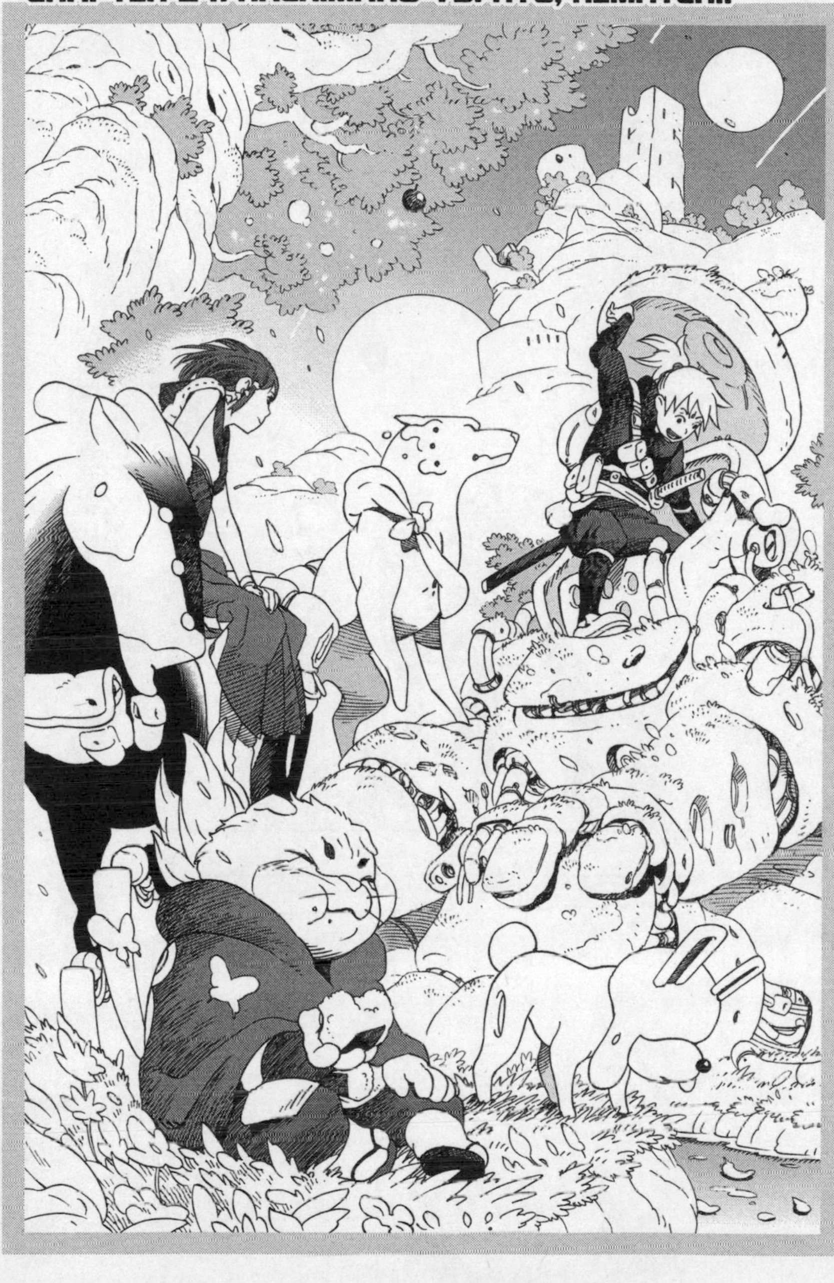

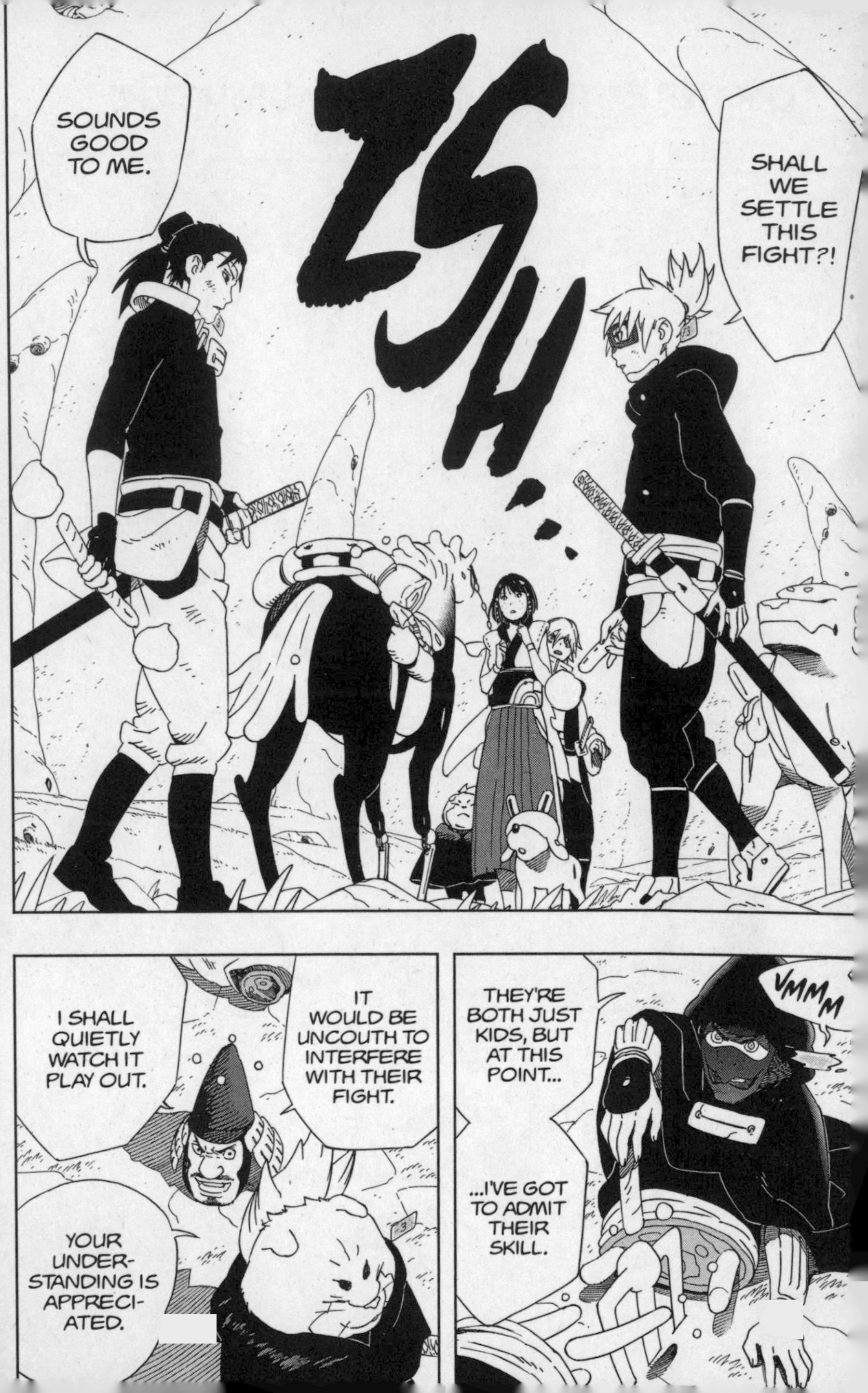
SHALL WE SETTLE THIS FIGHT?!
ZSH
SOUNDS GOOD TO ME.
VMMM
THEY'RE BOTH JUST KIDS, BUT AT THIS POINT...
...I'VE GOT TO ADMIT THEIR SKILL.
IT WOULD BE UNCOUTH TO INTERFERE WITH THEIR FIGHT.
I SHALL QUIETLY WATCH IT PLAY OUT.
YOUR UNDER-STANDING IS APPRECI-ATED.

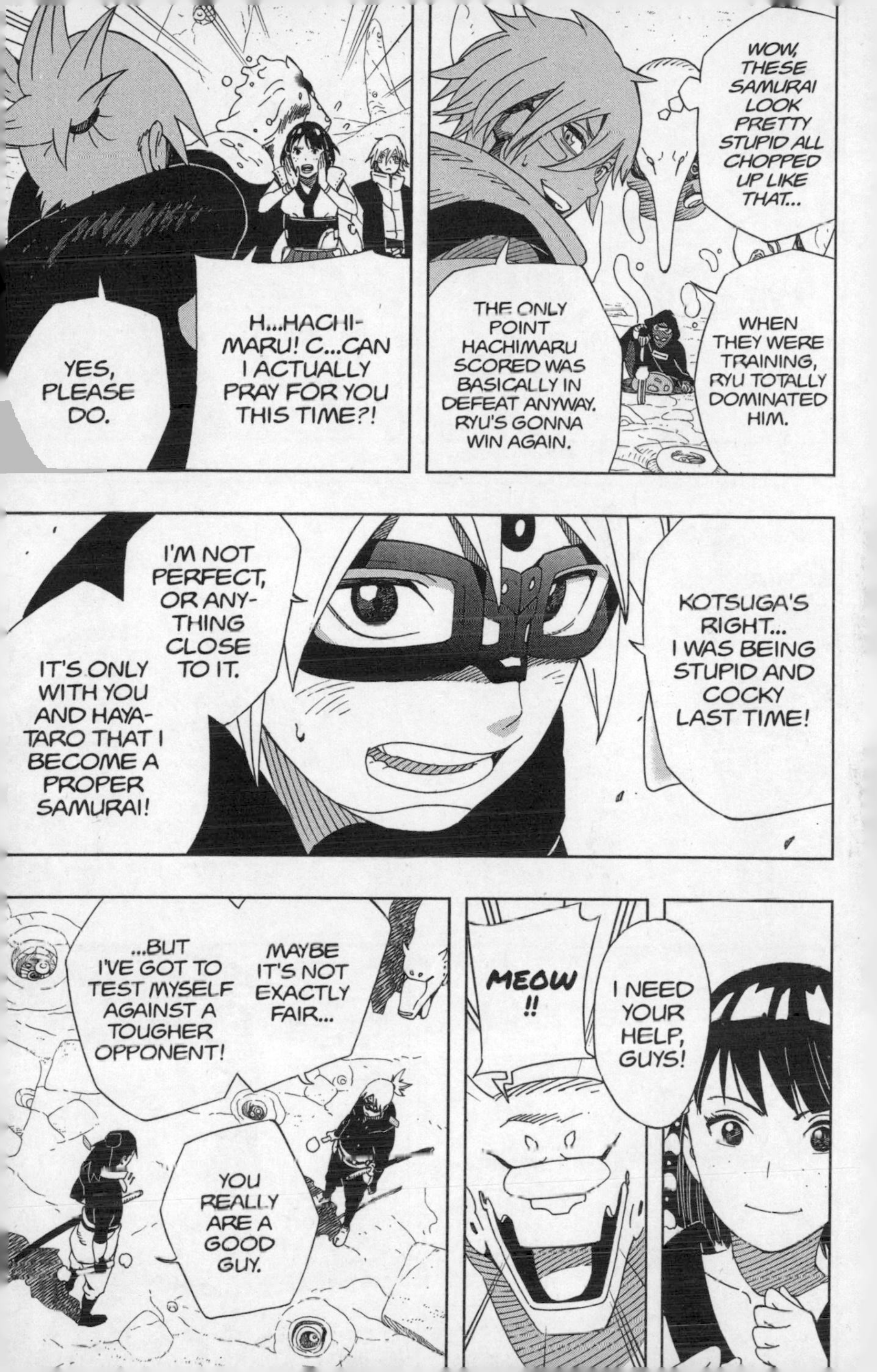
WOW, THESE SAMURAI LOOK PRETTY STUPID ALL CHOPPED UP LIKE THAT...
WHEN THEY WERE TRAINING, RYU TOTALLY DOMINATED HIM.
THE ONLY POINT HACHIMARU SCORED WAS BASICALLY IN DEFEAT ANYWAY. RYU'S GONNA WIN AGAIN.
H...HACHI-MARU! C...CAN I ACTUALLY PRAY FOR YOU THIS TIME?!
YES, PLEASE DO.
KOTSUGA'S RIGHT... I WAS BEING STUPID AND COCKY LAST TIME!
I'M NOT PERFECT, OR ANY-THING CLOSE TO IT.
IT'S ONLY WITH YOU AND HAYA-TARO THAT I BECOME A PROPER SAMURAI!
I NEED YOUR HELP, GUYS!
MEOW !!
MAYBE IT'S NOT EXACTLY FAIR...
...BUT I'VE GOT TO TEST MYSELF AGAINST A TOUGHER OPPONENT!
YOU REALLY ARE A GOOD GUY.

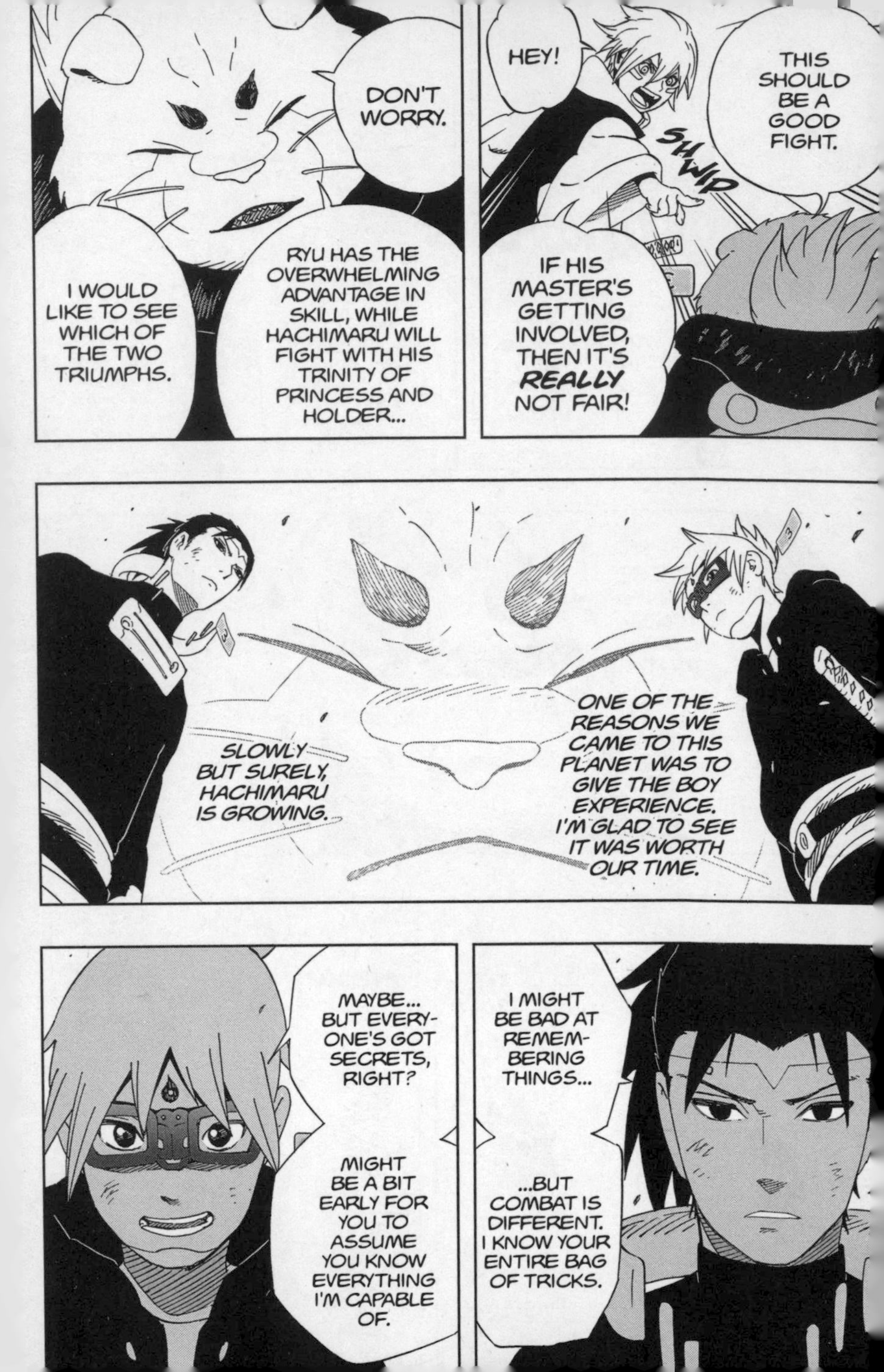
THIS SHOULD BE A GOOD FIGHT.
HEY!
SHWIP
IF HIS MASTER'S GETTING INVOLVED, THEN IT'S *REALLY* NOT FAIR!
DON'T WORRY.
RYU HAS THE OVERWHELMING ADVANTAGE IN SKILL, WHILE HACHIMARU WILL FIGHT WITH HIS TRINITY OF PRINCESS AND HOLDER...
I WOULD LIKE TO SEE WHICH OF THE TWO TRIUMPHS.
ONE OF THE REASONS WE CAME TO THIS PLANET WAS TO GIVE THE BOY EXPERIENCE. I'M GLAD TO SEE IT WAS WORTH OUR TIME.
SLOWLY BUT SURELY, HACHIMARU IS GROWING.
I MIGHT BE BAD AT REMEM-BERING THINGS...
...BUT COMBAT IS DIFFERENT. I KNOW YOUR ENTIRE BAG OF TRICKS.
MAYBE... BUT EVERY-ONE'S GOT SECRETS, RIGHT?
MIGHT BE A BIT EARLY FOR YOU TO ASSUME YOU KNOW EVERYTHING I'M CAPABLE OF.

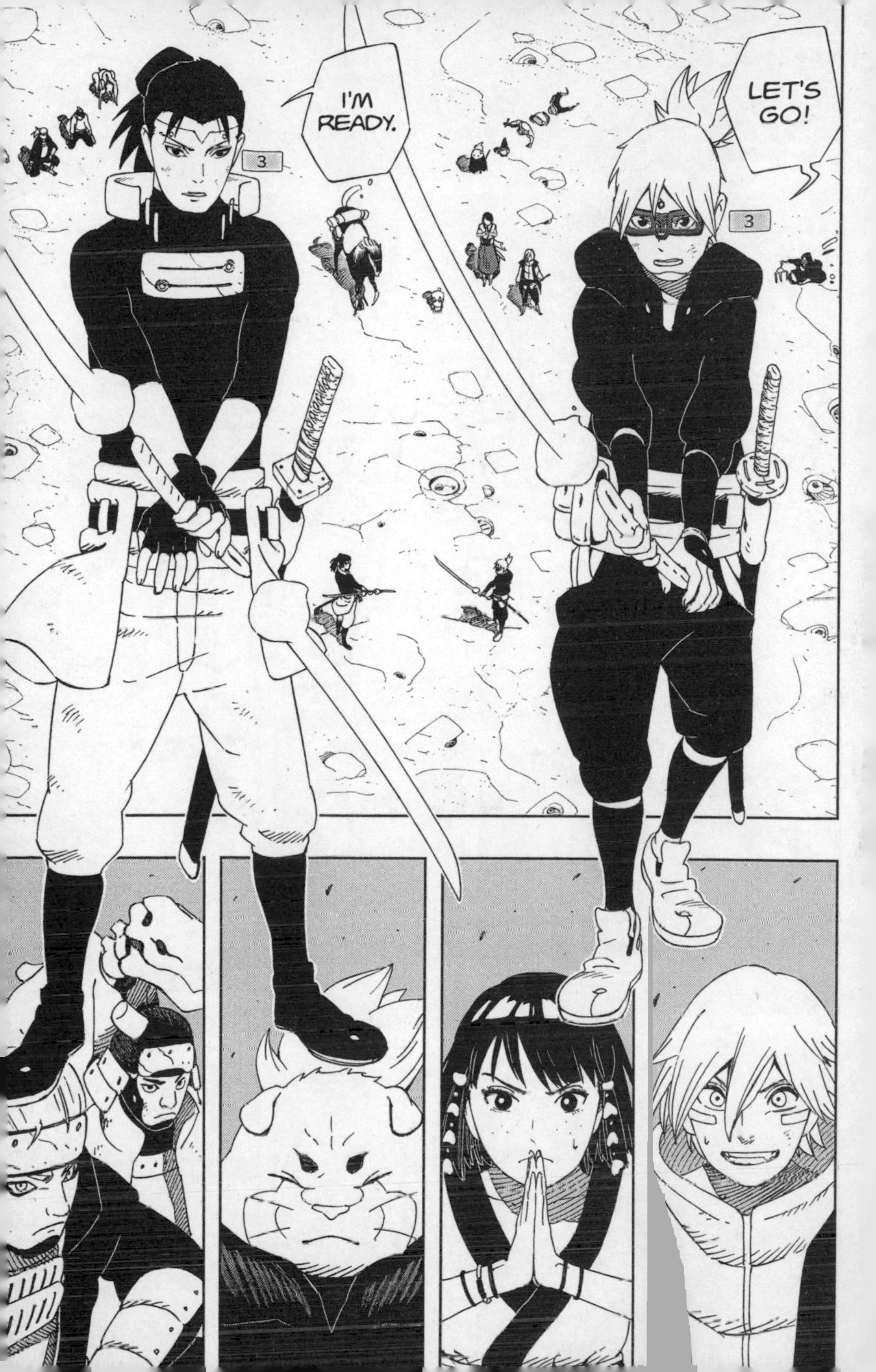
LET'S GO!
3
I'M READY.
3

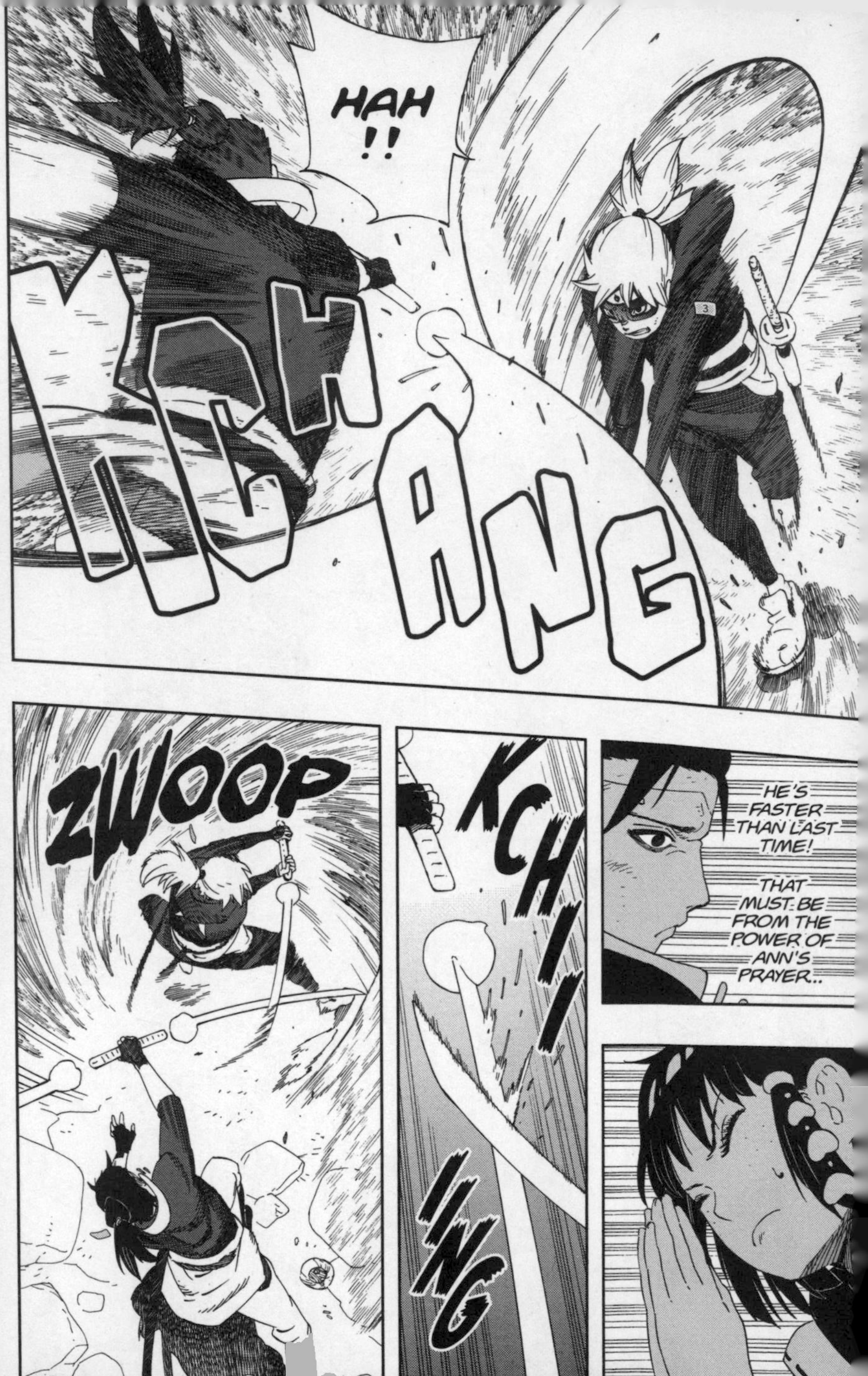
HAH !!
KACHANG
HE'S FASTER THAN LAST TIME!
THAT MUST BE FROM THE POWER OF ANN'S PRAYER..
KCHIIIING
ZWOOP

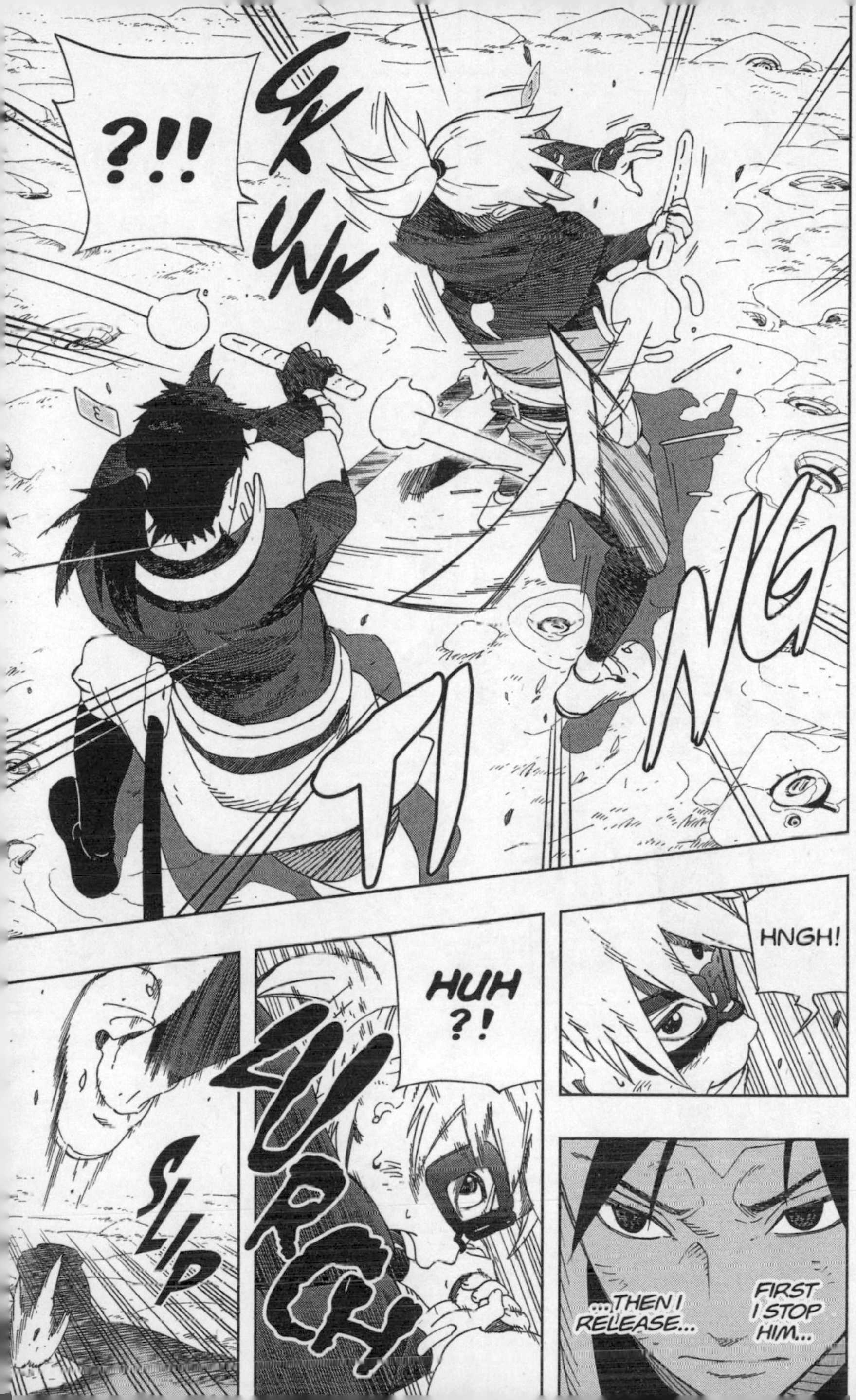
?!!
TING
HNGH!
HUH ?!
SLIP
FIRST I STOP HIM...
...THEN I RELEASE...

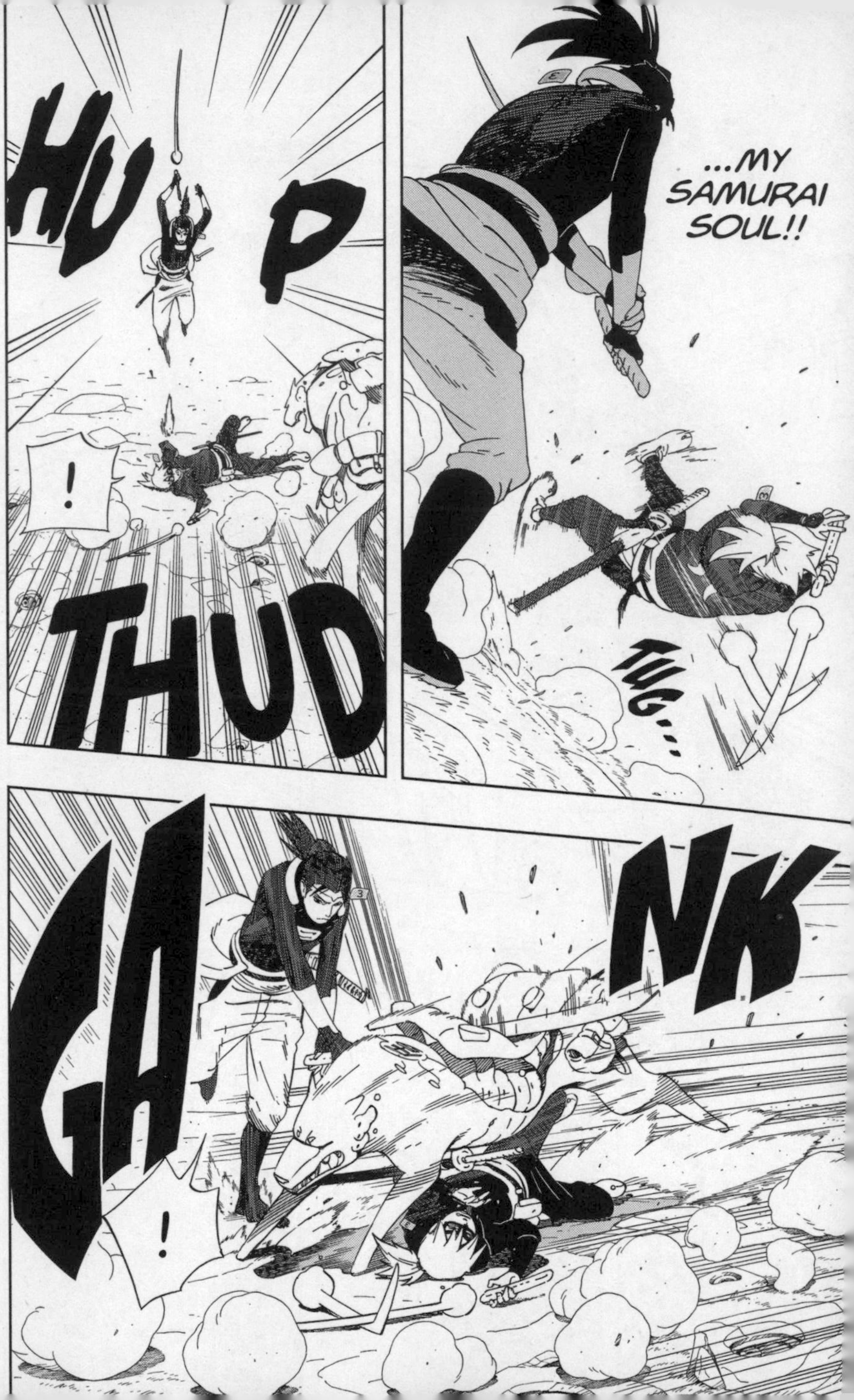

...MY SAMURAI SOUL!!
TUG...
HUP
!
THUD
GANK
!

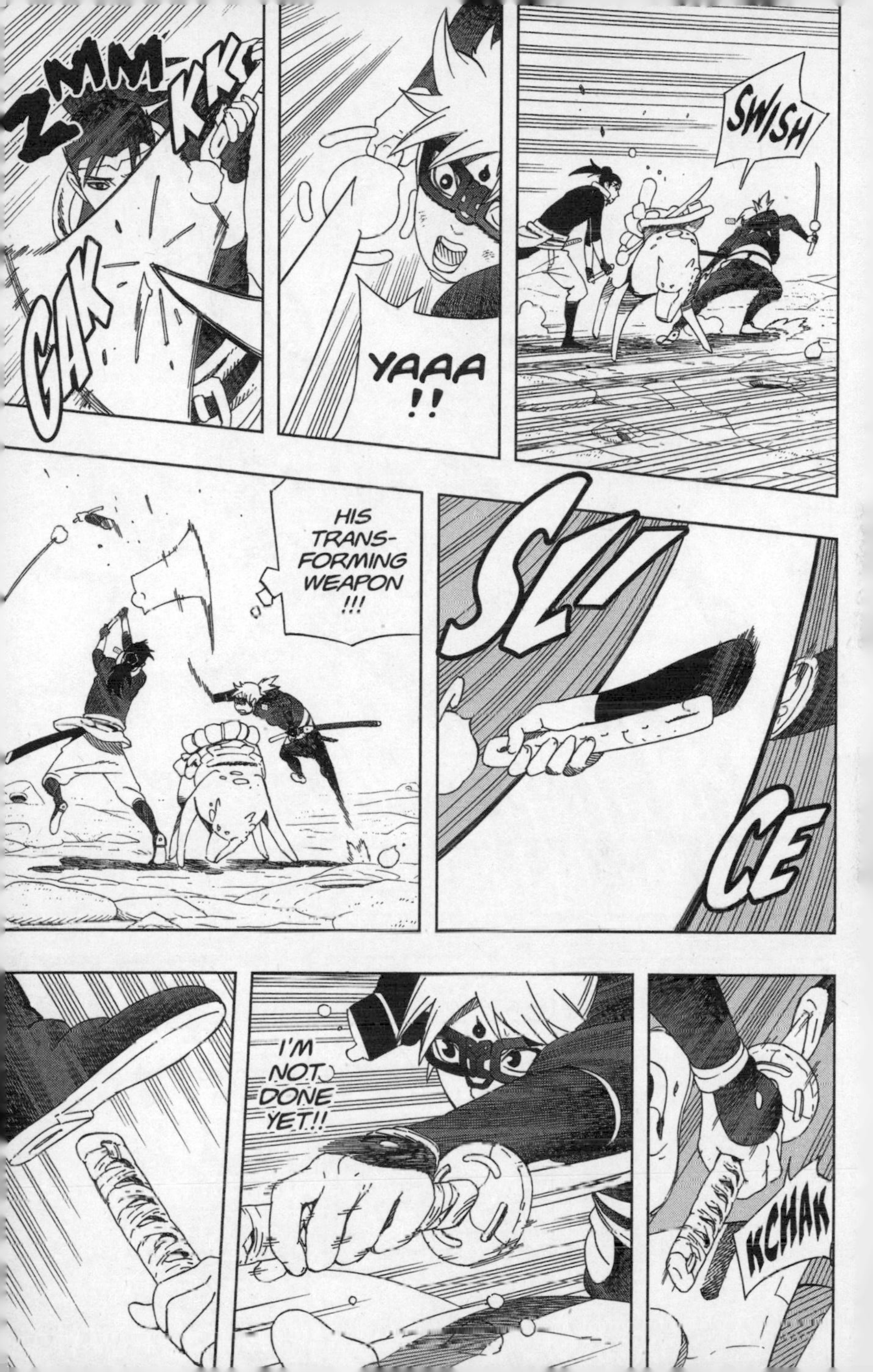
SWISH
YAAA!!
ZMM-KK
GAK
SLICE
HIS TRANS-FORMING WEAPON!!!
KCHAK
I'M NOT DONE YET!!

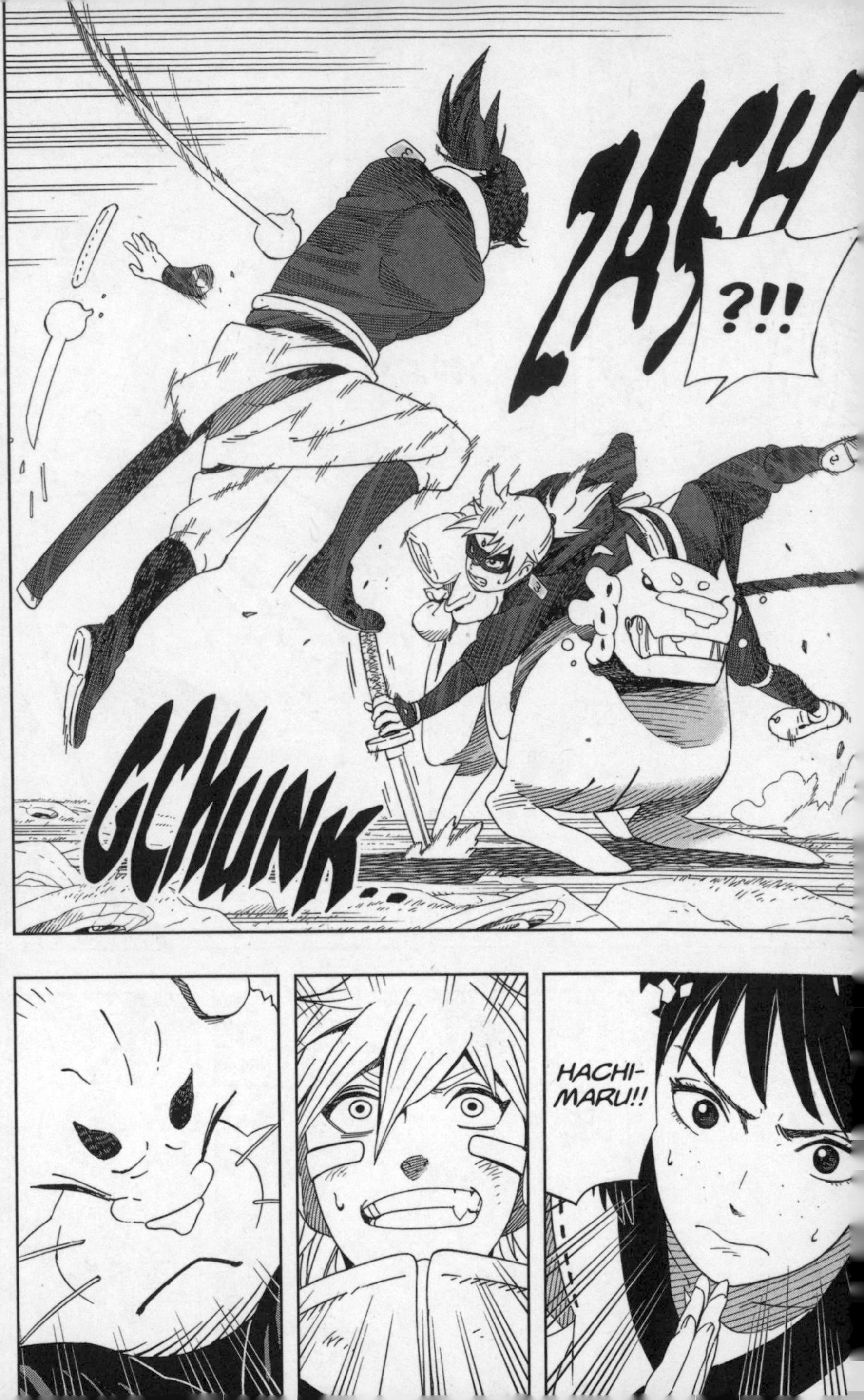
ZASH
?!!
GCHUNK
HACHI-
MARU!!

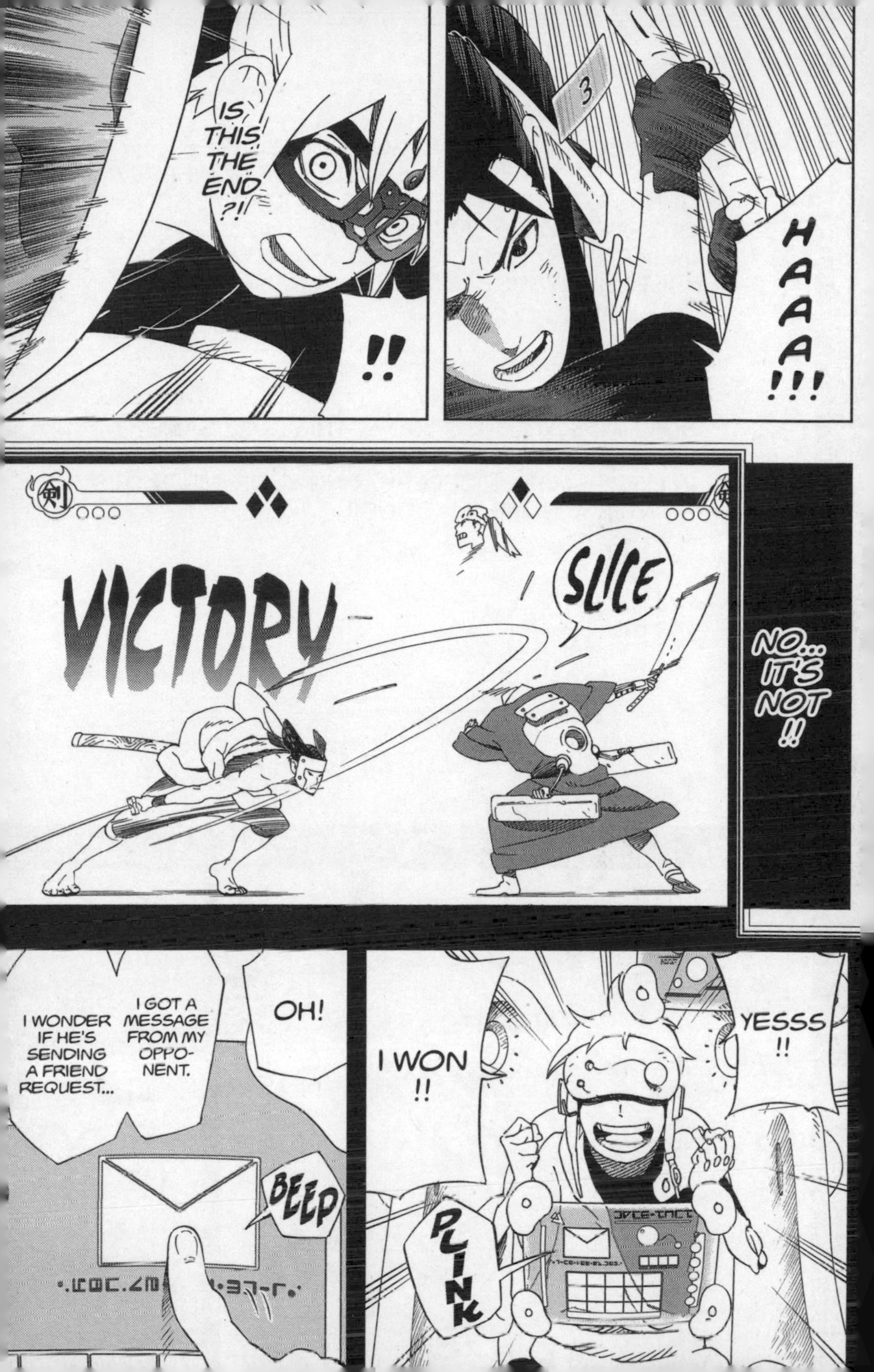
HAAAA!!!
IS THIS THE END?!
!!
NO... IT'S NOT!!
SLICE
VICTORY
YESSS!!
I WON!!
PLINK
OH!
I GOT A MESSAGE FROM MY OPPONENT.
I WONDER IF HE'S SENDING A FRIEND REQUEST...
BEEP

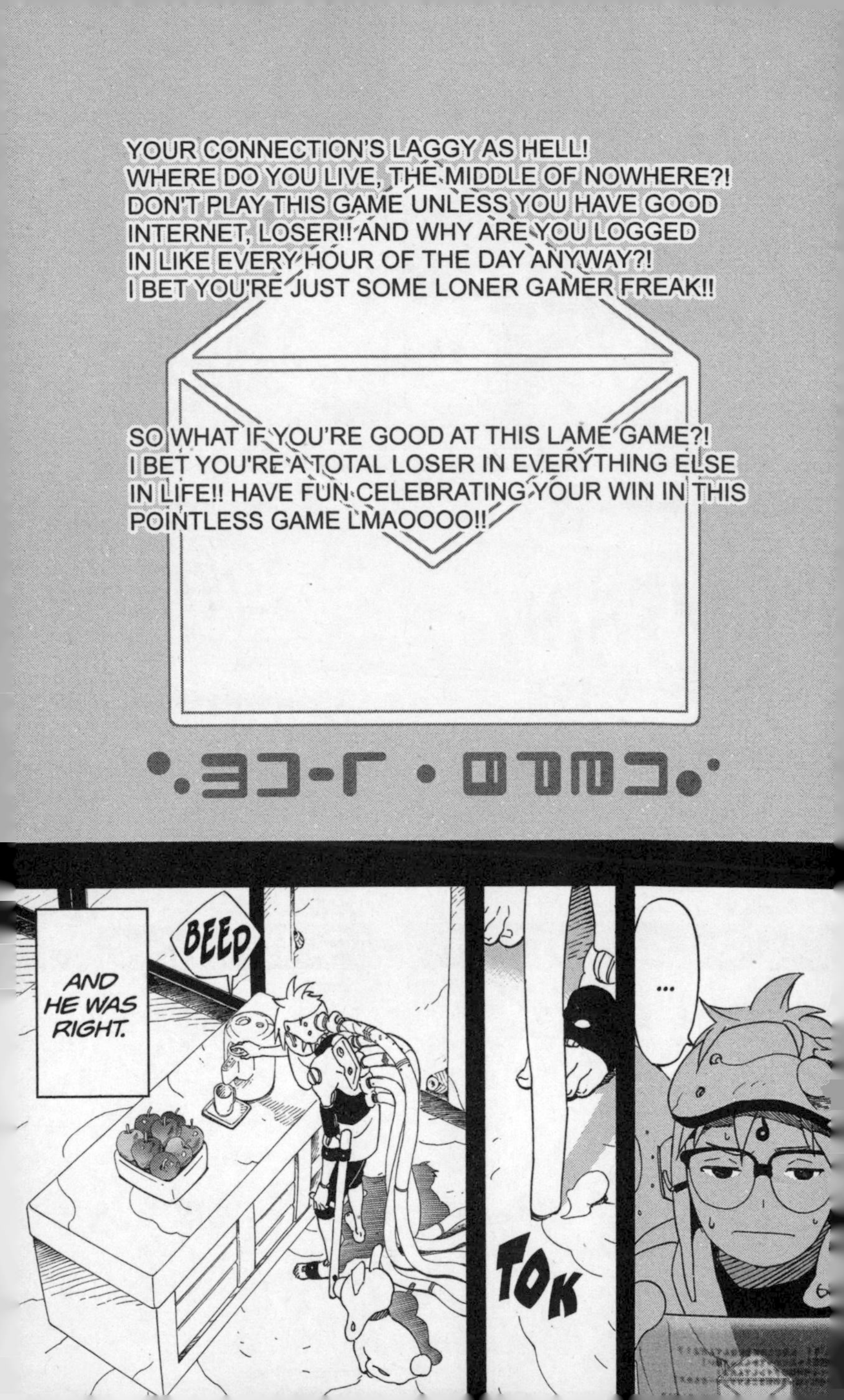
YOUR CONNECTION'S LAGGY AS HELL! WHERE DO YOU LIVE, THE MIDDLE OF NOWHERE?! DON'T PLAY THIS GAME UNLESS YOU HAVE GOOD INTERNET, LOSER!! AND WHY ARE YOU LOGGED IN LIKE EVERY HOUR OF THE DAY ANYWAY?! I BET YOU'RE JUST SOME LONER GAMER FREAK!!
SO WHAT IF YOU'RE GOOD AT THIS LAME GAME?! I BET YOU'RE A TOTAL LOSER IN EVERYTHING ELSE IN LIFE!! HAVE FUN CELEBRATING YOUR WIN IN THIS POINTLESS GAME LMAOOOO!!
...
TOK
BEEP
AND HE WAS RIGHT.

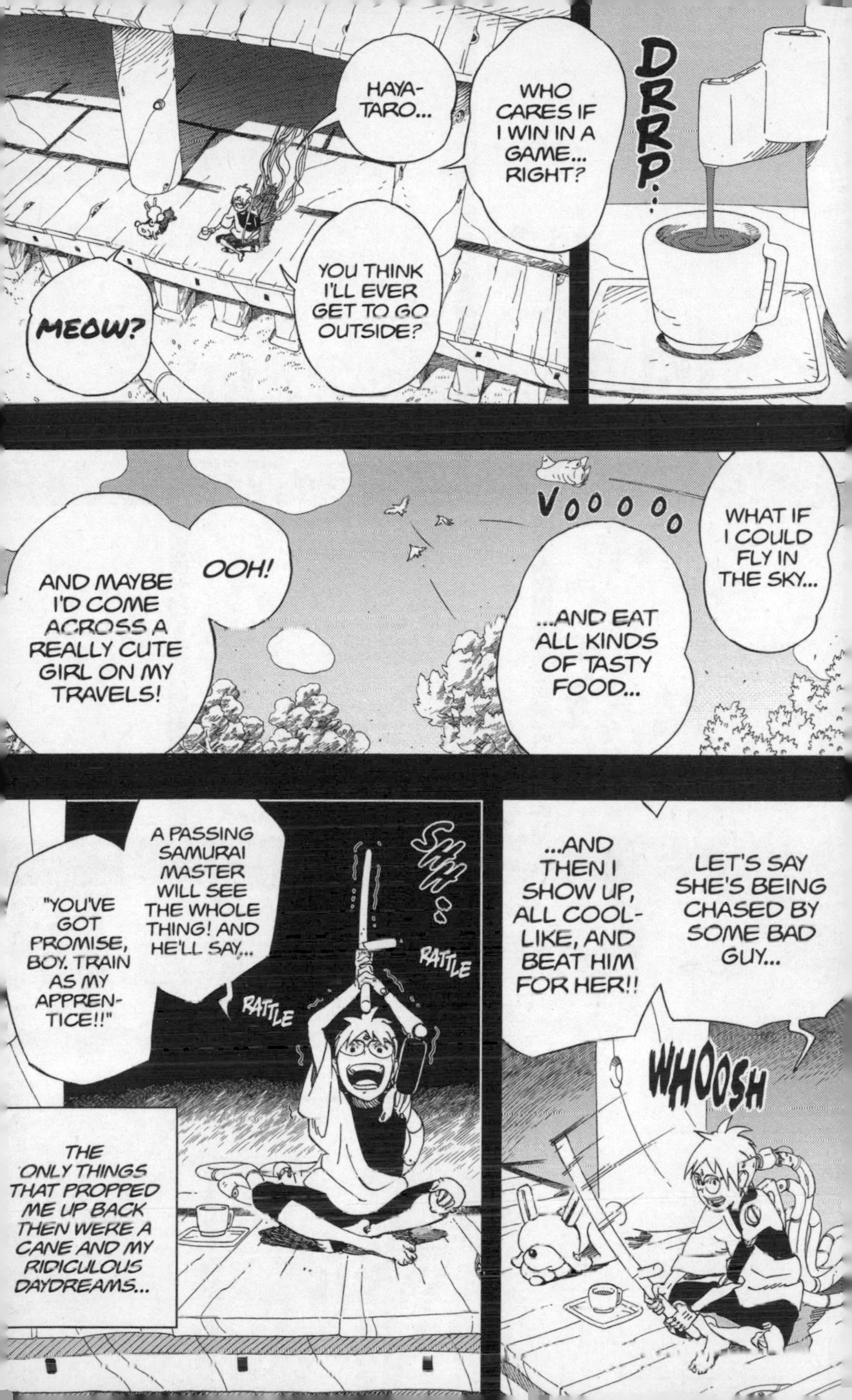
DRRP...
WHO CARES IF I WIN IN A GAME... RIGHT?
HAYA-TARO...
YOU THINK I'LL EVER GET TO GO OUTSIDE?
MEOW?
WHAT IF I COULD FLY IN THE SKY...
VOOOOO
...AND EAT ALL KINDS OF TASTY FOOD...
OOH!
AND MAYBE I'D COME ACROSS A REALLY CUTE GIRL ON MY TRAVELS!
LET'S SAY SHE'S BEING CHASED BY SOME BAD GUY...
...AND THEN I SHOW UP, ALL COOL-LIKE, AND BEAT HIM FOR HER!!
WHOOSH
SHP
RATTLE
A PASSING SAMURAI MASTER WILL SEE THE WHOLE THING! AND HE'LL SAY...
RATTLE
"YOU'VE GOT PROMISE, BOY. TRAIN AS MY APPRENTICE!!"
THE ONLY THINGS THAT PROPPED ME UP BACK THEN WERE A CANE AND MY RIDICULOUS DAYDREAMS...

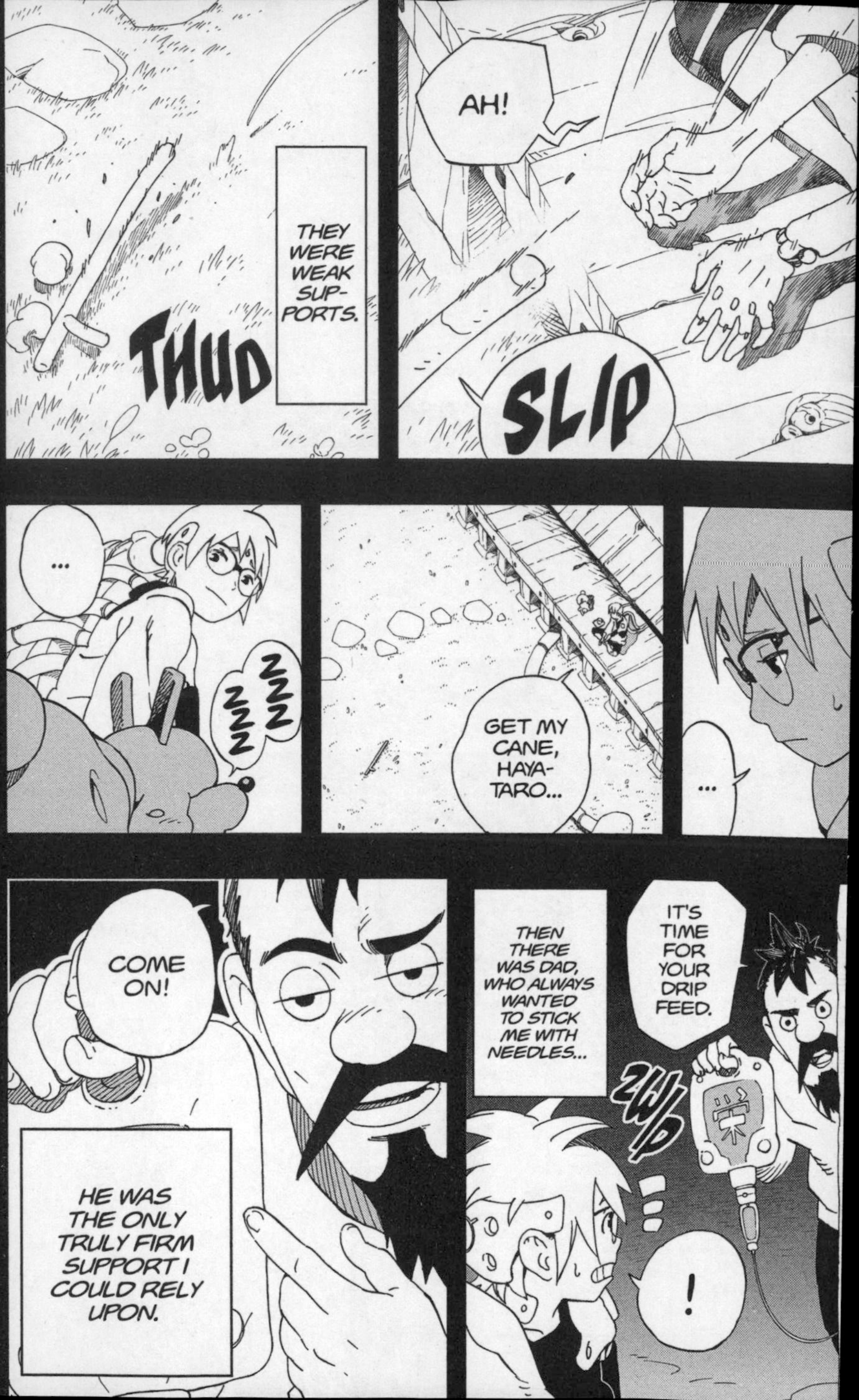
AH!
SLIP
THEY WERE WEAK SUP-PORTS.
THUD
...
GET MY CANE, HAYA-TARO...
...
ZZZ ZZZ
IT'S TIME FOR YOUR DRIP FEED.
THEN THERE WAS DAD, WHO ALWAYS WANTED TO STICK ME WITH NEEDLES...
ZWIP
!
COME ON!
HE WAS THE ONLY TRULY FIRM SUPPORT I COULD RELY UPON.

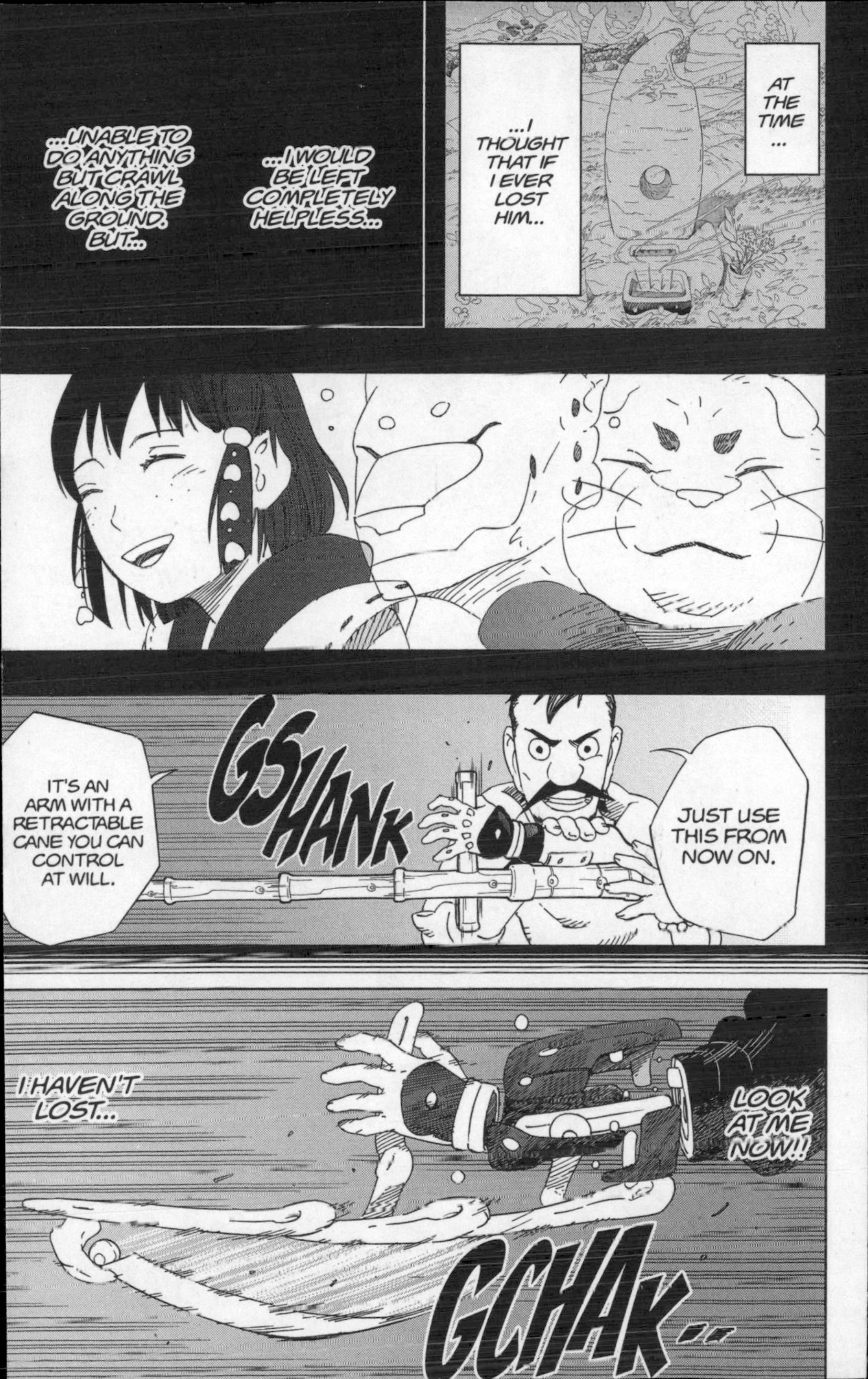

AT THE TIME...
...I THOUGHT THAT IF I EVER LOST HIM...
...I WOULD BE LEFT COMPLETELY HELPLESS...
...UNABLE TO DO ANYTHING BUT CRAWL ALONG THE GROUND. BUT...
JUST USE THIS FROM NOW ON.
GSHANK
IT'S AN ARM WITH A RETRACTABLE CANE YOU CAN CONTROL AT WILL.
LOOK AT ME NOW!!
I HAVEN'T LOST...
GCHAK..

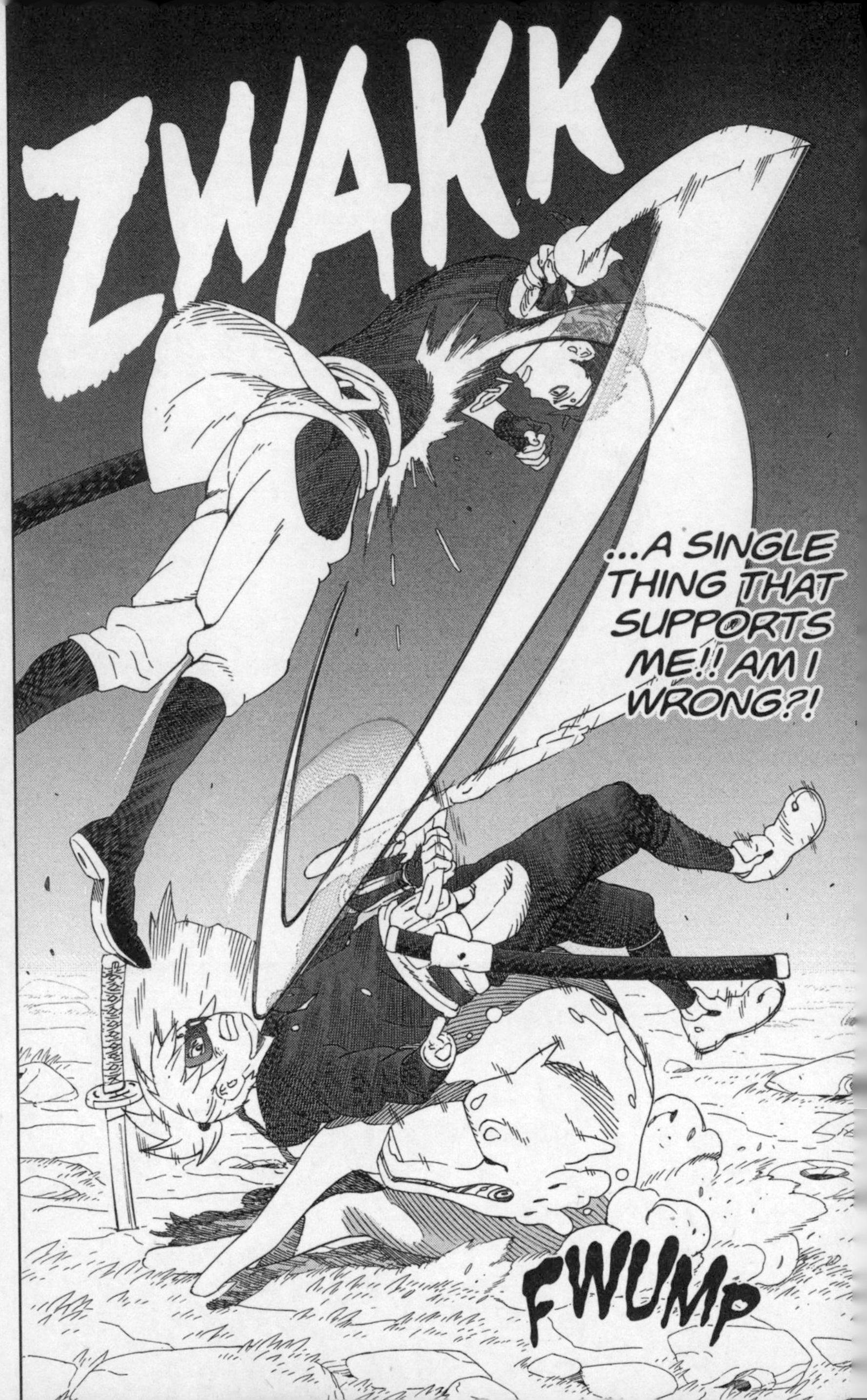
ZWAKK
...A SINGLE THING THAT SUPPORTS ME!! AM I WRONG?!
FWUMP

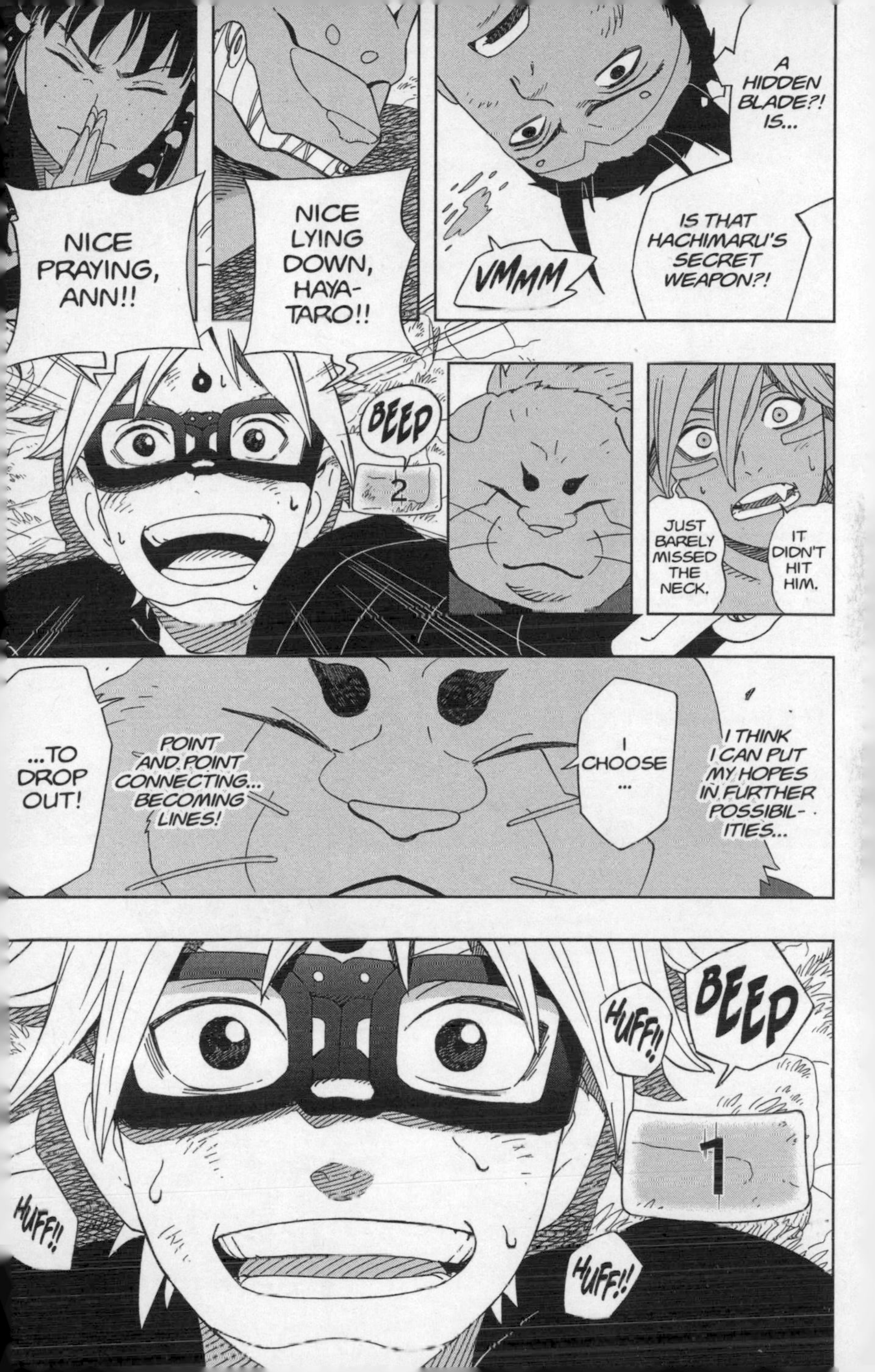

A HIDDEN BLADE?! IS...
IS THAT HACHIMARU'S SECRET WEAPON?!
VMMM
NICE LYING DOWN, HAYA-TARO!!
NICE PRAYING, ANN!!
IT DIDN'T HIT HIM.
JUST BARELY MISSED THE NECK.
BEEP
2
I THINK I CAN PUT MY HOPES IN FURTHER POSSIBIL-ITIES...
I CHOOSE...
POINT AND POINT CONNECTING... BECOMING LINES!
...TO DROP OUT!
BEEP
HUFF!!
1
HUFF!!
HUFF!!

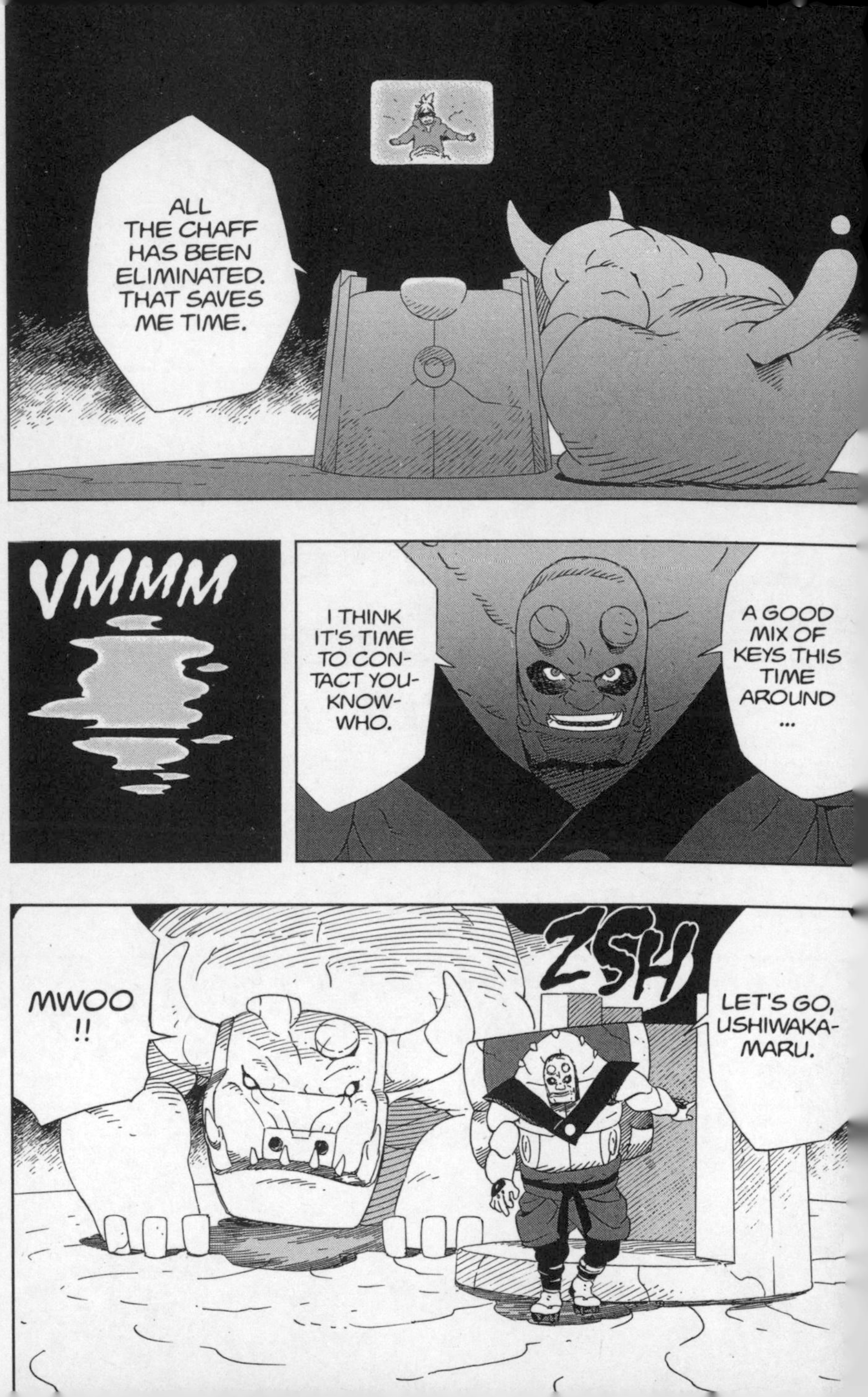
ALL THE CHAFF HAS BEEN ELIMINATED. THAT SAVES ME TIME.
A GOOD MIX OF KEYS THIS TIME AROUND ...
I THINK IT'S TIME TO CONTACT YOU-KNOW-WHO.
VMMM
LET'S GO, USHIWAKA-MARU.
ZSH
MWOO !!

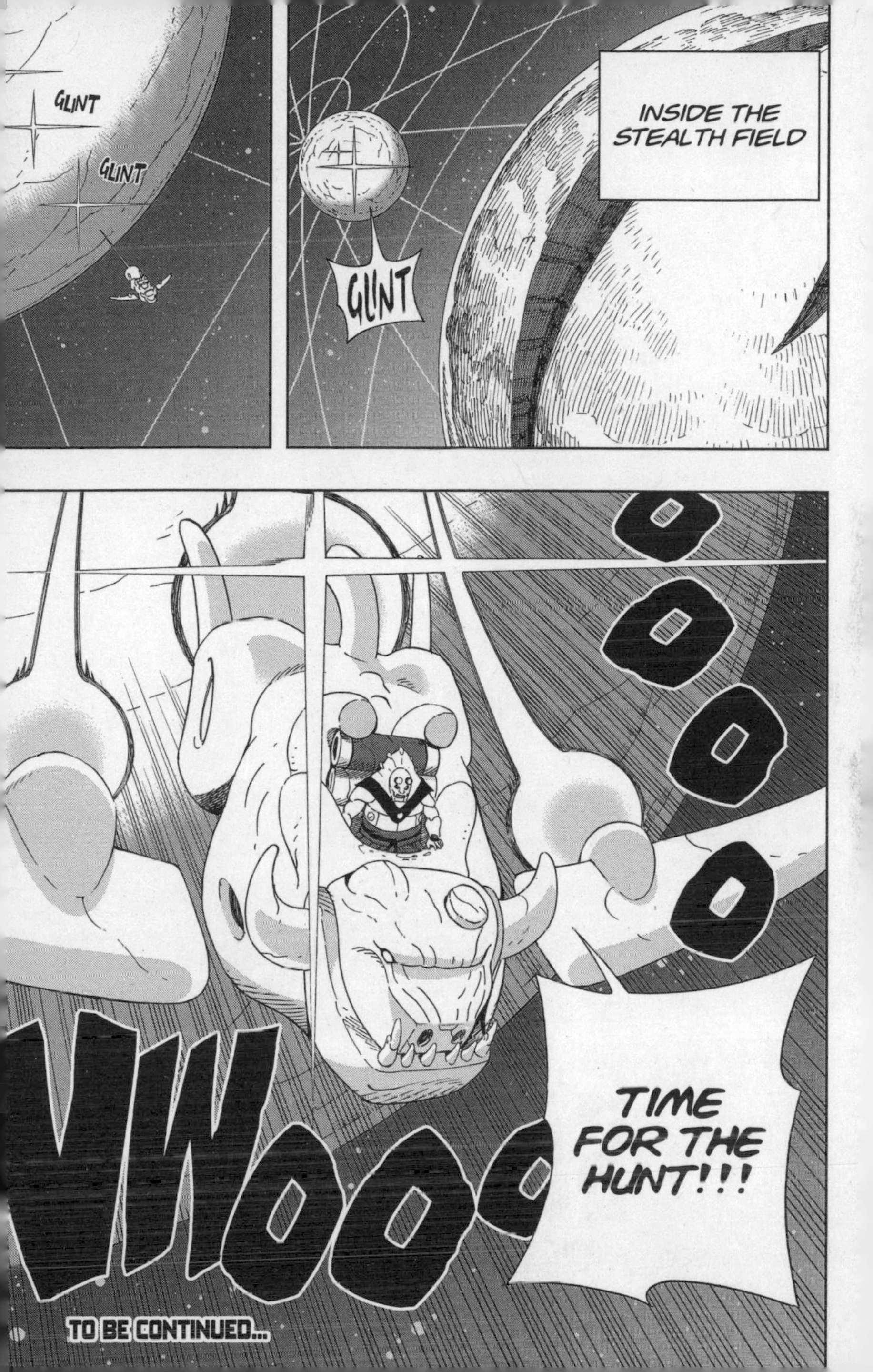
INSIDE THE STEALTH FIELD
GLINT
GLINT
GLINT
VWOOOOOOOO
TIME FOR THE HUNT!!!
TO BE CONTINUED...

SAMURAI 8
THE TALE OF HACHIMARU

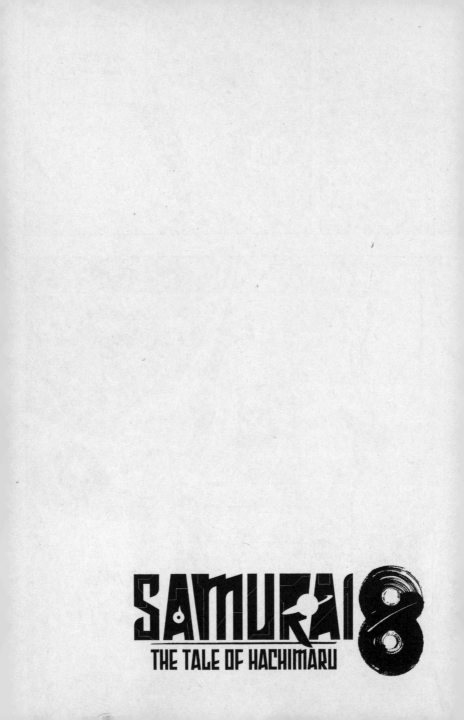

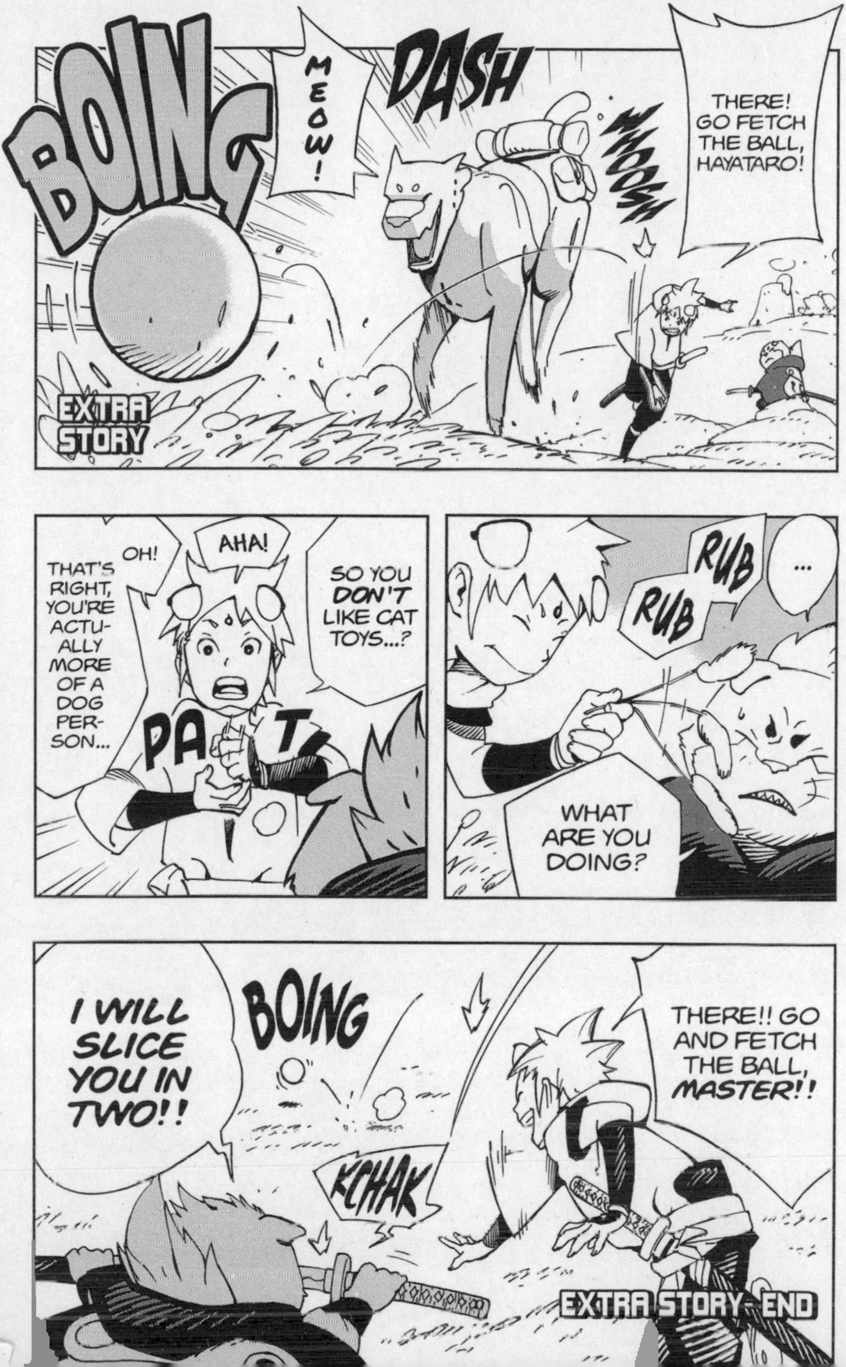
THERE! GO FETCH THE BALL, HAYATARO!
WHOOSH
DASH
MEOW!
BOING
EXTRA STORY
...
RUB
RUB
WHAT ARE YOU DOING?
SO YOU DON'T LIKE CAT TOYS...?
AHA!
OH!
THAT'S RIGHT, YOU'RE ACTUALLY MORE OF A DOG PERSON...
PAT
THERE!! GO AND FETCH THE BALL, MASTER!!
BOING
KCHAK
I WILL SLICE YOU IN TWO!!
EXTRA STORY-END

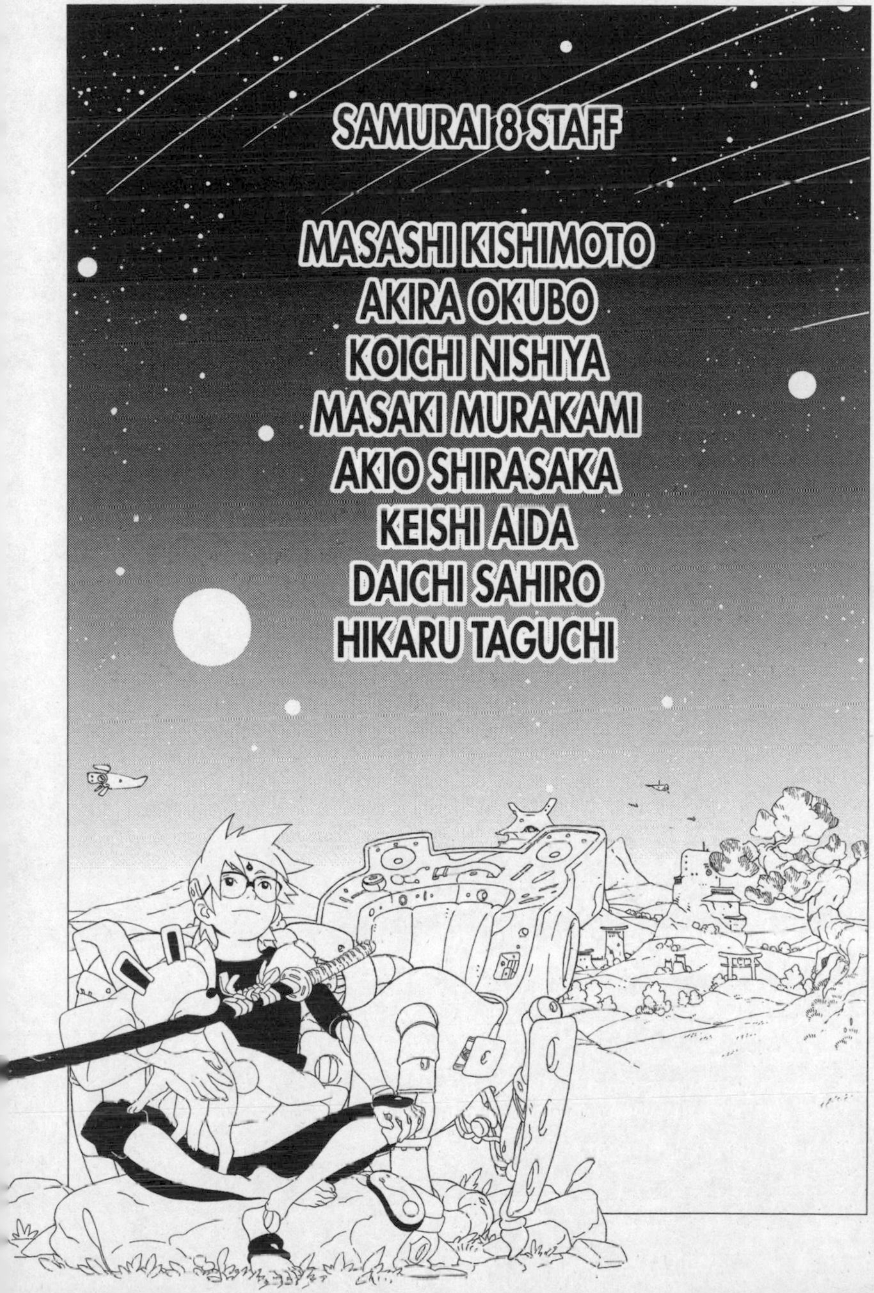
SAMURAI 8 STAFF
MASASHI KISHIMOTO
AKIRA OKUBO
KOICHI NISHIYA
MASAKI MURAKAMI
AKIO SHIRASAKA
KEISHI AIDA
DAICHI SAHIRO
HIKARU TAGUCHI

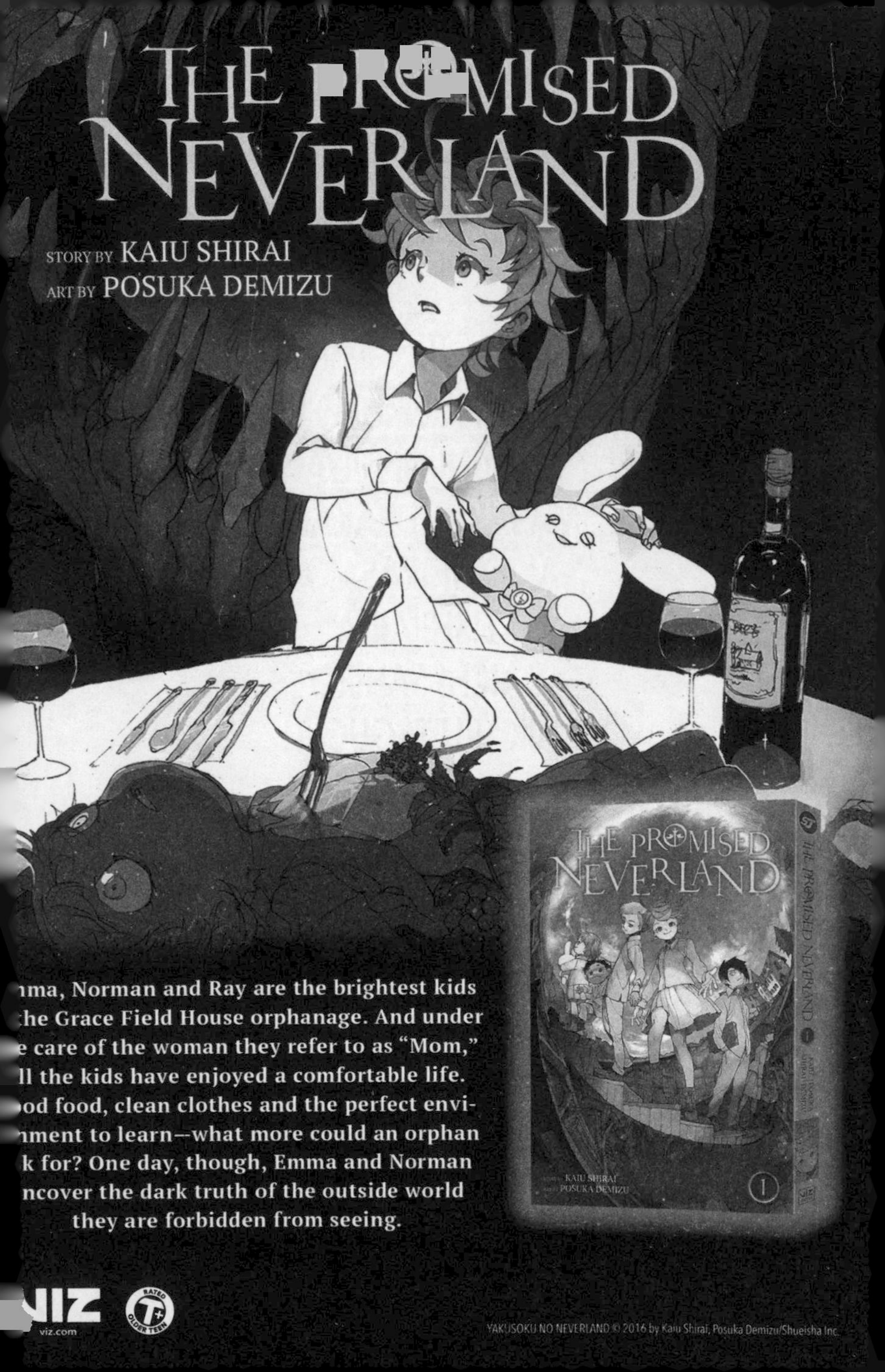
THE PROMISED NEVERLAND
STORY BY KAIU SHIRAI
ART BY POSUKA DEMIZU
THE PROMISED NEVERLAND
KAIU SHIRAI
POSUKA DEMIZU
1
ıma, Norman and Ray are the brightest kids
:he Grace Field House orphanage. And under
e care of the woman they refer to as "Mom,"
ll the kids have enjoyed a comfortable life.
ood food, clean clothes and the perfect envi-
ıment to learn—what more could an orphan
k for? One day, though, Emma and Norman
ncover the dark truth of the outside world
they are forbidden from seeing.
VIZ
viz.com
RATED T+ OLDER TEEN
YAKUSOKU NO NEVERLAND © 2016 by Kaiu Shirai, Posuka Demizu/Shueisha Inc.

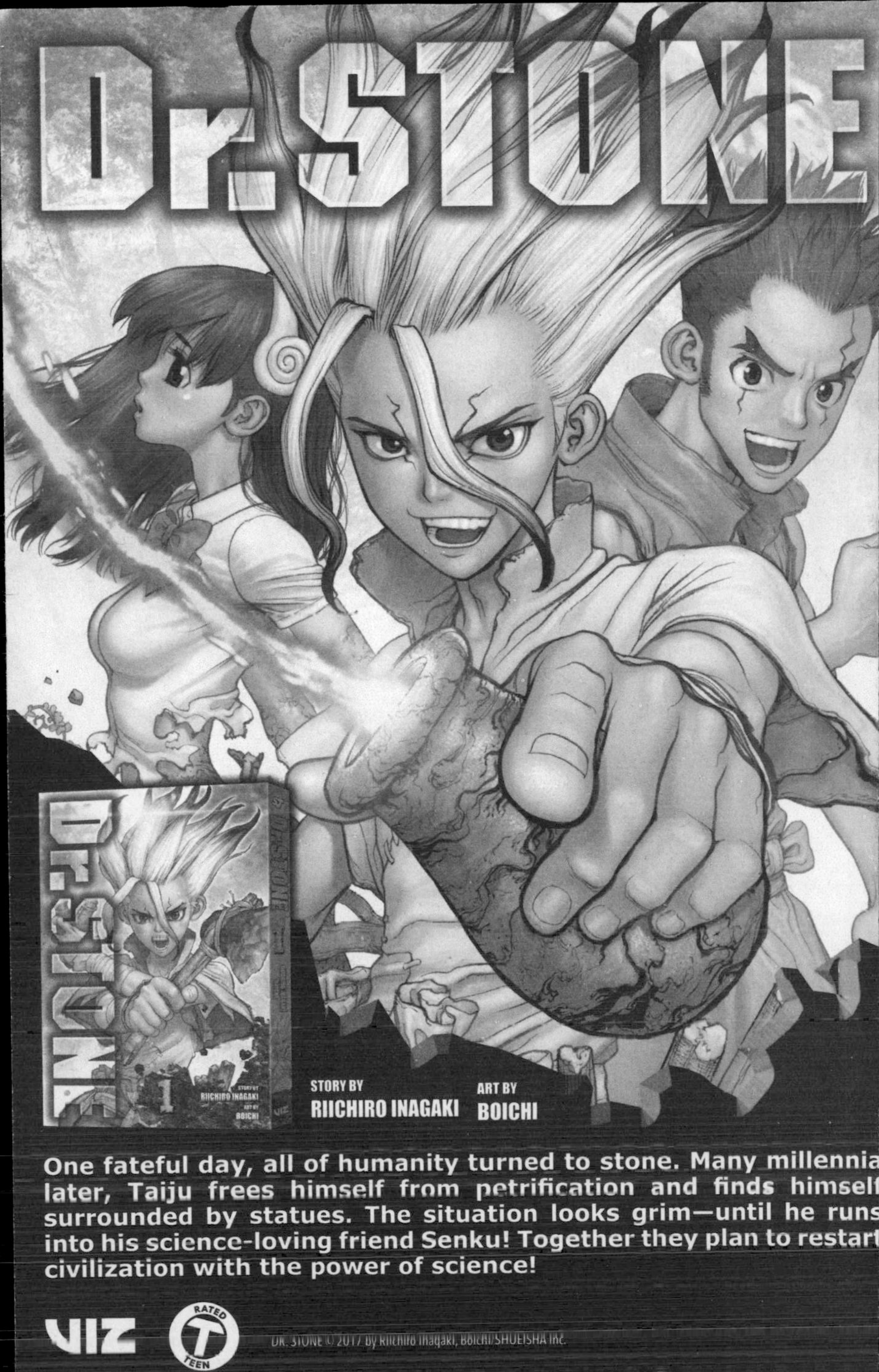
Dr.STONE
Dr.STONE 1
STORY BY RIICHIRO INAGAKI
ART BY BOICHI
STORY BY
RIICHIRO INAGAKI
ART BY
BOICHI

One fateful day, all of humanity turned to stone. Many millennia later, Taiju frees himself from petrification and finds himself surrounded by statues. The situation looks grim—until he runs into his science-loving friend Senku! Together they plan to restart civilization with the power of science!

VIZ

RATED T TEEN

YOU'RE READING THE WRO

SAMURA

THE TALE OF HACHIMARU

reads from right to left, starting in the upper-right corner. Japanese is read from right to left, meaning that action, sound effects and word-balloon order are completely reversed from English order.

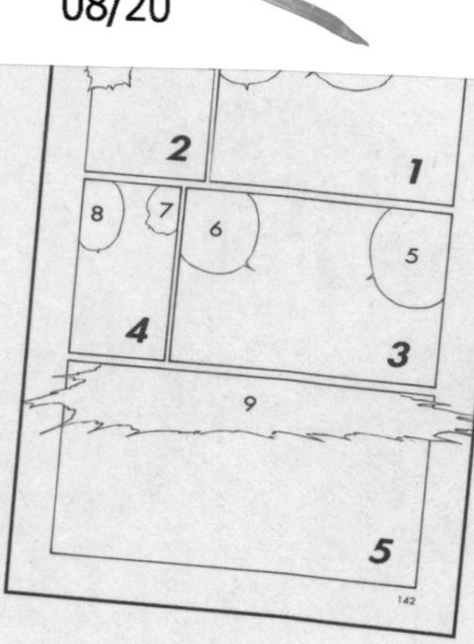
1
2
5
6
7
8
3
4
9
5
142

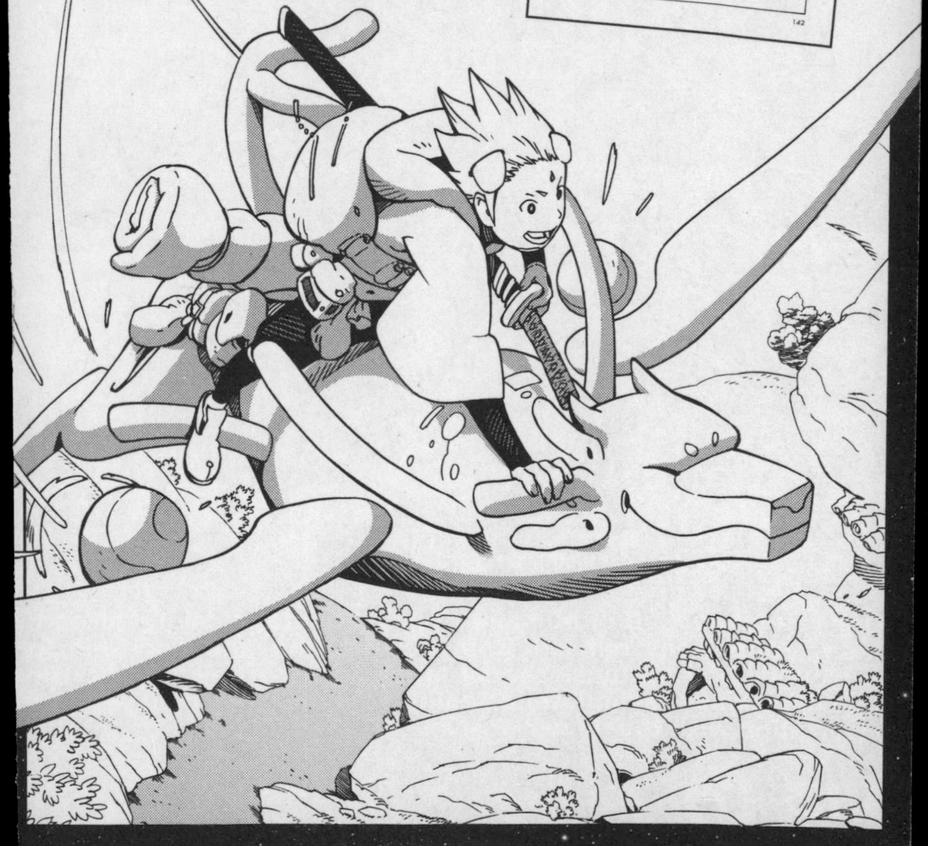

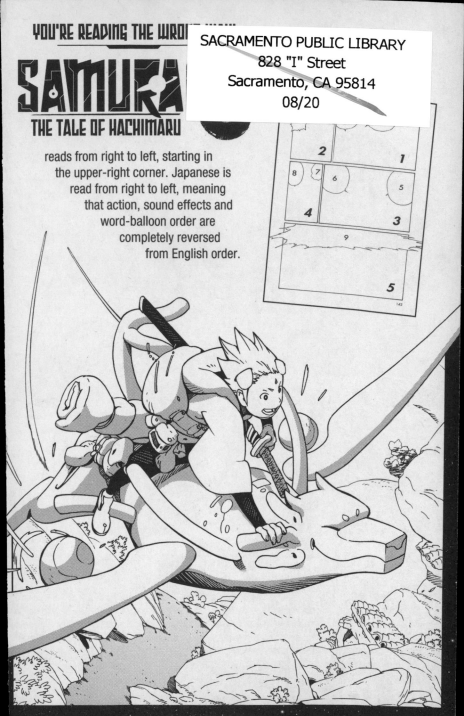